365 Devotions

TO ENCOURAGE YOUR WALK OF FAITH

TRUST

AND

OBEY

Paul Chappell

First published in 2018 by Striving Together Publications, a ministry of Lancaster Baptist Church, Lancaster, CA 93535. Striving Together Publications is committed to providing tried, trusted, and proven books that will further equip local churches to carry out the Great Commission. Your comments and suggestions are valued.

Striving Together Publications
4020 E. Lancaster Blvd.
Lancaster, CA 93535
800.201.7748

Cover design by Andrew Jones
Writing assistance by Robert Byers

The contents of this book are the result of decades of spiritual growth in life and ministry. It is not our intent to claim originality with any quote or thought that could not readily be tied to an original source.

ISBN 978-1-59894-380-1

Printed in the United States of America

Table of Contents

A Word from the Author

Dear Friend,

The entry point for the Christian life is simply faith. To become a child of God, we simply trust in Jesus Christ's substitutionary atonement—His sacrifice on the cross to pay for our sins. We call out to Him in faith and we are saved from the penalty of sin. It's that simple, which makes it incredibly wonderful.

But faith is not just the starting point of our Christian life. It is the way we grow in our relationship with God as well. Hebrews 11:6 tells us, "But without faith it is impossible to please him: for he that cometh to God must believe that he is, and that he is a rewarder of them that diligently seek him."

And how do we demonstrate that faith? By obedience. When we take God at His Word, we follow in the ways He has directed, even when they do not immediately make sense. This is the heart of Christian growth—to trust and obey.

Each of the daily readings in *Trust and Obey* are written to encourage you in your relationship with the Lord. Each reading includes a Scripture passage, a devotional truth based on that passage, and a "Today's Growth Principle"—a solid takeaway truth which you can apply to your life immediately. Also at the bottom of each page are references for your Bible reading. You can follow these to read through the entire Bible or simply the New Testament in a year.

In the back of the book, I've included some tools for effective Christian growth as well as a few Bible reading schedules. Also in the back is a Scripture index listing on which page each verse or reference in the book is mentioned.

It is my prayer that each devotion in *Trust and Obey* will help you in your spiritual growth and encourage you in your walk of faith.

Sincerely in Christ,
Paul Chappell

JANUARY

Trusting God with the Unseen Future

I will instruct thee and teach thee in the way which thou shalt go:
I will guide thee with mine eye. Be ye not as the horse, or as the mule,
which have no understanding: whose mouth must be held in with bit
and bridle, lest they come near unto thee. Many sorrows shall be to the
wicked: but he that trusteth in the LORD, mercy shall compass him about.
—PSALM 32:8–10

I read a fascinating story from the final days of World War II. An American B-29 bomber team was tasked with attacking targets in Kokura, Japan. As was normal procedure, they were assigned a secondary target in case the weather kept them from reaching their primary objective. Sure enough, they found the clouds over Kokura too thick to find their targets. After an hour of circling, they diverted to their secondary objective with some frustration. It was not until weeks later they learned that, unknown to American intelligence, the Japanese had transferred a huge number of American prisoners of war to Kokura just days before the scheduled raid. The officer who received this news said, "Thank God for that protecting cloud! If the city hadn't been hidden from the bomber, it would have been destroyed and thousands of American boys would have died."

Each new year we enter into territory that is clouded and unclear to our eyes. While we may expect certain things to happen, none of us know what the future holds. When we cannot see the path, it is more important than ever that we trust in God. So many times we are tempted to take matters into our own hands when God does not work as quickly as we think He should. But He never makes a mistake, and we can trust in Him no matter what seeming delays we experience. Often it is only as we look back over the years that we see how God has worked.

Today's Growth Principle: You can always trust God even when you cannot see the way ahead or what He is doing.

The God Who Knows Our Sorrows

And the LORD said, I have surely seen the affliction of my people which are in Egypt, and have heard their cry by reason of their taskmasters; for I know their sorrows; And I am come down to deliver them out of the hand of the Egyptians, and to bring them up out of that land unto a good land and a large, unto a land flowing with milk and honey; unto the place of the Canaanites, and the Hittites, and the Amorites, and the Perizzites, and the Hivites, and the Jebusites. Now therefore, behold, the cry of the children of Israel is come unto me: and I have also seen the oppression wherewith the Egyptians oppress them.—EXODUS 3:7-9

Frank Graeff spent much of his life as a pastor working with children and teens. He was known for his cheerful outlook on life. One friend described him as "a spiritual optimist, a great friend of children; his bright sun-shining disposition attracts him not only to children, but to all with whom he comes in contact." But Graeff suffered from frequent serious illnesses that limited his work for God. One day in despair he turned to the pages of Scripture for comfort and was greatly encouraged by 1 Peter 5:7, "Casting all your care upon him; for he careth for you."

Not long after, Graeff penned the words we now sing:

Does Jesus care when my heart is pained too deeply for mirth or song,
As the burdens press, and the cares distress, and the way grows weary and long?
Oh, yes, He cares, I know He cares, His heart is touched with my grief;
When the days are weary, the long nights dreary, I know my Saviour cares.

God is not oblivious to our pain and suffering. He knows our sorrows. And in the fullness of His time and His plan, He brings comfort. God has never abandoned or forsaken His children. We should never doubt that God cares about what brings pain and suffering into our lives.

Today's Growth Principle: The heart of God is touched when His children suffer, and He always cares for our needs.

The Choices of Faith

By faith Moses, when he was born, was hid three months of his parents, because they saw he was a proper child; and they were not afraid of the king's commandment. By faith Moses, when he was come to years, refused to be called the son of Pharaoh's daughter; Choosing rather to suffer affliction with the people of God, than to enjoy the pleasures of sin for a season; Esteeming the reproach of Christ greater riches than the treasures in Egypt: for he had respect unto the recompence of the reward.
—HEBREWS 11:23–26

The courses of our lives are determined by the choices we make. It is not our wishes, our intentions, or our resolutions that shape our destiny, but the actions we choose when confronted by decision points in life. There are not a few miraculously blessed people who coast through life without any problems, never having to make a hard choice. Every one of us comes to points when we must turn left or turn right—and what we do in those moments determines where we will end up in life.

Moses would not have lived to adulthood without the choice of his parents to hide him from Pharaoh's evil decree that all the Hebrew baby boys be murdered. And Moses would not have been chosen by God to lead Israel out of bondage in Egypt had he not chosen to turn his back on the pleasures he was offered as a young man in the palace of the king and stand with God's people instead.

The thing about difficult choices is that we do not know how they will turn out, even if we choose what is right to the best of our knowledge. Sometimes there is great earthly reward for obedience to God. But sometimes the reward of faith is only seen later. But the correctness of our decision is not determined based on earthly outcome. It is determined by whether or not we act in obedience and faith.

Today's Growth Principle: Faith chooses to believe that what God has said is true and to act upon it with confidence.

The Importance of Faithfulness

Preach the word; be instant in season, out of season; reprove, rebuke, exhort with all longsuffering and doctrine. For the time will come when they will not endure sound doctrine; but after their own lusts shall they heap to themselves teachers, having itching ears; And they shall turn away their ears from the truth, and shall be turned unto fables. But watch thou in all things, endure afflictions, do the work of an evangelist, make full proof of thy ministry.—2 TIMOTHY 4:2–5

It is tempting to look around at a society that is increasingly anti-Christian and think that we are going through something unprecedented. But as Paul's final letter to Timothy makes clear, the problem of people's rejection of the truth is not new. It may take different forms from one generation to the next, but the allure of listening to comfortable lies rather than to painful truth is hard to resist. Indeed we need to be on guard in our own lives to reject the teaching that simply tells us what we want to hear.

Our mission is not to correct, by argument or logic, all those who believe error. Instead, we are simply to stick to proclaiming the truth and trust God to provide the harvest. "I have planted, Apollos watered; but God gave the increase" (1 Corinthians 3:6). Our responsibility is to be faithful to present the truth. There are times when there are great results and times when there are none. These outcomes do not reflect on us if we remain faithful in either circumstance.

The temptation is to judge ourselves by whether or not we are seeing great harvests. But while we should do everything we can to reach others, as President John Quincy Adams liked to say, "Duties are ours, results are God's." The seasons may come and go and the harvest will change with them, but He always honors those who remain faithful in His service.

Today's Growth Principle: God is looking for those who are willing to remain faithful to the truth in every season of life.

What Only God Can Do

Daniel answered in the presence of the king, and said, The secret which the king hath demanded cannot the wise men, the astrologers, the magicians, the soothsayers, shew unto the king; But there is a God in heaven that revealeth secrets, and maketh known to the king Nebuchadnezzar what shall be in the latter days. Thy dream, and the visions of thy head upon thy bed, are these; As for thee, O king, thy thoughts came into thy mind upon thy bed, what should come to pass hereafter: and he that revealeth secrets maketh known to thee what shall come to pass.—DANIEL 2:27–29

Years ago, I heard a story of a missionary who had a problem with his car—it wouldn't start without being pushed. Each time he went somewhere, he had to make sure he was parked facing a downhill grade so he would be able to get the car started again when he was ready to leave. After two years went by, a new missionary came to replace him at that station. After he explained his procedure for ensuring he wouldn't be stranded, the new man lifted the hood of the car. He saw that the battery cable was loose, tightened it, and the car started right away. The problem was the connection, not the power source.

All of us who are children of God have access to an unlimited array of power and resources to do His work. Yet, if we are honest, we have to admit that many times we do not see anything of the divine or supernatural. Too often, we settle instead for what we are able to accomplish rather than checking for a "loose cable" to the power source. Jesus said, "I am the vine, ye are the branches: He that abideth in me, and I in him, the same bringeth forth much fruit: for without me ye can do nothing" (John 15:5). Although every harvest calls for a season of faithfulness before the fruit is mature and the results are visible, sometimes we don't see harvest because we're not abiding in the vine. Too often, we struggle on with no spiritual fruit simply because we are trying to manufacture it on our own.

Today's Growth Principle: Do not settle for what you can do on your own—tap into God's divine power through His promises.

　　　Genesis 13–15　　//　　Matthew 5:1–26

Don't Be Conformed to the World

And what agreement hath the temple of God with idols? for ye are the temple of the living God; as God hath said, I will dwell in them, and walk in them; and I will be their God, and they shall be my people. Wherefore come out from among them, and be ye separate, saith the Lord, and touch not the unclean thing; and I will receive you, And will be a Father unto you, and ye shall be my sons and daughters, saith the Lord Almighty.
—2 CORINTHIANS 6:16–18

There is a great temptation to adapt ourselves to our surroundings so we fit in rather than standing apart as the people of God. Even many churches are becoming more and more like the world. There is too often an unwillingness on the part of Christians to be looked down on or mocked for being different.

This is not the first time this issue has been faced, however. Charles Spurgeon decried the danger of compromising with the world in an effort to reach the world in a sermon he preached 130 years ago saying, "This is the suggestion of the present hour: If the world will not come to Jesus...Shall not the church go down to the world? Instead of bidding men be converted, and come out from among sinners, and be separate from them, let us join with the ungodly world, enter into union with it, and so pervade it with our influence by allowing it to influence us. Let us have a Christian world."

The plan of becoming more like the world did not work in Spurgeon's day, and it will not work in ours. God is still looking for faithful men and women who are willing to endure reproach for the cause of Christ as they share the message of the gospel.

Today's Growth Principle: Being like Jesus is not the path of least resistance, but it is a path of growth and blessing.

What God Has Done

I will remember the works of the LORD: surely I will remember thy wonders of old. I will meditate also of all thy work, and talk of thy doings. Thy way, O God, is in the sanctuary: who is so great a God as our God? Thou art the God that doest wonders: thou hast declared thy strength among the people.—PSALM 77:11–14

All Christians, and perhaps especially those of us who grew up in Christian homes and were saved at a young age, face the danger of forgetting all God has done for us. Over time we become accustomed to His grace and greatness and take for granted the blessings from which we benefit so often.

This is a tragedy for us on multiple levels. First, it is a tragedy for us because when we cease to be grateful, we soon will turn away from following Him. But it is also a tragedy for those who come after us. Parents, grandparents, and older believers play a powerful role in keeping the faith alive for coming generations. There are no guarantees that those who follow us will see God as a real power and presence in their lives. In fact, it was not many years after the death of Joshua that God's power became only dimly remembered by the Israelites: "And Gideon said unto him, Oh my Lord, if the LORD be with us, why then is all this befallen us? and where be all his miracles which our fathers told us of, saying, Did not the LORD bring us up from Egypt? but now the LORD hath forsaken us, and delivered us into the hands of the Midianites" (Judges 6:13).

Each time we rejoice and give thanks for God's goodness, we not only build our own faith, but we also invest in the future. We must remind ourselves and share with others the mighty works of God in our lives so that they will never be forgotten.

Today's Growth Principle: Our responsibility is to remember what God has done for us and pass our faith on to others.

God Makes Us Able

*But straightway Jesus spake unto them, saying, Be of good cheer;
it is I; be not afraid. And Peter answered him and said, Lord, if it
be thou, bid me come unto thee on the water. And he said, Come.
And when Peter was come down out of the ship, he walked on the
water, to go to Jesus. But when he saw the wind boisterous, he was
afraid; and beginning to sink, he cried, saying, Lord, save me.*
—MATTHEW 14:27–30

When Jesus came walking on the water to where the disciples were
fighting a fierce storm, He was doing something none of them
had seen before. Remember that many of the disciples were experienced
fishermen who knew the difference between a minor downpour and a
life-threatening storm. And these experienced sailors were terrified. But
then Jesus showed up. Rather than being comforted, however, they were
initially even more terrified, thinking they were seeing some kind of
ghost. Even after Jesus spoke to them they were still unsure.

Then Peter, with his customary impetuousness, came up with a
way to confirm that it was really Jesus. He asked Jesus if it really were
Him, that He would call Peter out onto the water. And in response to
the command of Jesus, Peter got out of the boat and successfully walked
across the water just as Jesus was doing…until he took his eyes off Jesus
and began to focus on his surroundings.

This story is a powerful demonstration of God's equipping and
enabling that prepares us for His service. None of us are likely to need to
join Peter on the surface of the Sea of Galilee, but all of us are called to
get out of our "boats"—to go beyond what we have done before and take
on new challenges and responsibilities. In those moments, we must not
rely on our own strength and resources, and we must not focus on the
difficulties around us. Instead, we must look to Jesus and follow His voice.

Today's Growth Principle: Only in the power of God can we find the
ability to accomplish His will and experience His peace in storms.

Salvation Changes Everything

Know ye not that the unrighteous shall not inherit the kingdom of God?
Be not deceived: neither fornicators, nor idolaters, nor adulterers, nor
effeminate, nor abusers of themselves with mankind, Nor thieves, nor
covetous, nor drunkards, nor revilers, nor extortioners, shall inherit the
kingdom of God. And such were some of you: but ye are washed, but ye are
sanctified, but ye are justified in the name of the Lord Jesus, and by the
Spirit of our God.—1 CORINTHIANS 6:9–11

One of the people who did the most to reach people through rescue missions was Mel Trotter. He knew firsthand the power of the gospel to change a life. Trotter was an alcoholic who returned home from one of his benders to find that his two-year-old son had died. Believing that he was to blame, he swore that he would never drink again. Two hours later, he was staggering out of a saloon. He took a train to Chicago, where he sold his shoes for enough money to buy one more drink, planning to kill himself. On his way to Lake Michigan he passed the Pacific Garden Rescue Mission and went inside. When he heard the message of salvation through Jesus Christ, he trusted Christ as his Saviour and was wonderfully transformed. He was reunited with his wife and devoted the rest of his life to helping reach others.

The salvation that God offers freely by grace through faith to all those who come to Christ and trust Him as their Saviour changes far more than just their eternal destiny. It changes everything about this life as well. The word *gospel* means "good news," and the message of salvation—that God gave Himself as a substitutionary sacrifice for us to be cleansed from our sins through His blood—is the best news anyone can ever receive. The only hope that we have is in Jesus, for our sins separate us from God, and nothing we do can bridge that gap. We have only to trust in what Jesus has already done for us to be saved.

Today's Growth Principle: There is no genuine salvation which does not produce a new nature and new character.

Certainty in the Scriptures

And this is the record, that God hath given to us eternal life, and this life is in his Son. He that hath the Son hath life; and he that hath not the Son of God hath not life. These things have I written unto you that believe on the name of the Son of God; that ye may know that ye have eternal life, and that ye may believe on the name of the Son of God.—1 JOHN 5:11–13

One of the great Bible teachers and preachers of the past, G. Campbell Morgan, had already enjoyed some success as a preacher by the time he was nineteen years old. But he began to read Charles Darwin and other critics of biblical truth, and his mind filled with doubt about the Bible. Finally, knowing he could not continue to preach with such doubts, he canceled his upcoming speaking engagements and put away all the books he had been reading. He went to the store and purchased a new, unmarked Bible, then sat down and began reading it—reading nothing else until he completed it from beginning to end. His doubts fled away, and he spent the rest of his life preaching the Word of God he had come to fully trust.

There are many wonderful resources available to Christians in our day, and I am thankful for every one of them. But nothing can ever take the place of the Word of God. We need to hear it preached and taught on a regular basis. We need to read it for ourselves. We should memorize it, hiding it in our hearts. We should fill our thoughts and meditations with the Bible. When we do, our faith grows as we become rooted and grounded in the truth.

The only completely perfect and trustworthy tool given to us is the Bible. We can fully believe everything it says and must fully obey everything it commands.

Today's Growth Principle: Unless your life is filled with the Word of God, your faith will be weak and uncertain.

Characteristics of False Teachers

Now the Spirit speaketh expressly, that in the latter times some shall depart from the faith, giving heed to seducing spirits, and doctrines of devils; Speaking lies in hypocrisy; having their conscience seared with a hot iron; Forbidding to marry, and commanding to abstain from meats, which God hath created to be received with thanksgiving of them which believe and know the truth. —1 TIMOTHY 4:1–3

It is easy for anyone with discernment and a basic knowledge of the Bible to see that our world is awash in false teaching. And yet almost all of us know people who have been deceived by those whose purpose is to lead others astray. It is important for us to be fully grounded in the truth, and it is important that we understand the traits and characteristics of false teachers so we can resist their doctrine.

One of the characteristics of false teachers is that they place restrictions where God has not. Certainly there are many things God forbids, and no matter how many of them society or even churches decide to accept, all of those are still wrong and should be forbidden. Sin is still sin, no matter how many people decide that things have changed. But false teachers go beyond forbidding what God has condemned and add their own interpretations and doctrines on top of the Scriptures, claiming biblical authority and requiring people to follow their teaching. This gives them power and control, even though they often do not obey those restrictions themselves. This was the tactic of the Pharisees who opposed Jesus. "For they bind heavy burdens and grievous to be borne, and lay them on men's shoulders; but they themselves will not move them with one of their fingers" (Matthew 23:4). The Bible is the standard by which all preaching and teaching must be measured for truth.

Today's Growth Principle: Only follow those who draw the lines that govern life in the same places that God does in His Word.

Genesis 27–28 // Matthew 8:18–34

The Value of Struggle

James, a servant of God and of the Lord Jesus Christ, to the twelve tribes which are scattered abroad, greeting. My brethren, count it all joy when ye fall into divers temptations; Knowing this, that the trying of your faith worketh patience. But let patience have her perfect work, that ye may be perfect and entire, wanting nothing. —JAMES 1:1-4

In 1921, Franklin D. Roosevelt was a rising star in the political world. But when he contracted polio and was left unable to walk on his own, it seemed that his dreams had been shattered. Roosevelt embarked on a grueling physical rehabilitation program, and though he never regained the use of his legs, he was able to return to public life. He would be elected President in 1932, overcoming great obstacles to reach the peak of the political world. Roosevelt said, "A smooth sea never made a skilled sailor."

Given the choice, most of us would not select great trials and hardship in our lives. Yet, God often uses difficulty to accomplish growth that cannot come in any other way. Like a sculptor chiseling away at a block of marble, God sometimes strikes us with seemingly heavy blows to remove the things that are not part of His design. The process of growth and spiritual development is not painless, nor did God ever guarantee that it would be.

In our moments of pain and trial, it is vital that we not lose sight of God's plan for our lives. Bad things are not necessarily a sign of His displeasure or punishment, though we should examine our lives to see if we are being chastened. Often they are simply God bringing us to a higher level of faith and trust in Him, as He uses struggles to shape and refine our character. There is a great comfort in knowing that nothing takes God by surprise, and that we can always trust Him to do what is best for us.

Today's Growth Principle: Rejoicing in trials only happens when we recognize God's control and purpose for what is happening.

Are You Ready?

In those days was Hezekiah sick unto death. And the prophet Isaiah the son of Amoz came to him, and said unto him, Thus saith the LORD, Set thine house in order; for thou shalt die, and not live. Then he turned his face to the wall, and prayed unto the LORD, saying, I beseech thee, O LORD, remember now how I have walked before thee in truth and with a perfect heart, and have done that which is good in thy sight. And Hezekiah wept sore. —2 KINGS 20:1–3

Early on Saturday morning, January 13, 2018, thousands of people all across Hawaii were shocked to receive an official warning message on their phones. It said, "Ballistic missile threat inbound to Hawaii. Seek immediate shelter. This is not a drill." The frightening message was official, but thankfully it was sent in error. About thirty minutes later, people began receiving messages and updates that confirmed there was no attack. But for a period of time, it seemed things were about to become deadly serious.

Here is the reality. Though most people go through life day by day without any real thought that a given day might be their last, none of us know how much time we have. While we hope for long and active lives, there are no guarantees. We spend a great deal of time and effort in our society working on ways to overlook the fact that life will end, but sooner or later, that day is coming for all of us. The question we must answer is whether or not we are living each day in such a way that we are prepared to stand before God. If you have not trusted Christ as your Saviour, you are not ready for eternity. If you have trusted Christ as your Saviour, you will certainly spend eternity with Him in Heaven. But are you investing your time in that which matters? The truth that life will end should motivate us to effective service and holy living. "So teach us to number our days, that we may apply our hearts unto wisdom" (Psalm 90:12).

Today's Growth Principle: Live today the same way you would if you were to learn it was your last.

The Witness of Creation

The heavens declare the glory of God; and the firmament sheweth his handywork. Day unto day uttereth speech, and night unto night sheweth knowledge. There is no speech nor language, where their voice is not heard. Their line is gone out through all the earth, and their words to the end of the world. In them hath he set a tabernacle for the sun,
—Psalm 19:1–4

In 1998, John Glenn, who had been the first American to orbit our planet thirty-six years earlier, became the oldest man ever to go into space when he joined the *Discovery* space shuttle mission. The seventy-six-year-old was greatly touched by his experience. Later Glenn described his second voyage to space this way: "To look at the window…as I did that first day…to look out at this kind of creation and not believe in God is to me impossible."

Though much of our world today tries its best to deny and discredit the Creator, the evidence of God's handiwork is not hard to find. It takes a more willful decision to disbelieve than to believe what the Bible tells us about how the world came to be. In fact, our surroundings are a powerful voice that speaks to God's existence and the fact that one day we will answer to Him. "For the invisible things of him from the creation of the world are clearly seen, being understood by the things that are made, even his eternal power and Godhead; so that they are without excuse" (Romans 1:20).

While lost people must hear the gospel in order to be saved, the very world around them is a reminder of their need of a Saviour. And the lengths to which people go to avoid dealing with this truth should not discourage us from our vital task of being witnesses, but should instead motivate us to increase our efforts to reach the lost before it is too late.

Today's Growth Principle: If the heavens and earth declare God's glory, how can we who have received His salvation stay silent?

God's Approval Matters Most

*Then said the Lord to him, Put off thy shoes from thy feet: for the place where thou standest is holy ground. I have seen, I have seen the affliction of my people which is in Egypt, and I have heard their groaning, and am come down to deliver them. And now come, I will send thee into Egypt. This Moses whom they refused, saying, Who made thee a ruler and a judge? the same did God send to be a ruler and a deliverer by the hand of the angel which appeared to him in the bush.—*ACTS 7:33–35

When T. DeWitt Talmage took the pastorate at Central Presbyterian Church in Brooklyn, New York, there were just seventeen members. His fervent preaching and emphasis on evangelism sparked massive growth. Just a few years later the church built an auditorium seating six thousand, but it frequently held as many as seven thousand with people sitting in aisles and even on the platform. Talmage kept his focus on God's approval rather than man's, often preaching against the powerful forces behind the drinking, gambling, and prostitution that flourished in the city. At one point, after a series of sermons on evil amusements, Talmage's life was so severely threatened that the Brooklyn police chief stationed twenty-four officers in shifts around the clock at the church to protect the pointed preacher's life. Talmage later said that the threats "frightened everyone but me."

If our focus is on what God thinks of us and what we are doing, we will not be deterred from doing right by either flattery or criticism from others. Jesus was able to say, "And he that sent me is with me: the Father hath not left me alone; for I do always those things that please him" (John 8:29). Nothing that we do is hidden from the eyes of God, and it is His approval that should motivate us rather than the fleeting opinions of men.

Today's Growth Principle: Since we must answer to God, we must keep His pleasure foremost in our minds and hearts.

The Lamb of God

John answered them, saying, I baptize with water: but there standeth one among you, whom ye know not; He it is, who coming after me is preferred before me, whose shoe's latchet I am not worthy to unloose. These things were done in Bethabara beyond Jordan, where John was baptizing. The next day John seeth Jesus coming unto him, and saith, Behold the Lamb of God, which taketh away the sin of the world.—JOHN 1:26–29

At the very beginning of the Old Testament, following the entry of sin into the world, God instituted a system of animal sacrifices. These offerings did not in and of themselves make an atonement for sin. "For it is not possible that the blood of bulls and of goats should take away sins" (Hebrews 10:4). Rather, they were a reminder that the penalty of sin is death (Romans 6:23) and were offered as a tangible expression of faith in God's promise of the coming Messiah who would provide salvation for those who believed in His substitutionary death.

Many years later, just before the beginning of Jesus' public ministry, John the Baptist had been preaching with power and effectiveness of the need for repentance and preparation for the Lord's coming. Huge crowds left the cities and went out across the Jordan River into the desert to hear John preach. When John saw Jesus, he could have announced Him in any number of ways. There are dozens of names for Jesus found throughout Scripture. The one that John chose to use, "The Lamb of God," is a statement of the purpose of Jesus' life. He came into the world to be the willing sacrifice for our sins. "How much more shall the blood of Christ, who through the eternal Spirit offered himself without spot to God, purge your conscience from dead works to serve the living God?" (Hebrews 9:14). This is our hope and confidence of eternal life—the Substitute who paid for our sins in full.

Today's Growth Principle: Take time today to specifically thank God for the amazing gift of salvation through Jesus Christ.

The Power of a Loving Heart

I am the good shepherd: the good shepherd giveth his life for the sheep. But he that is an hireling, and not the shepherd, whose own the sheep are not, seeth the wolf coming, and leaveth the sheep, and fleeth: and the wolf catcheth them, and scattereth the sheep. The hireling fleeth, because he is an hireling, and careth not for the sheep.—JOHN 10:11–13

The British pastor John Fawcett was saved under the ministry of George Whitefield when he was a teenager. After several years of effective ministry in a small rural church in Yorkshire, England, Fawcett was called to pastor the London church where the renowned John Gill had held the pulpit for many years. Fawcett agreed to make the move. He preached his farewell sermon and had his belongings loaded onto wagons. But as Fawcett looked at the people into whom he had poured his life and saw them weeping, he was struck with the realization that he could not leave them behind. Fawcett turned down the well-known and well-paid pulpit in London, and spent another thirty-five years in virtual obscurity with his flock. Not long after making the decision to stay, he penned these words that became a famous hymn:

> Blest be the tie that binds our hearts in Christian love;
> The fellowship of kindred minds is like to that above.
> We share our mutual woes, our mutual burdens bear,
> And often for each other flows the sympathizing tear.

Not just pastors but all of God's people need to have hearts that beat with love and concern for others. There are many excuses and reasons people give to reject the message of the gospel, but a loving heart is hard to refuse. And Christians need other believers to love, care for, and encourage as well. Our hearts must be joined together if the body of Christ is to be healthy.

Today's Growth Principle: Our attitude toward others is not determined by their behavior toward us, but by our hearts toward them.

Genesis 41–42   //   Matthew 12:1–23

The Importance of Commitment

And he said unto another, Follow me. But he said, Lord, suffer me first to go and bury my father. Jesus said unto him, Let the dead bury their dead: but go thou and preach the kingdom of God. And another also said, Lord, I will follow thee; but let me first go bid them farewell, which are at home at my house. And Jesus said unto him, No man, having put his hand to the plough, and looking back, is fit for the kingdom of God.
—LUKE 9:59–62

When the Continental Congress met in Philadelphia in 1775, they unanimously elected John Hancock from Massachusetts as their president. He presided over the representatives of the colonies as they debated the proper response to England. As the war had already begun, they soon set a course for declaring America as an independent nation. After Jefferson's draft of the Declaration of Independence was revised and passed, Hancock placed his large, flourishing signature on the document. According to some accounts he claimed that "King George would be able to read it without his spectacles." John Hancock literally put his life on the line by signing his name.

The Lord calls us to follow Him regardless of the cost. He does not call us to serve Him only when it is easy or convenient, nor is He honored if we abandon our work for Him in the face of opposition. The changing culture around us may mean that one day soon being a committed Christian who wants to believe and practice what the Bible says will be regarded as not just old-fashioned or bigoted, but criminal. Already many have been sued or fired for taking a stand for what they believe. Is your faith strong enough and your commitment to stand firm enough to overcome persecution? "If thou faint in the day of adversity, thy strength is small" (Proverbs 24:10).

Today's Growth Principle: Nothing must be allowed to deter us from following Jesus wherever He leads and commands us to go.

Utterly Secure

Blessed be the God and Father of our Lord Jesus Christ, which according to his abundant mercy hath begotten us again unto a lively hope by the resurrection of Jesus Christ from the dead, To an inheritance incorruptible, and undefiled, and that fadeth not away, reserved in heaven for you, Who are kept by the power of God through faith unto salvation ready to be revealed in the last time.—1 PETER 1:3–5

Many Christians are besieged with doubt and uncertainty regarding their salvation. Yet no one who has truly entered God's family should ever fear leaving it—it is impossible. We are not saved by our own work, but by grace alone. If our salvation depended on us then we would risk losing it, but since salvation is all of God, the keeping of those who come to Him is also completely His responsibility. And that is a responsibility He never fails to meet.

Preaching on this wonderful truth of eternal security, H. A. Ironside said, "You may have heard of the Irishman who was converted but was seized with a dreadful fear that some day he might commit some great sin and lose his soul, that he might be lost after all, and he trembled at the thought. He went to a meeting and heard the words read, 'For ye are dead, and your life is hid with Christ in God' [Colossians 3:3]. 'Glory to God!' the man shouted, 'Whoever heard of a man drowning with his head that high above water?'"

Rather than living with fear, the child of God can live with confidence. Our family relationship allows us access to Him, and we should claim it in faith. "Let us therefore come boldly unto the throne of grace, that we may obtain mercy, and find grace to help in time of need" (Hebrews 4:16). Do not allow the devil to cripple your work for God by causing you to doubt what He has promised regarding your destiny.

Today's Growth Principle: The eternal security promised to every child of God is our strength and confidence.

The Long-Range View

And he said unto Abram, Know of a surety that thy seed shall be a stranger in a land that is not theirs, and shall serve them; and they shall afflict them four hundred years; And also that nation, whom they shall serve, will I judge: and afterward shall they come out with great substance. And thou shalt go to thy fathers in peace; thou shalt be buried in a good old age. But in the fourth generation they shall come hither again: for the iniquity of the Amorites is not yet full.—GENESIS 15:13–16

We live in a society marked by impatience. We want what we want, and we want it right now. I read recently of large companies testing same-day delivery options for their customers who are willing to pay for the privilege. It seems there is a large market for this service because we have become accustomed to instant satisfaction. There are some who seem to regard thinking about next week as "long-term planning."

God works on a different schedule. He exists outside of time, and there is no hurry or haste in His program. Peter wrote, "But, beloved, be not ignorant of this one thing, that one day is with the Lord as a thousand years, and a thousand years as one day" (2 Peter 3:8). Because of that, God is not in a hurry. He is looking at the future in a different way than we are. His plans encompass hundreds and even thousands of years, and His purposes are deeper and richer than ours as well. Whereas we usually simply want change that makes our lives more comfortable, God is working out purposes that are much bigger and better than we could know to desire.

What does that mean for us in a rushed and hurried world? It means that we can relax and trust God with the timing of His plans. We are not ready today for what He has for us to do tomorrow—otherwise He would give it to us today. Instead of worrying about the future, we should trust in His wisdom and care.

Today's Growth Principle: We must not fall into the trap of demanding God to work on our schedule, but instead trust His perfect timing.

The God Who Cleanses

So Naaman came with his horses and with his chariot, and stood at the door of the house of Elisha. And Elisha sent a messenger unto him, saying, Go and wash in Jordan seven times, and thy flesh shall come again to thee, and thou shalt be clean. But Naaman was wroth, and went away, and said, Behold, I thought, He will surely come out to me, and stand, and call on the name of the LORD his God, and strike his hand over the place, and recover the leper.
—2 KINGS 5:9–11

In Bible times, leprosy was one of the most dreaded diseases known to man. The contagious effect meant that unless those suffering from it were isolated, it would quickly spread through a community. The disease was no respecter of persons, and even a powerful general like Naaman of Syria could contract it. The young Israeli girl who had been captured and taken into his home as a slave told Naaman's wife that Elisha, the prophet of God, would be able to help. So Naaman made his way to Elisha, and Elisha told him to go to the Jordan River and immerse himself seven times. After Naaman's initial reluctance to comply, his servants convinced him to obey. Not only was his leprosy completely healed, but the Bible says, "His flesh came again like unto the flesh of a little child, and he was clean" (2 Kings 5:14).

The Bible uses leprosy as a picture of sin. In our own strength and power, we have no hope of dealing with our sin. But as we see in the story of Naaman, we are often reluctant to accept God's plan for dealing with our problem and prefer to do things our own way. That approach never works. It is not until we come to the point where we realize what we have done and yield to God's plan that we receive His cleansing work. "If we confess our sins, he is faithful and just to forgive us our sins, and to cleanse us from all unrighteousness" (1 John 1:9).

Today's Growth Principle: Those who confess and forsake their sin find cleansing in the blood of Jesus Christ.

The Value of Dependability

And the LORD said, Shall I hide from Abraham that thing which I do;
Seeing that Abraham shall surely become a great and mighty nation,
and all the nations of the earth shall be blessed in him? For I know him,
that he will command his children and his household after him, and
they shall keep the way of the LORD, to do justice and judgment; that
the LORD may bring upon Abraham that which he hath spoken of him.
—GENESIS 18:17–19

I read about a man who was preparing to leave for an important business trip when he realized that one of his suits was badly in need of cleaning. Remembering that there was a cleaners with a huge "One Hour Dry Cleaning" sign, he drove across town to drop off his suit. As he filled out his ticket, he told the clerk, "I'll come back in an hour on my way to the airport to pick this up." "Oh no," she said, "It won't be ready until next Thursday." Somewhat taken back he pointed out the sign hanging over the door. "That's just the name of the business," she responded. "We don't do dry cleaning in an hour."

Sometimes there is a gap between our reputation and our character. Sometimes we present ourselves in a more favorable light than we really are willing to deliver. In truth, our character is more important than our reputation. Yet it is still important that we maintain our testimony. It should never be accurately said of a child of God that he or she cannot be counted on to do what is right. Others should learn from their interactions with us that we live up to our "advertising" in terms of our lives matching what we say we believe.

The best way to develop a reputation for dependability is to simply do what we say we will do—over and over and over again. Each of us should desire to have the reputation of Abraham, as God described him as a person who could be trusted to do what was right.

Today's Growth Principle: Each day you either enhance or detract from your reputation as someone who can be relied on.

Rest in the Yoke

Come unto me, all ye that labour and are heavy laden, and I will give you rest. Take my yoke upon you, and learn of me; for I am meek and lowly in heart: and ye shall find rest unto your souls. For my yoke is easy, and my burden is light.—MATTHEW 11:28–30

In Bible times, oxen often worked the fields and carried heavy loads. To distribute the weight of the farm equipment or wagons and to assist the animals in synergistic work, wooden yokes were made to fit over the shoulders of a team of two oxen. If you ever see an old wooden yoke, you will find it quite large and very heavy. If a yoke were not made properly, it would greatly irritate the animal wearing it so that they would find it nearly impossible to work. Additionally, if a diligent animal were placed in a yoke with a distracted or stubborn animal, both would find the yoke unpleasant and difficult.

Jesus did not promise His followers that they would be freed from wearing a yoke. God has service for Him that each of us is to carry out—if not there would be no reason not to take us to Heaven immediately upon our salvation. Rather Jesus promised that when we go to Him we will find that His yoke rests easy upon us, and we will not be burdened by His service. Best of all, we share in His yoke and thus enjoy fellowship with Christ as we serve with Him.

Many people "burn out" after they have served God for a period of time. When once they were faithful to do His work, now they find it burdensome and have laid it aside. What is the problem? Though there are many reasons, one of the biggest is that too many Christians try to work for God in their own strength. Jesus said that we are to learn of Him, which speaks of a growing and deepening relationship. When we work in His strength, we will not find the burdens more than we can bear. Instead we will find rest, even while we labor and share His yoke.

Today's Growth Principle: Rather than complaining about what our service for God requires, we should rejoice in the privilege.

Why the Law Lacks Power

For the law of the Spirit of life in Christ Jesus hath made me free from the law of sin and death. For what the law could not do, in that it was weak through the flesh, God sending his own Son in the likeness of sinful flesh, and for sin, condemned sin in the flesh: That the righteousness of the law might be fulfilled in us, who walk not after the flesh, but after the Spirit.—ROMANS 8:2-4

Many people all around the world think that if they can do enough good things or follow the moral law laid out in the Bible or other religious teachings, they will be acceptable in God's sight. The reality, however, is that no amount of doing good or following laws, no matter how sincere or diligent we are, can remove the stain of sin that each of us carry from the moment of our birth. Charles Spurgeon highlighted the reason for the law's inability when he said, "The law, as originally given to Adam, a perfect man, had he carried it out, would have glorified God, and would have produced in him a perfect life. But we are not in the same position towards God as Adam was, and we are not free from the taint of evil as he was. We have fallen."

The same principle that applies to our salvation applies to our ongoing walk with Christ. There is no way that we can live out the Christian life as God commands in our own strength. We simply lack the ability to overcome sin. It is only as we let the life of Jesus live through us that we can live in victory. This is what Galatians 2:20 speaks of when it says, "I am crucified with Christ: nevertheless I live; yet not I, but Christ liveth in me: and the life which I now live in the flesh I live by the faith of the Son of God, who loved me, and gave himself for me." If we work to obey God by following the law in our strength, we are doomed to failure. But if we yield to the Holy Spirit, allowing Christ to live through us, we can walk in victory.

Today's Growth Principle: Rather than seeking to overcome sin in our strength, we must rely on God's Spirit for victory.

How to Overcome Fear

If thou shalt say in thine heart, These nations are more than I; how can I dispossess them? Thou shalt not be afraid of them: but shalt well remember what the LORD thy God did unto Pharaoh, and unto all Egypt; The great temptations which thine eyes saw, and the signs, and the wonders, and the mighty hand, and the stretched out arm, whereby the LORD thy God brought thee out: so shall the LORD thy God do unto all the people of whom thou art afraid.—DEUTERONOMY 7:17–19

Winston Churchill was famous for his ability as a public speaker to grab an audience and inspire them. One of his most famous addresses was given at the boarding school he had attended as a boy, Harrow School, which had been badly damaged by German bombers during the Blitz on London. Churchill knew that he was speaking to a nation facing a powerful foe as well as to the young boys seated before him. At the conclusion of his address, Churchill said, "This is the lesson: never give in, never give in, never, never, never, never—in nothing, great or small, large or petty—never give in except to convictions of honour and good sense. Never yield to force; never yield to the apparently overwhelming might of the enemy."

The Christian life is a battle, not a pleasure cruise. And in those battles, we often face powerful foes. The temptation we face is to focus on our enemies rather than on God, and when we give in to that temptation, we will find our hearts filled with fear. This is what happened to the Israelites when they heard the report from the ten spies about the giants in the land. Despite what Joshua and Caleb said, they refused to trust God. Fear, and the disobedience that followed because of it, kept Israel in the wilderness for forty years, without the victory God would have given. Years later, however, Joshua led the people to conquer the land and their own fear by relying on the presence of God.

Today's Growth Principle: If you recognize God's power available to you and His presence with you, you will not be overcome by fear.

Stretched out Arms

*Ah Lord God! behold, thou hast made the heaven and the earth by thy great power and stretched out arm, and there is nothing too hard for thee: Thou shewest lovingkindness unto thousands, and recompensest the iniquity of the fathers into the bosom of their children after them: the Great, the Mighty God, the LORD of hosts, is his name, Great in counsel, and mighty in work: for thine eyes are open upon all the ways of the sons of men: to give every one according to his ways, and according to the fruit of his doings:—*JEREMIAH 32:17–19

The first and most visible evidence of the power of God that any of us experience is His creation. Despite the efforts of scientists and educators to convince people otherwise, there is proof of God everywhere we look in our world. The precise distance of the Earth from the sun and the precise angle of the Earth's tilt on its axis are both required for life to exist. Change either by a tiny amount, and we would either burn up or freeze and there would be no life. Yet we are told to believe that it is all a matter of random chance over the passing of billions of years. How foolish! Jeremiah described creation as the result of God's "stretched out arm."

Recently as I was thinking on this passage from Jeremiah, I was reminded of another place where God's arms were stretched out—in the death of Jesus on the cross. The nails themselves could not have held the Son of God. A single word from the lips of the One who created everything by speaking it into existence would have freed Him. Yet that word never came. "He was oppressed, and he was afflicted, yet he opened not his mouth: he is brought as a lamb to the slaughter, and as a sheep before her shearers is dumb, so he openeth not his mouth" (Isaiah 53:7). Although God's power is clearly seen in creation, His powerful love is clearly seen at the cross.

Today's Growth Principle: The amazing love God has for us is measured by the sacrifice of Jesus on the cross.

Recognizing God's Presence

It came even to pass, as the trumpeters and singers were as one, to make one sound to be heard in praising and thanking the LORD; and when they lifted up their voice with the trumpets and cymbals and instruments of musick, and praised the LORD, saying, For he is good; for his mercy endureth for ever: that then the house was filled with a cloud, even the house of the LORD; So that the priests could not stand to minister by reason of the cloud: for the glory of the LORD had filled the house of God.
—2 CHRONICLES 5:13–14

There never has been a building to compare with the amazing temple constructed by Solomon to provide a place of worship for God. The vision for the building was originally David's and when God told the great king it would be his son who would carry out the project, David spent the final years of his life and reign preparing materials and helping Solomon plan for the sacred place that would house the Ark of the Covenant. After years of careful work, when the building was finally complete, Solomon held a great dedication service. During that service, the visible presence of the Spirit of God filled the building in such power that the people could not stay inside.

Many people read this story and think how wonderful it would be to see God's presence displayed like that. Yet in truth, every believer has the same Holy Spirit in his life from the moment of conversion. Jesus said, "And I will pray the Father, and he shall give you another Comforter, that he may abide with you for ever;" (John 14:16). The problem is not that we do not have God's presence, but that we often do things that obscure and hinder His work. First Thessalonians 5:19 instructs us simply, "Quench not the Spirit." The Holy Spirit delights to work through His people, but sometimes—although we would like to experience great, outward manifestations of His presence—we hinder His daily work within us.

Today's Growth Principle: Do not allow anything in your life to hinder the working of the Holy Spirit's power.

The Priority of Service

For, brethren, ye have been called unto liberty; only use not liberty for an occasion to the flesh, but by love serve one another. For all the law is fulfilled in one word, even in this; Thou shalt love thy neighbour as thyself. But if ye bite and devour one another, take heed that ye be not consumed one of another.—GALATIANS 5:13–15

I read a story written by a doctor in which he described having to give a man a terminal diagnosis of pancreatic cancer. It was his last appointment of the day, and after the patient left, the doctor prepared to go home. When he reached the parking lot, he saw an elderly man with the hood of his car raised. As he got closer, the doctor realized someone was on the ground underneath the car working on the engine. In a moment he realized it was his patient. When the car started and the elderly man drove away, the doctor asked what the patient had been doing. "Helping out," the answer came. "My cancer didn't say I couldn't help someone who needed it."

There are always excuses we can find to avoid serving and helping others. There are always other priorities to which we could devote our time and attention. But if we are to live as Jesus lived and follow in His footsteps, then we must be willing to make the sacrifices necessary to serve. Again and again Jesus gave up time and strength for the sake of others. Though He was God, healing others took a toll on Jesus—a toll He thought worth paying. "And Jesus, immediately knowing in himself that virtue had gone out of him, turned him about in the press, and said, Who touched my clothes?" (Mark 5:30). If we see others as Jesus did, as precious people with great needs, we will be more willing to humble ourselves and serve them.

Today's Growth Principle: We have no higher calling than to be humble servants of others just as Jesus was.

It's Not about Us

And I, brethren, when I came to you, came not with excellency of speech or of wisdom, declaring unto you the testimony of God. For I determined not to know any thing among you, save Jesus Christ, and him crucified. And I was with you in weakness, and in fear, and in much trembling. And my speech and my preaching was not with enticing words of man's wisdom, but in demonstration of the Spirit and of power:—1 CORINTHIANS 2:1-4

In 1973, after decades of preaching the gospel, Dr. Lee Roberson woke up one morning unable to speak above a whisper. He had to cancel all of his meetings, and for an entire year he was unable to preach in his church. He traveled all over the country to see various specialists, but none of them could help. Finally, a local surgeon operated, and after a few weeks' recovery, Dr. Roberson was preaching again, which he continued until he was almost ninety-seven years old.

Looking back later, Dr. Roberson remarked how greatly God had blessed the church during the year when he could only sit silently on the platform while someone else filled the pulpit. He said it was one of the most blessed years of ministry he had ever known. Attendance, salvations, baptisms, and even offerings increased. Dr. Roberson said, "That just showed this preacher something. It didn't depend so much on what I was doing. It depended on the working of the power of God through our lives."

Too many times we rely on our talent and efforts rather than depending on God. The results of our labor for the Lord are not on our shoulders. If we want God's power and blessing, we must abandon both self-reliance and self-focus. Our service isn't about us—it's about Jesus! "But he giveth more grace. Wherefore he saith, God resisteth the proud, but giveth grace unto the humble" (James 4:6).

Today's Growth Principle: We must rely on God's strength rather than ours if we hope to accomplish anything lasting for Him.

Even the Philistines Knew Better

Wherefore then do ye harden your hearts, as the Egyptians and Pharaoh hardened their hearts? when he had wrought wonderfully among them, did they not let the people go, and they departed? Now therefore make a new cart, and take two milch kine, on which there hath come no yoke, and tie the kine to the cart, and bring their calves home from them: And take the ark of the Lord, and lay it upon the cart; and put the jewels of gold, which ye return him for a trespass offering, in a coffer by the side thereof; and send it away, that it may go. —1 Samuel 6:6–8

Because of the wickedness of the sons of Eli and their father's failure as the High Priest to stop them, God gave the Philistines victory over the Israelites in battle. They captured the Ark of the Covenant and placed it in the temples of their gods as part of the spoils of war. God destroyed the idols, making the stone statues bow down before the Ark. And He brought great diseases to the Philistine cities. They quickly realized what was going on and determined to return the Ark to Israel. They remembered the story of God's judgment on the Egyptians when they would not let the Israelites go in the days of Moses, and did not want to experience His judgment any longer.

Too often we cling to our sin, hardening our hearts against the convicting voice of the Holy Spirit and reproving words of the Bible. We love our sin and do not want to let it go. As a result we suffer the correction God brings on His children. He loves us too much to allow us to continue in sin. "Now no chastening for the present seemeth to be joyous, but grievous: nevertheless afterward it yieldeth the peaceable fruit of righteousness unto them which are exercised thereby" (Hebrews 12:11).

Today's Growth Principle: Rather than hardening our hearts, we should quickly turn back to God when He corrects us.

Don't Forget Where You Were

And you hath he quickened, who were dead in trespasses and sins; Wherein in time past ye walked according to the course of this world, according to the prince of the power of the air, the spirit that now worketh in the children of disobedience: Among whom also we all had our conversation in times past in the lusts of our flesh, fulfilling the desires of the flesh and of the mind; and were by nature the children of wrath, even as others.
—EPHESIANS 2:1–3

There is no question that our society is filled with evil, and that we are seeing evil not only *accepted* but actively *promoted*. Those who hold to the truth are scorned and mocked, and a number of people have faced legal battles for trying to hold to what they believed was right.

It is easy for us to fall into the trap of condemning evil in the world while forgetting that we were once a part of the world. Even those who were saved at an early age without ever going deep into a blatantly sinful lifestyle were dead in their sin. Their outward lives may not have been scarred and marked because of the things they were protected from doing, but they were just as much sinners in need of a Saviour as someone who has lived apart from God in the worst sins the world has to offer.

All of us needed God's salvation. And those who have not yet received God's gift are not to be scorned, but to be the objects of both compassion and outreach. We must never forget that Satan is actively working to keep them from recognizing the truth. "In whom the god of this world hath blinded the minds of them which believe not, lest the light of the glorious gospel of Christ, who is the image of God, should shine unto them" (2 Corinthians 4:4). We who carry the light should remember what it was like to be in darkness and should consistently and persistently share the truth of the gospel with those who need Christ.

Today's Growth Principle: Since we were once lost, it is our duty to reach out to those who have not yet responded to the truth.

FEBRUARY

Look and Live

And the LORD said unto Moses, Make thee a fiery serpent, and set it upon a pole: and it shall come to pass, that every one that is bitten, when he looketh upon it, shall live. And Moses made a serpent of brass, and put it upon a pole, and it came to pass, that if a serpent had bitten any man, when he beheld the serpent of brass, he lived.—NUMBERS 21:8–9

Though the great preacher Charles Spurgeon was raised in a Christian home, he had not yet been saved when one Sunday morning as a teenager, he decided to go to a different church than the one he normally attended. A snowstorm changed his plans, and he stopped at a small church with only a dozen or so people in attendance. The weather had kept the pastor from reaching the church, and an untrained layman filled the pulpit. He preached a simple salvation message from Isaiah 45:22, "Look unto me, and be ye saved…"

Spurgeon later recounted, "Just fixing his eyes on me, as if he knew all my heart, he said, 'Young man, you look very miserable. And you will always be miserable—miserable in life and miserable in death—if you don't obey my text; but if you obey now, this moment, you will be saved.' Then lifting up his hands, he shouted, 'Young man, look to Jesus Christ. Look! Look! Look! You have nothing to do but look and live!' I saw at once the way of salvation. I had been waiting to do fifty things, but when I heard that word, 'Look!'…the cloud was gone."

Salvation is not the result of our labors and efforts. It cannot be gained by avoiding evil or by doing good. It is not earned by going to church or following the golden rule or serving our fellowman. It is only when we look to Jesus, receiving in faith the free gift of salvation purchased for us by His death on the cross, that our sins are forgiven and we have eternal life.

Today's Growth Principle: No one, no matter how good, has any hope of salvation apart from looking to Jesus alone.

The Triumphant Power of God

And Moses and Aaron went in unto Pharaoh, and they did so as the LORD had commanded: and Aaron cast down his rod before Pharaoh, and before his servants, and it became a serpent. Then Pharaoh also called the wise men and the sorcerers: now the magicians of Egypt, they also did in like manner with their enchantments. For they cast down every man his rod, and they became serpents: but Aaron's rod swallowed up their rods.—EXODUS 7:10–12

When God sent Moses to Egypt to free the Israelites from bondage, He did not send Moses to work alone. God sent Aaron, Moses' older brother, to be his partner and supporter in the work. But there was something far more important God promised, which was that His powerful hand would be with Moses. Just as He always does, God kept that promise.

Pharaoh had no interest in giving up the benefits of hundreds of thousands of Israelites who worked for him in forced slavery. When Moses confronted him with God's demand, Pharaoh refused. Before the ten plagues which devastated Egypt and finally forced the reluctant ruler to concede, there was a demonstration of God's power which should have been all Pharaoh needed. When Aaron's rod became a snake after he threw it on the ground, Pharaoh's sorcerers duplicated the feat—but then all their "snakes" were eaten by the one God brought forth.

Though we do face a powerful enemy in the devil, his power pales in comparison to the power of God. God is more than able to overcome every obstacle and opposition that Satan can offer. God never sweats or calls for reserves or back up. He is never challenged in any way. He has all power and authority, and remains in control, no matter what our circumstances. The battles we face are real, but they are not a threat to God's overcoming power which is available to us as His children.

Today's Growth Principle: When we trust God and claim the victory He provides, we cannot be defeated by the enemy.

The Transformed Life

Therefore we are buried with him by baptism into death: that like as Christ was raised up from the dead by the glory of the Father, even so we also should walk in newness of life. For if we have been planted together in the likeness of his death, we shall be also in the likeness of his resurrection: Knowing this, that our old man is crucified with him, that the body of sin might be destroyed, that henceforth we should not serve sin.
—ROMANS 6:4–6

Some years ago, I received a card from a little girl in our church. She wrote: "Dear Pastor, Thank you for this church and for your preaching. I know that you work very hard to do that stuff. We are very happy to have you here. This year my dad learned not to drink and smoke and how to be nice. Thank you and God bless you. Love, Anna."

The Lord does not save us simply to change our eternal destiny, though the gift of salvation does change our course from headed toward Hell to headed toward Heaven. But God has plans for us in this life as well. He intends for us to be changed by our salvation on a practical, day-to-day level. The fact that we are Christians does not automatically remake our temperament, personality, or character traits, but it should mean that Christ is seen through us in the way those are expressed in our daily lives.

The Apostle Paul expressed this goal for each believer when he wrote, "That ye might walk worthy of the Lord unto all pleasing, being fruitful in every good work, and increasing in the knowledge of God" (Colossians 1:10). If there is no ongoing transformation in your life as a result of your salvation, something is very wrong. While no Christian is sinless, we should be sinning less and less as we become more and more like Jesus through our walk with Him.

Today's Growth Principle: It is not in our own strength but in the power of the Holy Spirit that our lives are transformed.

A Desire to Be Like Jesus

Yea doubtless, and I count all things but loss for the excellency of the knowledge of Christ Jesus my Lord: for whom I have suffered the loss of all things, and do count them but dung, that I may win Christ, And be found in him, not having mine own righteousness, which is of the law, but that which is through the faith of Christ, the righteousness which is of God by faith: That I may know him, and the power of his resurrection, and the fellowship of his sufferings, being made conformable unto his death; If by any means I might attain unto the resurrection of the dead.
—PHILIPPIANS 3:8–11

Though Ulysses S. Grant received a congressional appointment to West Point, he was far from a model student. Grant did not like the classes, preferring to read adventure stories from authors like James Fenimore Cooper to studying. As a result, his grades suffered, and he frequently considered dropping out of school. Then General Winfield Scott, a hero from both the War of 1812 and the Mexican-American War, visited the campus. Grant was struck by Scott's personal appearance and his bearing, and determined that he would stay in the military and one day be a great general as well. Eventually Grant would be placed in overall command of the Union Army and win the Civil War.

The model that we should be following every day of our lives is the example of Jesus Christ. He is the pattern for each of us. The highest aspiration we should have is to live in His power so that we become more like Him. "I am crucified with Christ: nevertheless I live; yet not I, but Christ liveth in me: and the life which I now live in the flesh I live by the faith of the Son of God, who loved me, and gave himself for me" (Galatians 2:20).

Today's Growth Principle: The more we read and study the life of Christ from the Bible, the more His image will be impressed on us.

The Benefits of Clear Boundaries

And what agreement hath the temple of God with idols? for ye are the temple of the living God; as God hath said, I will dwell in them, and walk in them; and I will be their God, and they shall be my people. Wherefore come out from among them, and be ye separate, saith the Lord, and touch not the unclean thing; and I will receive you, And will be a Father unto you, and ye shall be my sons and daughters, saith the Lord Almighty.
—2 CORINTHIANS 6:16–18

Unlike a football field or basketball court where the boundaries are permanently painted, the line markers on the baseball field are made with chalk. This means that over the course of a game the lines—especially around home plate where there is a lot of coming and going—start to get blurred. Often the umpire will take a moment to wipe the dust off the plate so he can clearly see where the boundaries of the strike zone should be. And if the foot traffic is heavy enough, he may even call for the batter's box to be re-chalked so the places where it is legal for the batter to stand are clearly visible.

The lines in life serve a purpose. This is just as true in important matters as it is in sports. God has given us clear guidelines, both in specific commandments and in specific principles. God has made His way plain to us in His Word. We do sometimes come to difficult choices and decisions that require us to carefully study the Bible to determine which principles apply. But in most cases, the blurring of the lines comes not from a lack of understanding what is right, but from our not really wanting to do what we know to be right, and from looking for alternatives. God calls us to live in such a way that we clearly and distinctly identify with Him.

Today's Growth Principle: A close relationship with God requires that we draw clear lines of distinction between ourselves and the world.

Life-Changing Impact

Wherewithal shall a young man cleanse his way? by taking heed thereto according to thy word. With my whole heart have I sought thee: O let me not wander from thy commandments. Thy word have I hid in mine heart, that I might not sin against thee. Blessed art thou, O LORD: teach me thy statutes.—PSALM 119:9–12

The evangelist Rodney "Gipsy" Smith was known not only for his pulpit ministry, which was powerful and effective, but also for his personal evangelism as well. He would talk to everyone he met about their need for Jesus. After his services, he would often stay for long periods of time to talk to those who were concerned about their souls and to counsel Christians who sought a deeper relationship with God. After one service, a man told Smith that the Bible hadn't done anything for him even though he had "gone through it several times." Smith replied, "Let it once go through you, and you will tell a different story."

The Bible was not given to us primarily for informational purposes, even though it is perfect and without error, and everything it says is correct and true. The Bible was given to us to guide our paths and keep us from sin. But it must be applied to our lives in order to have that effect. Just as having a state-of-the-art GPS system in your car will not get you to your destination unless you actually follow the directions it gives, so owning or even simply knowing God's Word won't change your life unless you apply it to your life.

It is true that there are things in the Bible that require deep study to grasp and truths that a lifetime of learning will never reach. It was inspired by an infinite and unlimited God. But rather than being discouraged by what we haven't yet learned, we need to focus on putting into practice everything we know. God reveals more truth to us when we follow what we have already been given.

Today's Growth Principle: If we look to the Bible as an unfailing guide and take heed to its directions, our lives will be transformed.

Following Through

Finally, brethren, whatsoever things are true, whatsoever things are honest, whatsoever things are just, whatsoever things are pure, whatsoever things are lovely, whatsoever things are of good report; if there be any virtue, and if there be any praise, think on these things. Those things, which ye have both learned, and received, and heard, and seen in me, do: and the God of peace shall be with you.—PHILIPPIANS 4:8–9

Perhaps the most famous battle in history, Waterloo, marked the final defeat of Napoleon by the combined British and Prussian armies. Knowing that he would be outnumbered if his two opponents combined their forces, Napoleon had ordered Marshall Emmanuel de Grouchy to attack the Prussian forces who were retreating from an earlier battle. Napoleon believed that this would give him time to deal with the British under Wellington separately before turning his attention back to the Prussians. Grouchy was slow to respond to his orders, and though he carried them out, eventually defeating the Prussian rear-guard, he failed to stop the main column from advancing. They reached the battlefield in the nick of time, and with those reinforcements, Wellington defeated Napoleon.

The Lord has given us a number of instructions in His Word. Knowing them is good, but it is not enough. We must actually do the things we are commanded to do. We must execute our orders. Many people fail to accomplish what they should for God because they are not putting what they know and have learned into practice. Bible study and learning what God intends is critical, but it is only the first step of the process. To be who God calls us to be, we must put forth whatever effort and obedience is required to actually *do* the things He says. In the Upper Room Jesus said, "Ye are my friends, if ye *do* whatsoever I command you" (John 15:14).

Today's Growth Principle: There is no victory apart from action.

Gracious and Salty Speech

Continue in prayer, and watch in the same with thanksgiving; Withal praying also for us, that God would open unto us a door of utterance, to speak the mystery of Christ, for which I am also in bonds: That I may make it manifest, as I ought to speak. Walk in wisdom toward them that are without, redeeming the time. Let your speech be alway with grace, seasoned with salt, that ye may know how ye ought to answer every man."—COLOSSIANS 4:2–6

Perhaps you heard about the elderly man whose hearing had declined over the years to where he could hardly understand what those around him were saying. Finally he went to the doctor and got a hearing aid. When he went back after a month for a checkup, the doctor asked how his family members liked being able to be heard when they spoke to him. "I didn't tell them about the hearing aid," the man replied. "I just sit there and listen. So far I've changed my will three times!"

God tells us in His Word that our speech should be wisely balanced with both grace and salt coming from our tongues. There are times to correct and times to praise, times to instruct and times to listen, times to teach and times to testify. There are no times, however, when it is right to gossip, murmur, or criticize with a harsh spirit. Many times we speak carelessly and thoughtlessly, not taking time to consider the impact of the words we use on those who hear them.

The same passage in which Paul asked for people to pray for his speaking to be effective when he preached the gospel, contains the instruction about our daily conversation. Have you ever prayed that God would guide and guard your words as you talk to others? A person who does that will not casually speak because of the reminder of the importance of what we say to those who hear us.

Today's Growth Principle: Choose your words with great care, for they have a powerful impact on the lives of others.

The Key to Bearing Fruit

And Jesus answered them, saying, The hour is come, that the Son of man should be glorified. Verily, verily, I say unto you, Except a corn of wheat fall into the ground and die, it abideth alone: but if it die, it bringeth forth much fruit. He that loveth his life shall lose it; and he that hateth his life in this world shall keep it unto life eternal.—JOHN 12:23–25

Every Christian should have a desire to live a fruitful and productive life for God. The gratitude for His salvation and the desire for obedience to His commands should compel us to seek to be busy about His work. But if we wish to be truly fruitful, there is a necessity—we must die to self. This is where many people are derailed. They want to accomplish things for God, but are not willing to pay the price. There is no way to detour around death to self and still reach the goal of bearing fruit.

One of the great men of faith in history was George Müller. His work of providing for the needs of thousands and thousands of orphans was carried out and financed completely through faith. Müller refused to seek financial support, instead trusting God to touch the hearts of people to support the work. His faith has challenged people for many years, adding another level of fruitfulness to his direct ministry during his life.

George Müller said, "There was a day when I died, utterly died, died to George Müller, his opinions, preferences, tastes and will, died to the world, its approval or censure, died to the approval or blame even of my brethren and friends, and since then I have studied to show myself approved unto God." Each of us must make this choice.

Just as a seed must be planted in the ground and die unseen by others if it is to bear fruit, so we also must die to self, surrendering our lives to Christ. If we are willing to die to self, then God will accomplish His harvest in our lives.

Today's Growth Principle: If we cling to our lives and our desires, we will never accomplish what God has called us to do.

Trusting God's Unseen Hand

Hold your peace, let me alone, that I may speak, and let come on me what will. Wherefore do I take my flesh in my teeth, and put my life in mine hand? Though he slay me, yet will I trust in him: but I will maintain mine own ways before him. He also shall be my salvation: for an hypocrite shall not come before him.—JOB 13:13–16

In the depths of his suffering and despair, when he had lost his possessions and his health, when he had been falsely accused by friends who should have comforted him, and when God was silent, Job maintained his faith. Though he did not have the Bible as a source of instruction and encouragement as we do, Job's relationship with God was strong enough to withstand the most severe trial of his life when he had to stand alone.

In November of 2017, twenty-six people were murdered during the worship service at the First Baptist Church in Sutherland Springs, Texas. The pastor, Frank Pomeroy, was out of town that Sunday, and he returned home to conduct funerals for nearly half of his congregation. One of the victims was his fourteen-year-old daughter. Asked how he could explain this tragedy, Pomeroy replied, "I don't understand, but I know my God does."

God does not owe us an explanation of what He is doing in our lives, or a justification for the methods He chooses to bring about His will. He is God and we are not. It is our responsibility to trust Him whether or not we can see His plan. God does not stop working just because we cannot see what He is doing. He is still there, lovingly working through the circumstances of our lives to conform us to become more like Jesus. Often it is the things that are most painful in the moment that produce the greatest harvest of God's work in our lives.

Today's Growth Principle: Faith is not created in hard times, but it is revealed when it is put to the test.

Obedience and Happiness

If I then, your Lord and Master, have washed your feet; ye also ought to wash one another's feet. For I have given you an example, that ye should do as I have done to you. Verily, verily, I say unto you, The servant is not greater than his lord; neither he that is sent greater than he that sent him. If ye know these things, happy are ye if ye do them.—JOHN 13:14–17

The false belief that happiness could be found in getting just one more thing than we have now—a newer car, a bigger house, a larger paycheck, a different spouse, or a better church—has been around since the Garden of Eden. Even in a perfect world with no sin and only one restriction, Adam and Eve still looked on the forbidden fruit with longing, and eventually ate it despite God's command. "And when the woman saw that the tree was good for food, and that it was pleasant to the eyes, and a tree to be desired to make one wise, she took of the fruit thereof, and did eat, and gave also unto her husband with her; and he did eat" (Genesis 3:6).

Lasting happiness is never found in getting what God has decreed to be off limits. Instead it is found when we submit our will and our desires to His command and obey. Dr. John Rice said, "Sin in the Christian brings the smiting of the conscience. It brings the rebuke of the Holy Spirit. No Christian can be a happy Christian, except as he day by day seeks to live in the smile of God's approval. Godly living does not earn salvation, but it does bring happiness."

True happiness is not discovered by getting forbidden fruit, but rather by proactive obedience. God knows better than we do what will promote and what will hinder happiness in our lives, and He only wants what is best for us.

Today's Growth Principle: When we trust God and follow His commands, we reap the benefit of an improved relationship with Him, which is the source of true joy.

Stop Complaining

And the people spake against God, and against Moses, Wherefore have ye brought us up out of Egypt to die in the wilderness? for there is no bread, neither is there any water; and our soul loatheth this light bread. And the LORD sent fiery serpents among the people, and they bit the people; and much people of Israel died. Therefore the people came to Moses, and said, We have sinned, for we have spoken against the LORD, and against thee; pray unto the LORD, that he take away the serpents from us. And Moses prayed for the people.—NUMBERS 21:5-7

It seems that Christians today often divide sins into two categories: those they think are really bad, and those that don't seem to them to be all that serious. Often people draw that line precisely between the sins that really tempt them and the ones that don't. That way, they feel good in evaluating themselves compared to those around them. But that doesn't change the way God views sins. He hates all of them, even the ones we deem to be "little" sins. And one of the worst of those that we so often overlook or excuse is complaining.

Mark Twain said, "Don't complain and talk about your problems. Eighty percent of the people won't care and the other twenty percent will think you deserve them." But complaining is far worse than just ineffective—it is wrong.

Complaining reveals that we are not thankful for the multitude of blessings we have received. The way God views complaining is vividly illustrated for us by the poisonous snakes God sent among the Israelites when they complained about God's provision for them. God had graciously freed them from slavery, taken them across the Red Sea, and fed them with manna from Heaven, yet they still complained. Murmuring is not an "acceptable" sin.

Today's Growth Principle: When we murmur and complain, we are insulting God's love and care for us.

Unfailing Promises

And it was so, that when Solomon had made an end of praying all this prayer and supplication unto the LORD, he arose from before the altar of the LORD, from kneeling on his knees with his hands spread up to heaven. And he stood, and blessed all the congregation of Israel with a loud voice, saying, Blessed be the LORD, that hath given rest unto his people Israel, according to all that he promised: there hath not failed one word of all his good promise, which he promised by the hand of Moses his servant.
—1 KINGS 8:54–56

Charles Spurgeon said, "I sometimes liken the promises to the smith's great bunch of keys which he brings when you have lost the key of your chest, and cannot unlock it. He feels pretty sure that out of all the keys upon the ring some one or other will fit, and he tries them with patient industry. At last—yes—that is it, he has loosened the bolt, and you can get at your treasures. There is always a promise in the volume of inspiration suitable to your present case."

The challenges that we face as we go through life require strength, wisdom, and resources that are beyond our ability to produce. But for every trial and burden, there is a promise in the Word of God on which we can lean for help—and not one of those promises God makes has ever been broken. No child of God has ever been turned away because the Father in Heaven did not have the resources or ability to meet his need. God even knows our needs before we bring them to Him.

While many Bible promises are conditioned on our obedience and cannot be claimed unless we fulfill the conditions, all of them are utterly reliable. Our task is to fill our hearts and minds with the Bible so that we know what God has said, and then to claim His promises in faith. When we do, we will receive what God offers.

Today's Growth Principle: We can rely on the promises of God with complete confidence in every situation of life.

The Unfailing Love of God

Nay, in all these things we are more than conquerors through him that loved us. For I am persuaded, that neither death, nor life, nor angels, nor principalities, nor powers, nor things present, nor things to come, Nor height, nor depth, nor any other creature, shall be able to separate us from the love of God, which is in Christ Jesus our Lord.—ROMANS 8:37–39

The wonderful hymn "The Love of God" was written by Frederick Lehman during a break from work one day at his job in California. Seated on an empty lemon box, he took a pencil and wrote the chorus and first two stanzas. The third stanza is actually much older, based on a poem written by a Jewish rabbi more than a thousand years ago:

> Could we with ink the ocean fill, And were the skies of parchment made;
> Were every stalk on earth a quill, And every man a scribe by trade:
> To write the love of God above Would drain the ocean dry,
> Nor could the scroll contain the whole Though stretched from sky to sky.

There is nothing more powerful than the love of God. This is the reason that Jesus came into the world. "For God so loved the world, that he gave his only begotten Son, that whosoever believeth in him should not perish, but have everlasting life" (John 3:16). God's love made possible the salvation that has changed the course of our eternal destiny and given us the incredible gift of eternal life and a relationship with God through Christ.

God's love is not meant to be hoarded. In fact, one of the wonderful things about God's love is that it is not diminished when it is shared. As we obey the Great Commission and reach others with the gospel, we bring God's love to those who so urgently need it. We should be living in the fullness of God's love so much that sharing it is the natural result.

Today's Growth Principle: Having been blessed to receive the wonderful gift of God's love in our lives, we have a privileged responsibility to share it with others.

Finding Courage in God's Presence

Let your conversation be without covetousness; and be content with such things as ye have: for he hath said, I will never leave thee, nor forsake thee. So that we may boldly say, The Lord is my helper, and I will not fear what man shall do unto me.—HEBREWS 13:5–6

The evangelist D. L. Moody loved to tell the story of a preacher he knew in Scotland who went once a week to a children's hospital to try to comfort sick little ones. On one trip, he met a boy of six who was facing having his leg amputated. The preacher asked if the boy had anyone to stay with him as he waited for the surgery. The boy explained that his father was dead and his mother was too ill to leave their home. Feeling sorry for him, the preacher talked about how caring and loving the hospital staff were, trying to find some way to offer him comfort. The boy, however, didn't seem troubled. He simply explained, "Jesus will be with me."

There will never be a day as a Christian when you must face the trials and burdens of life alone. God is always with us, and nothing can separate us from Him or His love (Romans 8:38–39). There may be days when we do not feel His presence as we would like, but there will never be days when He is not there.

The delight of experiencing God's presence in a real way should motivate us to live in such a way that we would not be ashamed if we could physically see Him with us. The reality of His presence should give us a sense of confidence and boldness that equips us to take on whatever threats or challenges would keep us from walking with Him. We should not expect the devil to leave us alone if we are trying to do right, but we should expect victory through God's power.

Today's Growth Principle: Even when we cannot feel His presence close to us, God never abandons or forsakes one of His children.

Be Still

Come, behold the works of the LORD, what desolations he hath made in the earth. He maketh wars to cease unto the end of the earth; he breaketh the bow, and cutteth the spear in sunder; he burneth the chariot in the fire. Be still, and know that I am God: I will be exalted among the heathen, I will be exalted in the earth. The LORD of hosts is with us; the God of Jacob is our refuge. Selah.—PSALM 46:8–11

There is not a great deal of description in the Bible of the emotional state of the Israelites as they left Egypt the night of the first Passover. The final plague, the death of the firstborn of Egypt, had convinced Pharaoh to let them go. After over four hundred years, they would finally be going to the land God had promised Abraham. There must have been enormous elation and gratitude in their hearts. Yet in just a few hours all of that was gone. They faced what seemed to be certain destruction, trapped between the Red Sea and the pursuing Egyptian army.

In that moment, the Israelites received one of the most difficult instructions from God—to do nothing. "And Moses said unto the people, Fear ye not, stand still, and see the salvation of the LORD, which he will shew to you to-day: for the Egyptians whom ye have seen to-day, ye shall see them again no more for ever" (Exodus 14:13).

There are certainly times when our action is required, and God does not do for us what He has enabled and equipped us to do for ourselves. But there are also times when we must be patient and wait for God to work. Our understanding of both the present and the future is necessarily limited, but God's understanding is not. He knows full well what we will face and what the outcome of His plan for our lives will be. Sometimes God tells us to move forward in bold and courageous faith. And sometimes he tells us to wait on Him, demonstrating our faith by bold and courageous patience.

Today's Growth Principle: Do not miss seeing God's power displayed because you insisted on taking matters into your own hands.

Rejoicing from Pain

Let the heavens be glad, and let the earth rejoice: and let men say among the nations, The LORD reigneth. Let the sea roar, and the fulness thereof: let the fields rejoice, and all that is therein. Then shall the trees of the wood sing out at the presence of the LORD, because he cometh to judge the earth. O give thanks unto the LORD; for he is good; for his mercy endureth for ever.—1 CHRONICLES 16:31–34

David's heart was in the right place when he first attempted to bring the Ark of the Covenant to Jerusalem, but his methods were not right. God does not grant exceptions to His commands for good intentions, and David did not follow the instructions Moses had given for transporting this visible symbol of God's presence among His people. As a result of going against those instructions, Uzzah was killed when he reached out to steady the Ark. After some time passed, David set out to do the job again using the methods God had laid out. This time the process was successful, and the arrival of the Ark in the Holy City was a time of national praise and rejoicing, when David penned one of his greatest songs of gratitude to God.

Many times it is our moments of failure and judgment that lead to a deeper level of relationship and joy in God's work in our lives. F. B. Meyer wrote, "Often God seems to place His children in positions of profound difficulty.…It is a platform for the display of His almighty grace and power. He will not only deliver you, but in doing so He will give you a lesson that you will never forget; and to which, in many a psalm and song in after days, you will revert. You will never be able to thank God enough for having done just as He has." Sometimes, in the middle of difficult circumstances, we become discouraged and feel forsaken by God. Yet these times are a special opportunity for us to draw near to God and to know that He is preparing us to see His hand in our lives.

Today's Growth Principle: When we endure difficult circumstances, we have an opportunity to see God work in mighty ways.

A Desire to Be with the Father

When I was a child, I spake as a child, I understood as a child, I thought as a child: but when I became a man, I put away childish things. For now we see through a glass, darkly; but then face to face: now I know in part; but then shall I know even as also I am known. And now abideth faith, hope, charity, these three; but the greatest of these is charity.
—1 CORINTHIANS 13:11–13

The first railroads represented an amazing increase in the speed of travel compared to what had come before, but they were still very slow by modern standards. And passenger comfort was limited by the noise, the smoke, and the very uneven ride of early trains. I read about a little boy who was making a lengthy trip on a train by himself. At one point, a lady who had been watching him asked if he was getting tired after so long a trip. He quickly replied that he wasn't tired. "I'm going to see my father as soon as we arrive," he explained. Anticipating his destination gave him hope and encouragement.

If our focus is on God as it should be, our greatest longing will be to be in His presence. Although we have the certainty of spending eternity with Him through the salvation provided by grace through faith, His presence is not just something we have to wait to experience in the future. Jesus said, "And this is life eternal, that they might know thee the only true God, and Jesus Christ, whom thou hast sent" (John 17:3). Our eternal life began the moment we were saved, and we have the opportunity to spend time in God's presence *now.* Certainly our fellowship with God will be on a much higher level in Heaven, but for those who seek His face, His presence can be experienced and enjoyed here on Earth. David wrote, "Thou wilt shew me the path of life: in thy presence is fulness of joy…" (Psalm 16:11). There is no such thing as a powerful, victorious Christian life apart from the abiding presence of God.

Today's Growth Principle: If our hearts do not long for a real sense of God's presence, it is a sign that something is wrong in our lives.

When You Include God

And the angel answered and said unto her, The Holy Ghost shall come upon thee, and the power of the Highest shall overshadow thee: therefore also that holy thing which shall be born of thee shall be called the Son of God. And, behold, thy cousin Elisabeth, she hath also conceived a son in her old age: and this is the sixth month with her, who was called barren. For with God nothing shall be impossible.—LUKE 1:35–37

On the way home from church one Sunday morning, little Billy's dad asked him what they learned in Sunday school. Billy launched into a dramatic account of the crossing of the Red Sea, complete with fighter jets, amphibious naval assault craft, and a dramatic bomb strike at the crucial moment. When his dad asked if that was really the way they told the story, he replied, "Well not exactly. But I didn't think you'd believe it if I told you what they said really happened!"

The power of God is truly amazing. And just as the miraculous accounts recorded in the Bible could not have taken place without His power, a victorious Christian life cannot be lived without God. Yet too many times we fail to trust in the amazing power we have been given to do His purpose and will in this world. There is great opposition from the devil when we try to do what is right, but that opposition cannot overcome God's people operating in God's strength. "And I say also unto thee, That thou art Peter, and upon this rock I will build my church; and the gates of hell shall not prevail against it" (Matthew 16:18).

The problem is that when we try to overcome opposition and obstacles in our own strength, we are certain to fail. None of us have the wisdom, power, and ability to triumph on our own. God never intended us to have those. Instead, He intends for us to rely on Him alone. Then He not only gives us the victory, but He also gets the credit and glory for it, just as He deserves.

Today's Growth Principle: No challenge that you will ever face exceeds God's ability to overcome it.

Leviticus 25   //   Mark 1:23–45

The Necessity of Evangelism

When therefore the Lord knew how the Pharisees had heard that Jesus made and baptized more disciples than John, (Though Jesus himself baptized not, but his disciples,) He left Judaea, and departed again into Galilee. And he must needs go through Samaria.—JOHN 4:1–4

In Bible times, Jewish people would go to great lengths to avoid going through Samaria. There was considerable tension between the Jews and the Samaritans, tracing back to the time of the Babylonian captivity. Yet when Jesus was returning to His home near Galilee, He was compelled to go through Samaria by the reality that there were people in Sychar who needed to hear that the Messiah had come.

When the Bible uses the expression "must needs go," it is a strong statement—a declaration of necessity. This was not a preference or a whim. Instead, Jesus was responding to God's commission on His life. He had to go there and tell first the woman He met at the well and then the entire town the good news. To Jesus, no one was insignificant or unworthy of hearing the message of the gospel—not even a single woman whom others despised. Jesus was driven by the urgency of reaching people. This was not a casual afterthought to Christ. He didn't just invite people to trust Him when it was convenient for His schedule and when they happened to be present. He purposefully sought out those who needed salvation, and before He returned to Heaven He commanded us to take up that mission and make it our priority (Matthew 28:19–20).

The church today has many good and helpful programs, and I'm thankful for them. But if we are not careful we can lose sight of the vital importance of evangelism. Nothing can substitute for it. Nothing can be allowed to crowd it out or diminish it. Jesus said, "And other sheep I have, which are not of this fold: them also I must bring, and they shall hear my voice; and there shall be one fold, and one shepherd" (John 10:16).

Today's Growth Principle: We must be diligent about reaching the lost with the gospel before it is too late.

A God Who Keeps His Promises

Prove all things; hold fast that which is good. Abstain from all appearance
of evil. And the very God of peace sanctify you wholly; and I pray God
your whole spirit and soul and body be preserved blameless unto the
coming of our Lord Jesus Christ. Faithful is he that calleth you, who also
will do it.—1 THESSALONIANS 5:21–24

In 1916, Woodrow Wilson ran for re-election as President of the United
States. What we now call World War I had been going on in Europe for
two years, and there was great disagreement over whether or not the US
should get involved. Wilson had been favorable toward the British and
French, who were fighting the Germans, but the official US policy was
neutrality. During the campaign, the slogan "He kept us out of war" was
used by Wilson's supporters to encourage people to vote for him. Wilson
won the election and was sworn in for his second term in office on March
4, 1917. On April 2, however, he asked Congress for a declaration of war
against Germany, and the US entered the conflict.

The promises made by men are not always reliable. Though there
may be a few people whom we have learned that we can trust, and
though we should always have the character and integrity to do what we
say we will do, the reality is that as fallible and sinful human beings, our
promises are not always certain. Almost all of us have had the experience
of being let down by someone we counted on.

No one who relies on God, however, ever has that experience. God
does not drop a task before He has done all that He said He will do. We
can have faith in Him because He is always faithful. "God is not a man,
that he should lie; neither the son of man, that he should repent: hath he
said, and shall he not do it? or hath he spoken, and shall he not make it
good?" (Numbers 23:19). He cannot make a promise beyond His ability
to fulfill, and nothing can deter Him from His purpose.

Today's Growth Principle: God has never failed to keep a promise—He
always completes what He says He will do.

What Is in Your Record?

And this is the record, that God hath given to us eternal life, and this life is in his Son. He that hath the Son hath life; and he that hath not the Son of God hath not life. These things have I written unto you that believe on the name of the Son of God; that ye may know that ye have eternal life, and that ye may believe on the name of the Son of God.—1 JOHN 5:11–13

Though for many of us it has been quite some time since we were in school, vivid memories of those days remain. We remember favorite classes and teachers, maybe a particular field trip or science project, or perhaps concerts or athletic competitions. If you go back to your alma mater now, even though years have passed, somewhere there will be a record of your time there. You can find a transcript of your grades as part of your permanent record. The one thing you cannot do now is change it. What happened was written down and recorded, and it is set.

The grace of God offers us a different approach to a far more important record—our standing with Him. The record we have established is not good. Our sin nature manifests itself even when we are very young. There are no "good" people, only sinners. Though some may be worse than others, all fall short of God's demand of perfection. That is why we needed Jesus so desperately.

Grace applies the perfect righteousness of the Son of God to our record. Instead of seeing a list of our many faults and failings, God sees us as justified in His sight, standing in the righteousness of Christ. "For he hath made him to be sin for us, who knew no sin; that we might be made the righteousness of God in him" (2 Corinthians 5:21). What a blessing! Yet, sadly, we often take it for granted. Salvation is so wonderful and so marvelous that we never need another reason to constantly praise and thank God for what He has done for us.

Today's Growth Principle: No matter how many years we may have been saved, we must never lose sight of God's amazing grace.

The Importance of Friendship

Two are better than one; because they have a good reward for their labour. For if they fall, the one will lift up his fellow: but woe to him that is alone when he falleth; for he hath not another to help him up. Again, if two lie together, then they have heat: but how can one be warm alone? And if one prevail against him, two shall withstand him; and a threefold cord is not quickly broken.—ECCLESIASTES 4:9–12

Following the coach's success at Kansas, UCLA hired Franklin "Pepper" Rodgers to be their head football coach in 1971. The season started with four straight losses, and alumni and fans loudly expressed their displeasure with the new leader. Later, Rodgers looked back on that painful season, which ended with only two wins and a last place finish in their conference. "My dog was my only true friend," he wrote. "I told my wife that every man needs at least two good friends. She bought me another dog."

There are tough times in everyone's life, and one of the things that make it easier for us to handle difficult days is the presence of a true friend. Much of the pain we experience comes not just from the circumstances, but from the feeling that no one else really knows or cares what we are going through. The Apostle Paul knew this feeling. Late in his life looking back under the direction of the Holy Spirit he wrote to Timothy, "At my first answer no man stood with me, but all men forsook me: I pray God that it may not be laid to their charge" (2 Timothy 4:16).

While we cannot control whether or not we have a friend in moments of crisis (though certainly there are things we can do to establish and strengthen friendships), we can control whether or not we are a true friend to others who are hurting.

Today's Growth Principle: Reach out today to someone who is going through a hard time and offer them comfort and encouragement.

Christian Soldiers

And the things that thou hast heard of me among many witnesses, the same commit thou to faithful men, who shall be able to teach others also. Thou therefore endure hardness, as a good soldier of Jesus Christ. No man that warreth entangleth himself with the affairs of this life; that he may please him who hath chosen him to be a soldier.—2 TIMOTHY 2:2–4

Isaac Watts wrote some of the most powerful and influential hymns in all of church history. He grew up in the home of a non-comformist pastor. Because his father refused to be part of the official Church of England, he was persecuted and even put in jail twice. When Watts was a baby, his mother would take him to the prison so his father could pray over him. Though religious liberty had increased by the time Watts became a pastor himself, he never forgot that following Jesus Christ carries a price. In 1709 Isaac Watts wrote these words:

> Am I a soldier of the cross, a follower of the Lamb?
> And shall I fear to own His cause or blush to speak His name?
>
> Sure I must fight if I would reign: increase my courage, Lord;
> I'll bear the toil, endure the pain, supported by Thy Word.

The notion that following Christ leads to a life of ease and comfort is attractive, but false. Jesus came into the world with the message of hope and salvation that mankind needed, but that did not mean He was greeted with acceptance and open arms. Instead, He was hated by many and lived without what we consider to be the basic necessities of life for much of His time on Earth. "And Jesus saith unto him, The foxes have holes, and the birds of the air have nests; but the Son of man hath not where to lay his head" (Matthew 8:20). Soldiers are not surprised when the battle brings difficulties, and we should not be either.

Today's Growth Principle: No one can serve as a soldier of Christ unless he is willing to endure hardship and suffering.

"Just and the Justifier"

*Being justified freely by his grace through the redemption that is in Christ Jesus: Whom God hath set forth to be a propitiation through faith in his blood, to declare his righteousness for the remission of sins that are past, through the forbearance of God; To declare, I say, at this time his righteousness: that he might be just, and the justifier of him which believeth in Jesus.—*ROMANS 3:24–26

In 1981, a man named Lenny Chow appeared in the courtroom of Judge Thomas Maloney in Chicago to face a charge of murder. The accused was a hit man for a Chicago gang, and he could have faced the death penalty if convicted. After the judge ruled that a key piece of evidence was unreliable, Chow was acquitted of the charge and set free. What no one knew at the time was that Judge Maloney was a corrupt judge, who had taken a $100,000 bribe to ensure the guilty defendant got off. It was not until ten years later that an FBI undercover sting revealed the plot, and the crooked judge was finally arrested and convicted of taking bribes.

The love of God for us is beyond measure, but His love does not mean that He is willing to overlook our sin. He is a just Judge. The only way that we can come into His holy presence is if our sins have been paid for. No one can bribe God to let him off the hook.

But the depth of God's love meant that He was willing to provide a way of salvation for us. Though the cost was great, Jesus paid it on our behalf, and as a result we can be justified without God sacrificing His perfect justice. "He shall see of the travail of his soul, and shall be satisfied: by his knowledge shall my righteous servant justify many; for he shall bear their iniquities" (Isaiah 53:11). Jesus is not only our judge, but He is also our deliverer. He set the payment for sin, and He paid it for us.

Today's Growth Principle: The sacrifice of Jesus on the cross should quell any doubts we have about God's love for us.

The Ongoing Work of Grace

For I am the least of the apostles, that am not meet to be called an apostle, because I persecuted the church of God. But by the grace of God I am what I am: and his grace which was bestowed upon me was not in vain; but I laboured more abundantly than they all: yet not I, but the grace of God which was with me. Therefore whether it were I or they, so we preach, and so ye believed.—1 CORINTHIANS 15:9–11

The cartoon character Popeye made his first appearance in 1929 just before the start of the Great Depression. First introduced as a character in another comic strip, Popeye quickly became one of the most popular fictional characters of the 1930s in both print and film. The spinach-eating sailor dispatched bad guys and saved the day, while singing his famous theme song:

> I'm Popeye the Sailor Man,
> I'm Popeye the Sailor Man...

None of us have the power to save ourselves. We are utterly dependent on God's grace. But that grace is not just extended to us for salvation—it brings change into our lives, making us more like Christ. And it equips and enables us for lives of service. All that we are, for good and for God, is a result of grace. Truly understanding this fact allows us both to remain humble and to recognize and praise God for His goodness to us.

Paul realized all that he was and all that he had done was because of God's grace. He had done much of which he could have been proud, but he recognized that all of that was the work of God in him and through him. The devil has destroyed many promising lives and ministries by pride. When we attempt to work in our own strength, apart from God's grace, we can never accomplish anything of lasting value.

Today's Growth Principle: When we forget the role God's grace plays in our lives, we are headed for pride and destruction.

Numbers 12–14   //   Mark 5:21–43

Showing God to the World

But we have this treasure in earthen vessels, that the excellency of the power may be of God, and not of us. We are troubled on every side, yet not distressed; we are perplexed, but not in despair; Persecuted, but not forsaken; cast down, but not destroyed; Always bearing about in the body the dying of the Lord Jesus, that the life also of Jesus might be made manifest in our body.—2 CORINTHIANS 4:7-10

From the earliest records of human history, man has been making idols and images to worship. The false gods are merely an imitation of the real thing, a diversion designed by Satan to substitute for true worship. But their creation across so many cultures and centuries reveals a truth about the human heart—we have a longing to see something that is greater than we are. Even the most ardent atheist has this void of longing inside, no matter how much he tries to conceal it. God is real, and we need Him. Because God is invisible, we cannot see Him. "No man hath seen God at any time; the only begotten Son, which is in the bosom of the Father, he hath declared him" (John 1:18). Jesus was only present on the Earth for a few years, and while He was fully and completely God, He did not appear in glory and power except for brief moments. Instead, He revealed God to the world through His actions, His words, and His compassion and love for others. Today, it falls on us to show the world the true nature of God.

Annie Johnson Flint wrote:

> We are the only Bible the careless world will read;
> We are the sinner's gospel; we are the scoffer's creed.
> We are the Lord's last message, given in deed and word.
>
> What if the type is crooked? What if the print is blurred?
> What if our hands are busy with other work than His?

Today's Growth Principle: It is our privilege and responsibility to show the world a true picture of what God is like.

Building Blocks

To whom coming, as unto a living stone, disallowed indeed of men, but chosen of God, and precious, Ye also, as lively stones, are built up a spiritual house, an holy priesthood, to offer up spiritual sacrifices, acceptable to God by Jesus Christ. Wherefore also it is contained in the scripture, Behold, I lay in Sion a chief corner stone, elect, precious: and he that believeth on him shall not be confounded.—1 PETER 2:4–6

Very few buildings in our day are made of stone. There may be a stone veneer added to the outside for appearances, but generally rock is not considered the best material for most construction projects. But there was a time when stone was the major building block of any significant building. In the Old Testament, we read about the construction of Solomon's Temple where the blocks were so carefully cut in advance that they could be assembled without being hammered into place. It was critical when building with stone that the cornerstone and foundation be laid right so that the massive weight would be distributed safely and the building would not fall.

But there was another necessary element—the joining of many stones together. Each of us stands before God on our own. We do not need a priest or mediator to go to God on our behalf. That is the role Jesus alone can play. "For there is one God, and one mediator between God and men, the man Christ Jesus" (1 Timothy 2:5).

That does not mean, however, that we are to live and serve Him as isolated individuals. Instead, His plan is for us to be joined together in a local church to build His work. Each stone has a place to fill in the wall so that it is complete. Each stone brings something to a role that no one else can fill in exactly the same way. Each stone is necessary for the strength and stability of the whole building.

Today's Growth Principle: God's work requires each of us doing our part for the local church to be fully effective as He designed.

God Has Whatever We Need

The LORD your God which goeth before you, he shall fight for you, according to all that he did for you in Egypt before your eyes; And in the wilderness, where thou hast seen how that the LORD thy God bare thee, as a man doth bear his son, in all the way that ye went, until ye came into this place. Yet in this thing ye did not believe the LORD your God, Who went in the way before you, to search you out a place to pitch your tents in, in fire by night, to shew you by what way ye should go, and in a cloud by day.—DEUTERONOMY 1:30–33

When God led the Children of Israel out of bondage in Egypt, He did not just give them freedom. He led them through the wilderness, providing them with everything they needed along the way. The visible symbol of God's presence with His people was a constant reminder to them that He would meet their needs. In the daytime, when the desert sun was hot, it was seen as a cloud, offering shade and protection. At night, when the cold winds blew, it appeared as a fire, providing warmth. And day by day, when it was time to travel, the cloud led them toward their next destination.

God has not changed. He still has unlimited resources available to meet every need that we have. Yet too often Christians live without accessing what God has promised to provide. We try to make our way on our own. We do not realize our inability to orchestrate life alone, and we do not claim what God has promised. "Ye lust, and have not: ye kill, and desire to have, and cannot obtain: ye fight and war, yet ye have not, because ye ask not" (James 4:2).

It is a tragedy for a child of God to live as if he were an orphan. We are not desolate, and we do not need to rely on our limited resources. We have a Heavenly Father who delights to provide for our needs.

Today's Growth Principle: Do not live without the provision for your needs God would give you if you would simply ask.

MARCH

Motivated to Action

If after the manner of men I have fought with beasts at Ephesus, what advantageth it me, if the dead rise not? let us eat and drink; for to-morrow we die. Be not deceived: evil communications corrupt good manners. Awake to righteousness, and sin not; for some have not the knowledge of God: I speak this to your shame.—1 CORINTHIANS 15:32–34

According to recent statistics, the world's population is rapidly approaching eight billion people. Never before have so many been alive on Earth at one time. Though the typical lifespan varies greatly from country to country, on average, a person born today will live about sixty-seven years. At the end of each life—whether long or short—lies eternity. Though many teach other concepts, the Bible makes it clear that there are only two destinations for that eternity—Heaven or Hell.

The fact that billions of people have never heard a clear presentation of the gospel should motivate us to actively work and support missionary efforts, both around the globe and across the street from where we live. Paul told the church at Corinth that the fact that "some have not the knowledge of God" should bring shame to them. Charles Spurgeon said, "If there be any one point in which the Christian church ought to keep its fervor at a white heat, it is concerning missions. If there be anything about which we cannot tolerate lukewarmness, it is in the matter of sending the gospel to a dying world."

The primary mission of the church and of each Christian is to fulfill the command to reach the lost. This was the heartbeat of Jesus throughout His life and ministry and it should be ours as well. "But when he saw the multitudes, he was moved with compassion on them, because they fainted, and were scattered abroad, as sheep having no shepherd" (Matthew 9:36).

Today's Growth Principle: We cannot say we are truly like Jesus if we are not burdened to action by the fate of a lost and dying world.

Specific Prayers

And Isaiah said, This sign shalt thou have of the LORD, that the LORD will do the thing that he hath spoken: shall the shadow go forward ten degrees, or go back ten degrees? And Hezekiah answered, It is a light thing for the shadow to go down ten degrees: nay, but let the shadow return backward ten degrees. And Isaiah the prophet cried unto the LORD: and he brought the shadow ten degrees backward, by which it had gone down in the dial of Ahaz.—2 KINGS 20:9-11

It is true that our prayers must be in subjection to God's will, but that does not mean that they have to be general and vague. God has invited us to come before His throne in boldness and confidence as we present our petitions to Him: "Let us therefore come boldly unto the throne of grace, that we may obtain mercy, and find grace to help in time of need" (Hebrews 4:16). Furthermore, God tells us that He does not want us to carry our burdens ourselves, but to take them to Him in prayer: "Be careful for nothing; but in every thing by prayer and supplication with thanksgiving let your requests be made known unto God" (Philippians 4:6).

Sometimes people do not offer specific prayers because they do not have confidence that they will receive an answer. By generalizing, they make it so that it is not clear if an answer is received. This is the opposite of how we should pray. We should be clear and precise in what we ask so that we know when God answers. While we should not ask selfishly or presumptuously, God cares and wants us to take that need to Him in faith.

If you have a lost loved one or friend, do not pray just for God to save the lost—ask God for his or her salvation. If you have a financial burden, do not pray just for blessing, but for that specific need. Such definite prayer shows confidence in God's promises.

Today's Growth Principle: Pray with confidence for specifics, and rejoice when God answers.

Faint, Yet Pursuing

And Gideon came to Jordan, and passed over, he, and the three hundred men that were with him, faint, yet pursuing them. And he said unto the men of Succoth, Give, I pray you, loaves of bread unto the people that follow me; for they be faint, and I am pursuing after Zebah and Zalmunna, kings of Midian. And the princes of Succoth said, Are the hands of Zebah and Zalmunna now in thine hand, that we should give bread unto thine army?—JUDGES 8:4-6

After the amazing victory God gave Gideon over the Midianites, most of the enemy army was destroyed, but those who remained alive fled. Rather than settling for a partial victory, Gideon and his band of three hundred courageous warriors chased after them. Despite the fact that they were tired, hungry, and greatly outnumbered, they were committed to tracking down and destroying those who threatened their land. Even when they were refused help by those who could and should have aided them, they simply refused to stop.

Dr. Bob Jones, Sr. said, "The test of a man's character is what it takes to stop him." Every worthwhile task is going to encounter obstacles and difficulties. There will always be excuses that could be made for quitting. There will always be reasons why we have done enough and someone else should pick up the cause and run with it. There will always be fatigue from labor and a desire to stop and rest. There will always be those who could help but choose to criticize instead. But if the cause is burning in our hearts, we will not stop.

Sometimes we give up too easily in pursuing opportunities which God has placed in our paths because we become weary in overcoming the obstacles. We should remember Gideon and his men who, even when they were faint, continued pursuing.

Today's Growth Principle: The thing that stops people is not an obstacle, but a lack of commitment to their cause.

Hold On for Dear Life

For a bishop must be blameless, as the steward of God; not selfwilled, not soon angry, not given to wine, no striker, not given to filthy lucre; But a lover of hospitality, a lover of good men, sober, just, holy, temperate; Holding fast the faithful word as he hath been taught, that he may be able by sound doctrine both to exhort and to convince the gainsayers.
—TITUS 1:7–9

Nik Wallenda comes from a famous family of circus performers, and he is the seventh generation of the "Flying Wallendas" to perform as an aerialist. His best-known high wire feats include crossing Niagara Falls as well as a gorge at the Grand Canyon suspended far above the ground. He proposed to his wife, who is also from a circus family, on a high wire thirty feet in the air. One of Wallenda's more incredible performances was while suspended from a helicopter 250 feet above the ground while dangling by his toes from the harness. He may have been using his feet rather than his hands, but he was still hanging on for dear life.

That kind of tenacity is the approach God calls each of us to have with the truth. We are to cling to the Bible as if our lives depend on it—because they do. There are many things that are helpful and useful to our walk with God, but the Bible is essential. It is more important that our spiritual life be fed than that our bodies receive nourishment. Job said, "Neither have I gone back from the commandment of his lips; I have esteemed the words of his mouth more than my necessary food" (Job 23:12). Yet if we are honest, faced with a choice between skipping Bible reading or skipping breakfast, which would we choose? It is vital that God's people take the spiritual battles they are facing seriously and use the tool He has given us to fight these battles: His Word.

Today's Growth Principle: The Bible is the most important resource God has given us, and we should hold to it tightly.

Pleasing Sacrifices

Not because I desire a gift: but I desire fruit that may abound to your account. But I have all, and abound: I am full, having received of Epaphroditus the things which were sent from you, an odour of a sweet smell, a sacrifice acceptable, well-pleasing to God. But my God shall supply all your need according to his riches in glory by Christ Jesus.
—PHILIPPIANS 4:17–19

D r. Curtis Hutson was a full-time mailman and part-time pastor when he started out in the ministry. His small church wasn't able to pay enough for him to support his family. So he continued to work day after day delivering mail and fitting his ministry around his job schedule. God began to work on his heart to give up the mail route and enter the ministry full-time despite the fact that his starting salary would be $75 a month. Years later when he told the story, Dr. Hutson said, "I finally told God I'd do it, even though I wasn't sure how we could. I told Gerri [his wife], 'If I starve to death, you tell the devil I was fasting!'" God blessed him with an amazingly fruitful ministry first as a pastor and then as an evangelist. His faith was honored.

When it comes to making sacrifices for the work of God, whether it involves our time, talent, or treasure, we must remember three things: First, God doesn't need our help. He has infinite resources. We do not add to His supply in any way when we give to His work. He allows us to give and reap the benefits even though He does not need what we contribute. Second, giving to the work of the Lord is an opportunity for us to invest ourselves in that which has eternal value. Third, God doesn't overlook our help. When we step out in faith to be part of His work, He sees what we have done and rewards us. Our giving is pleasant in the sight of God not for the gift itself, but for the heart that gives it.

Today's Growth Principle: No one ever makes a sacrifice for God that goes unnoticed or unrewarded.

The Power of Encouragement

But exhort one another daily, while it is called To-day; lest any of you be hardened through the deceitfulness of sin. For we are made partakers of Christ, if we hold the beginning of our confidence stedfast unto the end; While it is said, To-day if ye will hear his voice, harden not your hearts, as in the provocation.—HEBREWS 3:13–15

In April of 2016, Jim Herman fulfilled a lifelong dream when he won his first PGA (Professional Golfers' Association) tournament at the age of thirty-eight. Ten years earlier, after trying and failing repeatedly to qualify as a professional golfer, Herman gave up on his dream and got a job at a golf course in New Jersey as an assistant pro. A conversation with the owner of the club, Donald Trump, changed the course of his life. After his win, Herman told an interviewer, "I got into a conversation with Mr. Trump. He said, 'Why are you folding shirts and giving lessons? Why aren't you on the Tour? I've played with Tour players—you're good enough!'" Inspired to try again, Herman did make the tour and reached his dream by winning the Shell Houston Open.

Our words have enormous power in the lives of others (and the words we tell ourselves silently have enormous power in our own lives). So it is vital that we use that great power for good rather than evil. The careless words we speak without thinking, the cruel words we utter without caring, and the critical words we declare without rightly judging are not harmless. They can leave deep wounds and echo for years in someone's heart and mind.

God commands us to use our words to encourage and lift up others. Eliphaz gave this testimony about his friend Job: "Behold, thou hast instructed many, and thou hast strengthened the weak hands. Thy words have upholden him that was falling, and thou hast strengthened the feeble knees" (Job 4:3–4). Could the same be said of you?

Today's Growth Principle: The tongue has great power—use yours wisely to encourage and build up others.

Making Things Right

And he made haste, and came down, and received him joyfully. And when they saw it, they all murmured, saying, That he was gone to be guest with a man that is a sinner. And Zacchaeus stood, and said unto the Lord; Behold, Lord, the half of my goods I give to the poor; and if I have taken any thing from any man by false accusation, I restore him fourfold.
—LUKE 19:6–8

In 1985, a young mother named Cathleen Webb contacted the Cook County State's Attorney with a shocking revelation. Eight years before, she had falsely claimed that she had been raped. She had identified a man named Gary Dotson as her assailant, and he had been convicted and sentenced to prison. But in the interim she had gotten saved, and after talking to her husband and her pastor, decided that even though it put her at great legal and financial risk, she had to come forward with the truth.

At first the authorities did not believe her story. It would take three years, and a DNA test before Dotson was finally released from prison. Webb wrote a book about the situation, donating the proceeds to Gary Dotson. She later died of cancer. Her husband spoke about her after her death. "She fully expected to pay more of a price than she actually did. There was a good chance that she might have had to go to jail. She couldn't give Gary back his years, but at that point she did everything she could to make it right."

If we are genuinely repentant for what we have done wrong, we will not only confess it to God, but also do whatever is possible to rectify the harm we have caused. There are some things that cannot be undone, but as much as is possible, it should be our desire to address the pain of those we have wronged.

Today's Growth Principle: It is not enough to feel sorry for what we do wrong—we must do whatever we can to make things right.

A Fractured Family Background Isn't Fatal

Now Israel loved Joseph more than all his children, because he was the son of his old age: and he made him a coat of many colours. And when his brethren saw that their father loved him more than all his brethren, they hated him, and could not speak peaceably unto him. —GENESIS 37:3–4

For an example of a deeply dysfunctional family, we have only to look to the one in which Joseph grew up. His father Jacob played favorites with his many children, especially with his son Joseph. Because of that favoritism, Joseph's brothers hated him, and when the opportunity arose, they seized him and were going to kill him. They decided instead to sell him into slavery and pocket the money. When they got home they told their father Jacob that they had found Joseph's coat of many colors which he had given Joseph covered in blood, letting their father assume he had been killed by a wild animal. Joseph certainly had every reason to hold a grudge about his experiences growing up.

Yet though his pain was real, Joseph was not bound by his past, even as a slave. Joseph recognized that God could use even the worst things that happened to him for good—provided that he was willing to trust God with the process. We see Joseph's understanding of this truth revealed in the birth and naming of his children. "And Joseph called the name of the firstborn Manasseh: For God, said he, hath made me forget all my toil, and all my father's house. And the name of the second called he Ephraim: For God hath caused me to be fruitful in the land of my affliction" (Genesis 41:51–52). Before we can be fruitful, we have to forget the past—not in the sense that we pretend it didn't happen, but that we release our claim to retaliation against those who have done us wrong. Only then can we enjoy God's fruitfulness in our lives.

Today's Growth Principle: Though our upbringing may leave scars, God is able to use even painful experiences for His purposes.

Failure Isn't Final

Do thy diligence to come shortly unto me: For Demas hath forsaken me, having loved this present world, and is departed unto Thessalonica; Crescens to Galatia, Titus unto Dalmatia. Only Luke is with me. Take Mark, and bring him with thee: for he is profitable to me for the ministry. And Tychicus have I sent to Ephesus.—2 TIMOTHY 4:9–12

When G. Campbell Morgan was starting out in the ministry, he was part of a group of 150 young men who applied for ordination in 1888. To qualify, they had to pass doctrinal examinations and then preach a sermon. Morgan did fine on the test, but his trial sermon was a disaster. Two weeks later Morgan found his name on the list of candidates who had failed. A despondent Morgan telegraphed his father one word: "Rejected." Soon he received a reply: "Rejected on Earth. Accepted in Heaven." Morgan did not give up, and became one of the preachers of his generation who were greatly used by God.

When Paul and Barnabas went on their first missionary trip, they took Mark with them, but he gave up and went home. When it came time to leave for the second trip, Paul refused to allow Mark to go, and the tension between him and Barnabas over that decision was so great that it separated two men who had been dear friends and co-workers in the ministry for many years. But near the end of his life, Paul had a different opinion. Over the years Mark had proven himself to be faithful in the work. His initial failure did not keep him from trying again. And in Paul's final epistle, he described Mark as an asset in God's work.

Every one of us knows what it is like to fail. Some people allow those failures to become the definition of their lives. Others decide instead to get up and try again…and again…and again. These are the people who accomplish things. We do not have to stop trying just because our last attempt didn't work.

Today's Growth Principle: Failure may leave scars, but it is never final unless we allow it to be.

Don't Forget Those Who Helped

Then spake the chief butler unto Pharaoh, saying, I do remember my faults this day: Pharaoh was wroth with his servants, and put me in ward in the captain of the guard's house, both me and the chief baker: And we dreamed a dream in one night, I and he; we dreamed each man according to the interpretation of his dream. —GENESIS 41:9–11

When Joseph was unjustly imprisoned in Egypt, his attitude and God's blessing gave him great favor with the jailers. As a result, he was able to interact with the other prisoners. When Pharaoh's butler was in prison, Joseph interpreted a dream for him that promised he would be restored to his former position. Joseph asked the butler remember him and bring his case before Pharaoh. But when the butler got back to the palace, he forgot all about Joseph. Two full years passed before Pharaoh had a dream, and only then did the butler remember Joseph and that he could interpret dreams.

Too many times we take the help we receive from others for granted. Yet, in truth, all of us have benefited in ways both large and small from parents, teachers, pastors, youth workers, relatives, and friends who have invested in our lives. How often do we stop to thank them? How often do we take the time to let them know that what they did made a difference? How often do we express the simple words that would mean so much to them?

Sometimes, like the butler, we get busy with the duties and responsibilities of life and simply forget those who have helped. Other times our pride does not want to acknowledge the contributions of others so we can give ourselves more credit for what we have accomplished. But as the old saying goes, if you see a turtle sitting on a fence post, he probably didn't get there by himself. Do not let pride render you ungrateful.

Today's Growth Principle: Take the time to reach out and express gratitude to those who have contributed to your life.

Letting Go of the Past

This is the covenant that I will make with them after those days, saith the Lord, I will put my laws into their hearts, and in their minds will I write them; And their sins and iniquities will I remember no more. Now where remission of these is, there is no more offering for sin.
—HEBREWS 10:16–18

I read a humorous story about a couple who were having a problem in their marriage. Years before, Albert had done something really dumb, and Ethel had chewed him out royally. After he apologized, they made up. But as time passed, Ethel would from time to time bring up what he had done. Finally Albert said, "Honey, why do you keep bringing up what I did? I thought you said you would forgive and forget." "I have," Ethel replied, "But I don't want you to forget that I've forgiven and forgotten!"

All of us have suffered from unfair treatment at one point or another. Many have endured abuse, hardship, and suffering that they in no way deserved. The world is filled with sinful people, and sinful people act in sinful ways. While there are scars that do not go away, there is a plan laid out for us in the Word of God to keep us from having to live with the pain of the past on an ongoing basis. And that plan centers around forgiveness.

Many people struggle to forgive and let go because they think it means they have to say that what happened to them was justified. But forgiveness is not an admission that you deserved what happened. Forgiveness is an expression of your faith and obedience to God. Following the example that He set for us, we do not hold on to the things of the past, but replace them with a new future through grace He provides. We who have benefited from the forgiveness God has shown to us should be the most ready to forgive others. Ephesians 4:32 tells us, "And be ye kind one to another, tenderhearted, forgiving one another, even as God for Christ's sake hath forgiven you."

Today's Growth Principle: Do not let a lack of forgiveness keep you trapped in the hurts of the past for the rest of your life.

The Test of Faith

Then Daniel went in, and desired of the king that he would give him time, and that he would shew the king the interpretation. Then Daniel went to his house, and made the thing known to Hananiah, Mishael, and Azariah, his companions: That they would desire mercies of the God of heaven concerning this secret; that Daniel and his fellows should not perish with the rest of the wise men of Babylon.—DANIEL 2:16–18

Daniel had risen through the ranks of the captives carried to Babylon and was recognized in that heathen country as a man of wisdom and learning. The thing that set Daniel and his three friends apart from hundreds of others taken from Israel and many other lands conquered by Nebuchadnezzar as he expanded his empire, was their faith in God and their faithfulness to Him. Their faith was not theoretical—it was tested in the most severe ways possible.

When Nebuchadnezzar's personal guard showed up to kill Daniel and his friends because none of the other wise men had been able to interpret the king's dream, they were literally facing a life or death moment. Yet Daniel did not panic. He did not condemn God for abandoning him, nor did he bewail the injustice of being threatened because someone else had made impossible demands. He did not criticize the Babylonian form of government that placed his life in peril. He prayed!

Daniel's faith was expressed in his response to trouble. He believed that even in a foreign country, surrounded by danger and facing a death sentence, God was able to intervene. He threw himself on the mercy of God and received the answer that he needed.

Our faith is not measured by how loudly we speak of it in public, but by how consistently we exercise it in private. If we rely on ourselves when we are tested, we reveal that we don't trust God as we should.

Today's Growth Principle: Through good times and bad we must remember that God never fails to keep His promises.

Crying Out for Deliverance

The face of the LORD is against them that do evil, to cut off the remembrance of them from the earth. The righteous cry, and the LORD heareth, and delivereth them out of all their troubles. The LORD is nigh unto them that are of a broken heart; and saveth such as be of a contrite spirit. Many are the afflictions of the righteous: but the LORD delivereth him out of them all.—PSALM 34:16–19

David knew what it was like to be truly desperate. We often think of him as a great king ruling over an expanding nation and winning victories against Israel's enemies. But those triumphs only came after many years of difficult circumstances. During those years, Saul's jealousy toward David was a real threat. The old king God had rejected viewed the hero of the battle against Goliath as a challenge to his throne. As a result, Saul set out to kill David.

At one point, David even resorted to leaving Israel and going to the Philistines—to the hometown of the giant he had famously killed. Think about how desperate he must have been to take that step. When the Philistines recognized David as the one who killed Goliath, David realized he was in trouble and pretended to be crazy. "And David laid up these words in his heart, and was sore afraid of Achish the king of Gath. And he changed his behaviour before them, and feigned himself mad in their hands, and scrabbled on the doors of the gate, and let his spittle fall down upon his beard" (1 Samuel 21:12–13). Achish let David go, and David's heart was full of praise.

In fact, it was against that background and in those dark days that the Holy Spirit inspired David to write the words of praise that we know as Psalm 34. He had seen the goodness and faithfulness of God in a severe trial. David was both expressing his thanks to God for his deliverance and encouraging others to turn to Him when they were in distress.

Today's Growth Principle: You will never face a trial or danger from which God cannot deliver you—cry out for His help.

Taken out of the Furnace

But the LORD hath taken you, and brought you forth out of the iron furnace, even out of Egypt, to be unto him a people of inheritance, as ye are this day. Furthermore the LORD was angry with me for your sakes, and sware that I should not go over Jordan, and that I should not go in unto that good land, which the LORD thy God giveth thee for an inheritance: But I must die in this land, I must not go over Jordan: but ye shall go over, and possess that good land.
—DEUTERONOMY 4:20–22

The popular teaching in many religious circles of our day is that life for God's children should not have any bumps in the road—raises, promotions, better houses and cars, good health, and continued advancement should be expected. It's easy to understand why people like to hear such teaching, but it contradicts what the Bible actually says. God's Word reveals that God's plan for His beloved children often includes great trials and severe testing.

The reality is that often the very troubles that are so painful prepare us for the plan God has for our lives. The experiences we endure are the equipping God knows we will need for what He has in store for us. At a difficult time in the life of the nation of Israel, God sent this message through the prophet Isaiah: "Behold, I have refined thee, but not with silver; I have chosen thee in the furnace of affliction" (Isaiah 48:10).

If we refuse to remain in the fire until God's work is done, our lives will not be refined and made more useful. But we have the wonderful promise from God, "…I will never leave thee, nor forsake thee. So that we may boldly say, The Lord is my helper, and I will not fear what man shall do unto me" (Hebrews 13:5–6). If His plan involves placing us into the furnace, we will find Him there with us, just as the three Hebrew children did in their day (Daniel 3:24–25).

Today's Growth Principle: We must be willing to endure the afflictions and trials God brings if we are to be valuable in His service.

Don't Look Back

Not as though I had already attained, either were already perfect: but I follow after, if that I may apprehend that for which also I am apprehended of Christ Jesus. Brethren, I count not myself to have apprehended: but this one thing I do, forgetting those things which are behind, and reaching forth unto those things which are before, I press toward the mark for the prize of the high calling of God in Christ Jesus.—PHILIPPIANS 3:12–14

Author and motivational speaker Erick Reahm recounted a story from his days as a student at West Point. During the summer between his junior and senior years, he was stationed at Fort Hood in Texas. He was asked to represent his company in a 10K race. About two hundred runners, both soldiers and civilians, entered. As the race went on and the field thinned out, Reahm saw there was only one runner ahead of him.

He wrote, "With little over a mile to go, I noticed that he started to look back to see where I was. I observed that his form was deteriorating, and I knew I had a chance to beat him. The more he looked back, the more confident I became. As I closed the gap on him, I would wave at him and smile every time he looked back at me. By the time I passed him, he was demoralized and could not match my surge. I won the race easily and solidified a lesson I learned early in my running career—NEVER LOOK BACK!"

All of us have things in the past that we would like to change, but it is impossible to change the past. We can do our best to make up for things left undone and try to make wrong things right, but we cannot change the past. It's a grave error to spend your life looking over your shoulder. The sins and failures we have confessed and forsaken are covered with the blood of Jesus Christ. If we spend our days looking back, we won't very well follow the instruction of Hebrews 12:1, "…let us run with patience the race that is set before us."

Today's Growth Principle: A life spent looking backward will make little forward progress toward what matters most.

Forgetting the Things of Earth

If ye then be risen with Christ, seek those things which are above, where Christ sitteth on the right hand of God. Set your affection on things above, not on things on the earth. For ye are dead, and your life is hid with Christ in God. When Christ, who is our life, shall appear, then shall ye also appear with him in glory.—COLOSSIANS 3:1-4

I read a fascinating interview with astronaut John Blaha who spent several months on the Russian Mir space station back in the 1990s. This veteran astronaut flew six space shuttle missions, but spending months with people he didn't know and with whom he had a significant language barrier proved challenging. Blaha said that his first month was pretty miserable. "I kept longing for things that I loved on earth. Finally, I decided that I had to forget them. When I did that, then I loved being on the Space Station."

No matter what country a Christian lives in here on Earth, our true citizenship is in Heaven. "For our conversation is in heaven; from whence also we look for the Saviour, the Lord Jesus Christ" (Philippians 3:20). And while we do have concerns of daily living that must be met, when our focus settles on earthly things, we cannot love Heaven and the things of God as we should. Everything around us is temporal, and one day all that is material will be destroyed.

Whole-hearted living for the things of God requires more than our action; it requires our affection. It is no mistake that Jesus said the greatest commandment is to love God above all else. Obedience and holiness are primarily matters of the heart. No matter what temptations or inducements are offered to someone who loves God as he should, he will remain focused on pleasing the One he loves. This is how we glorify and obey God.

Today's Growth Principle: A Christian fixated on the things of Earth will not have his affections on Christ or eternity.

Acceptable Service

And this word, Yet once more, signifieth the removing of those things that are shaken, as of things that are made, that those things which cannot be shaken may remain. Wherefore we receiving a kingdom which cannot be moved, let us have grace, whereby we may serve God acceptably with reverence and godly fear: For our God is a consuming fire.
—HEBREWS 12:27–29

One of the most popular books of the 1800s was Jules Verne's adventure story *Around the World in Eighty Days* which highlighted the way travel and technology improvements of the 1860s had brought the world closer together. At the beginning of the book, the eccentric Englishman Phileas Fogg, who would soon set out on the great trip around the globe, fires his valet, James Forster. The offense that led to his dismissal? "Forster had brought him shaving water that was 84 degrees instead of 86!"

God is not an unreasonable or capricious master, but He is our sovereign Lord, and He has every right to demand our full obedience. Throughout the Bible, we see examples of people doing things their own way, in disobedience to God's clear instructions, and finding God's disfavor—Nadab and Abihu bringing strange fire to the altar, Uzzah touching the Ark of the Covenant, Saul saving animals for a sacrifice when God had commanded him to destroy them, and Ananias and Sapphira lying about their partial offering.

God is not a negotiator. He doesn't settle for less than He demands and decide it is close enough. We are justified in God's sight through the blood of Jesus (Romans 5:1), and we are "accepted in the beloved" (Ephesians 1:6). As we serve Christ, however, we should remember that He has given us instructions for how He wants His work to be done, and we must follow His Word rather than our own whims.

Today's Growth Principle: The way we view God will determine how we serve Him.

The Basis of Faith

Wherefore say unto the children of Israel, I am the LORD, and I will bring you out from under the burdens of the Egyptians, and I will rid you out of their bondage, and I will redeem you with a stretched out arm, and with great judgments: And I will take you to me for a people, and I will be to you a God: and ye shall know that I am the LORD your God, which bringeth you out from under the burdens of the Egyptians. And I will bring you in unto the land, concerning the which I did swear to give it to Abraham, to Isaac, and to Jacob; and I will give it you for an heritage: I am the LORD.
—EXODUS 6:6–8

All of us have had the unpleasant experience of having someone we trusted let us down. Perhaps it was something as simple as a friend not showing up to give you a ride or failing to return a book you lent them. Perhaps it was a serious breach of trust in a marriage or a financial relationship that left devastation. The reason people fail to keep their word to us—and if we're honest, the reason we sometimes fail to keep our word to others—is because of our nature. We are sinners, and sinners fail to do what is right from time to time.

By contrast, when God was making promises to Moses for the Israelites, He was speaking of things that seemed to be impossible— delivering the Israelites from bondage to Pharaoh in Egypt. But there was no hope humanly speaking of changing Pharaoh's mind. The slave labor of the Israelites was a valuable resource for Egypt and would not be willingly abandoned. The military might of Egypt meant no revolt could hope to succeed. Yet what God promised happened exactly as He said. This is because His promise was based on His unfailing nature. God's character causes Him to fulfill these promises, and we can always trust that He will.

Today's Growth Principle: Our faith rests on the unshakable foundation of God's nature and character.

A Life Transformed

And you hath he quickened, who were dead in trespasses and sins; Wherein in time past ye walked according to the course of this world, according to the prince of the power of the air, the spirit that now worketh in the children of disobedience: Among whom also we all had our conversation in times past in the lusts of our flesh, fulfilling the desires of the flesh and of the mind; and were by nature the children of wrath, even as others.
—EPHESIANS 2:1–3

Billy Sunday's father died during the Civil War, and he grew up in the Iowa Soldiers' Orphans Home. His amazing athletic ability provided him a lavish lifestyle as a professional baseball player in the 1880s. Known as only an average hitter, his amazing speed (he was the fastest player in the National League) made him an outstanding fielder and a feared base runner. On a day off in Chicago, Sunday and some of his teammates watched as a group from the Pacific Garden Mission sang and preached. Sunday went to the mission where he heard the gospel and trusted Christ as his Saviour.

Sunday's entire life was transformed. He gave up his drinking and gambling and, in 1891, turned down a contract worth $3,100 per year for a job at the Rescue Mission paying less than $1,000 a year. Not long after, he went into full time evangelism and saw hundreds of thousands saved. Many years later, a Chicago policeman walking his beat saw a man standing outside the Pacific Garden Mission. Not recognizing the famous preacher, he went up to ask what was going on. "My name is Billy Sunday," the reply came, "and I was saved right inside here many years ago. If I am ever in town, I always come by and pray to thank God for saving a sinner like me."

We do nothing to earn or deserve salvation—we only accept it. But it transforms everything about our lives.

Today's Growth Principle: Never lose your sense of gratitude for the gift of God's salvation that you received.

The Christian and the Bible

*And let the peace of God rule in your hearts, to the which also ye are called in one body; and be ye thankful. Let the word of Christ dwell in you richly in all wisdom; teaching and admonishing one another in psalms and hymns and spiritual songs, singing with grace in your hearts to the Lord. And whatsoever ye do in word or deed, do all in the name of the Lord Jesus, giving thanks to God and the Father by him.—*COLOSSIANS 3:15–17

I heard about a pastor who was talking to a little girl after the Sunday service. He asked her, "Do you know what's in the Bible?" "Yes, sir," she replied confidently. "I know everything that's in the Bible." So he asked, "Okay, tell me what's in the Bible." She said, "There's a picture of my brother's girlfriend, a ticket from the dry cleaner, a curl of my hair, and a pizza coupon."

The Bible has all of the information God knows we need to live according to His purpose. Yet too many Christians have only a casual relationship with their Bible. They carry it with them to church, but it often never gets opened again until the following Sunday. That is not enough. George Müller correctly observed, "The vigor of our spiritual life will be in exact proportion to the place held by the Bible in our life and thoughts."

There needs to be more Bible reading, more Bible study, more Bible memorization, and more Bible meditation in every one of our lives. Nothing is more important to our spiritual health and well-being. The Bible is our resource, our guide, our spiritual food, our strength, our corrector, and our comfort. "All scripture is given by inspiration of God, and is profitable for doctrine, for reproof, for correction, for instruction in righteousness: That the man of God may be perfect, throughly furnished unto all good works" (2 Timothy 3:16–17).

Today's Growth Principle: If the Bible does not fill your heart and mind, you will not walk in holiness and wisdom.

Make the Right Choice

Ye lust, and have not: ye kill, and desire to have, and cannot obtain: ye fight and war, yet ye have not, because ye ask not. Ye ask, and receive not, because ye ask amiss, that ye may consume it upon your lusts. Ye adulterers and adulteresses, know ye not that the friendship of the world is enmity with God? whosoever therefore will be a friend of the world is the enemy of God.—JAMES 4:2-4

When Willie Nelson was starting out in his musical career, he quickly developed a following among the honky tonks and bars around Fort Worth, Texas, where he would play and sing. Yet nearly every Sunday morning, he could be found teaching Sunday school. Before long, this double life became a problem, and the pastor of his church confronted him regarding his testimony. The pastor explained that he must either give up his class or his lifestyle. Nelson later said, "I decided to stay with the beer joints. The preacher sounded so wrong to me that I quit the Baptist church."

While many people try to live with one foot in the world and one foot in God's kingdom, that never works for very long. "And Elijah came unto all the people, and said, How long halt ye between two opinions? if the LORD be God, follow him: but if Baal, then follow him. And the people answered him not a word" (1 Kings 18:21). Yet too often when that moment of decision comes, we choose the allure of the world over the truth of God.

The world tries to convince us that sin isn't really so bad, or that God will not be upset if we indulge a little in our carnal desires. But the Bible doesn't have a "not really all that bad" category. There is right and wrong, good and evil, sin and obedience. The harder we try to cling to the things of the world, the less we are able to follow God.

Today's Growth Principle: There is no middle ground between God and the world—we will eventually love and serve one and leave the other.

Grace for Every Difficulty

And lest I should be exalted above measure through the abundance of the revelations, there was given to me a thorn in the flesh, the messenger of Satan to buffet me, lest I should be exalted above measure. For this thing I besought the Lord thrice, that it might depart from me. And he said unto me, My grace is sufficient for thee: for my strength is made perfect in weakness. Most gladly therefore will I rather glory in my infirmities, that the power of Christ may rest upon me.—2 CORINTHIANS 12:7–9

One of the reasons the Peanuts comics were popular for so many years is the level of insight into adult issues that come from the mouths of young children. In one strip, Linus, talking to Charlie Brown, says, "I don't like to face problems head on. I think the best way to solve problems is to avoid them. In fact, this is a distinct philosophy of mine. No problem is so big or so complicated that it can't be run away from."

While that approach to problems may be attractive, it certainly doesn't resolve anything. In fact, problems that we refuse to deal with do not somehow magically disappear. They usually become even greater. The right approach, of course, is to take our problems to the Lord and ask Him for His wisdom in dealing with them. First Peter 5:7 graciously instructs, "Casting all your care upon him; for he careth for you." And James 1:5 invites, "If any of you lack wisdom, let him ask of God, that giveth to all men liberally, and upbraideth not; and it shall be given him."

But what about those problems that don't go away even with our repeated prayers and willingness to take action? What about the difficulties that are outside of our control? Paul had this kind of a problem—a "thorn in the flesh" that God chose not to remove. What Paul discovered, however, is that, while all difficulties provide an opportunity to receive God's grace, the problems that just won't go away give us a special opportunity to continually experience His grace in a special way.

Today's Growth Principle: Every difficulty we face is an opportunity to experience God's strength and grace.

Joshua 10–12   //   Luke 1:39–56   85

Fiery Trials

Beloved, think it not strange concerning the fiery trial which is to try you, as though some strange thing happened unto you: But rejoice, inasmuch as ye are partakers of Christ's sufferings; that, when his glory shall be revealed, ye may be glad also with exceeding joy. If ye be reproached for the name of Christ, happy are ye; for the spirit of glory and of God resteth upon you: on their part he is evil spoken of, but on your part he is glorified.—1 PETER 4:12–14

When Peter wrote to suffering Christians on the subject of persecution, trials, and tested faith, he was not writing about something he had not experienced. Peter's own faith had faced a trial the night before Jesus was crucified, and he had failed the test. After Christ restored him, Peter became one of the faith-filled leaders of the early church. He experienced great suffering firsthand—being beaten, jailed, and threatened with execution. Many of his fellow disciples lost their lives because of their faithful witness, and Peter himself would eventually be crucified.

The appearance of hardships, trials, and even persecution in our lives should not come as a surprise to us. The popular notion that the Christian life is meant to be easy and that we should expect to only receive blessings leaves people poorly prepared when difficulty does come. The Bible instead tells us that if we are committed to doing right, we should expect to experience difficulties and challenges. "Yea, and all that will live godly in Christ Jesus shall suffer persecution" (2 Timothy 3:12).

The thing that sustains us through trials and testing is our faith that God is still in control. Though we are often surprised by what happens, God never is. As someone once said, "All of our fiery trials are Father-filtered." When we remember that God is in control even when things go wrong according to our expectation and understanding, we are reminded to keep our faith in Him.

Today's Growth Principle: No trial ever comes into your life that has not first passed through the hands of your loving Father in Heaven.

The Power of Praise

Because thy lovingkindness is better than life, my lips shall praise thee. Thus will I bless thee while I live: I will lift up my hands in thy name. My soul shall be satisfied as with marrow and fatness; and my mouth shall praise thee with joyful lips: When I remember thee upon my bed, and meditate on thee in the night watches.—PSALM 63:3-6

David penned this Holy Spirit-inspired song of praise, not at a time of ease, but at a time when he was running for his life. Yet even while living in the wilderness and hiding from Saul, David recognized that God was faithful to him. So often we equate God's goodness with our comfort, but He is always good, no matter our circumstances. Every good thing we receive comes from His hand, and in every trial, He remains faithful.

I read about an older Christian singer who had been diagnosed with cancer of the tongue. When he was told that it would require surgery, he was also informed that following the surgery, he would no longer be able to sing. In the operating room he told the doctor, "I've had many good times singing the praises of God. Now you tell me I can never sing again. I have one song that will be my last." He began to sing the old hymn by Isaac Watts:

> I'll praise my Maker while I've breath,
> And when my voice is lost in death,
> Praise shall employ my nobler power;
> My days of praise shall ne'er be past,
> While life, and thought, and being last,
> Or immortality endures.

The praise we offer to God, especially in hard times, guards us from despair and defeat. When we remember all that God has done for us in the past, we are encouraged to seek His help for the present.

Today's Growth Principle: When we praise God in difficult times, our faith is strengthened and our hope renewed.

Keeping the Stones Silent

And when he was come nigh, even now at the descent of the mount of Olives, the whole multitude of the disciples began to rejoice and praise God with a loud voice for all the mighty works that they had seen; Saying, Blessed be the King that cometh in the name of the Lord: peace in heaven, and glory in the highest. And some of the Pharisees from among the multitude said unto him, Master, rebuke thy disciples. And he answered and said unto them, I tell you that, if these should hold their peace, the stones would immediately cry out.—LUKE 19:37–40

When Jesus rode into Jerusalem on a donkey, He was fulfilling prophecies that were hundreds of years old. Every detail happened just as God had said, according to the time line revealed to Daniel centuries earlier. There were many who welcomed Jesus, but most of them wanted Him to be a king who would overthrow the Romans rather than the Saviour who would rescue them from their sin. For the Pharisees, even a political deliverer was too much. They feared the loss of their prestigious and profitable positions. "If we let him thus alone, all men will believe on him: and the Romans shall come and take away both our place and nation" (John 11:48). So they demanded that Jesus quiet the throngs who had gathered.

In response, Jesus told them that if the people were silenced, the very stones would cry out. The praise, glory, and greatness of God is beyond human ability to properly express, but that should not stop us from doing our best to let everyone know of our love and gratitude toward God. The gift of salvation alone would be worthy of a lifetime of praise and worship, to say nothing of the daily blessings and provision we receive. Yet, too often our praise is tepid at best, rather than filled with sincere joy and appreciation as it should be.

Today's Growth Principle: Praise in the heart is good, but praise expressed outwardly so that others see and hear it is far better.

The Preparation of Separation

But in a great house there are not only vessels of gold and of silver, but also of wood and of earth; and some to honour, and some to dishonour. If a man therefore purge himself from these, he shall be a vessel unto honour, sanctified, and meet for the master's use, and prepared unto every good work. Flee also youthful lusts: but follow righteousness, faith, charity, peace, with them that call on the Lord out of a pure heart.
—2 TIMOTHY 2:20–22

Today there are many pressures for us to become more and more like the world in an effort to reach the world. But this direction is doomed to failure. It will not work to reach the lost, but it will destroy the spiritual health and well-being of those who take that route.

The work to which God has called us is greater than we can do in our power or reach by human philosophy. It is only as we surrender our lives to the Lord as His instruments that He uses us by His power. Rather than borrowing worldly methods or adjusting to sinful lifestyles, we should recognize our need for the filling of the Holy Spirit and strive to live in such a way that we will be clean vessels through which His power will flow. Charles Spurgeon said, "A church which, in a living way, holds fast the truth once for all delivered to the saints will also separate itself from the ways of the world: in fact, the world and the worldly church will shun it and push it into the place of separation. The more separated we are after our Master's fashion, the more fit we shall be to do His bidding."

Consider the incredible privilege of being a vessel used of God! A vessel, of course, is not a source of power, but it can be a container through which power flows. The work of God must be done in the power of God if it is to have a genuine impact, and we cannot expect to have His power unless we are walking in obedience.

Today's Growth Principle: If we want to be effective tools in the hands of God for His work, we must walk in obedience to Him.

The Limits of Suffering

Be sober, be vigilant; because your adversary the devil, as a roaring lion, walketh about, seeking whom he may devour: Whom resist stedfast in the faith, knowing that the same afflictions are accomplished in your brethren that are in the world. But the God of all grace, who hath called us unto his eternal glory by Christ Jesus, after that ye have suffered a while, make you perfect, stablish, strengthen, settle you. To him be glory and dominion for ever and ever. Amen.—1 PETER 5:8–11

In 1957, a professor at Johns Hopkins University named Curt Richter published the findings of a study he had conducted on rats to measure the effect of hope in response to hardship and difficulty. He placed a number of rats in water and took note of how long they could swim before drowning.

Then he took a second set of rats and put them in the same conditions. With this group, just before the average time of survival was reached, his team would take the rats out of the water. After they had rested a while and dried off, the rats were placed back into the water to be timed again. This time they were able to swim for a much longer period of time. "In this way," Richter reported, "the rats quickly learn that the situation is not actually hopeless. After elimination of hopelessness the rats do not die."

Most, if not all, of us know the feeling of enduring a trial or time of suffering that feels like it will never end. It is tempting for us to lose hope and give up, or to blame God and become bitter against Him. But Peter reminds us that all of our suffering is limited. It only lasts for "a while." That does not mean it doesn't hurt or even that our outward circumstances will improve this side of eternity. What it does mean is that there is hope. We have a loving Father who will never fail or forsake us. With this hope, we can endure with joyful confidence.

Today's Growth Priniple: God's goodness and grace ensures that our suffering is limited and that we are never without hope.

Judges 1–3   //   Luke 4:1–30

An Empowered Church

The former treatise have I made, O Theophilus, of all that Jesus began both to do and teach, Until the day in which he was taken up, after that he through the Holy Ghost had given commandments unto the apostles whom he had chosen: To whom also he shewed himself alive after his passion by many infallible proofs, being seen of them forty days, and speaking of the things pertaining to the kingdom of God:—ACTS 1:1–3

The early church in Jerusalem saw a staggering level of growth. Just days after three thousand were saved on the Day of Pentecost, five thousand more were saved after Peter healed the lame man at the Temple and preached again. Every day new converts were being added to the church. What explains the phenomenal impact it made? That church had none of the things we think are important—no facilities, no advanced educational training, no books or seminars or ability to see how others were ministering. Yet they changed the world. The impact of the Jerusalem church has a simple explanation: they had the teaching of Jesus, and they worked in the power of the Holy Spirit.

That explanation raises an obvious question: why aren't we making the same impact? We have the teachings of Jesus and the completed Word of God. We have the same Holy Spirit living within, who has the same power. Nothing has changed on God's end. The problem lies with us.

We have far too many churches that have traded power for programs and divine enabling for human effort. We work in our strength, gather the latest research, follow the latest trends, and try to produce what only God can perform. There is nothing wrong with strategy, research, or programs. We need to be wise in how we spend our time and resources. But the bottom line is that we need a return to the Word of God and the power of His Holy Spirit.

Today's Growth Principle: If we fail to see God's power working in our lives, the problem does not lie with Him.

"I Would Prefer Not To"

Ye stiffnecked and uncircumcised in heart and ears, ye do always resist the Holy Ghost: as your fathers did, so do ye. Which of the prophets have not your fathers persecuted? and they have slain them which shewed before of the coming of the Just One; of whom ye have been now the betrayers and murderers: Who have received the law by the disposition of angels, and have not kept it.—ACTS 7:51-53

Though Herman Melville is best remembered now for writing the whaling tale *Moby Dick*, he was better known in his lifetime for his short stories. One of the most influential was "Bartleby, the Scrivener: A Story of Wall Street," which told of a man hired to copy legal documents in a busy law firm. After a period of productive work, Bartleby fell into a deep depression and stopped accepting assignments. Every order or suggestion was met with the phrase, "I would prefer not to." Eventually Bartleby lost his job and his home, and even refused to eat, until he died.

It is a tragic story, and we find it hard to believe that someone could be so obstinate with such negative results. Yet if we're honest, we must admit that there are times when we know exactly what God has directed and commanded, but our response is anything but obedience. We come up with all kinds of excuses and explanations to justify our rebellion, but in the final analysis it comes down to a matter of the will—we either bend our necks to God's yoke or we stubbornly insist on going our own way. Too often, we simply decide, "I would prefer not to."

It is often easier to diagnose rebellion in others than in our own hearts. But we must not allow our preferences and desires to be placed ahead of God's command. The only proper response that a Christian can make to a directive from the Lord is cheerful, prompt, and complete obedience.

Today's Growth Principle: The Lord's will and work cannot be done by those who refuse to yield their desires to Him.

Responding to the Preaching of Jesus

And all they in the synagogue, when they heard these things, were filled with wrath, And rose up, and thrust him out of the city, and led him unto the brow of the hill whereon their city was built, that they might cast him down headlong. But he passing through the midst of them went his way, And came down to Capernaum, a city of Galilee, and taught them on the sabbath days.—LUKE 4:28–31

There are many events recorded in Scripture that would be amazing to have witnessed in person. We think of David's battle with Goliath, Daniel in the den of lions, or Elijah calling down fire on Mt. Carmel and picture the events in our minds. But what would it have been like to have heard Jesus preach in person? We tell ourselves that we would eagerly receive His teaching and hang on every word, but often that was not the response of those who heard Him.

When Jesus returned to His hometown of Nazareth and preached in the synagogue, those who had watched Him grow up and *should* have been the first to respond and follow Him did not like what they heard. In fact, they were so outraged that they tried to kill Jesus. If you visit Nazareth today, you can still visit the place overlooking the city where that attempted murder took place. After their response, Jesus moved His headquarters to Capernaum on the shores of the Sea of Galilee.

What a tragedy to have Jesus in your presence but reject His message. We do not have Jesus physically present to hear His voice, but we can read His Word. What is our response? Do we gladly obey what He says, or do we find, like the people of Nazareth, that the message compels us to make changes we are unwilling to make?

Today's Growth Principle: Rejecting what God tells us to do robs us of the blessing of obedience and limits us in what God will do in our lives.

When Things Seem Hopeless

And as they were afraid, and bowed down their faces to the earth, they said unto them, Why seek ye the living among the dead? He is not here, but is risen: remember how he spake unto you when he was yet in Galilee, Saying, The Son of man must be delivered into the hands of sinful men, and be crucified, and the third day rise again. And they remembered his words,—LUKE 24:5–8

The three days that Jesus was in the grave were dark indeed for the disciples who had followed and loved Him. Despite the fact that He had told them of His impending death, they did not seem to grasp the reality of God's plan for redemption. As those around them celebrated Passover and the Feast of Unleavened Bread, they huddled together in hiding. Fear and doubt filled their minds. Their problem was revealed by the angels at the empty tomb—*they had forgotten what Jesus said.*

If we are honest, many of us live in fear and doubt rather than in confidence and faith. There are times when our fears have a real foundation. Of course, not all of the things that concern us are imaginary; some are real. But just as the disciples faced the loss of the Lord, when we face real threats we do not have to give in to hopelessness and despair. Even when all of the evidence, all of our senses, all of our experience, and all those around us say that there is no hope, we can know that with God all things are possible.

The faithfulness of God recorded in His Word is our comfort and strength in times of distress, but only if we remember what He has promised us. Too often, we allow bad circumstances to fill our minds, so that the only thing we remember is how bad things are. When we pause to read and recall the unfailing promises we have been given, we will not give in to despair.

Today's Growth Principle: Even in the darkest days, there is hope to be found in claiming the unchanging promises of God.

APRIL

Faith in the Resurrection

For I know that my redeemer liveth, and that he shall stand at the latter day upon the earth: And though after my skin worms destroy this body, yet in my flesh shall I see God: Whom I shall see for myself, and mine eyes shall behold, and not another; though my reins be consumed within me.—JOB 19:25–27

Thousands of years before Jesus came to the world as the Saviour and Messiah who had been promised, those who knew and believed God had a great faith that this life is not the end—that there is an eternity beyond this life. Job lived long before there was a written promise of the resurrection recorded in Scripture, yet in the midst of his great trial, he declared with confidence that after his death he would see God in his physical body.

The death of Christ alone could not be the end of the story for us to have salvation. It was necessary that He also rise from the dead. Paul wrote, "For I delivered unto you first of all that which I also received, how that Christ died for our sins according to the scriptures; And that he was buried, and that he rose again the third day according to the scriptures" (1 Corinthians 15:3–4). The Resurrection is just as much a part of the gospel as the cross.

The fact—not a myth, a legend, or a tradition, but a historical, demonstrated fact—that Jesus rose from the dead is the evidence that all of God's promises concerning our future are reliable. The power that overcame death and the grave guarantees our future resurrection as well. The Resurrection is the center and source of our hope. It is the greatest miracle in all of human history. The empty tomb is an assurance that God will fulfill all of His commitments to us, and that one day the Lord will return to take us home.

Today's Growth Principle: We should live every day in the reality of the resurrection and the certainty of Christ's return.

Jesus Does All Things Well

And straightway his ears were opened, and the string of his tongue was loosed, and he spake plain. And he charged them that they should tell no man: but the more he charged them, so much the more a great deal they published it; And were beyond measure astonished, saying, He hath done all things well: he maketh both the deaf to hear, and the dumb to speak.
—MARK 7:35–37

Because she was blind and unable to work a traditional job, Fanny Crosby relied on the sale of her poems and hymns for her financial income. Despite her popularity, there were often times when money was short. On one particular day, she had a pressing need for five dollars. Though the sum was not huge, she had no prospect of getting the money, so she began to pray for God's help. Only a few minutes passed before a stranger knocked on her door and gave her exactly five dollars. She wrote, "I have no way of accounting for this, except to believe that God, in answer to my prayer, put it into the heart of this good man to bring the money." My first thought was, "It is so wonderful the way the Lord leads me." Not long after, she wrote the words to the song we still sing today, "All the Way My Saviour Leads Me":

> All the way my Saviour leads me; what have I to ask beside
> Can I doubt His tender mercy, who through life has been my guide?
> Heavenly peace, divinest comfort, here by faith in Him to dwell!
> For I know what 'er befall me, Jesus doeth all things well.

There is great peace in remembering that God always knows what is best for us. Many times, it is the very things that bring us hardship and pain that He is using to mold us to be more like Jesus. We must trust our Father who knows and does what is best.

Today's Growth Principle: Never forget God's perfect knowledge and love; He makes no mistakes.

The Foundation of Truth

Till we all come in the unity of the faith, and of the knowledge of the Son of God, unto a perfect man, unto the measure of the stature of the fulness of Christ: That we henceforth be no more children, tossed to and fro, and carried about with every wind of doctrine, by the sleight of men, and cunning craftiness, whereby they lie in wait to deceive; But speaking the truth in love, may grow up into him in all things, which is the head, even Christ:—EPHESIANS 4:13–15

In our society, it has become common to hear people referring to "my truth" or "your truth." But there is no such thing as subjective truth. Truth is not a commodity that varies based on the person. Truth is an absolute. There are things that are true, and there are things that are false. Our perceptions and experiences may vary, but that does not change the truth. The truth is absolute, certain, and unchanging. It is not and never has been relative to conditions, circumstances, or personalities.

The truth is what the truth is, because the truth is set and settled by the nature and character of God. "That by two immutable things, in which it was impossible for God to lie, we might have a strong consolation, who have fled for refuge to lay hold upon the hope set before us" (Hebrews 6:18). People change. Scientific understanding is altered and updated. History is rewritten as new discoveries are made. Educational methods and ideologies are adjusted. Truth remains.

If we want a sure and certain source of truth upon which to build our lives, we must fill our hearts and minds with the only unchanging record of truth—the Word of God. The night before His crucifixion, Jesus prayed: "Sanctify them through thy truth: thy word is truth" (John 17:17). We must know the truth to overcome error.

Today's Growth Principle: If we want a solid foundation for uncertain times, we must build on the unchanging truth of the Bible.

Making Copies

Let us therefore, as many as be perfect, be thus minded: and if in any thing ye be otherwise minded, God shall reveal even this unto you. Nevertheless, whereto we have already attained, let us walk by the same rule, let us mind the same thing. Brethren, be followers together of me, and mark them which walk so as ye have us for an ensample.—PHILIPPIANS 3:15-17

In 1938, a patent lawyer and inventor named Chester Carlson revolutionized the business world with his work in what was known at the time as electrophotography—making exact copies using a machine. He soon begin calling his process *xerography,* from the Greek for "dry writing." The Xerox machine was one of the most successful inventions in history. The ability to reproduce page after page of duplicates changed the way people kept records and did business.

God's plan for His work in the world also revolves around making copies. Paul wrote to Timothy, "And the things that thou hast heard of me among many witnesses, the same commit thou to faithful men, who shall be able to teach others also" (2 Timothy 2:2). The process we are commanded to follow is patterned after the work Jesus did with twelve chosen men—discipleship, and it is nothing less than living in such a way that our lives are patterned after Christ, and others can see in us a pattern as they live the Christian life.

This is not a matter of setting ourselves up in pride as great examples, but a matter of living like Jesus so much that we can say as Paul did to the church at Corinth, "Be ye followers of me, even as I also am of Christ" (1 Corinthians 11:1) and to the church at Philippi, "be followers together of me." The more closely we adhere to the example of Jesus, the better copies our lives will produce. We must never forget that whether or not we intend it, we have great influence on those around us. We must be careful to live so that our pattern is a good one for others to follow.

Today's Growth Principle: If those you influence turn out to be copies of your life, would you be pleased with the result?

Created for a Purpose

And when those beasts give glory and honour and thanks to him that sat on the throne, who liveth for ever and ever, The four and twenty elders fall down before him that sat on the throne, and worship him that liveth for ever and ever, and cast their crowns before the throne, saying, Thou art worthy, O Lord, to receive glory and honour and power: for thou hast created all things, and for thy pleasure they are and were created.
—REVELATION 4:9–11

Many of us have faced the challenge of hanging a picture when we didn't have a hammer close at hand. The number of tools and other objects that we have used to drive nails is impressive. People have used shoes, books, screwdriver handles, and many other things, but nothing does the job in the same way that a hammer does. Hammers are designed and created with a specific purpose in mind, and they're very good at doing what they were made to do. If we could stretch the analogy a little more and give personality to hammers, we could also note that they don't spend their days wishing they could do something else. Hammers are quite content being used for their original purpose. They don't seek to bring glory to themselves. They were made to drive nails. When we pick up a hammer, it does the job.

People, on the other hand, were also created for a purpose—to glorify God. Yet far too often we are not content with our purpose and designs, and seek fulfillment on our own rather than yielding to God's creation and calling on our lives. Everything that God made plays its role except for man. This is not something new in our day. Thousands of years ago God spoke to Isaiah and said, "The ox knoweth his owner, and the ass his master's crib: but Israel doth not know, my people doth not consider" (Isaiah 1:3). There is no greater or higher purpose we can reach than to bring glory to our Creator.

Today's Growth Principle: Glorifying God should always be the number one priority of the Christian life.

The Gift of a Family

Behold, what manner of love the Father hath bestowed upon us, that we should be called the sons of God: therefore the world knoweth us not, because it knew him not. Beloved, now are we the sons of God, and it doth not yet appear what we shall be: but we know that, when he shall appear, we shall be like him; for we shall see him as he is. And every man that hath this hope in him purifieth himself, even as he is pure.—1 John 3:1–3

One of the biggest stars of radio and the early days of television was Art Linkletter. He described his success simply: "Put regular people, especially kids, in front a camera and let them be themselves." Linkletter had a long and successful life and career, but things could have gone very differently for him. He was born in 1912 in Moose Jaw, Saskatchewan, Canada, as Arthur Kelly. His parents abandoned him on the steps of a local church when he was just a few weeks old, and Art was adopted by a pastor and his wife. In an interview given in his nineties, Linkletter talked about all he had experienced and then said, "But I'm still the preacher's kid."

All of us were born into the wrong family. Jesus said, "Ye are of your father the devil, and the lusts of your father ye will do. He was a murderer from the beginning, and abode not in the truth, because there is no truth in him. When he speaketh a lie, he speaketh of his own: for he is a liar, and the father of it" (John 8:44). But the love of God for us was so great, that, even when we did not know Him or love Him, He reached out to us by sending His Son to be the Saviour of all who believe.

Think about it! We, who were lost in sin, are now "… heirs of God, and joint-heirs with Christ…" (Romans 8:17). God Himself has lavished His love on us and made us His own. Our adoption is the measure of His devotion.

Today's Growth Principle: Never lose sight of the amazing love of God that offered you a place in His family.

Who Owns the Wool?

What? know ye not that your body is the temple of the Holy Ghost which is in you, which ye have of God, and ye are not your own? For ye are bought with a price: therefore glorify God in your body, and in your spirit, which are God's.—1 CORINTHIANS 6:19–20

Dr. John Rice said that one of the sermons he heard as a young man had a powerful influence on his life. An old Texas preacher named Dr. J. B. Gambrell delivered a message entitled "Who Owns the Wool?" Dr. Rice remembered, "His argument was very simple. He who owns the sheep owns the wool. And if God owns the Christian, then He owns all his time. He owns all his money. He owns all his family. A Christian ought to say, 'All I am, all I have belongs to God. I want to use it for Him.'"

There is no circumstance in which a Christian has a right to say "No" to God's command. It is an act of defiance and rebellion to disobey what the Lord says we are to do—not to mention an act that demonstrates we do not love Him. Jesus said, "If ye love me, keep my commandments" (John 14:15).

Surely there have been times when people have misinterpreted Scripture and incorrectly claimed Divine support for a position. In those cases, it is not disobedience to God to do what He says rather than what men may declare God wants. But where the Bible is clear, we must obey. We have no right to do otherwise. Because God owns us, both by right of creation and by right of redemption, everything that we are and everything that we have is His.

We belong to Christ—not just our spirits, but our bodies as well—because of the price that was paid for our salvation. A Christian who holds back from full surrender to the Lord has lost sight of the incredible sacrifice Christ made when He purchased our salvation.

Today's Growth Principle: Remembering God's ownership of our lives and all we possess has a powerful impact on all we do.

The Only Door to Heaven

Then said Jesus unto them again, Verily, verily, I say unto you, I am the door of the sheep. All that ever came before me are thieves and robbers: but the sheep did not hear them. I am the door: by me if any man enter in, he shall be saved, and shall go in and out, and find pasture. The thief cometh not, but for to steal, and to kill, and to destroy: I am come that they might have life, and that they might have it more abundantly.—John 10:7-10

In our increasingly pluralistic society, it is becoming more and more unpopular to declare that Jesus is the only way to Heaven. But that was His message while He was here on Earth, and it is the message all of His faithful followers must declare. Though God is love, and He loves the world, He is also holy, and the only way we can enter His presence is if our sins have been cleansed through the blood of Jesus Christ.

Many churches have backed away from this truth. Writing to Eygenio Scalfari, editor of the *La Repubblica* newspaper, Pope Francis wrote: "You ask me if the God of the Christians forgives those who don't believe and who don't seek the faith. I start by saying—and this is the fundamental thing—that God's mercy has no limits if you go to him with a sincere and contrite heart. The issue for those who do not believe in God is to obey their conscience."

In truth, no one comes to God by following his conscience. No one comes to God by following the Pope, the Dalai Lama, or any other religious leader. In fact, no one comes to God by joining a church, getting baptized, being kind, or doing any other work to earn salvation. We only come to God by accepting the sacrifice of Jesus in our place.

Have you trusted Christ as your personal Saviour? If so, give thanks for the wonderful gift of salvation, and look for an opportunity to share it with someone else today. If not, place your faith in Him right now. He promises, "…him that cometh to me I will in no wise cast out" (John 6:37).

Today's Growth Principle: Jesus is the only door to Heaven, and we must accept His salvation by grace through faith to see Heaven.

1 Samuel 10–12   //   Luke 9:37–62   103

Sacrificial Love

Hereby perceive we the love of God, because he laid down his life for us: and we ought to lay down our lives for the brethren. But whoso hath this world's good, and seeth his brother have need, and shutteth up his bowels of compassion from him, how dwelleth the love of God in him? My little children, let us not love in word, neither in tongue; but in deed and in truth.— 1 JOHN 3:16–18

On October 1, 2017, concert goers at an outdoor venue in Las Vegas, Nevada, were attacked in what became one of the deadliest mass shootings in American history. As bullets flew among the shocked crowds, people rushed for safety, seeking a way to escape. Among the more than twenty thousand who attended the concert was a couple from Tennessee, Sonny and Heather Melton. Sonny placed his body between his wife and the shooter and kept the bullets from reaching her. He was shot, but her life was spared by his sacrifice.

Most of us will, hopefully, never face a life and death choice where we would have to protect someone else with our own bodies. Yet each day we are faced with choices of whether we will live for self or for others. There is no way to emulate the life of Christ without loving others to the point where we are willing to sacrifice for them. "For ye know the grace of our Lord Jesus Christ, that, though he was rich, yet for your sakes he became poor, that ye through his poverty might be rich" (2 Corinthians 8:9).

We live in a world that glorifies selfishness. The value of sacrifice in God's eyes is still great, but it is little valued by most of those around us. We are not called, however, to be like the world or to be great in its eyes. We are called to lay down our lives, pick up our crosses, and walk in the footsteps of Jesus.

Today's Growth Principle: The Christian life is not about serving ourselves, but rather sacrificially loving and caring for others.

Being a Blessing to Others

And it came to pass, when Rachel had born Joseph, that Jacob said unto Laban, Send me away, that I may go unto mine own place, and to my country. Give me my wives and my children, for whom I have served thee, and let me go: for thou knowest my service which I have done thee. And Laban said unto him, I pray thee, if I have found favour in thine eyes, tarry: for I have learned by experience that the LORD hath blessed me for thy sake.—GENESIS 30:25–27

Jacob was hardly an example of faithful Christian living. He cheated his brother and lied to his father, and he took advantage of every opportunity to increase his wealth at any cost. Despite the pain of growing up in a family where the parents were divided by their favorites, he played favorites with *his* sons. Yet for all of his failings, Jacob trusted God.

As an expression of his faith, Jacob promised to honor God with a tithe of all his resources. At Bethel where he saw the vision of angels ascending and descending from Heaven, Jacob promised, "And this stone, which I have set for a pillar, shall be God's house: and of all that thou shalt give me I will surely give the tenth unto thee" (Genesis 28:22). God honored Jacob's faith and blessed him with great wealth. But the blessing of God was not limited to Jacob alone. Jacob's father-in-law, Laban, recognized that God was at work in Jacob's life and that he (Laban) had been blessed as a result of their association.

We often make two mistaken assumptions about the blessings of God. First, we assume they are only material. But some of God's richest blessings come through His Word, His church, the relationships He gives us, and more. Second, we think of the blessing of God solely in terms of what it means to us. But if we are living in such a way that allows God's blessing to flow, the impact is not limited—it helps others as well as us.

Today's Growth Principle: When we are obedient to God and honor Him, the blessings spill over beyond our own lives to help others.

Selfie Theology

What shall we say then? Is there unrighteousness with God? God forbid. For he saith to Moses, I will have mercy on whom I will have mercy, and I will have compassion on whom I will have compassion. So then it is not of him that willeth, nor of him that runneth, but of God that sheweth mercy. —ROMANS 9:14–16

We live in a self-obsessed culture. People are more and more focused inwardly. The networks and connections that once bound communities and society together have frayed. Everything you need to know about what we value can be seen on the ubiquitous cell phone where the camera doesn't just take pictures of what you are looking at it—it quickly changes to take selfies. I read recently that most celebrities are no longer asked for autographs. Instead, they are now asked to pose for a picture, not of themselves, but with the fan. Even those that many look up to are included in memory only to the extent that they reinforce the image of self.

God's plan is not focused on us. He is not impressed by our strength, our intelligence, or our resources, which pale in comparison to His perfection. Yet despite our shortcomings by God's standard, we find it easy to be proud because we measure ourselves by whatever standard will make us feel better. We nurture and feed our pride, even though it is at the very top of the list of sins that God despises. "These six things doth the LORD hate: yea, seven are an abomination unto him: A proud look, a lying tongue, and hands that shed innocent blood" (Proverbs 6:16–17).

This self-obsession is not limited to the world. We see its effects in God's work as well. The temptation to focus on and rely on self has led to the destruction of many Christians and many ministries. The only hope we have is God.

Today's Growth Principle: We can either have our pride and what we can accomplish on our own, or we can choose humility and have God's power.

God's Plan Includes Every Part of Life

And Joseph said unto them, Fear not: for am I in the place of God? But as for you, ye thought evil against me; but God meant it unto good, to bring to pass, as it is this day, to save much people alive. Now therefore fear ye not: I will nourish you, and your little ones. And he comforted them, and spake kindly unto them.—GENESIS 50:19–21

In his autobiography, *An American Life,* Ronald Reagan wrote, "I was raised to believe that God had a plan for everyone and that seemingly random twists of fate are all a part of His plan. My mother—a small woman with auburn hair and a sense of optimism that ran as deep as the cosmos—told me that everything in life happened for a purpose. She said all things were part of God's plan, even the most disheartening setbacks, and in the end, everything worked out for the best. If something went wrong, she said, you didn't let it get you down: You stepped away from it, stepped over it, and moved on."

The trials and difficulties of life are not pleasant to endure, but we must learn to view them as God views them—as tools to work His plan in our lives. "My brethren, count it all joy when ye fall into divers temptations; Knowing this, that the trying of your faith worketh patience" (James 1:2–3). Many times we miss the opportunity trouble brings because we fail to believe that God is working in and through it to prepare and equip us for His purpose.

The way we respond to trouble is determined by our focus. Joseph could have become bitter toward his brothers and used his powerful position to exact revenge. That is what they expected and feared. But because Joseph was focused on God, he forgave them and cared for their needs just as God had designed.

Today's Growth Principle: Rather than complaining about our troubles, we should look for the opportunities God is creating.

Finishing God's Purpose

Wherefore he saith also in another psalm, Thou shalt not suffer thine Holy One to see corruption. For David, after he had served his own generation by the will of God, fell on sleep, and was laid unto his fathers, and saw corruption: But he, whom God raised again, saw no corruption.
—ACTS 13:35–37

There were many times in David's life when he was in great danger. He fought with wild animals as a boy keeping his father's sheep. He faced a trained warrior in the giant Goliath with nothing but a sling. Saul tried to kill him repeatedly. The Philistines wanted him dead. His own son, Absalom, raised an armed insurrection against him and sought his life. Yet through all of those dangers and threats, David survived because God's purpose for his life was not finished. David died at an old age, only after he had completed the mission God gave him.

The great missionary David Livingstone said, "I am immortal until the will of God is accomplished in my life." While we should not be foolish or cavalier in our approach to life, we should also not live in fear and bondage, no matter how difficult our circumstances may be. Some people die unexpectedly in accidents or a sudden health crisis, while others have plenty of time to prepare for an end that seems long in advance. But in none of those cases is God taken by surprise.

God knows His plan and purpose, and He knows exactly how long we will live. Every one of those days, including the final one, will be under His care. "Surely goodness and mercy shall follow me all the days of my life: and I will dwell in the house of the LORD for ever" (Psalm 23:6). Rather than living with fear and worry, we should live joyfully, committing our lives to fulfilling God's calling and purpose.

Today's Growth Principle: Just as we trust God for our daily needs and our eternity, we can trust Him to enable us to complete His purpose for our lives.

The Case for Confidence

*Being confident of this very thing, that he which hath begun a good work in you will perform it until the day of Jesus Christ: Even as it is meet for me to think this of you all, because I have you in my heart; inasmuch as both in my bonds, and in the defence and confirmation of the gospel, ye all are partakers of my grace. For God is my record, how greatly I long after you all in the bowels of Jesus Christ.—*PHILIPPIANS 1:6–8

One of the great naval heroes of the American Civil War was Admiral David Farragut. Though he had been born in Tennessee and lived in Virginia, he opposed secession and fought for the Union. He was renowned for his personal courage, and willing to take risks to win a victory. The story goes that he met with another officer named DuPont who had failed in an attack on Charleston Harbor. Farragut asked, "Why didn't you get into Charleston?"

DuPont responded, "It was because the channel was crooked."

"No," Farragut said, "That is not the reason."

"The rebel fire was perfectly horrible," DuPont added.

"Yes, but it wasn't that," Farragut said.

DuPont asked, "Then what was it?"

Farragut replied, "It was because you didn't believe you could get in."

The successful and victorious Christian life is not a life of self-confidence. Rather, it is a life of confidence, faith, and trust in the promises of God. We can have a true confidence, not based on arrogance or presumption, because God has committed Himself, and He never fails. "God is not a man, that he should lie; neither the son of man, that he should repent: hath he said, and shall he not do it? or hath he spoken, and shall he not make it good?" (Numbers 23:19). Our confidence is not in our limited strength but in His boundless power and might.

Today's Growth Principle: Because our work for God relies on His strength and provision instead of ours, we can be confident of success.

Smelling Good to God

For even in Thessalonica ye sent once and again unto my necessity. Not because I desire a gift: but I desire fruit that may abound to your account. But I have all, and abound: I am full, having received of Epaphroditus the things which were sent from you, an odour of a sweet smell, a sacrifice acceptable, well-pleasing to God.—PHILIPPIANS 4:16–18

Of all our senses, smell is the one that produces the strongest memory and emotional effect. Repeated scientific studies show that an odor triggers more brain activity than sight, sound, touch, or taste. *Psychology Today* reported a study of a veteran with PTSD: "On one occasion, the smell of diesel from a neighborhood fire instantly conjured the memory of an accident in Vietnam. In his mind he could vividly see the burning vehicle, doors ajar, and billows of fire and smoke. The patient couldn't save his fellow soldiers that day. The smell of diesel frequently caused him to re-experience the overwhelming feelings of guilt and helplessness that he initially experienced more than thirty years ago."

The Lord certainly does not need reminders—He never forgets. Yet again and again the Bible speaks of things we do such as our gifts and our prayers being a pleasant aroma to God. Using the same metaphor of smell, God spoke to Isaiah of His displeasure in the hypocritical self-righteousness of the Israelites who worshiped idols while claiming to love Him. "Which say, Stand by thyself, come not near to me; for I am holier than thou. These are a smoke in my nose, a fire that burneth all the day" (Isaiah 65:5). In contrast, Revelation 5:8 speaks of "...golden vials full of odours, which are the prayers of saints." And, of course, our verse above speaks of sacrificial giving as being a "sweet smell" to God.

How incredible to realize that our self-righteousness is repulsive to God, while our tender dependence on and obedience to Him is pleasing to Him in one of the strongest ways.

Today's Growth Principle: God is pleased by our basic expressions of dependence on and obedience to Him.

1 Samuel 27–29   //   Luke 13:1–22

Grace in Severe Trials

Then they cried out with a loud voice, and stopped their ears, and ran upon him with one accord, And cast him out of the city, and stoned him: and the witnesses laid down their clothes at a young man's feet, whose name was Saul. And they stoned Stephen, calling upon God, and saying, Lord Jesus, receive my spirit. And he kneeled down, and cried with a loud voice, Lord, lay not this sin to their charge. And when he had said this, he fell asleep.—ACTS 7:57-60

Joseph Parker, a powerful preacher and contemporary of Charles Spurgeon, spent a great deal of time, especially in his younger years, speaking in public parks and gathering places, presenting the gospel to atheists and skeptics who came together to discuss the topics of the day. Once he was confronted by an infidel who shouted at him, "What did Christ do for Stephen when he was stoned?" Parker responded, "He gave him grace to pray for those who stoned him."

God's grace does not always deliver us from the suffering of trials. Some of the greatest Christians in history endured great hardship and persecution, and multiplied thousands have perished for their faith. What grace does, however, is overcome the hardship, so that we endure with faith, and even in our darkest moments we are an unmistakable witness to the world. It is not by accident that the Bible tells us Saul was present at Stephen's death. The attitude Saul saw displayed by the dying martyr helped prepare his heart to receive Christ.

Just as Jesus on the cross asked the Father to forgive those who were killing Him, Stephen sought God's mercy on his unjust murderers. Most of us will not face that ultimate test, but we all endure physical, emotional, and spiritual trials. And for every trial, God's grace is sufficient if we apply it and allow it to govern our responses.

Today's Growth Principle: Rather than asking God for ease and comfort, we should ask for grace to reflect Jesus in our trials.

The Power of Prayer

And now, behold, the children of Ammon and Moab and mount Seir, whom thou wouldest not let Israel invade, when they came out of the land of Egypt, but they turned from them, and destroyed them not; Behold, I say, how they reward us, to come to cast us out of thy possession, which thou hast given us to inherit. O our God, wilt thou not judge them? for we have no might against this great company that cometh against us; neither know we what to do: but our eyes are upon thee.
—2 CHRONICLES 20:10–12

William Cowper lost his mother when he was very young and grew up struggling with depression. Though a gifted student and poet, Cowper sought in vain for a purpose and direction for his life. Amid his depression, he tried to commit suicide and was sent to an asylum for a time. There at the asylum he heard and understood the gospel and put his faith in Christ. On his release, he moved to Olney, England, where he met John Newton. The former slave trader was a great help to Cowper, and it was during this time that he wrote the song, "There Is a Fountain Filled with Blood." Cowper was physically weak and often ill, and continued to battle depression. But he learned profound lessons during his battles as he found himself forced to rely on God for his every need. Cowper wrote:

> Restraining prayer, we cease to fight;
> Prayer makes the Christian's armor bright;
> And Satan trembles, when he sees
> The weakest saint upon his knees.

The constant temptation we face is to go our own way and to work in our own strength. Yet in truth, we are completely unable to serve and live for God apart from His power. And that power can only be found on our knees. We do not need more strength and ability. We need more prayer.

Today's Growth Principle: Through prayer we seek and receive God's power and provision for our daily lives.

Keep On Doing Right

Be not deceived; God is not mocked: for whatsoever a man soweth, that shall he also reap. For he that soweth to his flesh shall of the flesh reap corruption; but he that soweth to the Spirit shall of the Spirit reap life everlasting. And let us not be weary in well doing: for in due season we shall reap, if we faint not. —GALATIANS 6:7–9

When William Carey went to India, the concept of missionaries was sadly unknown and unpracticed among most of the people he knew. There was a great deal of resistance to Carey's plan to take the gospel to a foreign land. Carey was not a pastor or theologian; he ran a shoe repair business. But his burning zeal to reach the lost compelled him to leave his home and country behind. His first years on the field were hard. His son Peter died, his wife suffered a mental breakdown, and it was seven long years before he baptized his first convert. There was little to indicate a mighty work from God was about to happen.

On a trip to England, I was able to visit Regents Park College at Oxford where they have preserved the letters William Carey wrote to his family and supporters during his time in India. They are filled with news of various difficulties and hardships, but also with an unwavering commitment to continue the work. He closed one of the letters to his sisters with the admonition, "Be strong in the Lord." Carey remained faithful, and his work eventually made a major impact on India and challenged thousands of others to take up the missionary cause. But none of this would have happened had he not persevered.

No one has accomplished anything lasting and great for God who was not willing to pay the price of faithfulness. Those who shrink or give up when things get hard will not see the harvest. Only those who remain faithful and keep doing what is right will reap.

Today's Growth Principle: God did not promise us ease or comfort, but He did promise a fruitful harvest to those who endure.

Where Is Your Focus?

That being justified by his grace, we should be made heirs according to the hope of eternal life. This is a faithful saying, and these things I will that thou affirm constantly, that they which have believed in God might be careful to maintain good works. These things are good and profitable unto men. But avoid foolish questions, and genealogies, and contentions, and strivings about the law; for they are unprofitable and vain.
—TITUS 3:7–9

How we receive instruction and correction from the Word of God depends in large measure on whether we understand that it is meant for us, or if we instead think that it is meant for others to apply. It's like the elderly church member shaking hands with the pastor after the service on a Sunday morning. "That was a wonderful sermon—just wonderful," she said. "Everything you said applies to someone I know!"

The temptation to apply truth to the lives of others rather than to our own is not new, but it is misleading. The truth that God wants us to internalize does us no good if we are only concerned with those around us. We see this in the life of Peter after the Resurrection. When Jesus had finished their memorable conversation, designed to bring Peter back to a right relationship with Him, by the Sea of Galilee, Peter immediately turned his focus to John. "Peter seeing him saith to Jesus, Lord, and what shall this man do? Jesus saith unto him, If I will that he tarry till I come, what is that to thee? follow thou me" (John 21:21–22).

We must resist the temptation to worry about correcting others instead of taking care of our own spiritual condition. We cannot make progress unless we are willing to focus on our own lives and make the necessary changes to bring us in line with what the Bible commands. All spiritual progress begins here.

Today's Growth Principle: By focusing on your personal spiritual condition, you will benefit from the teaching and preaching you hear.

A Certain Appointment

For then must he often have suffered since the foundation of the world: but now once in the end of the world hath he appeared to put away sin by the sacrifice of himself. And as it is appointed unto men once to die, but after this the judgment: So Christ was once offered to bear the sins of many; and unto them that look for him shall he appear the second time without sin unto salvation.—HEBREWS 9:26–28

When William Campbell was buried near Atlanta, Georgia, in April of 1962, there was one unique feature that set his funeral apart from normal—nearly twenty years earlier, Campbell had built his own casket. He owned a lumberyard and a construction business, and his hobby was wood working. So Campbell got some western fir and began the three-month process of making his own casket. He said, "It takes a lot of money to come into the world and to leave it as well, and I want to be as little expense to my folks as possible." When the casket was finished, it was placed in storage until Campbell's death at the age of eighty-five.

Most people don't want to think about the reality of death, but the certain reality is that, unless the Lord returns during our lifetime, all of us will one day keep that appointment. The question is not whether we will die, but whether we will be prepared when that moment comes. The only preparation for death is to put our faith in the payment Christ made for our sins on the cross by His substitutionary death—to place our faith in Jesus as our risen Saviour.

For those of us who know the Lord as our personal Saviour, we also want to live in such a way that we will not be ashamed to see Christ when He returns or calls us home. Although our salvation is sure, we want to invest our lives in that which will count for eternity.

Today's Growth Principle: Use the time that you have today wisely—none of us know how long we have to live for God.

The Necessity of Gratitude

And be not drunk with wine, wherein is excess; but be filled with the Spirit; Speaking to yourselves in psalms and hymns and spiritual songs, singing and making melody in your heart to the Lord; Giving thanks always for all things unto God and the Father in the name of our Lord Jesus Christ; Submitting yourselves one to another in the fear of God.
—EPHESIANS 5:18–21

There are two major enemies of gratitude that keep many people from being thankful. The first is a sense of entitlement—feeling that we deserve all of the good things we get. The second is a sense of greed—feeling we deserve even more than we get. Both of these attitudes stand in the way of living as thankful people.

There is an old joke about a husband who wanted to get his wife something special for Christmas but didn't have much money. He bought her a fur coat made of skunks. When she opened the package she said, "I can't see how such a nice coat can come from such a foul smelling little beast." Her husband responded, "I don't ask for thanks, but I do demand some respect!"

Too many times we look at God's good and gracious gifts, things which we do not deserve to receive at all, with contempt rather than with thanksgiving. What we deserve is eternity in Hell, but God has promised us eternity in Heaven and daily gives us so much more. The folly of Christians, who have received salvation and innumerable blessings solely by God's grace, complaining because they do not have everything they think they deserve is great indeed. The Spirit-filled Christian does not gripe and murmur, but gives thanks always and in every situation. If our focus is on the Lord and His goodness to us, there are no times in which we cannot find great cause for heartfelt gratitude.

Today's Growth Principle: God's grace gives us far more than we deserve, and in every circumstance we can find cause for gratitude.

Choosing a Legacy

I will extol thee, my God, O king; and I will bless thy name for ever and ever. Every day will I bless thee; and I will praise thy name for ever and ever. Great is the LORD, and greatly to be praised; and his greatness is unsearchable. One generation shall praise thy works to another, and shall declare thy mighty acts.—PSALM 145:1-4

Every one of us is going to leave a legacy of some kind. If you think of those who have gone before, whether friends or family, usually there are one or two words that sum up the main thrust of their lives. People are remembered for their generosity, their courage, their attitude, or perhaps a particular hobby or interest. Sometimes this legacy is a positive one, and sometimes it is negative.

Whatever our legacy, however, it isn't something we choose at the end of our lives. It's not like a will where we set aside a period of time to determine what we want others to remember about us and simply write it down. Rather, we build our legacy one day at a time over the course of our lives.

There are few things that are more fitting for a Christian than to be known as a person who praises God. The impact of praise to God on our own lives is great, but the impact of that praise on others may be even more important. The stories passed down about what God did for Dad or how He answered a special prayer for Grandma are of enormous value. So verbalize that praise to others. For many of us, the problem isn't that we never *feel* thankful, but that we don't express our thanks audibly—directly to God and to others about God.

Each of us has so much for which to praise God, but unless we tell those stories to others, they will be lost. We have a responsibility to the future to be people of praise.

Today's Growth Principle: Every day you have the opportunity to build a legacy of praise.

God Leads His Children

Then shalt thou call, and the LORD shall answer; thou shalt cry, and he shall say, Here I am. If thou take away from the midst of thee the yoke, the putting forth of the finger, and speaking vanity; And if thou draw out thy soul to the hungry, and satisfy the afflicted soul; then shall thy light rise in obscurity, and thy darkness be as the noon day: And the LORD shall guide thee continually, and satisfy thy soul in drought, and make fat thy bones: and thou shalt be like a watered garden, and like a spring of water, whose waters fail not.—ISAIAH 58:9–11

When Haldor Lillenas was putting together one of his first hymnals, he recalled a song he had learned soon after moving to America and learning English, "God Leads Us Along." He wanted to include it, but needed permission from the writer. Lillenas tracked down the author's widow whom he found living in, what was called in those days, a county poor house.

Not only was she delighted to have her husband's song shared with others, but despite her circumstances, she was rejoicing. She told Lillenas, "My husband and I were married while we were very young. God gave us a wonderful life together; he led us from day to day. But then God took my husband. Now God has led me here, and I'm so excited and glad about it! God has used me in this place. Many people come to this place and they are so sad and in such great need. They need help and comfort. I have been able to cheer many of them and lead scores of them to the Lord Jesus Christ."

God does not promise us ease and comfort, but He does promise to guide us through this life and never leave us. He is just as present and loving in our moments of pain as in our moments of joy. And when we trust His guidance, we find that our joy is increased.

Today's Growth Principle: Our responsibility is not to make our own path, but to follow wherever God leads us in trust.

Beware the Danger of Unintentional Idolatry

And the weight of the golden earrings that he requested was a thousand and seven hundred shekels of gold; beside ornaments, and collars, and purple raiment that was on the kings of Midian, and beside the chains that were about their camels' necks. And Gideon made an ephod thereof, and put it in his city, even in Ophrah: and all Israel went thither a whoring after it: which thing became a snare unto Gideon, and to his house.—JUDGES 8:26–27

God granted Gideon a miraculous victory over the Midianites that brought deliverance from painful bondage to the Jewish people. With a tiny group of three hundred men, Gideon routed a massive enemy army and put them to flight. Then, once the victory had been won, in one of the great tragedies of Scripture, Gideon took the spoils of war that had been gained only by God's power and grace, and used them to make an object that eventually he and many others began to worship.

While most people do not carve statues of gold or silver to worship in our day, there are many who worship something in place of God. Charles Spurgeon said, "If you love anything better than God, you are idolaters: if there is anything you would not give up for God it is your idol: if there is anything that you seek with greater fervor than you seek the glory of God, that is your idol."

It is not by coincidence that the first commandment said, "I am the LORD thy God, which have brought thee out of the land of Egypt, out of the house of bondage. Thou shalt have no other gods before me" (Exodus 20:2–3). God is not willing to be one among many or even first among equals. He is God alone, and nothing and no one will be allowed to take His place. The throne of our hearts must be His completely.

Today's Growth Principle: The only rightful place for God is on the throne of our hearts, and He will accept nothing less.

Which Direction Are You Facing?

And Lot lifted up his eyes, and beheld all the plain of Jordan, that it was well watered every where, before the LORD destroyed Sodom and Gomorrah, even as the garden of the LORD, like the land of Egypt, as thou comest unto Zoar. Then Lot chose him all the plain of Jordan; and Lot journeyed east: and they separated themselves the one from the other. Abram dwelled in the land of Canaan, and Lot dwelled in the cities of the plain, and pitched his tent toward Sodom.—GENESIS 13:10–12

L ot had a close relationship with one of the greatest men of faith in all of human history. His uncle, Abraham, brought Lot with him when he left his home to follow God's leading to a new land. As a result of their time together, Lot not only learned about God but profited materially in a great way as well. Yet he was not wise enough to want to stay with Abraham, and when the men who kept their large herds began to argue over land, Abraham graciously gave Lot first choice of where to go. Lot not only chose the area around Sodom, the most wicked city of the day, but when he set up camp, his tent looked toward Sodom. That choice led to great loss and sin for Lot and his family.

A. W. Tozer said, "If I look at the world, I will conform to the ways of the world. If I look at the Word, I will conform to the will of God." When we long to get as close to the world as we can and still feel good about ourselves as Christians, it will not be long before we pull back in our pursuit of God. There is a great drawing power in the things of the world. Satan is a master of temptation, and we must remain on guard to keep our hearts fixed on God.

Today's Growth Principle: The direction you lean will be the direction you fall, so take great care in what holds your affections.

Rejoice in the Lord

I will greatly rejoice in the LORD, my soul shall be joyful in my God; for he hath clothed me with the garments of salvation, he hath covered me with the robe of righteousness, as a bridegroom decketh himself with ornaments, and as a bride adorneth herself with her jewels. For as the earth bringeth forth her bud, and as the garden causeth the things that are sown in it to spring forth; so the Lord GOD will cause righteousness and praise to spring forth before all the nations.—ISAIAH 61:10–11

An English preacher named William Burt described how he visited the home of a family during his school days. The father he described as a good man but a "chronic growler." As he sat with the family, their young daughter began describing the favorite food of each of her siblings. The father asked, "What do I like, Nancy?" After a brief pause the little girl replied, "Well, you mostly like everything we haven't got." Burt said that from that day forward he resolved to be careful not to complain.

Every Christian endures hardship and trouble. There are no people who float through life without problems. The difference between those who rejoice and those who complain is not their circumstances, but their focus. Some look at their troubles, while others look to the Lord.

When Jesus sent the disciples out they returned with great joy over the results they had seen from their ministry. Jesus responded, "Notwithstanding in this rejoice not, that the spirits are subject unto you; but rather rejoice, because your names are written in heaven" (Luke 10:20).

The expression "rejoice in the Lord" is not meant to be a motto or a phrase we use without thinking. It is an instruction. Jesus is the source of our joy, and His promises and faithfulness are the guarantee that we will receive all that He has offered, despite the circumstances of the moment.

Today's Growth Principle: A Christian who thinks he has no cause for rejoicing has lost sight of God's salvation.

Everlasting Love

Thus saith the LORD, The people which were left of the sword found grace in the wilderness; even Israel, when I went to cause him to rest. The LORD hath appeared of old unto me, saying, Yea, I have loved thee with an everlasting love: therefore with lovingkindness have I drawn thee. Again I will build thee, and thou shalt be built, O virgin of Israel: thou shalt again be adorned with thy tabrets, and shalt go forth in the dances of them that make merry.—JEREMIAH 31:2–4

From the time it appeared on the cover of *The Saturday Evening Post* on June 11, 1955, Norman Rockwell's "Marriage License" proved to be one of his most popular and enduring paintings. It depicts a young couple trying to get the paperwork for their upcoming wedding finished before the office closes for the day. For his models, Rockwell used Joan Lahart and Francis Mahoney, a real life couple preparing for their wedding who lived near his studio in Stockbridge, Massachusetts. Rockwell touched so many hearts because he captured the genuine love and affection the two young people had for each other—and he later gave them an oil sketch of that painting as a wedding gift.

Human love is wonderful, but it is always subject to the limitations we experience as fallen beings. God's love is different. It is unlimited and because it is part of His very nature and character, it can never change. No power is able to take God's love away from His children. "For I am persuaded, that neither death, nor life, nor angels, nor principalities, nor powers, nor things present, nor things to come, Nor height, nor depth, nor any other creature, shall be able to separate us from the love of God, which is in Christ Jesus our Lord" (Romans 8:38–39). We can live in complete and glad confidence, rather than with fear or doubt, because God's love for us is everlasting.

Today's Growth Principle: The love of God never fails, and nothing we can do will separate His children from His love for them.

Keep On Doing What Is Right

And this is life eternal, that they might know thee the only true God, and Jesus Christ, whom thou hast sent. I have glorified thee on the earth: I have finished the work which thou gavest me to do. And now, O Father, glorify thou me with thine own self with the glory which I had with thee before the world was. —JOHN 17:3–5

There are many reasons people fail to accomplish all that they could or should in God's work. One of the most common explanations for failure is that people simply stop doing what is right. The walls of Jericho did not fall down when the Israelites marched around the city on the first day, or the third, or even the sixth. It was not until they completed the seventh circuit on the seventh day that God stepped in to give them the victory. It is not always fun or exciting to do God's will—it is simply obedience, again and again, that leads us to the place we should be.

It is easy to allow ourselves to become discouraged and decide that it doesn't matter whether we keep going. Many have missed victories that could have been won if they had simply remained faithful and kept going. There will always be reasons and excuses for those who want to quit, but that is the time when it is most important that we do not give up. "And let us not be weary in well doing: for in due season we shall reap, if we faint not" (Galatians 6:9). As the old poem puts it:

> Success is failure turned inside out—
> The silver tint of the clouds of doubt,
> And you never can tell just how close you are,
> It may be near when it seems so far;
> So stick to the fight when you're hardest hit—
> It's when things seem worst that you must not quit.

Today's Growth Principle: You will never finish God's course for your life if you are not faithful to stay on it.

Bringing Joy to Heaven

*And when he hath found it, he layeth it on his shoulders, rejoicing. And when he cometh home, he calleth together his friends and neighbours, saying unto them, Rejoice with me; for I have found my sheep which was lost. I say unto you, that likewise joy shall be in heaven over one sinner that repenteth, more than over ninety and nine just persons, which need no repentance.—*LUKE 15:5-7

Because this world is all we have ever known, it is hard for us to comprehend the perfection of Heaven. The place where those who have trusted Christ as Saviour will spend eternity has none of the flaws that are part of daily life here. There is no sin, no sickness, no sadness, and no night. Best of all, there is the constant presence of God Himself.

As wonderful and glorious and perfect as Heaven is, there is something that we can do here on Earth that brings rejoicing even there—bringing other people to Jesus. There is no more important task given to God's children than for us to follow the example of Jesus and work to reach the lost. There are many good and right things that can and should be done, but the essential mission of every believer is to be a witness to others of the salvation we have received. There is an eternal Heaven and an eternal Hell, and every person we meet will spend forever in one of those places.

It is our task to see to it that we warn the lost. We are their only hope. And if we fail in this assignment, the consequences are grave, both for others and for our own lives. "For though I preach the gospel, I have nothing to glory of: for necessity is laid upon me; yea, woe is unto me, if I preach not the gospel!" (1 Corinthians 9:16).

Today's Growth Principle: The material things of Earth will one day vanish, but the souls of those around us endure into eternity.

People Who Care for Others

But thanks be to God, which put the same earnest care into the heart of Titus for you. For indeed he accepted the exhortation; but being more forward, of his own accord he went unto you. And we have sent with him the brother, whose praise is in the gospel throughout all the churches;
—2 CORINTHIANS 8:16–18

When Catherine Booth died of cancer in 1890 after many years of faithful service with her husband William in the Salvation Army, her body lay in state at Congress Hall in London. Thousands filed past her body, giving honor to the lady who had given so much to so many. The cream of London society and the rich and powerful filed by next to children from the slums and former drunkards. It is recorded that one elderly man paused by her casket and said, "I've come sixty miles to see her again. She was the means of saving my two boys."

The impact that we make on the lives of others is a direct result of the amount of care and compassion we have for them. That is because it is that care that drives our actions. There is no more powerful motivation than love. It changes the way we view other people, and it changes the way we allocate our resources, time, and energy. We invest in what we care about, and when we care, others can tell. "And of some have compassion, making a difference" (Jude 1:22).

The world has many ways to counterfeit a number of the good things God calls us to do and be, but there is no substitute for compassion. The people with whom we work and to whom we minister will know whether or not they genuinely matter to us. And the more we care for others, the more we will devote ourselves to meeting their needs and reaching them with the gospel.

Today's Growth Principle: Only those who truly care for the needs of others are prepared to make a major impact on their lives.

MAY

The Purpose of Christ's Coming

For God so loved the world, that he gave his only begotten Son, that whosoever believeth in him should not perish, but have everlasting life. For God sent not his Son into the world to condemn the world; but that the world through him might be saved. He that believeth on him is not condemned: but he that believeth not is condemned already, because he hath not believed in the name of the only begotten Son of God.
—JOHN 3:16–18

Jesus lived a perfect life, but He did not come to us primarily as an example. Jesus never said anything that was false, but He did not come just to be a teacher. Jesus healed many who were sick, but He did not come to work miracles. Jesus had great compassion on the people He met, but He did not come to be a helper. Jesus came into the world to be the Saviour of those who believe—"to give his life a ransom for many" (Mark 10:45). He is the only way that we can have a personal relationship with God and a future home in Heaven.

All around us, people are pursuing different paths to God, and we often hear that there are many ways to Him, but that is false. Jesus is the only way. Charles Spurgeon said, "That which saves the soul is not coming to a human priest, nor even attending the assemblies of God's saints; it is coming to Jesus Christ, the great exalted Saviour, once slain, but now enthroned in glory. You must get to Him, or else you have nothing upon which your soul can rely."

Salvation is freely offered to those who will come to Jesus, but there are no alternate plans. God provides salvation only through His Son. No substitutes or replacements will be accepted. God's holy justice demands the payment for sin that only Jesus could provide for others. "For there is one God, and one mediator between God and men, the man Christ Jesus" (1 Timothy 2:5).

Today's Growth Principle: Salvation is only found by faith in the finished work of Jesus Christ on the cross.

The Ministry of Reconciliation

And all things are of God, who hath reconciled us to himself by Jesus Christ, and hath given to us the ministry of reconciliation; To wit, that God was in Christ, reconciling the world unto himself, not imputing their trespasses unto them; and hath committed unto us the word of reconciliation. Now then we are ambassadors for Christ, as though God did beseech you by us: we pray you in Christ's stead, be ye reconciled to God.—2 CORINTHIANS 5:18–20

Jonathan Dolliver served as United States Senator from Iowa from 1900 to 1910. During much of the time he was in Washington, his elderly father lived with him and his family. When his father passed away, Senator Dolliver was surprised when the Italian ambassador sent flowers and asked if he could sit with the family at the funeral. When Senator Dolliver asked why he wanted to come, the ambassador replied, "He was the only person who thought enough of me to speak to me about my soul."

Many, if not most, of the people we meet day after day are living in this world with little, if any, thought or concern of eternity. Our society does its best to ignore and obscure the reality of death. People go to great lengths to extend their lives. Even the product that pays people's heirs money upon their death is packaged and sold as "life insurance." Yet, no matter how much we try, we cannot escape the reality that death is coming to everyone.

This reality should be at the front of our minds as we meet people in different walks of life. Whether it is neighbors, co-workers, friends or family members, every person we meet has an eternal destiny. And we must try to reach them. "Knowing therefore the terror of the Lord, we persuade men; but we are made manifest unto God; and I trust also are made manifest in your consciences" (2 Corinthians 5:11).

Today's Growth Principle: We cannot force anyone to be saved, but we should not let anyone go to Hell unwarned.

A God Who Provides

Therefore I say unto you, Take no thought for your life, what ye shall eat, or what ye shall drink; nor yet for your body, what ye shall put on. Is not the life more than meat, and the body than raiment? Behold the fowls of the air: for they sow not, neither do they reap, nor gather into barns; yet your heavenly Father feedeth them. Are ye not much better than they? Which of you by taking thought can add one cubit unto his stature?
—MATTHEW 6:25–27

David Brainerd, the great pioneer missionary to the American Indians, traveled across the growing American colonies to take the gospel to places where it had never been heard. He suffered greatly from tuberculosis, which would lead to his death at just twenty-nine years of age. Yet despite his physical struggles, his faith was strong.

In his journal, Brainerd recorded being forced to take shelter in a hollow log as a severe storm raged. Unsure what he would eat as his stay lengthened, he prayed. In a few minutes a squirrel came and left a few nuts in the tree where Brainerd was staying. This happened for three days in a row until the storm finally passed and it was safe to travel again.

God is able to meet our needs even when it seems humanly impossible. But He usually works in response to our faith. When Jesus returned to Nazareth after doing miracles across the land of Israel, the people who had watched Him grow up did not believe on Him. They down played His power and authority asking, "Is not this the carpenter's son? is not his mother called Mary? and his brethren…And his sisters, are they not all with us?…And they were offended in him…" (Matthew 13:55–57). As a result, Jesus "…did not many mighty works there because of their unbelief" (Matthew 13:58). The problem was not a lack of power on Jesus' part, but a lack of faith in their hearts.

Today's Growth Principle: Never lose heart because your circumstances seem to be impossible. God delights in demonstrating His power on behalf of those who trust in Him.

The God Who Saves

But when the fulness of the time was come, God sent forth his Son, made of a woman, made under the law, To redeem them that were under the law, that we might receive the adoption of sons. And because ye are sons, God hath sent forth the Spirit of his Son into your hearts, crying, Abba, Father. Wherefore thou art no more a servant, but a son; and if a son, then an heir of God through Christ. —GALATIANS 4:4–7

In his letter to the churches of Galatia, Paul describes the incredible work of God for our salvation. He reminds them that God sent His Son for our redemption *and* that, at the moment of our salvation, He has put His Holy Spirit in our hearts assuring us that we are indeed God's children. The relationship between man and God, broken by Adam's sin in the Garden of Eden, could not be restored without the work of Christ and the Holy Spirit. God of course has the power to compel men to salvation, but He has chosen instead to invite them to be saved, and then allow them to either respond to the gospel or to reject it.

A. W. Tozer wrote, "Students of the Scriptures are aware that the Old Testament prophets and the writing apostles of New Testament times foresaw and proclaimed God's coming day of judgment—the consummate settling of accounts between the Sovereign God and His rebellious and sinful creation. How desperately we would like to believe that in the face of coming judgment, all lost men and women will cry out to God, but such will not be the case."

Salvation is never about us, but rather wholly the work of God. It is not our effort, sincerity, or emotion that determines our salvation, but our faith in what God has already done. It is only when we lay aside our own righteousness that we can claim the righteousness of Jesus Christ applied to our account. It is God alone who saves.

Today's Growth Principle: If we lose sight of the gift of God's salvation, we will not live in gratitude and obedience as we should.

Unfailing Power

For he whom God hath sent speaketh the words of God: for God giveth not the Spirit by measure unto him. The Father loveth the Son, and hath given all things into his hand. He that believeth on the Son hath everlasting life: and he that believeth not the Son shall not see life; but the wrath of God abideth on him.—JOHN 3:34–36

Here in the States, we easily take electricity for granted, but in the early days following its invention, there were often times when the supply simply was not equal to the demand. There is an old story of a pastor going down the street one day and being surprised to find one of the members of his church sitting on the porch instead of at work. He stopped to ask if everything was okay—if he had been laid off or was sick. The man explained that there was plenty of work, but there wasn't enough power to run the machines, and all the workers had been sent home for the day.

Many churches have impressive programs and outreaches. They have invested in technology, planning, resources, and equipment to be effective in reaching people. They have programs and procedures in place to deal with almost any situation. Yet it quickly becomes obvious that while there is plenty of work to be done and lots of tools, there is no spiritual power.

The Bible teaches us that while nothing we do can change the amount of *God's* power, we can certainly limit how much of that power we allow to flow through our lives and ministries. Jesus said, "Abide in me, and I in you. As the branch cannot bear fruit of itself, except it abide in the vine; no more can ye, except ye abide in me" (John 15:4). As Christians, we must remain connected to Christ and be aware of our dependence upon Him. God desires to give us His power to do His will, but sometimes we ourselves neglect it.

Today's Growth Principle: The work of God requires the power of God to be effective.

Taking a Stand for What Is Right

But neither Titus, who was with me, being a Greek, was compelled to be circumcised: And that because of false brethren unawares brought in, who came in privily to spy out our liberty which we have in Christ Jesus, that they might bring us into bondage: To whom we gave place by subjection, no, not for an hour; that the truth of the gospel might continue with you.—GALATIANS 2:3–5

There were several points of dispute in the early church regarding Gentile converts. Some people believed that they needed to basically become Jews, keeping not just the moral law but the ceremonial law as well in order to be saved. Paul soundly rejected this teaching. There is no salvation apart from grace alone. "I do not frustrate the grace of God: for if righteousness come by the law, then Christ is dead in vain" (Galatians 2:21).

Paul would have faced fewer battles if he had been willing to compromise on this issue, but it was too important to allow any confusion to remain. So when he took Titus, a Greek convert, with him to Jerusalem, Paul not only refused to compel Titus to be circumcised, but he publicly rejected the false teaching of those who pushed for that. What Paul referred to as the "truth of the gospel" is so important that no compromises can be made on what the Scriptures teach.

There is no value in being contentious and fighting over things that don't matter. But there is great value in holding so firmly to the truth that we will not bend even an inch from what is right. Even if it costs us greatly, we should be willing to endure battle for the sake of the truth.

Today's Growth Principle: While peace is more pleasant than conflict, there are times when defending the truth requires us to "earnestly contend for the faith which was once delivered unto the saints" (Jude 3).

What You Have Is Enough with God

And Moses answered and said, But, behold, they will not believe me, nor hearken unto my voice: for they will say, The LORD hath not appeared unto thee. And the LORD said unto him, What is that in thine hand? And he said, A rod. And he said, Cast it on the ground. And he cast it on the ground, and it became a serpent; and Moses fled from before it.
—EXODUS 4:1–3

The devil often keeps God's people from doing what they should for God's Kingdom by convincing them that they lack the resources to accomplish what needs to be done. The feeling of inadequacy—that what we have or can contribute is not enough to do the job—may keep us from doing anything at all. Yet the Bible is filled with examples of small things being used by God to accomplish mighty works once they are given to Him. The question is not whether what is already in our hand is sufficient, but whether or not we are willing to launch out in faith and trust God to work in a great way. The preacher F. B. Meyer wrote, "God is looking for people through whom He can do the impossible. What a pity that we plan only the things we can do by ourselves."

I believe in wise planning and careful living, but at the same time, we must not leave God out of our thinking. As Paul wrote to the church at Corinth, "For we walk by faith, not by sight:" (2 Corinthians 5:7). The God who took a shepherd's rod and parted the Red Sea, who took a boy's sling and killed a giant, and who took another boy's lunch and fed thousands is able to supply whatever we need to do His work. God, however, does not work with what we hold back. We must be willing to give what we have and trust Him to see Him supply what is lacking.

Today's Growth Principle: Faith reaches beyond what is seen and depends on God to do what He has promised.

It's a Small Thing to God

Then Rabshakeh stood and cried with a loud voice in the Jews' language, and spake, saying, Hear the word of the great king, the king of Assyria: Thus saith the king, Let not Hezekiah deceive you: for he shall not be able to deliver you out of his hand: Neither let Hezekiah make you trust in the LORD, saying, The LORD will surely deliver us, and this city shall not be delivered into the hand of the king of Assyria.—2 KINGS 18:28–30

Sennacherib greatly expanded the Assyrian Empire through a series of military conquests. He had defeated other nations both large and small, and when he prepared to attack Jerusalem, he was fully confident of victory. His messenger was instructed to warn the Jews not to depend on their God. The gods of the other nations had fallen before his armies, and the Assyrians expected nothing to be different about the kingdom of Judah. Their massive army was camped nearby, ready to attack once the order was given.

Despite the Assyrian message not to trust in God, King Hezekiah went directly to the Temple and prayed. There the prophet Isaiah met him and assured the outnumbered king that God had heard his prayers, and that a complete and total victory was coming without a battle at all. "And it came to pass that night, that the angel of the LORD went out, and smote in the camp of the Assyrians an hundred fourscore and five thousand: and when they arose early in the morning, behold, they were all dead corpses" (2 Kings 19:35).

Someone said, "It is far more important to pray with a sense of the greatness of God than with a sense of the greatness of the problem." We are sometimes overwhelmed by the weight of the obstacles we face, but God never is. His power is unlimited, and all we need is faith in Him to see His might displayed.

Today's Growth Principle: No challenge you face will ever cause God to wonder or worry about the solution—it is a small thing to Him.

A Command for All Who Breathe

Praise him with the sound of the trumpet: praise him with the psaltery and harp. Praise him with the timbrel and dance: praise him with stringed instruments and organs. Praise him upon the loud cymbals: praise him upon the high sounding cymbals. Let every thing that hath breath praise the LORD. Praise ye the LORD.—PSALM 150:3–6

The story goes that a man traveling for business ended up attending a church that was much more formal and liturgical than his regular place of worship. At one point when the preacher said something that really touched his heart, he said, "Praise the Lord" out loud. The congregation was shocked by the unexpected interruption. One man leaned forward and whispered to him, "We don't praise the Lord here." Another congregant responded, "Yes we do. It's on page 15 of the Lectionary."

Praise is not something that is supposed to be uncommon for those who know God. As long as we have breath in our lungs, we should praise Him. Too many times we only praise God when everything is going the way we think it should. But even in our worst moments, His praise should fill our mouths. After being unjustly arrested, beaten and thrown in jail, Paul and Silas had reason to complain. They did not. "And at midnight Paul and Silas prayed, and sang praises unto God: and the prisoners heard them" (Acts 16:25).

Praising God is not restricted to Sundays at church. It should be a regular part of our days—in our prayers, our thoughts, and even in our conversation with others. The words of praise that come out of our mouths are proceeded by thoughts of gratitude that build in our hearts until they cannot be contained.

Today's Growth Principle: When we praise God, it pleases Him, changes us for the better, and encourages others around us.

Equal in God's Eyes

Immediately therefore I sent to thee; and thou hast well done that thou art come. Now therefore are we all here present before God, to hear all things that are commanded thee of God. Then Peter opened his mouth, and said, Of a truth I perceive that God is no respecter of persons: But in every nation he that feareth him, and worketh righteousness, is accepted with him.—Acts 10:33–35

Because humans are fallible, our idea of justice is often slanted and skewed. Despite the best efforts to set up our legal system with safeguards, there are times when the outcome is influenced by much more than the facts of the case. Differences in age, income, education, or background sometimes matter more than the evidence when the outcome is being weighed. In a startling look at the way our assumptions can affect justice, repeated studies have shown that even appearance can make a large difference. Good-looking defendants are more likely to be found not guilty by a jury than are less-attractive defendants.

God does not treat us that way. He judges justly, without regard to who we are or where we come from. And He expects the same from His children. God demands that we use the same standard in treating others, regardless of what those around us may do. "If ye fulfil the royal law according to the scripture, Thou shalt love thy neighbour as thyself, ye do well: But if ye have respect to persons, ye commit sin, and are convinced of the law as transgressors" (James 2:8–9).

The world around us is divided by many factors, and too often people are treated differently because of something over which they have no control. It is wrong to allow the divisions and prejudices that are part of our society to creep into the church. All men stand equal before God, and the ground is level at the foot of the cross.

Today's Growth Principle: We must not allow any prejudice to keep us from treating all people with equal love and respect.

Qualified for Service

But in a great house there are not only vessels of gold and of silver, but also of wood and of earth; and some to honour, and some to dishonour. If a man therefore purge himself from these, he shall be a vessel unto honour, sanctified, and meet for the master's use, and prepared unto every good work. Flee also youthful lusts: but follow righteousness, faith, charity, peace, with them that call on the Lord out of a pure heart.
—2 TIMOTHY 2:20–22

Most professions require training to become proficient. Many also require examination, certification, and continuing education. This is not random or arbitrary, but instead is intended to protect those who receive services. I certainly don't want a surgeon who has never been to medical school or a lawyer who didn't pass the bar exam working on my behalf. I want someone who is qualified and prepared to do the best possible job.

Service for God also requires qualification, but this qualification is not primarily a matter of the head, but of the heart. There's certainly nothing wrong with education, and all of us should strive to learn as much as we can. But the most important thing that God is looking for is someone whose heart is devoted to Him. "And when he had removed him, he raised up unto them David to be their king; to whom also he gave testimony, and said, I have found David the son of Jesse, a man after mine own heart, which shall fulfil all my will" (Acts 13:22).

To qualify for God's service, we do not have to be brilliant or gifted, but we do have to be cleansed by the blood of Christ and to walk with the Lord in purity and truth. Just as none of us would choose to drink out of a dirty cup, God is not going to select us for His service when we harbor sin in our lives rather than confessing and forsaking it.

Today's Growth Principle: God chooses to use those who are available through surrendered hearts for His service.

A Picture of Love

But Zion said, The LORD hath forsaken me, and my Lord hath forgotten me. Can a woman forget her sucking child, that she should not have compassion on the son of her womb? yea, they may forget, yet will I not forget thee. Behold, I have graven thee upon the palms of my hands; thy walls are continually before me.—ISAIAH 49:14–16

When torrential rains from Hurricane Harvey slammed into southern Texas in 2017, there was massive flooding. Many people were trapped in their cars by swiftly rising water. One of those was a woman named Colette Sulcer who was in her car driving near I-10 with her three-year-old daughter. Trying to flee from the flooding, they were swept off the interstate by the rapid current. When Beaumont police officers were finally able to rescue them, Colette had propped her child up on her own body to keep her out of the water. Both were suffering from hypothermia, but while Colette later died, the baby was saved. Officer Carol Riley said, "The mother did the best she could to keep her child up over the water. She absolutely saved the child's life."

God has blessed the world with mothers who love their children, and that love is meant to be a picture of His love and compassion toward us. It is natural when mothers love and sacrifice for their children. While thankfully most are never called on to lay down their lives, it does not surprise us when they do.

God's love infinitely exceeds that of even the most devoted mother. He never forgets or forsakes His children. He never abandons us. He never allows us to go through hardship and suffering without offering us comfort. "And we have known and believed the love that God hath to us. God is love; and he that dwelleth in love dwelleth in God, and God in him" (1 John 4:16).

Today's Growth Principle: Give thanks to God for His love today, and if your mother is living, take time to thank her as well.

Everyone Has a Testimony

Moreover thou shalt provide out of all the people able men, such as fear God, men of truth, hating covetousness; and place such over them, to be rulers of thousands, and rulers of hundreds, rulers of fifties, and rulers of tens: And let them judge the people at all seasons: and it shall be, that every great matter they shall bring unto thee, but every small matter they shall judge: so shall it be easier for thyself, and they shall bear the burden with thee.—EXODUS 18:21–22

When Moses found himself overwhelmed by the task of judging the disputes and questions between the huge number of Israelites who had left Egypt and were traveling through the wilderness, his father-in-law advised him to pick subordinates who would be able to handle routine details, leaving Moses to adjudicate the major issues that those under him could not settle. These helpers were not picked at random. They would have enormous power and be subject to great temptation. There was tremendous potential for abuse if the wrong people were put in power. In order to get the right people, the rulers were selected on the basis of their prior reputation as being "able men, such as fear God, men of truth, hating covetousness."

Each of us has a testimony—not just a recounting of the events that led to our conversion, but the way in which we have lived that has created a story about who and what we are. While it is true that character matters more than reputation, it is also true that reputation, largely, is the harvest of the seeds we have been planting. We may not be thinking about the impact we are having, but every day we are enhancing or destroying our witness to others. It is said that a friend once approached Plato with news of a serious false accusation that had been leveled against the philosopher and asked what they should do. Plato replied, "We must simply live in such a way that all people will know it is false.

Today's Growth Principle: Our actions and reactions combine to make up the reputation by which we are known.

A Question of Focus

These all died in faith, not having received the promises, but having seen them afar off, and were persuaded of them, and embraced them, and confessed that they were strangers and pilgrims on the earth. For they that say such things declare plainly that they seek a country. And truly, if they had been mindful of that country from whence they came out, they might have had opportunity to have returned.—HEBREWS 11:13–15

Dr. John Rice said that because he grew up poor on a ranch in Texas, the only present he and his siblings received for Christmas was an orange. Before they ate their special gift, his mother told them to save the peels, setting them on top of the refrigerator, and she would later make candy from them for another treat. Dr. Rice said that he began thinking about those orange peels, and finally decided that since some of them were from his orange, no one would realize the difference if he ate a few of them. He said, "It wasn't long before I put my hand on top of the refrigerator and found that I had not only eaten my own orange peels. I had eaten all of the peels from every orange."

If our minds are constantly focused on things that we do not have, or things that we have left behind in the past, it will be easy for us to rationalize doing things to get what we want, even if we know they are wrong. Our focus is not neutral—it has a powerful impact on our conduct. The things that fill our minds determine what our feelings will be and eventually what our actions will be. This is why God told Joshua to focus his mind on His Word. "This book of the law shall not depart out of thy mouth; but thou shalt meditate therein day and night, that thou mayest observe to do according to all that is written therein: for then thou shalt make thy way prosperous, and then thou shalt have good success" (Joshua 1:8).

Today's Growth Principle: Just as a car tends to go in the direction we are focusing on, so our lives tend to go in the direction we look at the most.

Having the Word Living Within

If ye abide in me, and my words abide in you, ye shall ask what ye will, and it shall be done unto you. Herein is my Father glorified, that ye bear much fruit; so shall ye be my disciples.—JOHN 15:7–8

The disciples had the unique privilege of hearing Jesus speak nearly every day for over three years. They listened as He preached to others and as He taught them privately. They got to hear the very words of God spoken by God Himself—Jesus, the Living Word (John 1:1). Many years later John introduced one of his epistles by writing, "That which we have seen and heard declare we unto you, that ye also may have fellowship with us: and truly our fellowship is with the Father, and with his Son Jesus Christ" (1 John 1:3).

I wonder if—when the Holy Spirit inspired John to pen those words—he thought back to the day that Jesus called him to leave his fishing boat and become a disciple? Or perhaps he remembered the Mount of Transfiguration, or Jesus telling him from the cross to take care of Mary. John had kept those words that he had heard from Jesus in his heart, and they continued to abide in him. Though Jesus had returned to Heaven, His presence was still felt through the indwelling of the Holy Spirit and the power of the Word.

If we want to have the presence of Christ in our lives today, we must have His Word filling our hearts and minds. There is no substitute for the habit of regular, careful reading, studying, and hearing of the Scriptures. Paul wrote, "Let the word of Christ dwell in you richly in all wisdom; teaching and admonishing one another in psalms and hymns and spiritual songs, singing with grace in your hearts to the Lord" (Colossians 3:16). This thought is the key to walking daily in the presence of Christ, and it is the key to power in our spiritual lives as well.

Today's Growth Principle: Walk in the presence of Christ by reading, studying, and meditating on His Word.

Keep Calm and Carry On

And it came to pass from the time that he had made him overseer in his house, and over all that he had, that the LORD blessed the Egyptian's house for Joseph's sake; and the blessing of the LORD was upon all that he had in the house, and in the field. And he left all that he had in Joseph's hand; and he knew not ought he had, save the bread which he did eat. And Joseph was a goodly person, and well favoured.—GENESIS 39:5-6

In the months leading up to World War II, the British government printed several posters designed to encourage the people during what they knew would be a long and difficult war. The most famous of these now is the red and white sheet that simply says, "Keep Calm and Carry On." Interestingly, at the time of the war, this slogan didn't gain much popularity. In fact, although more than two million were printed, very few were posted during the war and the sign was largely forgotten. It was not until 2000 that a newly discovered sheet was posted in a bookstore. That generated so much attention that reprints began being issued, and it became known around the world.

The key to the message during the war, however, and the principle that holds a parallel meaning for us as Christians, was not in the words, but in the single image that appears on the poster. Above the plain white words is a picture of the crown of England. The message was this—whatever happens, there is an authority that is in control and can be trusted.

When we recognize this truth in the spiritual realm, we realize that no matter what our circumstances may be, God is still in control. This allows us to live in faith, continuing to do what is right regardless of the circumstances. The point of the poster was not to promise that bad things wouldn't happen, but to remind people what to do when they did.

Today's Growth Principle: Nothing that happens to you today will take God by surprise, and you can trust Him to see you through every trial.

Doing Your Work with Diligence

Servants, obey in all things your masters according to the flesh; not with eye-service, as menpleasers; but in singleness of heart, fearing God: And whatsoever ye do, do it heartily, as to the Lord, and not unto men; Knowing that of the Lord ye shall receive the reward of the inheritance: for ye serve the Lord Christ. But he that doeth wrong shall receive for the wrong which he hath done: and there is no respect of persons.—Colossians 3:22–25

There are all sorts of performance standards held at different jobs, depending on the requirements of the position. A surgeon preparing for an operation goes through a cleaning process that is rigorous and detailed, but a man who is going to paint houses all day isn't worried that there might be one tiny germ left when he washes his hands before work. The standard of cleanliness is not determined by the demands of the process, but by the need for results.

When there are parts of our jobs that require a certain level of performance, we should strive to reach that standard every time. Other areas may have more room for individual preferences or tastes. Some people are extremely careful about making sure not one paper is ever left on their desks. Others are like the pastor I read about whose deacon invited a man to visit the church. "I don't like organized religion," the man said. The deacon replied, "One look at our pastor's desk and you will see that we are not an organized religion!"

Whatever job we have to do, we have the opportunity and the obligation to work as we would if God were watching—after all, He is. The standard we should be aiming toward is not what people will think of our work, but whether we will be able to tell God, "I did the best that I could."

Today's Growth Principle: Our faith should motivate us to be the best we possibly can be as employees no matter what our jobs are.

Blending In

Ye are witnesses, and God also, how holily and justly and unblameably we behaved ourselves among you that believe: As ye know how we exhorted and comforted and charged every one of you, as a father doth his children, That ye would walk worthy of God, who hath called you unto his kingdom and glory.—1 THESSALONIANS 2:10–12

Though not all of the more than two hundred different kinds of chameleons can change colors, that is the trait we most associate with these small lizards. Through complex layers of skin and chemicals, they are able to regulate the way different wavelengths of light are reflected. Among the colors they can produce are basically all the colors of the rainbow, including combinations of pink, blue, red, orange, green, black, brown, yellow, turquoise, and purple. This is done for many reasons, including communication with other chameleons, as well as regulation of body temperature. But the main reason we think of when it comes to their ability to change colors is for camouflage. By blending in with their surroundings, chameleons are hard for predators to see, and so they are kept safe.

This is an astonishing miracle of God's creation work, but it is not a good model for His children. We are not called to fit in or blend into the background. We are called to stand out—to be worthy of the example of the Lord who saved us. The temptation to lower our standards and deny our association in an effort to stay out of trouble has been around for a long time. Peter fell victim to it when Jesus was arrested. "And after a while came unto him they that stood by, and said to Peter, Surely thou also art one of them; for thy speech bewrayeth thee. Then began he to curse and to swear, saying, I know not the man. And immediately the cock crew" (Matthew 26:73–74). Even if it is costly, our colors must remain clear.

Today's Growth Principle: Our lives should not blend in to the world around us, but should reveal that we walk with and serve Christ.

The World Is Always Watching

Withal praying also for us, that God would open unto us a door of utterance, to speak the mystery of Christ, for which I am also in bonds: That I may make it manifest, as I ought to speak. Walk in wisdom toward them that are without, redeeming the time. Let your speech be alway with grace, seasoned with salt, that ye may know how ye ought to answer every man. —COLOSSIANS 4:3-6

Perhaps you heard about a pastor who was building a wooden trellis to support a climbing vine he had planted by his house. As he pounded away, he noticed that there was a little boy who was watching him intently. The youngster didn't say a word, so the pastor kept on working, thinking the boy would get bored and eventually leave, but he didn't. Finally the pastor asked, "Well, son, are you trying to pick up some pointers on gardening or construction?" "No," the boy replied, "I'm waiting to hear what a preacher says when he hits his thumb with a hammer."

Whether or not we're aware of it, all of us are being watched. Whether it is by children, co-workers, neighbors, friends, or strangers, they are forming opinions of us—and, more importantly, of Jesus—based on what they see in our lives. There is never a time when we are not teaching others about our faith. Over the years I've heard many people share disappointment over ways they knew their testimonies had negatively influenced others—whether it was their own children, co-workers, or someone else. In the moment, they simply hadn't realized the impact their behavior would have on those who were watching.

None of us are perfect. But we should be careful that nothing we do would be a hindrance to someone else believing the gospel. Though each individual is responsible for his decisions, we do not want to be the cause of someone stumbling because of how we live.

Today's Growth Principle: Realizing that we are having an influence on others will help us respond properly in every circumstance.

Who Is in Charge?

But the fruit of the Spirit is love, joy, peace, longsuffering, gentleness, goodness, faith, Meekness, temperance: against such there is no law. And they that are Christ's have crucified the flesh with the affections and lusts. If we live in the Spirit, let us also walk in the Spirit.—GALATIANS 5:22–25

Evangelist D. L. Moody was one of the most famous preachers in the world during his lifetime. His conferences in Chicago and Northfield, Massachusetts, drew guests from many nations. Moody was known for having God's power on his ministry, and it made an impact on those who heard him. But many did not understand how the process worked. It is said that at one conference Moody was approached by a pastor who said, "I have come a hundred miles to get some of Moody's spirit." Moody replied, "You don't want my spirit. What you need is the Spirit of God."

Every day, we as Christians face the choice of who is going to be in charge of our lives. We can live, work, and act in our own strength and wisdom, or we can walk under the control of the Holy Spirit of God. When we insist on going our own way, we should not be surprised by the negative consequences that follow. God will not share control. He is the Lord and King, and He both calls for and deserves total surrender of our lives. In fact, Romans 12:1 reminds us that this surrender as a "living sacrifice" is simply our "reasonable service."

The Christians who accomplish great things for God do not do so on their own; they rely on His power and follow His leading. The Holy Spirit is given to every child of God, not to be an observer, but a director of our steps. "Howbeit when he, the Spirit of truth, is come, he will guide you into all truth: for he shall not speak of himself; but whatsoever he shall hear, that shall he speak: and he will shew you things to come" (John 16:13).

Today's Growth Principle: The devil destroys many Christians who refuse to yield control of their lives to the Holy Spirit.

Living in Truth

This then is the message which we have heard of him, and declare unto you, that God is light, and in him is no darkness at all. If we say that we have fellowship with him, and walk in darkness, we lie, and do not the truth: But if we walk in the light, as he is in the light, we have fellowship one with another, and the blood of Jesus Christ his Son cleanseth us from all sin. —1 JOHN 1:5–7

It has become quite common to hear people speak of "my truth" as if their perception is more valid and important than reality. Yet despite what a culture or society may say, there is such a thing as absolute, unchanging, eternal truth. There are principles God has laid out for us that are grounded and firm which apply to all people at all times in all circumstances.

It is easy to see why people reject the notion of absolute truth. It is far more demanding to have a set standard that never varies than to adjust demands and beliefs according to circumstances and personal desires. Most of us remember a class or two from the past where tests were graded on a curve. That meant that your score was not an absolute measure of how many questions you got right, but how you did in relation to the rest of the class. Even if you only got a few questions right, you could come out all right as long as most of the rest of the class was in the same boat.

God, however, doesn't grade on a curve. When we claim that truth adjusts and that we are therefore not really sinning, He says we are lying. He will not change His commands or what He calls sin just because what He declared is not popular with people. Instead, God calls us to walk in His light, allowing His truth to shine into every area of our lives so that we can have fellowship with Him. How much better it is to walk with God in the light learning His truth, than to create our own "truth" and walk on our own in darkness.

Today's Growth Principle: Jesus is the truth, and He invites us to walk with Him in the light as He leads us in the way of truth.

The Need for Thorough Cleansing

Behold, thou desirest truth in the inward parts: and in the hidden part thou shalt make me to know wisdom. Purge me with hyssop, and I shall be clean: wash me, and I shall be whiter than snow. Make me to hear joy and gladness; that the bones which thou hast broken may rejoice. Hide thy face from my sins, and blot out all mine iniquities.—PSALM 51:6-9

Those who have been in the military or attended a school with strict requirements for cleaning know what is meant by a "white glove" inspection. It is easy to put a few things away, run the vacuum over the middle of the floor and call a room clean. But that kind of cleaning won't pass white glove. In the literal sense of the phrase, the person doing the inspection would put on a pair of gloves before checking whether the room was actually clean. Those gloves would quickly reveal whether a thorough cleaning had taken place, or whether the occupant had done just the minimum to make things look good on the surface.

God looks at our lives and measures them against a standard of perfect holiness. He does not overlook sins just because we think they are small or insignificant. In fact, most of the major tragedies of character, the devastating public sins that seem to be so sudden, begin with small sins allowed to linger rather than being dealt with. Charles Spurgeon said, "Dread sin; though it be ever so small, dread it. You cannot see all that is in it. It is the mother of ten thousand mischiefs. The mother of mischief, they say, is as small as a midge's egg; and certainly, the smallest sin has ten thousand mischiefs sleeping within its bowels." If we treat sin casually, it will not be long before we find ourselves enslaved to it. If we bring them to the Lord in repentance, He will cleanse us and help us walk in freedom from them.

Today's Growth Principle: If you allow small sins to linger in your heart, it will not be long before they are joined by larger sins.

Grace Building Christians Up

For I know this, that after my departing shall grievous wolves enter in among you, not sparing the flock. Also of your own selves shall men arise, speaking perverse things, to draw away disciples after them. Therefore watch, and remember, that by the space of three years I ceased not to warn every one night and day with tears. And now, brethren, I commend you to God, and to the word of his grace, which is able to build you up, and to give you an inheritance among all them which are sanctified.
—ACTS 20:29–32

There is no doubt that grace is one of the most misunderstood doctrines in all of Scripture. People have many different ideas, and often they conflict with what God actually said. Grace is not a license to live in any way we choose. Instead, it is a powerful teacher and tool that molds and shapes the decisions, choices, and actions that make up our lives. Grace is a builder—a power given to us by God to help us become more like Jesus.

Before the world was created, God had a purpose and plan for our lives. "For whom he did foreknow, he also did predestinate to be conformed to the image of his Son, that he might be the firstborn among many brethren" (Romans 8:29). The Lord could certainly have saved us and taken us to Heaven at the moment of our conversion. All of the things necessary for us to enter His presence are settled and accomplished the moment we trust Him. Our sins are forgiven, and we have already been granted the gift of eternal life.

But God has more in mind for us. Dr. Curtis Hutson had a sermon he often preached called "Salvation Is More than Being Saved." The same grace that offers us entry into God's family stays with us to accomplish our sanctification. Through the process of God's grace being applied to our daily lives, we become more and more like His Son.

Today's Growth Principle: Grace is never content to leave us where we are—it works to build us up into Christlikeness.

A Prepared Heart

And he came to Jerusalem in the fifth month, which was in the seventh year of the king. For upon the first day of the first month began he to go up from Babylon, and on the first day of the fifth month came he to Jerusalem, according to the good hand of his God upon him. For Ezra had prepared his heart to seek the law of the LORD, and to do it, and to teach in Israel statutes and judgments.—EZRA 7:8-10

Through Moses and a number of prophets who followed, God warned the Israelites what would happen if they turned away from Him and began worshiping idols. They did not listen. One king after another led the people further and further astray. Things got so bad that a wicked king named Ahaz adopted the heathen practice of sacrificing his own son to a false god. "But he walked in the way of the kings of Israel, yea, and made his son to pass through the fire, according to the abominations of the heathen, whom the LORD cast out from before the children of Israel" (2 Kings 16:3).

So, just as God had said, the people were conquered by foreign armies. The God who had once defended Israel and given them victory in battle allowed them to be defeated. But even in those days of judgment, God did not forget His people. When the seventy years of the Babylonian captivity ended and the Israelites returned to the land, God sent a special teacher named Ezra to guide them to do what was right.

Before Ezra was equipped to teach and lead Israel, he first had to prepare his own heart. It was not primarily his natural talent or his training that made Ezra effective. It was his love and devotion to God and His Word that made him a powerful influence on those around him. Ezra's example of preparing his heart to seek God's Word and obey it before attempting to teach others is a good one for all of us to follow.

Today's Growth Principle: We will not be able to effectively minister to others until our own hearts are fixed on God.

The Power of Rewards

And this is love, that we walk after his commandments. This is the commandment, That, as ye have heard from the beginning, ye should walk in it. For many deceivers are entered into the world, who confess not that Jesus Christ is come in the flesh. This is a deceiver and an antichrist. Look to yourselves, that we lose not those things which we have wrought, but that we receive a full reward. —2 JOHN 1:6–8

For many years, *Reader's Digest* has published first person accounts of humorous happenings. In 1994, they ran a story from Marion Gilbert: "One morning I opened the door to get the newspaper and was surprised to see a strange little dog with our paper in his mouth. Delighted with this unexpected 'delivery service,' I fed him some treats. The following morning I was horrified to see the same dog sitting in front of our door, wagging his tail, surrounded by eight newspapers. I spent the rest of that morning returning the papers to their owners."

There is enormous power in rewards. God has created us with a need for affirmation and a desire to respond to praise. In fact, God Himself offers us rewards for our service. "And every man that striveth for the mastery is temperate in all things. Now they do it to obtain a corruptible crown; but we an incorruptible" (1 Corinthians 9:25). Our greatest reward will be to hear our Lord say, "Well done, thou good and faithful servant."

Because we recognize the power of rewards, it is very important for those of us who lead—parents, teachers, bosses, and influencers in any venue—to carefully consider what we are rewarding. Our words of praise or tangible expressions of affirmation will encourage others to continue the behavior that gained them. Yet many times, we encourage simple achievements rather than the character or attitudes that drive those accomplishments.

Today's Growth Principle: We should be sure that we are using the power of rewards to encourage the attitudes and character that encourage godly actions.

Standing Guard

Take heed therefore unto yourselves, and to all the flock, over the which the Holy Ghost hath made you overseers, to feed the church of God, which he hath purchased with his own blood. For I know this, that after my departing shall grievous wolves enter in among you, not sparing the flock. Also of your own selves shall men arise, speaking perverse things, to draw away disciples after them.—ACTS 20:28–30

Shepherds, especially in the Western part of the United States, face a real threat from predators. Wild animals like coyotes can devastate a flock in short order. Many methods to protect sheep have been tried, but one of the most effective is to introduce a guard llama to the flock. A single llama will bond with the sheep, and become intensely and fiercely protective. Studies show that using a guard llama reduces loss of sheep to predators by two-thirds. The llamas are not afraid of the attackers, and thus their mere presence can be a deterrent to attacks. When necessary, they will use their hooves as effective weapons to defend the sheep.

God's people are under attack in this world. The Bible uses the metaphor of shepherds for the role of the pastor, and those who lead churches are charged with a special level of care for those in the congregation. But whether or not we are in full-time ministry, each of us have a responsibility to our brothers and sisters in Christ. Many times a simple word of encouragement or caution from a friend is all that is needed to prevent great sin and suffering.

If our hearts are knit together as part of the body of Christ as they should be, we will care deeply about the needs of others, and do our best to strengthen and protect them from danger. "Wherefore comfort yourselves together, and edify one another, even as also ye do" (1 Thessalonians 5:11).

Today's Growth Principle: Our fellow believers are under assault, and we need to do all we can to encourage and defend them from danger.

Something Worth the Risk

Forasmuch as we have heard, that certain which went out from us have troubled you with words, subverting your souls, saying, Ye must be circumcised, and keep the law: to whom we gave no such commandment: It seemed good unto us, being assembled with one accord, to send chosen men unto you with our beloved Barnabas and Paul, Men that have hazarded their lives for the name of our Lord Jesus Christ.
—ACTS 15:24–26

On November 19, 1863, almost by accident, President Abraham Lincoln gave what is probably the most famous speech in American history. He was not the main speaker when he gave what is remembered today as the Gettysburg Address. But in his few words, Lincoln managed to capture both the purpose of the war and the American spirit. Recognizing the courage and spirit of those who had fought at Gettysburg, Lincoln said, "But, in a larger sense, we cannot dedicate—we cannot consecrate—we cannot hallow—this ground. The brave men, living and dead, who struggled here, have consecrated it, far above our poor power to add or detract."

The debt that we owe to those who have risked and given their lives for home and country is huge, and those sacrifices are fully worthy of honor and remembrance. Those who are willing to take on a great and dangerous task do so because they have found a cause that is worthy of sacrifice. The Bible often uses the metaphor of warfare for the Christian life. Just as soldiers defend our country for a great cause, Christians are called to fight and sacrifice for the truth. "Beloved, when I gave all diligence to write unto you of the common salvation, it was needful for me to write unto you, and exhort you that ye should earnestly contend for the faith which was once delivered unto the saints" (Jude 1:3).

Today's Growth Principle: We should remember those who have sacrificed both in the physical and spiritual realms.

The Importance of Listening to God

Because I have called, and ye refused; I have stretched out my hand, and no man regarded; But ye have set at nought all my counsel, and would none of my reproof: I also will laugh at your calamity; I will mock when your fear cometh; When your fear cometh as desolation, and your destruction cometh as a whirlwind; when distress and anguish cometh upon you.—PROVERBS 1:24–27

I read the following account from a pastor about a conversation he witnessed between a father and his first grade son.

Dad: "Max! Why didn't you answer me when I called you?"

Max: "I didn't hear you, Dad."

Dad: "What do you mean you didn't hear me?" Max did not respond.

Dad: "How many times didn't you hear me?"

Max: "I don't know, maybe three or four times."

The Bible is called "the Word of God" because it is indeed God's very words recorded and preserved for us. "All scripture is given by inspiration of God, and is profitable for doctrine, for reproof, for correction, for instruction in righteousness" (2 Timothy 3:16). God speaks to us through His Word, and it is our responsibility to listen and not ignore what God tells us to do. Saying that we do not hear His voice does not excuse us from the necessity of obedience.

Listening to God is primarily a matter of the heart. If we love Him as we should, we will not feel like we are being treated badly when we are told to do or not do a particular thing. "While it is said, To-day if ye will hear his voice, harden not your hearts, as in the provocation" (Hebrews 3:15). If we do not listen to what God says and respond, we have no reason to expect that we will escape the consequences of disobedience.

Today's Growth Principle: A soft heart toward God is eager and ready to hear His Word and obey what it says.

Look at the Source

O generation of vipers, how can ye, being evil, speak good things? for out of the abundance of the heart the mouth speaketh. A good man out of the good treasure of the heart bringeth forth good things: and an evil man out of the evil treasure bringeth forth evil things. But I say unto you, That every idle word that men shall speak, they shall give account thereof in the day of judgment.—MATTHEW 12:34–36

As part of his pioneering missionary work in Africa, David Livingstone spent time exploring routes to the interior of this great continent so future missionaries would be able to take the gospel to the heart of Africa. As an explorer, he made major geographical discoveries at a time when much of the continent was largely unknown to the outside world. Livingstone's final great expedition was a search to verify whether Lake Victoria in Tanzania was indeed the source of the Nile River as earlier explorers had speculated. Although Livingstone didn't reach Lake Victoria before he died, he was correct that it was the source of the Nile.

Just as understanding the source of the Nile would shape Europeans' understanding of the continent of Africa, so it is for us when we understand the source from which our words and actions flow—which is our hearts. It is what is inside rather than outward circumstances and events that dictates our responses. When people speak harsh and biting words or respond with a lack of compassion and love toward others, it shows that there is an internal problem. Too often we make excuses for ourselves or others, saying things like, "I didn't really mean that." Yet Jesus taught that our words are the overflow of our hearts. If we are focused on changing our behavior by changing our surroundings, we are doomed to failure. The only way we can make the outside what it should be is to first fix what is on the inside. "Keep thy heart with all diligence; for out of it are the issues of life" (Proverbs 4:23).

Today's Growth Principle: If you want your words and actions to be right, you must first make sure your heart is right.

The Danger of False Teachers

But there were false prophets also among the people, even as there shall be
false teachers among you, who privily shall bring in damnable heresies,
even denying the Lord that bought them, and bring upon themselves swift
destruction. And many shall follow their pernicious ways; by reason of
whom the way of truth shall be evil spoken of. And through covetousness
shall they with feigned words make merchandise of you: whose judgment
now of a long time lingereth not, and their damnation slumbereth not.
—2 PETER 2:1–3

There is an array of religious material and instruction available today. There are books, audio and video series, teaching programs, broadcasts, and online teaching on almost any topic you can imagine. Yet, when a vast quantity of those teachings are evaluated in light of God's Word, it quickly becomes apparent that they do not match. In fact, our world is overflowing with false doctrine and false teachers.

This spread of heretical teaching should not come as a surprise because it is not new. There may be more forms of communication and availability of such teaching in our day, but warnings about false prophets are thousands of years old. The Apostle John warned, "Beloved, believe not every spirit, but try the spirits whether they are of God: because many false prophets are gone out into the world" (1 John 4:1).

Each of us has a responsibility to be careful about the influences and teaching we allow into our hearts and minds. We cannot blindly accept a teacher just because he is popular or well-spoken. Some of the most eloquent pulpiteers of history have been purveyors of heresy. While we must also be careful not to become critical and harsh, we must not allow anyone or anything to draw us away from the unchanged and unchangeable truth of the Bible.

Today's Growth Principle: Do not accept any teaching or teacher, no matter how eloquent, who contradicts the Word of God.

Wrong Attitudes toward Money

If any man teach otherwise, and consent not to wholesome words, even the words of our Lord Jesus Christ, and to the doctrine which is according to godliness; He is proud, knowing nothing, but doting about questions and strifes of words, whereof cometh envy, strife, railings, evil surmisings, Perverse disputings of men of corrupt minds, and destitute of the truth, supposing that gain is godliness: from such withdraw thyself.
—1 Timothy 6:3–5

Shortly before World War II, a Dutch artist named Han van Meegern, who had been dismissed by critics, hatched a plan. He painted a work using the technique of Vermeer and submitted it as a genuine masterpiece. The critics hailed it, and it was exhibited as a newly discovered masterwork. Originally, van Meegern planned to reveal the hoax and his role in it to embarrass his detractors, but when he realized the huge price the painting would bring, he decided instead to sell it and pocket the money. He eventually sold the painting to a Nazi collector after German forces conquered the Netherlands. After the war, when the victorious Allies were returning artwork to original owners, they called on van Meegern. When he could not produce proof that he had purchased the painting (since he had forged it himself), he was arrested and charged as a collaborator. Officials did not believe his eventual confession until he painted an identical copy and revealed himself as a skilled forger.

The desire for material wealth has led many people astray. Most people do not go to the extreme of van Meegern, but many have sacrificed principles and truth for the sake of financial benefit. Jesus made it clear that we must choose between loving God and money. "No man can serve two masters: for either he will hate the one, and love the other; or else he will hold to the one, and despise the other. Ye cannot serve God and mammon" (Matthew 6:24).

Today's Growth Principle: If you love money, you will never be able to love God as you should.

JUNE

How the World Gives

Peace I leave with you, my peace I give unto you: not as the world giveth, give I unto you. Let not your heart be troubled, neither let it be afraid. Ye have heard how I said unto you, I go away, and come again unto you. If ye loved me, ye would rejoice, because I said, I go unto the Father: for my Father is greater than I. And now I have told you before it come to pass, that, when it is come to pass, ye might believe.—JOHN 14:27–29

Even though Jesus had told His disciples multiple times that He would be crucified, His warnings didn't sink in until the night before it happened. "But because I have said these things unto you, sorrow hath filled your heart" (John 16:6). Because Jesus knew what was about to happen, He knew that they were going to be in great need of comfort in the coming days, and He gave them a promise of peace.

Notice, however, in Jesus' words of promise, how He highlighted the difference between the way God gives His gifts and the way the world gives. The gifts of the world are usually not what they appear to be on the surface, and even when they are good things, they come with strings attached. The world does not give freely. Furthermore, the gifts of the world are not permanent. It was realizing this truth that prompted Moses to choose to endure the hardships of standing for the truth rather than taking the easy route and enjoying the temporary pleasures of Pharaoh's palace. "Choosing rather to suffer affliction with the people of God, than to enjoy the pleasures of sin for a season" (Hebrews 11:25).

God's gifts, however, are given both freely and permanently. There is nothing in this world that compares to the immeasurable love of God for His children. When we understand the depth of His love, we understand why He gives differently than the world does. He has no ulterior motives or hidden agendas. He only wants what is best for us.

Today's Growth Principle: All of God's good gifts are offered to us as His children freely and without any strings attached.

You Are Not Bound by the Past

And when he went out the second day, behold, two men of the Hebrews strove together: and he said to him that did the wrong, Wherefore smitest thou thy fellow? And he said, Who made thee a prince and a judge over us? intendest thou to kill me, as thou killedst the Egyptian? And Moses feared, and said, Surely this thing is known. Now when Pharaoh heard this thing, he sought to slay Moses. But Moses fled from the face of Pharaoh, and dwelt in the land of Midian: and he sat down by a well.—EXODUS 2:13–15

All of us have failures in our lives. There are moments we would like to change, moments when we did things we should not have done or failed to do the things we should have done. And there are consequences to some of those failures that remain with us, even after we have confessed and forsaken our sins and done what we can to make things right with those we have hurt. But past failure is not an unbreakable bondage that means we can never do anything for God with the rest of our lives—unless we allow ourselves to be bound by the past.

Paul knew something about living with the past. He was persistent in his persecution of the early church, going to great lengths to stamp out the new religion being preached by the followers of Jesus. But after Paul's conversion on the road to Damascus, his life took on a completely new direction. Whereas he had once been antagonistic toward Christianity and cruel toward Christians, he devoted the remainder of his life to preaching the gospel, starting new churches, and training others. I'm sure Paul thought of his own past when the Holy Spirit directed him to pen these words: "Therefore if any man be in Christ, he is a new creature: old things are passed away; behold, all things are become new" (2 Corinthians 5:17). While we should do what we can to undo damage we have brought on others in the past, we find freedom from our past confessing our sin to the Lord and trusting the pardon bought by His blood.

Today's Growth Principle: The past cannot bind us and render us ineffective to God's service unless we allow it to do so.

Seeing Ourselves and Others

And one cried unto another, and said, Holy, holy, holy, is the LORD of hosts: the whole earth is full of his glory. And the posts of the door moved at the voice of him that cried, and the house was filled with smoke. Then said I, Woe is me! for I am undone; because I am a man of unclean lips, and I dwell in the midst of a people of unclean lips: for mine eyes have seen the King, the LORD of hosts.—ISAIAH 6:3-5

I heard about a young couple who moved into a new home. As they ate breakfast together on their first morning there, the lady who lived next door was hanging her laundry on an old-fashioned clothes line to dry in the sun. "That laundry doesn't look very clean," the wife remarked to her husband. "Perhaps her washing machine doesn't work very well, or she should try a different laundry soap." Each time the neighbor hung her laundry, the lady made a comment on how dirty it looked. Then a few weeks later, something changed. "Wow her laundry looks clean this morning," the lady said. "She must have changed something." "Not really," her husband replied, "I washed our windows."

Many times we are quick to see the flaws and faults in others. Those failings may be imagined or real, but in either case they seem glaring to us. On the other hand, our own faults frequently seem to escape our attention. Isaiah was a prophet with a message from God for a people who were not living right. At first, Isaiah's focus was on the people, and if you read the first chapters of Isaiah, you will find "Woe to [them]" as a repeated theme.

But when the prophet saw *God*, his first concern was not for the people, but for himself. Measured against God's perfect holiness, all of us fall short and stand in need of God's mercy. When we compare ourselves to others, we'll either be proud or discouraged. But when we look to Christ, we'll see our need for Him and cry out to Him to change us.

Today's Growth Principle: Our first concern should always be our own lives rather than comparing ourselves to others.

The Path to a Strong Conscience

But this I confess unto thee, that after the way which they call heresy, so worship I the God of my fathers, believing all things which are written in the law and in the prophets: And have hope toward God, which they themselves also allow, that there shall be a resurrection of the dead, both of the just and unjust. And herein do I exercise myself, to have always a conscience void of offence toward God, and toward men.—ACTS 24:14–16

I came across a humorous story about a man who went to seek advice. He confessed to the counselor that he had been doing some things that he knew were wrong, and his conscience was bothering him. "So you're looking for some help strengthening your will power so you stop doing what you're doing?" he was asked. "No," the man replied. "I was hoping for something that would weaken my conscience."

While the Bible is the only unfailing and completely reliable guide to what is wrong, God has given each person an internal moral compass. The conscience can be a powerful voice that helps guide our behavior, but it can also be beaten into silence so that it no longer warns us that what we are about to do is wrong. First Timothy 4:2 describes this as a seared conscience: "Speaking lies in hypocrisy; having their conscience seared with a hot iron." If we want our conscience to play the role God intended, we have to keep it strong. Paul said, "I exercise myself" when it came to keeping his conscience right. The best way to strengthen our conscience is to fill our hearts and minds with God's Word. When we use that as our guide, our conscience will be giving us the right warnings before we act. The more we listen to those warnings, following Scripture and yielding to the Holy Spirit rather than just doing what seems best for us or convenient, the stronger our conscience will become.

Today's Growth Principle: Be careful not to silence your conscience— you need to be able to hear from it.

God's Plan for Saving Sinners

And Jesus said unto them, I am the bread of life: he that cometh to me shall never hunger; and he that believeth on me shall never thirst. But I said unto you, That ye also have seen me, and believe not. All that the Father giveth me shall come to me; and him that cometh to me I will in no wise cast out.—JOHN 6:35–37

Dr. John R. Rice told of witnessing to an elderly man following a funeral. The man had raised his hand to indicate that he was not saved, and when Dr. Rice asked him why not, he explained that he did not know how to be saved. After they talked for a few minutes, Dr. Rice explained it this way: "God furnished the Saviour, and you furnish the sinner." He later recounted, "He looked up to me startled and then his eyes lightened and he began to chuckle while the tears still ran down his gray, beard-stubbled face. 'Well, I can certainly furnish the sinner, if He is willing to furnish the Saviour,' he said."

So many people are working and struggling and laboring in an effort to procure salvation. They do certain things and avoid others, hoping to gain merit and favor with God. They live with fear hanging over their heads that they will somehow miss out despite their efforts. In reality, all of us fail to measure up to God's perfect standard of holiness. But the solution to that is not for us to do more or to do better. It is to turn from our sin and accept God's free offer of salvation. Jesus illustrated this truth by holding up the simple faith of children as our model. "Verily I say unto you, Whosoever shall not receive the kingdom of God as a little child shall in no wise enter therein" (Luke 18:17).

Just as if you were sick it would be foolish to wait to go to the doctor until you were well, so it is foolish to hold back from faith in Christ until you sin less. The reality is that our only contribution to salvation is our sin! We simply trust in Jesus because He already made the payment for it.

Today's Growth Principle: Jesus has done everything necessary for us to be saved—all we must do is claim His offer in faith.

The Cross and the Christian Life

*Saying, The Son of man must suffer many things, and be rejected of the elders and chief priests and scribes, and be slain, and be raised the third day. And he said to them all, If any man will come after me, let him deny himself, and take up his cross daily, and follow me. For whosoever will save his life shall lose it: but whosoever will lose his life for my sake, the same shall save it.—*LUKE 9:22–24

There is surely no more recognized symbol of Christianity than the cross. We see it on buildings, in art, in cemeteries, in churches, and on clothing and jewelry. Yet the actual cross was nothing less than an instrument of torture and execution perfected by the Romans. And while we often speak of the cross in metaphorical terms, the cross Jesus carried was real. It was made from heavy wood, and He was forced to carry his own means of death to the place where He would be crucified. When the weight caused Jesus to collapse, another was compelled to carry that cross in His place.

When Jesus instructs us to take up His cross and follow Him, He is not telling us how to have our "best life now." He is calling us to a life of service and sacrifice according to the example that He set. Of course, simply knowing this does not make doing what we should easy. Many times we are tempted to avoid a particular cross that entails hardship or suffering. Charles Spurgeon said, "'Any cross but the one I have,' cried one. Surely it would not be a cross if you had the choosing of it, for it is the essence of a cross that it should run counter to our likings." Being the Saviour was not free or easy for Jesus, and we should not expect our service to Him to come without cost.

Today's Growth Principle: What looks like sacrifice to us now can be a source of great blessing if we willingly surrender to the Lord and follow Him through it.

An Example of Grace

Ye have heard that it hath been said, Thou shalt love thy neighbour, and hate thine enemy. But I say unto you, Love your enemies, bless them that curse you, do good to them that hate you, and pray for them which despitefully use you, and persecute you; That ye may be the children of your Father which is in heaven: for he maketh his sun to rise on the evil and on the good, and sendeth rain on the just and on the unjust.
—MATTHEW 5:43–45

We often hear a great emphasis on justice. Many people are focused on making sure they get what they deserve, or at least what they think they deserve. The reality as taught in the Word of God, however, is that the last thing we should seek is what we deserve—for we deserve to spend eternity in Hell apart from God as the just consequence of our sins. Instead He freely offers salvation through Jesus Christ to those who believe. This gift is only by God's grace.

But even beyond the grace of salvation, God displays His grace day after day. He has the power to create physical distinctions so that Christians could have different weather from the general population. Indeed, during the plagues of Egypt, God did protect the Israelites from some of the suffering. "And I will sever in that day the land of Goshen, in which my people dwell, that no swarms of flies shall be there; to the end thou mayest know that I am the LORD in the midst of the earth" (Exodus 8:22). Yet, God allows the sun to shine on everyone, not just the righteous, and everyone to benefit from the rain that falls. We take these common mercies for granted, but they are gifts from God which we do not deserve. We receive them because of His grace. In the same spirit He calls us to extend grace to others, even those who do not deserve it.

Today's Growth Principle: Since God is willing to extend His grace to us, we in turn should be gracious toward others.

A Most Important Trait

And after he had spent some time there, he departed, and went over all the country of Galatia and Phrygia in order, strengthening all the disciples. And a certain Jew named Apollos, born at Alexandria, an eloquent man, and mighty in the scriptures, came to Ephesus. This man was instructed in the way of the Lord; and being fervent in the spirit, he spake and taught diligently the things of the Lord, knowing only the baptism of John.—Acts 18:23–25

John Broadus was a powerful preacher. But more than his impact in the pulpit, Broadus made an even greater impact on training preachers, helping to found seminaries, and serving as a teacher for many years. His book, *On the Preparation and Delivery of Sermons,* remains one of the most influential books on the subject nearly 150 years after it was first published.

Broadus died at just sixty-eight years of age. In his final lecture, delivered just nine days before his death, he told his students, "Gentlemen, if this were the last time I should ever be permitted to address you, I would feel amply repaid for consuming the whole hour endeavoring to impress upon you these two things: true piety, and, like Apollos, to be men 'mighty in the Scriptures.'"

There are many things that people do for God which require special gifts and abilities. Some are more talented in certain areas while others excel in different spheres. But every Christian can be powerful in the Word of God. It simply requires that we read, hear, study, learn, and meditate on the Bible. It is not a lack of talent, but a lack of work that keeps people from being strong in the Word. Some of God's greatest and most effective servants have not been the most gifted, but those who were willing to invest the time and effort to become people of the Word.

Today's Growth Principle: The more importance you place on the Word of God, the more effective your service for the Lord will be.

Relationship Maintenance

Therefore if thou bring thy gift to the altar, and there rememberest that thy brother hath ought against thee; Leave there thy gift before the altar, and go thy way; first be reconciled to thy brother, and then come and offer thy gift. Agree with thine adversary quickly, whiles thou art in the way with him; lest at any time the adversary deliver thee to the judge, and the judge deliver thee to the officer, and thou be cast into prison.
—MATTHEW 5:23-25

On January 31, 2000, Alaska Airlines Flight 261 took off from Puerto Vallarta, Mexico, to fly to Seattle, Washington. Tragically the plane crashed into the Pacific Ocean, killing everyone on board. The investigation into the accident revealed that the cause of the crash—a failure in the nut threads that controlled the horizontal stabilizer—could have been easily prevented. But the airline had reduced the frequency of lubrication on the parts and then falsified the maintenance logs to make it look like things had been taken care of when they had not. The results were fatal.

Every relationship we have requires regular maintenance if it is to survive. Most of us know people who were friends for a time, but now do not speak. It is sadly common for family relationships to be so ruptured that members will not even be in the same place. Church splits have become so acrimonious in some places that police had to be called in to keep order between Christian brothers and sisters.

While there are many things that can cause damage to a relationship, most of them can be overcome, if not prevented, by taking care of small things before they become major problems. If we are quick both to forgive and seek forgiveness, if we take our own responsibilities more seriously rather than demanding perfection from others, and if we make the relationship a priority, we will find far fewer crashes.

Today's Growth Principle: Every relationship requires grace and forgiveness in order to remain strong.

Uncertainty Is Not a Virtue

For the which cause I also suffer these things: nevertheless I am not ashamed: for I know whom I have believed, and am persuaded that he is able to keep that which I have committed unto him against that day. Hold fast the form of sound words, which thou hast heard of me, in faith and love which is in Christ Jesus. That good thing which was committed unto thee keep by the Holy Ghost which dwelleth in us.—2 TIMOTHY 1:12–14

In our society, it seems that one of the worst offenses a person can commit in public is to state with certainty that something is actually right or actually wrong—all the time, in every case, and for every person. That goes against the grain of our "tolerant" culture, which insists that any belief or idea, no matter how much it contradicts reality, must be accepted. Against that current, Christians are called to stand firm in defense of the truth. While we should not be unpleasant or rude in our demeanor, we should be clarion clear in declaring, "thus saith the Lord."

No one knows everything, but it is possible for us to know with confidence what God has said in His Word. And our commitment to the truth must be firm no matter what others may do. A. W. Tozer said, "Moral power has always accompanied definite beliefs. Great saints have always been dogmatic. We need a return to a gentle dogmatism that smiles while it stands stubborn and firm on the Word of God that lives and abides forever."

The less the world believes in absolute truth, the more important it is for us to take an unwavering stand for what God has said. There are those who tell us that to have influence we must not state truth with certainty. They are wrong. "For if the trumpet give an uncertain sound, who shall prepare himself to the battle?" (1 Corinthians 14:8).

Today's Growth Principle: The message of absolute truth may not be popular but it is still right—and still important.

Our Prayer Partner

Likewise the Spirit also helpeth our infirmities: for we know not what we should pray for as we ought: but the Spirit itself maketh intercession for us with groanings which cannot be uttered. And he that searcheth the hearts knoweth what is the mind of the Spirit, because he maketh intercession for the saints according to the will of God.—ROMANS 8:26–27

Many of us are blessed to have a few close friends who really know how to pray. When we are facing difficult circumstances or trials, we often turn to these people and ask them to join us in seeking God's help. It is a wonderful blessing to have such prayer support, and there is nothing wrong with asking others to pray for us and with us. It is a real encouragement to know that we are not alone in our praying.

But, as Christians, we have a far greater resource and partner in our praying—the Holy Spirit of God. All human prayer is necessarily limited. We lack full understanding of our circumstances, and we thus do not always know what the best solution to our problem is. Sometimes when we are convinced we know what God "should" do, we are completely off base. But our sincere prayers, offered in submission to the will of God, are heard and helped, even when they are misguided.

The Holy Spirit knows what is in our hearts and hears our sincere cries, even when they are not fully informed by His knowledge. In God's grace our prayers are interpreted to what is best. Even better, they are joined in by the Holy Spirit. And His intercession for us is not casual. Sometimes when we ask someone to pray with us about a need, their prayers are not intense. But the Holy Spirit is intensely involved in our prayer, interceding "for us with groanings which cannot be uttered... according to the will of God." This should give us great confidence as we wait for God to answer.

Today's Growth Principle: We can trust the Holy Spirit to take our limited prayers and perfectly express them to the Father.

An Open Invitation

I Jesus have sent mine angel to testify unto you these things in the churches. I am the root and the offspring of David, and the bright and morning star. And the Spirit and the bride say, Come. And let him that heareth say, Come. And let him that is athirst come. And whosoever will, let him take the water of life freely.—REVELATION 22:16-17

In 1872, Jerry McAuley opened the Water Street Mission in one of the worst neighborhoods in New York City. It is considered to be the first rescue mission dedicated to reaching those who were in great need. McAuley, who had been saved after he was sentenced to Sing Sing Prison at just nineteen years of age, had a real burden for reaching those who were often looked down on by others. One of his early converts was a man named Samuel Hadley, who had lost everything because of his habitual drunkeness. After his salvation, Hadley became one of the most effective workers at the mission. He summed up the mindset of the Water Street Mission with these words: "We don't want anyone here who is welcome anywhere else."

The world around us is filled with people who wonder if anyone cares for them. There are visible signs of brokenness all around. The challenge is to see past the wounds, the hurts, and the scars to the person within, and to reach out to them in love. The church should be firmly grounded in the truth, but it should also provide help and hope to those in need. We do not condone sin or lower God's holiness, but we do set forth God's offer of salvation through His forgiveness and new birth. This balanced approach is what Jesus displayed with the woman at the well. He didn't condone her sin, but He did offer her forgiveness and wholeness: "…whosoever drinketh of the water that I shall give him shall never thirst; but the water that I shall give him shall be in him a well of water springing up into everlasting life" (John 4:14).

Today's Growth Principle: Make an effort to reach out to those who are overlooked or ignored and invite them to Jesus.

Living for Others

Neglect not the gift that is in thee, which was given thee by prophecy, with the laying on of the hands of the presbytery. Meditate upon these things; give thyself wholly to them; that thy profiting may appear to all. Take heed unto thyself, and unto the doctrine; continue in them: for in doing this thou shalt both save thyself, and them that hear thee.
—1 Timothy 4:14–16

The famous evangelist J. Wilbur Chapman told the story of a hiker who became lost in the mountains during a snow storm. He tried to continue forward but could not find any landmarks. Realizing his peril, he looked for a place of safety but found none. Finally, he tripped and fell into the snow. Chapman said, "As he fell his hand struck the body of another man who had fallen in the same place. This first man was unconscious, and the man who had just fallen rose to his knees, and, bending over the prostrate form, began to chafe his hands and to rub his face, until by and by the man's eyes opened. He had saved another's life, but he had also saved himself, for the exercise had kept the life in his own body."

The temptation all of us face is to live our lives focused on our own needs, wants, goals, and ambitions rather than realizing the importance of investing our lives into others. The Christian life is not just about us. When we follow the pattern Jesus set and pour ourselves into helping others, we find great benefit for our own lives. When Jesus gave the gospel to the woman at the well while His disciples searched for food, it renewed His strength in a powerful way. "Jesus saith unto them, My meat is to do the will of him that sent me, and to finish his work" (John 4:34). God gives strength to those who seek to serve Him.

Today's Growth Principle: You cannot live like Jesus unless your heart is burdened and broken for the needs of others.

The Damage of Wounding Words

*There is a generation that are pure in their own eyes, and yet is not washed from their filthiness. There is a generation, O how lofty are their eyes! and their eyelids are lifted up. There is a generation, whose teeth are as swords, and their jaw teeth as knives, to devour the poor from off the earth, and the needy from among men.—*PROVERBS 30:12-14

I came across a powerful description that someone wrote of one of the most serious problems that undermines the effectiveness and unity of so many churches: "My name is Gossip. I have no respect for justice. I maim without killing. I break hearts and ruin lives. I am cunning and malicious and gather strength with age. The more I am quoted, the more I am believed. My victims are helpless. They cannot protect themselves against me because I have no name and face. To track me down is impossible. The harder you try, the more elusive I become. I am nobody's friend. Once I tarnish a reputation, it is never the same. I topple governments and wreck marriages. I make headlines and headaches. I ruin careers and cause sleepless nights, heartaches, and indigestion. I make innocent people cry in their pillows. Even my name hisses. I am called Gossip."

The words that we speak to and about others have enormous power, and we are going to one day answer to God for the words we have chosen to carelessly utter. "But I say unto you, That every idle word that men shall speak, they shall give account thereof in the day of judgment" (Matthew 12:36). Every Christian should make a deliberate and intentional effort to make sure that his speech is uplifting. This is equally true whether we are speaking to someone or about them. There are many things that even if true should not be spread to damage or destroy the reputation of others.

Today's Growth Principle: Use your words to strengthen, encourage, and build up others rather than tear them down.

Trusting God in Times of Trouble

But we have this treasure in earthen vessels, that the excellency of the power may be of God, and not of us. We are troubled on every side, yet not distressed; we are perplexed, but not in despair; Persecuted, but not forsaken; cast down, but not destroyed; Always bearing about in the body the dying of the Lord Jesus, that the life also of Jesus might be made manifest in our body.—2 CORINTHIANS 4:7–10

When he was narrowly defeated in his bid for re-election in 1888 by Benjamin Harrison, Grover Cleveland faced a choice—to retire from public life or to continue to fight for the principles he believed. Cleveland chose to continue his career, and in 1892, he became the only man in American history to serve as president twice in non-consecutive terms. He is listed as both the twenty-second and the twenty-fourth presidents. Early in his second term in office, Cleveland was diagnosed with a tumor which required part of his jaw to be removed. Following his surgery, Cleveland wrote, "I have learned how weak the strongest man is under God's decrees; and I see in a new light the necessity of doing my allotted work in the full apprehension of the coming night."

The fact that things are hard or that we suffer reversals and defeat does not mean that we are left hopeless. Instead, each hardship should remind us that God's grace is always sufficient, and that He has a plan for the future. One of the lessons of suffering is that God must always be exalted instead of our receiving the glory. And when hard times come, we can take heart knowing that God recognizes us as able to endure them in a manner which will bring praise to Him. "And they departed from the presence of the council, rejoicing that they were counted worthy to suffer shame for his name" (Acts 5:41).

Today's Growth Principle: Do not allow difficulty to discourage or defeat you. God is still in control no matter what happens.

A Father's Heart

When Israel was a child, then I loved him, and called my son out of Egypt. As they called them, so they went from them: they sacrificed unto Baalim, and burned incense to graven images. I taught Ephraim also to go, taking them by their arms; but they knew not that I healed them. —HOSEA 11:1–3

Evangelist D. L. Moody told the story of an interaction he had with his young daughter, Emma. She had been asking for a new muff to keep her hands warm in the winter, and one day her mother brought one home for her. Even though it was cold and snowing, she wanted to go out right away and try it. Moody said, "I went out with her, and I said, 'Emma, better let me take your hand.' She wanted to keep her hands in her muff, and so she refused to take my hand. Well, by and by she came to an icy place, her little feet slipped, and down she went.

"When I helped her up she said, 'Papa, you may give me your little finger.' 'No, my daughter, just take my hand.' 'No, no, Papa, give me your little finger.' Well, I gave my finger to her, and for a little way she got along nicely, but pretty soon we came to another icy place, and again she fell. This time she hurt herself a little, and she said, 'Papa, give me your hand,' and I gave her my hand, and closed my fingers about her wrist, and held her up so that she could not fall."

God takes great delight in His children and fully understands us. "Like as a father pitieth his children, so the LORD pitieth them that fear him. For he knoweth our frame; he remembereth that we are dust" (Psalm 103:13–14). He teaches us and invests in us and protects us. Earthly fathers fail us, but even when they do, our Heavenly father holds us. "When my father and my mother forsake me, then the LORD will take me up" (Psalm 27:10).

Today's Growth Principle: We can always trust the heart of our Heavenly Father.

The Priority of Wisdom

For I give you good doctrine, forsake ye not my law. For I was my father's son, tender and only beloved in the sight of my mother. He taught me also, and said unto me, Let thine heart retain my words: keep my commandments, and live. Get wisdom, get understanding: forget it not; neither decline from the words of my mouth.—PROVERBS 4:2–5

When Nebuchadnezzar had his dream of a great statue made of different materials that foretold the future empires of history, he recognized that it was important. But when he awoke he could no longer remember what his dream had been. When his wise men could not recall his dream for him, despite the fact that his demand was unrealistic and unfair, he ordered them to be put to death. Because Daniel and his three friends were among that group, they also faced death. As all of us should do in times of trouble, they turned to prayer.

Daniel's prayer was answered. God not only revealed the king's dream to him, but also told him what it meant, thus sparing Daniel's life. There is a wonderful reminder to us regarding wisdom in Daniel's resulting song of praise: "Daniel answered and said, Blessed be the name of God for ever and ever: for wisdom and might are his: And he changeth the times and the seasons: he removeth kings, and setteth up kings: he giveth wisdom unto the wise, and knowledge to them that know understanding" (Daniel 2:20–21).

Too often God's people do not live with wisdom because they do not turn to God to get it. We do not become wise by being more educated. There is a vast difference between knowledge and wisdom. Someone said, "Knowledge is recognizing a tomato is a fruit. Wisdom is not putting it in a fruit salad." God's wisdom enables us to live according to the precepts of His Word.

Today's Growth Principle: If we are to have godly wisdom, we must make the search of it from God's Word a priority in our lives.

God Loves the World

*O Jerusalem, Jerusalem, thou that killest the prophets, and stonest them which are sent unto thee, how often would I have gathered thy children together, even as a hen gathereth her chickens under her wings, and ye would not! Behold, your house is left unto you desolate. For I say unto you, Ye shall not see me henceforth, till ye shall say, Blessed is he that cometh in the name of the Lord.—*MATTHEW 23:37–39

Most of the world religions throughout history have featured stern and largely unapproachable gods. These gods often demanded great sacrifices in order to be appeased. One of the distinctive traits of Christianity is that God Himself provided the sacrifice for the atonement of men's sins. Rather than demanding that we make the payment for redemption, Jesus—God in the flesh—came to make it. John the Baptist was the first human voice to announce Jesus' redemptive role. "The next day John seeth Jesus coming unto him, and saith, Behold the Lamb of God, which taketh away the sin of the world" (John 1:29).

There are many things in the world around us that are in direct opposition to God, and it seems that the more that evil is displayed, the more it is applauded. Yet, God loves the whole world, and we too were once sinners. Even those raised in the most protective environments of church were still sinners in need of God's love and a Saviour.

Dr. John R. Rice wrote, "God loves this world! Let me say it again, because our hearts are so calloused to the blessed truth that it makes little impression upon us—God loves this world! He loves every sinner in it. The extent of His love is beyond human comprehension. He gave His own perfect Son, to be a man, to be tempted as a man, to live a perfect life, to minister among men and then to die a shameful death of agony that men might be saved."

Today's Growth Principle: When we spend time with the Lord, we will love the world around us with the same fervor and intensity that God loves them.

Remembering the Purpose of Life

But if a man live many years, and rejoice in them all; yet let him remember the days of darkness; for they shall be many. All that cometh is vanity. Rejoice, O young man, in thy youth; and let thy heart cheer thee in the days of thy youth, and walk in the ways of thine heart, and in the sight of thine eyes: but know thou, that for all these things God will bring thee into judgment. Therefore remove sorrow from thy heart, and put away evil from thy flesh: for childhood and youth are vanity.
—ECCLESIASTES 11:8–10

Oliver Wendell Holmes, Jr. lived through some of the most momentous events of American history. As a young officer in the Massachusetts militia, he was wounded three times during the Civil War. After a brilliant legal career, Holmes was appointed to the Supreme Court by President Teddy Roosevelt and served as a justice for nearly thirty years. He was widely respected, and on the occasion of his ninetieth birthday, a nationwide radio program was broadcast in his honor. Asked to say a few words, Holmes concluded his remarks this way: "And so I end with a line from a Latin poet who uttered the message more than fifteen hundred years ago: 'Death plucks my ear and says, Live—I am coming.'"

This life is often the sole focus of people's attention, but this life is only a brief moment in time in preparation for eternity. All of us will one day give an account to God for how we have used the time, energy, gifts, and resources He has provided. We only get one opportunity to live and serve God. There are no do-overs—no going back to claim wasted days or years. Each day comes but once and will never be replaced. As missionary Amy Carmichael pointed out, "We shall have all eternity to celebrate the victories, but we have only the few hours before sunset in which to win them."

Today's Growth Principle: Strive to use the time you have been given to accomplish as much as possible for the cause of Christ.

Staying Within the Rules

And every man that striveth for the mastery is temperate in all things. Now they do it to obtain a corruptible crown; but we an incorruptible. I therefore so run, not as uncertainly; so fight I, not as one that beateth the air: But I keep under my body, and bring it into subjection: lest that by any means, when I have preached to others, I myself should be a castaway.—1 CORINTHIANS 9:25–27

The most anticipated match up heading into the Seoul Olympic Games in 1988 was the 100-meter dash competition between American Carl Lewis, who had won the event in 1984, and Canadian Ben Johnson. The two athletes easily qualified into the final race, putting them side by side when the starter's gun sounded. Johnson led throughout the race, crossing the finish line with a new world record. In his post-victory press conference, Johnson said, "A gold medal—that's something no one can take away from you." The problem was that Johnson had cheated, and when the mandatory drug test after the event came back positive for steroid use, the gold medal was taken away from Johnson and awarded to Lewis, who had finished second on the track.

There are times when, in the name of expediency or getting results, people are tempted to cut corners and do things they know are not right. Even when these actions are motivated by good intentions, they are always wrong. As Dr. Bob Jones, Sr. put it, "It is never right to do wrong in order to get a chance to do right." God's principles and commandments are unchanging, and He does not excuse our violation of them no matter what our motive may be. No amount of work for God and no results justify disobedience to His Word. He will not reward those who excuse sin or take shortcuts in the name of doing good things for Him.

Today's Growth Principle: To win the race and gain the prize, we must stay within the limits and boundaries God has set for us.

Guard Your Tongue

Set a watch, O LORD, before my mouth; keep the door of my lips. Incline not my heart to any evil thing, to practise wicked works with men that work iniquity: and let me not eat of their dainties. Let the righteous smite me; it shall be a kindness: and let him reprove me; it shall be an excellent oil, which shall not break my head: for yet my prayer also shall be in their calamities.—PSALM 141:3–5

Have you ever heard the statement, "Among my most prized possessions are the words that I have never spoken"? The impact of our words goes much further than most people realize, and often we say things carelessly or thoughtlessly without considering the effect they will have on those who hear them. Many people have been wounded by casually spoken words that did not have hurtful intentions. And tragically there are even some cases when words are used to deliberately and purposefully wound others.

The power of words places an enormous responsibility on us to guard carefully what we say both to and about others. Most of us can remember either words of praise that encouraged us to keep going and do better or words of criticism that made us feel hopeless and want to give up—even though those words may have been spoken many years, even decades, ago. As we reflect on the power words have had in our lives, we should also consider the impact *our* words will have on those who hear them.

David wrote, "Let the words of my mouth, and the meditation of my heart, be acceptable in thy sight, O LORD, my strength, and my redeemer" (Psalm 19:14). The more care and consideration we give to our words before speaking, the more likely we are to say things that are helpful and uplifting. We must never forget that God is measuring every word that we utter.

Today's Growth Principle: Think before you speak so that you use the incredible power of words to accomplish good things.

Walking Wisely before the Eyes of the World

Having your conversation honest among the Gentiles: that, whereas they speak against you as evildoers, they may by your good works, which they shall behold, glorify God in the day of visitation. Submit yourselves to every ordinance of man for the Lord's sake: whether it be to the king, as supreme; Or unto governors, as unto them that are sent by him for the punishment of evildoers, and for the praise of them that do well. For so is the will of God, that with well doing ye may put to silence the ignorance of foolish men:—1 PETER 2:12–15

Many years ago, Dr. Bill Rice traveled and preached as an evangelist before founding a ministry geared to reaching deaf people with the gospel. He told the story that once he was riding a city bus through the town where he was holding a revival. When he paid his fare, the driver gave him back too much change. He pointed it out, returning the extra money. The driver responded, "I knew I gave you too much. I heard you preach last night and wanted to see if you were for real."

Every day we are being watched by those around us. Most of the time we are not even aware of who is looking. But our testimony—for good or for bad—has a powerful impact. In fact as the old saying goes, "Actions speak louder than words."

When our lives match what our words say, there is a confirmation that shows people we are for real. The fact that there are hypocrites in the church is a poor excuse for people not to go to church, but it is also a tragedy for our failings in daily life to be used by Satan to keep others away from the gospel. We should do all we can to live a consistent testimony that points others to Christ rather than distracting them from Him by hypocrisy in our lives.

Today's Growth Principle: Make sure that what you live from day to day aligns with what you declare your beliefs to be.

Comfort in Distress

I will call on the LORD, who is worthy to be praised: so shall I be saved from mine enemies. When the waves of death compassed me, the floods of ungodly men made me afraid; The sorrows of hell compassed me about; the snares of death prevented me; In my distress I called upon the LORD, and cried to my God: and he did hear my voice out of his temple, and my cry did enter into his ears. —2 SAMUEL 22:4–7

The Lord blessed David in so many ways, but that blessing did not mean that the shepherd boy who was anointed to be king over Israel had an easy life. David spent much of his life on fields of battle. There were many days when he did not know whether he would even survive until sundown. There were many nights where he slept in caves while hiding from those who wanted him dead. Throughout all of his dark days, David continued to trust in God. He knew that the hard times he endured did not mean that God had forsaken him. Sometimes others even used David's troubles to claim that God had abandoned him: "Many there be which say of my soul, There is no help for him in God. Selah" (Psalm 3:2). Yet David's faith remained steadfast.

God does not always cause our troubles to disappear, but He always comforts those who flee to Him for help. And it is often the very things that bring us the most grief and turmoil that God uses to shape our lives. Charles Spurgeon said, "Great hearts can only be made by great troubles. The spade of trouble digs the reservoir of comfort deeper, and makes more room for consolation." In 2 Corinthians 1:4, Paul explained that difficulty in our lives allows for us to experience God's comfort, which then allows us to give God's comfort to others: "Who comforteth us in all our tribulation, that we may be able to comfort them which are in any trouble, by the comfort wherewith we ourselves are comforted of God."

Today's Growth Principle: Trust God just as much when you are struggling with difficulty as you do when you are rejoicing in peace.

The Right Attitude toward Work

Go to the ant, thou sluggard; consider her ways, and be wise: Which having no guide, overseer, or ruler, Provideth her meat in the summer, and gathereth her food in the harvest. How long wilt thou sleep, O sluggard? when wilt thou arise out of thy sleep?—PROVERBS 6:6-9

Many people will work hard and get the job done if they know the boss is watching, but they otherwise do the minimum to get by. Some people will work hard consistently for more money or prestige or to advance their careers. But as Christians, we are to work hard at whatever job we have because we are servants of God. Our duty to be a good reflection of His character and nature should impact the way we perform any task we are assigned.

There is a constant temptation to grumble and complain about work, but it is one we should resist. Work is not a curse. Adam was given assignments from God that he carried out before the Fall. When sin entered into the world, work became more difficult, but work itself is a blessing. Besides profitably filling our time, work gives us an opportunity to glorify God: "And whatsoever ye do, do it heartily, as to the Lord, and not unto men; Knowing that of the Lord ye shall receive the reward of the inheritance: for ye serve the Lord Christ" (Colossians 3:23–24).

Christians should not be lazy or indifferent as they go about their jobs. They should work hard, keep a positive attitude, be respectful, and be diligent. There are few places in life that are more revealing of the state of our hearts than the way we approach our work. A Christian who is not diligent in his labor will not be an effective witness of the gospel.

Today's Growth Principle: Realizing that work is a gift from God and that He is our ultimate boss will change our attitudes toward our jobs.

The Value of Faithfulness

But the LORD was with Joseph, and shewed him mercy, and gave him favour in the sight of the keeper of the prison. And the keeper of the prison committed to Joseph's hand all the prisoners that were in the prison; and whatsoever they did there, he was the doer of it. The keeper of the prison looked not to any thing that was under his hand; because the LORD was with him, and that which he did, the LORD made it to prosper.
—GENESIS 39:21–23

Think about the various people you have worked with over the years. How many of them would you trust with your life if you knew you would not be checking up on them to make sure they took care of things on your behalf? That is exactly what the keeper of Pharaoh's prison did with Joseph. The jailer was responsible to keep the prisoners, and if any of them escaped, his own life would be forfeited as penalty. Yet, he placed that responsibility, and thus his own life, in the hands of a young foreign prisoner named Joseph.

Why would the jailer take such a drastic step? Because he recognized in Joseph a faithfulness to God that led to a faithfulness in accepting responsibilities. Matthew Henry wrote, "Faithfulness in a servant lies in the ready, punctual, and thorough execution of his master's orders; keeping his secrets and counsels, dispatching his affairs, and managing with frugality, and to as much just advantage for his master as he is able; looking well to his trusts, and preventing, as far as he can, all spoil, or loss, or damage." In a society where excuses run rampant and people routinely break commitments, God still rewards and honors those who fulfill their duties. This is not a secondary trait, but a necessity with Him. "Moreover it is required in stewards, that a man be found faithful" (1 Corinthians 4:2).

Today's Growth Principle: Faithfulness to human responsibilities starts with being faithful to God in all things.

Missing the Point

*Let us therefore fear, lest, a promise being left us of entering into his rest, any of you should seem to come short of it. For unto us was the gospel preached, as well as unto them: but the word preached did not profit them, not being mixed with faith in them that heard it. For we which have believed do enter into rest, as he said, As I have sworn in my wrath, if they shall enter into my rest: although the works were finished from the foundation of the world.—*HEBREWS 4:1-3

Queen Victoria had nine children and forty-two grandchildren, so besides the responsibilities she had as monarch of England, there were many family duties as well. The story goes that there was one grandson about whom she was particularly concerned. He was notably loose with his money, constantly asking for advances and gifts to allow him to keep spending. As his birthday was approaching, he wrote the queen a letter hinting that a cash gift would be most appreciated. She responded not with a gift but with a letter filled with advice regarding the importance of self control and the dangers of extravagance. After a little while he wrote back, thanking her for the letter—and telling her he had sold it to a collector for five pounds!

The Bible often speaks of the importance and value of seeking counsel from others. "Where no counsel is, the people fall: but in the multitude of counsellors there is safety" (Proverbs 11:14). As valuable as counsel is, however, it is of little value to us unless we put it into practice and do as we are counseled. There are times when we are reluctant to follow good advice we receive because it is simply not what we want to hear. Yet it is even more foolish to ignore good counsel than it is to not seek it in the first place.

Today's Growth Principle: There is no benefit gained from receiving good advice unless we also follow it.

Where the Anchor Is Found

Wherein God, willing more abundantly to shew unto the heirs of promise the immutability of his counsel, confirmed it by an oath: That by two immutable things, in which it was impossible for God to lie, we might have a strong consolation, who have fled for refuge to lay hold upon the hope set before us: Which hope we have as an anchor of the soul, both sure and stedfast, and which entereth into that within the veil;
—HEBREWS 6:17–19

There is an old story about a young naval officer being examined before assignment to his first command. The grizzled veteran asked what the prospective captain would do if he saw a storm approaching from the south. "Throw out an anchor at the stern," the reply came. The next question brought a storm from the north. "Throw out an anchor at the bow," the young officer said. The veteran continued bringing up potential storms, and the answer to every one was another anchor. Finally the exasperated old-timer asked, "Where are you getting all those anchors?" "From the same place you're getting all the storms, Sir," the young man replied.

Life is filled with storms that come at us from every direction. There are days when it feels like it's just one challenge and difficulty after another. But on every one of those days and for every one of those storms, we have an anchor that never fails. Just as there are many different kinds of trials and temptations, God's grace has many facets that allow us to win the victory in every situation. "As every man hath received the gift, even so minister the same one to another, as good stewards of the manifold grace of God" (1 Peter 4:10). No one ever went wrong by trusting what God has promised. We falter and sink when we take our eyes off of Him and rely on our own strength.

Today's Growth Principle: Those who trust the unfailing promises of God for strength have an anchor that will hold through the storms.

The Priority of Pleasing God

Then said Jesus unto them, When ye have lifted up the Son of man, then shall ye know that I am he, and that I do nothing of myself; but as my Father hath taught me, I speak these things. And he that sent me is with me: the Father hath not left me alone; for I do always those things that please him. As he spake these words, many believed on him.
— JOHN 8:28–30

Back in the late 1800s, rail travel revolutionized the way people moved across vast distances of the country as well as the way they traveled to work. I read about a new ticket collector who had been hired for work at a commuter station near New York City. His predecessor in the job had known many of the regular customers, and he had gotten in the habit of allowing them to board without showing their tickets. The new agent insisted on seeing every ticket, and this irritated several passengers. After a few days one of them said to him, "You're not at all popular with the traveling public." He responded by pointing toward the station master's office. "I don't mind that," he said. "It's the man in there with whom I want to be popular."

There are many times when we allow the concerns and opinions of others to become more important to us than what God thinks. While we should not be rude or careless regarding what others think or feel, ultimately the only judgment of our lives that really matters is the one that He will render. We must remember that we are not going to answer to God for others, but for our own actions, thoughts, and motives. "So then every one of us shall give account of himself to God" (Romans 14:12). Even if no one else is doing what is right, we can still follow God's path if we care about His opinion most.

Today's Growth Principle: If our primary purpose is pleasing God, we will not be deterred by criticism or disapproval from others.

Being Bold for Jesus

*Are not five sparrows sold for two farthings, and not one of them is forgotten before God? But even the very hairs of your head are all numbered. Fear not therefore: ye are of more value than many sparrows. Also I say unto you, Whosoever shall confess me before men, him shall the Son of man also confess before the angels of God:—*LUKE 12:6–8

The story goes that a young man who had been converted under John Wesley's preaching was so excited to be saved that he began attempting to preach on the streets, telling those who passed by about Jesus. He had little training or education and was not a greatly gifted speaker. After listening for a few moments, a man interrupted his message and said, "Young man, you cannot preach; you ought to be ashamed of yourself!" Immediately he responded, "So I am, but I am not ashamed of my Lord!"

One of the most effective tools of Satan to hinder our witness is the fear of embarrassment. Often when we have an opportunity to speak to someone about the gospel or to pray in public or to say something when others deride Christians in our presence, we remain silent. We allow the possibility that we might be made fun of or mocked to keep us from speaking. But the more we love God and the more we know of His Word and walk in the power of His Spirit, the more bold we will be. "And such as do wickedly against the covenant shall he corrupt by flatteries: but the people that do know their God shall be strong, and do exploits" (Daniel 11:32).

The further our society goes from the truth of God, the less welcoming they become to those who speak that truth. But we must not allow the scorn or criticism of others to keep us from boldly declaring what God has said.

Today's Growth Principle: Never stay silent when the Spirit of God prompts you to speak, no matter who is listening or watching.

Believing What God Said

If they return to thee with all their heart and with all their soul in the land of their captivity, whither they have carried them captives, and pray toward their land, which thou gavest unto their fathers, and toward the city which thou hast chosen, and toward the house which I have built for thy name: Then hear thou from the heavens, even from thy dwelling place, their prayer and their supplications, and maintain their cause, and forgive thy people which have sinned against thee.
—2 CHRONICLES 6:38–39

When Solomon completed the beautiful Temple in Jerusalem, he dedicated it with great ceremony and sacrifices. As part of the dedication, he prayed that God would guard His people and keep them following Him—but also that if they turned away from God and were judged, He would still remember them and still listen for their prayers. The Israelites did turn from God and were taken into captivity as a result of His judgment.

Yet even after that great defeat, there were those among God's people who loved and followed God and turned to Him in repentant prayer for their nation. Daniel was one of these. In fact, this helps us understand why Daniel had the obvious habit of prayer toward Jerusalem: "…he went into his house; and his windows being open in his chamber toward Jerusalem, he kneeled upon his knees three times a day, and prayed, and gave thanks before his God, as he did aforetime" (Daniel 6:10). What Daniel was doing, and had been doing long before the law was signed, was in response to Solomon's declaration of what God would do.

Daniel believed that God would be faithful to hear his prayers just as Solomon had asked. His faith was demonstrated in his actions. There is no such thing as a vibrant and living faith that does not produce obedience in our lives.

Today's Growth Principle: Only when we do what God says, do we reveal that we have genuine faith in His Word and His promises.

JULY

Look and Live

*If I have told you earthly things, and ye believe not, how shall ye believe, if I tell you of heavenly things? And no man hath ascended up to heaven, but he that came down from heaven, even the Son of man which is in heaven. And as Moses lifted up the serpent in the wilderness, even so must the Son of man be lifted up: That whosoever believeth in him should not perish, but have eternal life.—*JOHN 3:12–15

As the Israelites made their way toward the Promised Land, there were many days when they did not give thanks for their deliverance from slavery. Instead they often grumbled and complained. At one point, God sent poisonous snakes into the camp to judge the people for their unbelief. In desperation, the people cried out for forgiveness, and God instructed Moses to make a replica of the poisonous snakes from brass and lift it high in the center of the camp on a pole. Everyone who believed the promise of God for deliverance and looked at the brass serpent was healed. Those who tried another cure or who did not believe God's promise and look to the brass snake perished.

Jesus used this Old Testament story to explain to Nicodemus how God's plan of salvation worked. Jesus said that He would be lifted up—speaking of His death on the cross—to provide all that was needed for deliverance from sin. All over the world people are trying to find alternatives to accepting God's offer of salvation. Many want to do something—join a church, be baptized, be confirmed, or do good works—in order to gain their redemption.

All of these plans are doomed to failure, for salvation is only offered by grace through faith. We do nothing to earn or deserve it. Our efforts to justify ourselves to God cannot satisfy His perfect righteousness. Only by faith can we accept and receive God's salvation.

Today's Growth Principle: The only way of salvation is the one God provided through His Son Jesus Christ.

The Loss of Liberty

Stand fast therefore in the liberty wherewith Christ hath made us free, and be not entangled again with the yoke of bondage. Behold, I Paul say unto you, that if ye be circumcised, Christ shall profit you nothing. For I testify again to every man that is circumcised, that he is a debtor to do the whole law. Christ is become of no effect unto you, whosoever of you are justified by the law; ye are fallen from grace.—GALATIANS 5:1–4

On July 4, 1926, President Calvin Coolidge gave a speech in Philadelphia to mark the 150th anniversary of the Declaration of Independence. After recounting the many ways God had blessed and preserved the United States, he concluded with these words of warning: "If we are to maintain the great heritage which has been bequeathed to us, we must be like-minded as the fathers who created it. We must not sink into a pagan materialism. We must cultivate the reverence which they had for the things that are holy. We must follow the spiritual and moral leadership which they showed. We must keep replenished, that they may glow with a more compelling flame, the altar fires before which they worshiped."

Though they are enormous blessings, neither our political nor our religious liberty is guaranteed. Either or both may be lost if we are careless to maintain the things that produce them. So often we take for granted what many people can only dream of. There are enemies of liberty in both realms that seek to destroy freedom and bind others so that they can have control and power. The most important thing we can do for our nation and our political freedom is to exercise our religious freedom. And, more importantly, as we walk in the liberty Christ provided for us through our salvation, we have the ability to make a powerful impact on those around us, both for this world and for the next.

Today's Growth Principle: Do not allow your liberty to be lost through careless inattention to things that would take it away.

The Sound of Liberty

Then shalt thou cause the trumpet of the jubile to sound on the tenth day of the seventh month, in the day of atonement shall ye make the trumpet sound throughout all your land. And ye shall hallow the fiftieth year, and proclaim liberty throughout all the land unto all the inhabitants thereof: it shall be a jubile unto you; and ye shall return every man unto his possession, and ye shall return every man unto his family.
—LEVITICUS 25:9–10

In 1751, Isaac Norris, Speaker of the Pennsylvania Assembly, ordered a bell for the State House in Philadelphia. When the bell arrived from England, it cracked on the very first test ring. The metal was melted down and recast by John Pass and John Stow. Around the bell the words of Scripture from Leviticus 25:10, "Proclaim Liberty Throughout All the Land unto All the Inhabitants Thereof," carried a powerful message. The bell rang to call the members of the Continental Congress to assemble as they debated declaring independence from England. For many years after, it was rung on ceremonial occasions, until in the 1840s a major crack ended its life as a bell, but not its message.

The Lord has called us to be messengers of hope and liberty to a world in chains—not chains of political oppression, but chains of sin. When Jesus began His ministry, He selected a passage from Isaiah as the text for His sermon in the synagogue in Nazareth: "The Spirit of the Lord is upon me, because he hath anointed me to preach the gospel to the poor; he hath sent me to heal the brokenhearted, to preach deliverance to the captives, and recovering of sight to the blind, to set at liberty them that are bruised" (Luke 4:18). Freedom from sin has already been purchased through the blood of Christ, but the lost will not know that truth unless someone tells them. It is our duty to proclaim liberty.

Today's Growth Principle: We are most like Jesus when we tell those in bondage to sin that there is liberty in Him.

The Key to a Blessed Nation

The counsel of the LORD standeth for ever, the thoughts of his heart to all generations. Blessed is the nation whose God is the LORD; and the people whom he hath chosen for his own inheritance. The LORD looketh from heaven; he beholdeth all the sons of men. From the place of his habitation he looketh upon all the inhabitants of the earth.—PSALM 33:11–14

Speaking at a prayer breakfast in Dallas, Texas, in August of 1984, President Ronald Reagan said, "Those who created our country—the Founding Fathers and Mothers—understood that there is a divine order that transcends the human order. They saw the state, in fact, as a form of moral order and felt that the bedrock of moral order is religion. A state is nothing more than a reflection of its citizens; the more decent the citizens, the more decent the state. Without God, there is no virtue, because there's no prompting of the conscience. Without God, there is a coarsening of the society. And without God, democracy will not and cannot long endure. If we ever forget that we're one nation under God, then we will be a nation gone under."

As our nation moves further and further away from God, there is a temptation to despair. But in reality most of history has featured Christians living in hostile environments, both from government and from their surrounding culture. We are blessed in America with freedom of religion, but that is not a guarantee or a promise. And that freedom is under threat today as never before. The cure for America's ills is not primarily found in electing different politicians, but in a change of heart in the people. That change can only come about through the transforming power of new life from salvation in Christ. What America needs most is not new leaders or laws, but a revival of heart, turning to the Lord.

Today's Growth Principle: The best thing a believer can do for his country is to be a faithful servant of Jesus Christ.

Looking for the Lord's Return

For I am now ready to be offered, and the time of my departure is at hand.
I have fought a good fight, I have finished my course, I have kept the faith:
Henceforth there is laid up for me a crown of righteousness, which the
Lord, the righteous judge, shall give me at that day: and not to me only,
but unto all them also that love his appearing.—2 TIMOTHY 4:6–8

Nearly two thousand years have passed since Jesus made a promise to His disciples the night before His crucifixion: "And if I go and prepare a place for you, I will come again, and receive you unto myself; that where I am, there ye may be also" (John 14:3). Despite the passage of time, that promise is just as certain and secure as it was when it was first spoken. Jesus is going to return, and He will do so without notice or warning at a time which remains unknown to us.

Our duty is to look for His return and to live in such a way that we are prepared to meet Him with joy rather than shame. The old Scottish preacher Alexander MacLaren said, "The apostolic church thought more about the Second Coming of Jesus Christ than about death and Heaven. The early Christians were looking, not for a cleft in the ground called a grave, but for a cleavage in the sky called Glory."

The question is not *if* the Lord will return, but how we will meet Him when He does. We are not meant to know when that moment will be, in part, because it serves as motivation for us to live each day to the fullest to accomplish as much as possible for God's kingdom. Rather than saving up all our work, like a student cramming at the last minute for a test, we are to live every day expecting His return. Whether the end of our life on Earth comes through the rapture or through death, how wonderful it will be to look back and know we gave our hours and days fully to the Lord.

Today's Growth Principle: Since Jesus could return today, use every moment you have to prepare for His return.

The Comfort of God's Presence

*Whither shall I go from thy spirit? or whither shall I flee from thy presence? If I ascend up into heaven, thou art there: if I make my bed in hell, behold, thou art there. If I take the wings of the morning, and dwell in the uttermost parts of the sea; Even there shall thy hand lead me, and thy right hand shall hold me.—*PSALM 139:7–10

The evangelist D. L. Moody told of talking to an elderly Christian man. After serving the Lord for many years, his faith was shaken by a series of difficulties with his finances and his health. He described beginning to doubt God's love for him, and eventually wondering whether he was even a Christian. Then he told Moody, "I began to think what I would do if I ended up in Hell. My first thought was that I would start a prayer meeting—and after that I didn't worry about being lost any more!"

No one who has trusted Christ and received His free gift of salvation can ever lose it. Jesus said, "And I give unto them eternal life; and they shall never perish, neither shall any man pluck them out of my hand. My Father, which gave them me, is greater than all; and no man is able to pluck them out of my Father's hand" (John 10:28–29). There may be times when our fellowship is broken by something we have done or failed to do, but our standing as children of our Heavenly Father never changes. He will never leave us or forsake us (Hebrews 13:5).

Too many Christians do not live with the comforting presence of God as a daily reality. They do not draw strength from His Word and do not seek His face in prayer. They do not listen to the guidance of the Holy Spirit or fellowship with other believers around the things of God. That is a painful way to live, because it forfeits so much peace and comfort that God offers His children.

Today's Growth Principle: If your confidence is based on God's presence rather than circumstances, you will experience peace.

Seeking God's Help

And Asa in the thirty and ninth year of his reign was diseased in his feet, until his disease was exceeding great: yet in his disease he sought not to the LORD, but to the physicians. And Asa slept with his fathers, and died in the one and fortieth year of his reign. And they buried him in his own sepulchres, which he had made for himself in the city of David, and laid him in the bed which was filled with sweet odours and divers kinds of spices prepared by the apothecaries' art: and they made a very great burning for him.—2 CHRONICLES 16:12–14

Francis Ridley Havergal was one of England's best-known poets and hymnists of the nineteenth century. Among her best-known works are "Take My Life and Let it Be" and "Like a River Glorious." Once Havergal told a friend, "When I had great troubles I always went to God and was wondrously carried through; but my little trials I used to try to manage myself, and often most dismally failed."

God is not a last resort to whom we turn when all else fails. God should be our first source of refuge and comfort. He has the knowledge, the resources, and the power to meet any need. He has promised we can run to Him for help for any need—whether in our darkest hours or simply in a challenging time of temptation. "Let us therefore come boldly unto the throne of grace, that we may obtain mercy, and find grace to help in time of need" (Hebrews 4:16).

Yet despite the wonderful promises we have been given, many Christians insist on taking matters into their own hands and trying to deal with their problems without involving God. Like King Asa of Judah, they seek human help alone rather than tapping into the ultimate resource that is available simply by asking. We must set aside our pride and admit our utter dependence on God to receive His provision.

Today's Growth Principle: If you turn to yourself rather than to God in times of trouble, you are headed for defeat.

A Sacrifice with a Purpose

All that ever came before me are thieves and robbers: but the sheep did not hear them. I am the door: by me if any man enter in, he shall be saved, and shall go in and out, and find pasture. The thief cometh not, but for to steal, and to kill, and to destroy: I am come that they might have life, and that they might have it more abundantly. I am the good shepherd: the good shepherd giveth his life for the sheep.—JOHN 10:8–11

When Giuseppe Garibaldi was leading the struggle to unify the nation of Italy in the 1800s, he faced numerous military obstacles in addition to political foes. At the beginning of his campaign, the great general was forced to rely on volunteers to fight for his vision of Italy. After one rally, a young man came up and asked him what reward he might expect if he enlisted in the fighting. Garibaldi replied, "Wounds, scars, and perhaps death. But remember that through your bruises Italy will be free." The young man responded, "Then I will follow to the death."

The measure of a sacrifice is not just in how much is given up, but in how much is gained in return. The coming of Jesus into the world to provide salvation required the greatest sacrifice in all of history. The perfect Son of God left Heaven and exchanged His glory and wealth for poverty and scorn. Then He took upon Himself all of our sins and died on the cross. But Hebrews 12:2 tells us that even as He did so, He had us in mind: "Looking unto Jesus the author and finisher of our faith; who for the joy that was set before him endured the cross, despising the shame, and is set down at the right hand of the throne of God" (Hebrews 12:2).

Just as Jesus thought us worthy of His sacrifice, we should consider those around us important enough to reach even at great cost. The value we attach to a person or a cause is seen in what we are willing to sacrifice to reach it.

Today's Growth Principle: The work of God is worthy of any sacrifice that He calls us to make.

The Covering of the Blood

For I will pass through the land of Egypt this night, and will smite all the firstborn in the land of Egypt, both man and beast; and against all the gods of Egypt I will execute judgment: I am the LORD. And the blood shall be to you for a token upon the houses where ye are: and when I see the blood, I will pass over you, and the plague shall not be upon you to destroy you, when I smite the land of Egypt.—EXODUS 12:12–13

In 2008, a major terrorist raid was launched in Mumbai, India. Teams of gunmen went into hotels, randomly shooting people. By the time military and police responded and finally ended the raid, more than two hundred people were dead. One of the few survivors told a reporter who interviewed him that he had sought shelter under a table after several of those around him were shot. He said, "I suppose because I was covered in someone else's blood, that they took me for dead."

As Christians we are covered in the blood of Jesus Christ. The covering that was applied at salvation when we accepted His free gift by grace through faith remains applied to our daily lives, even when we as believers fall short of God's perfection: "But if we walk in the light, as he is in the light, we have fellowship one with another, and the blood of Jesus Christ his Son cleanseth us from all sin" (1 John 1:7).

In the Old Testament, God gave us a picture through the passover lamb of the future sacrifice He Himself would provide. Just as the Israelites were to place the blood of a spotless lamb around their door to avoid the judgment of the death angel, so we are protected from judgment by the blood of Christ shed for our sins. The blood of Jesus is the covering that allows us to enter into the presence of a perfect and holy God. It was shed on our behalf, and it grants us membership into a divine family and access to God's presence. It is the most precious treasure, and we should never lose our gratitude for it.

Today's Growth Principle: The precious blood of Jesus is the only avenue we have of God's forgiveness, both for this world and the next.

The Importance of Example

When I shall send Artemas unto thee, or Tychicus, be diligent to come unto me to Nicopolis: for I have determined there to winter. Bring Zenas the lawyer and Apollos on their journey diligently, that nothing be wanting unto them. And let ours also learn to maintain good works for necessary uses, that they be not unfruitful. All that are with me salute thee. Greet them that love us in the faith. Grace be with you all. Amen.
—TITUS 3:12–15

Dr. D. J. Fleming who worked as a medical missionary in both India and China recounted a powerful story from the Boxer Rebellion that swept over China. The movement was violently anti-foreign and anti-Christian, and when the soldiers captured one town they came to a mission school for children. They placed a cross on the ground by the gate and announced that those who would trample over the cross would be free to go. The first seven children walked on the cross and were spared, but the eighth, a young girl dropped to her knees. For her refusal to trample on the cross, she was shot. Every remaining student followed her example and died rather than deny their faith.

There are many who start out well and continue on the right path for a little while. But when the pressure is on, and their faith may actually cost them something, they wilt and turn back. "For Demas hath forsaken me, having loved this present world, and is departed unto Thessalonica; Crescens to Galatia, Titus unto Dalmatia" (2 Timothy 4:10). There are also, however, many, like the Apostle Paul, who have stood for Christ even in the face of death, unwilling to deny their Lord. The example of people who finish their course strong for Christ challenges and encourages our faith. We should strive to have that kind of testimony for those who come behind us.

Today's Growth Principle: Do not settle for less than finishing your course through a life victoriously committed to doing right.

Sorrow of Heart

And it came to pass in the month Nisan, in the twentieth year of Artaxerxes the king, that wine was before him: and I took up the wine, and gave it unto the king. Now I had not been beforetime sad in his presence. Wherefore the king said unto me, Why is thy countenance sad, seeing thou art not sick? this is nothing else but sorrow of heart. Then I was very sore afraid, And said unto the king, Let the king live for ever: why should not my countenance be sad, when the city, the place of my fathers' sepulchres, lieth waste, and the gates thereof are consumed with fire?—NEHEMIAH 2:1–3

When Charles Spurgeon was just twenty-two years of age, his church had already outgrown their building. While a new facility was under construction, they rented a large hall at Surrey Gardens for services. As Spurgeon prepared to preach to a crowd of thousands, someone yelled, "Fire" and the panicked audience rushed for the exits. Seven people were killed, trampled to death, and dozens more were injured in the confusion. Spurgeon himself fell into a deep depression and even believed he wasn't fit for the ministry. When he returned to the pulpit two weeks later, he told the people that he had feared he would never be able to speak to them again.

All around us there are hurting people. Sometimes that pain is noticeable, but often it is concealed beneath what seems to us to be bitterness, anger, or harshness. While we are responsible to respond correctly to the hardships of life, it is not unusual for even committed Christians to struggle with pain and sorrow. It is important for us to look beyond the surface to see what is causing the reactions of others. While some people are unkind and unpleasant, many times it is a result of a deep level of pain. We should be gentle toward them, knowing that we may not see their sorrow of heart.

Today's Growth Principle: It is never wrong to be a kind encouragement to those around you—they may need it far more than you know.

Psalms 1–3 // Acts 17:1–15

The Value of Courage

And Moses called unto Joshua, and said unto him in the sight of all Israel, Be strong and of a good courage: for thou must go with this people unto the land which the LORD hath sworn unto their fathers to give them; and thou shalt cause them to inherit it. And the LORD, he it is that doth go before thee; he will be with thee, he will not fail thee, neither forsake thee: fear not, neither be dismayed.—DEUTERONOMY 31:7–8

Peter was supremely confident of his commitment to Jesus. Even when the Lord Himself told Peter that before the rooster crowed the next morning he would three times deny Jesus, Peter scoffed. He said that he would be willing to even give his life before he would turn away from Christ. Yet, when the pressure was on after the arrest of Jesus, Peter did exactly what he had vowed never to do and denied even knowing Jesus in an effort to keep from being arrested and put on trial with Him. His courage failed in the moment of testing, and he did not do what he knew he should have done.

Before we condemn Peter too strongly, however, we must remember that there are times when we, too, have failed to take a stand. Though there are often multiple reasons for such failure, one of the central issues is whether we allow ourselves to be dominated by our fears or whether we respond in courage, regardless of the cost. In *Measure for Measure*, William Shakespeare wrote, "Our doubts are traitors, and make us lose the good we oft might win, by fearing to attempt."

Our courage must not be based on our own strength to withstand Satan's advances, or we will certainly collapse. But we can confidently base our courage on the presence of God. We have His unfailing promise to always be with us. With God to fight our battles for us, there is nothing we need fear.

Today's Growth Principle: If we are focused on the presence of God, we will find the courage to do right no matter what comes.

The Practice of Prayer

Wherefore king Darius signed the writing and the decree. Now when Daniel knew that the writing was signed, he went into his house; and his windows being open in his chamber toward Jerusalem, he kneeled upon his knees three times a day, and prayed, and gave thanks before his God, as he did aforetime. Then these men assembled, and found Daniel praying and making supplication before his God.—DANIEL 6:9–11

Daniel's enemies in the Medo-Persian Empire resented his status and his ability. As they schemed against him, they realized they had no grounds to denounce him, so they began a quest to find some leverage against him. In modern terms, they bugged his phone and hacked his email, but Daniel had no secrets that revealed wrong-doing or carelessness. He walked in integrity and did his work with diligence. (That should be true of all of us no matter what our field of work is in life.)

Yet Daniel's enemies did find one thing they could use, and that was his utter devotion to God. It was no secret to those around him that Daniel was a man of prayer. He had made it a habit for many years to pray at specific times during the day. This routine became the foundation of the plot they hatched against Daniel. Daniel did not start praying when a law was passed forbidding it—he just kept doing what he had always done.

Someone said that too many people use prayer like a spare tire, only pulling it out in case of an emergency. Prayer should be a constant, habitual, ongoing, and serious part of our lives. It should be apparent to those who know us that we are people of prayer. The modern trend toward self-reliance is a great hindrance to prayer, because it keeps us from acknowledging our utter dependence on God. Prayer attacks our pride at its root. And prayer allows us to access the provision God has promised to those who seek His face.

Today's Growth Principle: Christians who are faithful and diligent in prayer will be strong and effective in God's work.

A Faith that Makes a Difference

Ye are the light of the world. A city that is set on an hill cannot be hid. Neither do men light a candle, and put it under a bushel, but on a candlestick; and it giveth light unto all that are in the house. Let your light so shine before men, that they may see your good works, and glorify your Father which is in heaven.—MATTHEW 5:14–16

As an atheist, British historian and author, Niall Ferguson is not an expected source for kind words about the impact of religion on the world. Yet in his book *Civilization: The West and the Rest,* Ferguson included a revealing statement. He interviewed a member of the Chinese Academy of Social Sciences who told him they had diligently searched for the secret to the growth and influence of Western culture. He said, "We studied everything we could from the historical, political, economic, and cultural perspective. At first, we thought it was because you had more powerful guns than we had. Then we thought it was because you had the best political system. Next we focused on your economic system. But in the past twenty years, we have realized that the heart of your culture is your religion: Christianity. The Christian moral foundation of social and cultural life was what made possible the emergence of capitalism and then the successful transition to democratic politics. We don't have any doubt about this."

Of course many religious groups claim the name of Christianity without actually following what the Word of God teaches. But the impact of the followers of Jesus Christ on the world cannot be denied. That is exactly the way God intends for it to be. Our primary focus is to be on the spiritual and eternal things, but faithfully preaching and practicing the Bible day after day produces major changes in the temporal world as well.

Today's Growth Principle: God has called us to make a powerful impact on those around us by the way in which we live.

Filling a Town with the Truth

And when they had brought them, they set them before the council: and the high priest asked them, Saying, Did not we straitly command you that ye should not teach in this name? and, behold, ye have filled Jerusalem with your doctrine, and intend to bring this man's blood upon us. Then Peter and the other apostles answered and said, We ought to obey God rather than men.—ACTS 5:27-29

The first church in Jerusalem didn't have a lot of things we consider to be essential to a growing and successful church, but what they did have was a group of people who were committed to taking the truth to those around them. Though the church was led by the apostles, men who had spent three years with Jesus and had learned much from Him, it was not just the apostles doing the work. The entire church took responsibility for proclaiming the gospel to Jerusalem. "And daily in the temple, and in every house, they ceased not to teach and preach Jesus Christ" (Acts 5:42).

There is no substitute for talking to people about Jesus. I'm grateful for every means of technology that allows us to reach people in different ways, but we must never confuse the tools or the programs with the message. Those must never be allowed to take precedence over the simple and effective means of testifying to others about what we have experienced and learned from the Word of God.

There are churches all over the country that are surrounded by people who have never received a clear presentation of the gospel. We rightly work, pray, and give to send missionaries around the world, but we must not neglect our own responsibility to reach those close to us at home. If we want to change the world, we must do the work of telling those around us the truth. This is the only way to transform a town.

Today's Growth Principle: The more we tell others about Jesus, the greater an impact we will have on the cities in which we live.

God's Will for Uncertain Times

Wherefore he saith, Awake thou that sleepest, and arise from the dead, and Christ shall give thee light. See then that ye walk circumspectly, not as fools, but as wise, Redeeming the time, because the days are evil. Wherefore be ye not unwise, but understanding what the will of the Lord is.—EPHESIANS 5:14–17

We live in an age of massive technological change and progress. New discoveries and inventions constantly change the way people live. Often with such massive transformation, people assume that they can change things that have long been believed. While error (even if it is a long-held tradition) should always be replaced with truth, there are times when changing the past is not an improvement but represents throwing out uncomfortable truth for pleasing error

There is a great need in this day of change for people who are grounded in the truth and will not be moved. That confidence and stability only comes when we are rooted in the Bible. The church and society both are in desperate need of people who understand God's plan for our world and how to carry it out. Such a level of understanding does not come from our thoughts or philosophies, but from the Divine revelation that has been given to us as a guide for every part of life.

Vance Havner said, "The children of Issachar had understanding of the times and knew what Israel ought to do…(1 Chronicles 12:32). With all the news media of today, there is plenty of knowledge of the times, but little understanding. Such understanding will not be gained from news analysts and political experts. It must be based on God's Word, and it produces a practical knowledge of what God's people ought to do. We must know the times, we must understand them, and we must know what to do."

Today's Growth Principle: Only through the Word of God and the Spirit of God can we gain understanding of God's will for our time.

When Hidden Things Are Revealed

The disciple is not above his master, nor the servant above his lord. It is enough for the disciple that he be as his master, and the servant as his lord. If they have called the master of the house Beelzebub, how much more shall they call them of his household? Fear them not therefore: for there is nothing covered, that shall not be revealed; and hid, that shall not be known.—MATTHEW 10:24–26

One of Edgar Allan Poe's most famous stories is "The Tell-Tale Heart" which describes the effect of conscience and memory on a guilty man. A murderer thinks that he has gotten away with his crime and hidden the evidence, but when the police come to interview him, he begins to think that he hears the beating heart of his victim. When he is certain that the officers must be able to hear it too, he confesses his crime and shows them where the body was hidden.

Ever since the Garden of Eden, man's tendency and temptation has been to conceal sin rather than confess it and deal with the consequences. Although this may be the course that seems best in the short run, God is not deceived or mocked, and the impact of sin only increases the longer it remains hidden. "He that covereth his sins shall not prosper: but whoso confesseth and forsaketh them shall have mercy" (Proverbs 28:13).

God has a way of working to bring hidden things to light, and He will not tolerate our attempts to cling to and cover our sin. Even when we think all of the evidence is concealed, God sees. And of course the best way to live is in obedience. We never have a reason to fear people finding out about sins we don't commit. Will Rogers said, "Live in such a way that you would not be embarrassed to sell the family parrot to the town gossip."

Today's Growth Principle: Rather than attempting to hide sin in your life, confess and forsake it before it is revealed.

Eat with Your Shoes On

And thus shall ye eat it; with your loins girded, your shoes on your feet, and your staff in your hand; and ye shall eat it in haste: it is the LORD's passover. For I will pass through the land of Egypt this night, and will smite all the firstborn in the land of Egypt, both man and beast; and against all the gods of Egypt I will execute judgment: I am the LORD. And the blood shall be to you for a token upon the houses where ye are: and when I see the blood, I will pass over you, and the plague shall not be upon you to destroy you, when I smite the land of Egypt. —EXODUS 12:11–13

The custom in Old Testament times was that meals, especially the evening meal, were leisurely times to spend with family and friends. There was a relaxed atmosphere with the day's work concluded. Shoes would be set aside and feet washed, and then those eating the meal would gather around a low table leaning or reclining while reaching for the food. When God gave Moses the instructions for the Passover, however, He commanded something very different. This meal was to be eaten standing up with shoes on—in a position of readiness—because something important was about to happen.

There is a great picture and reminder for us in that instruction. The events and cares of this world may clamor for and even capture our attention, but there is a sure and certain promise—that one day the Lord will return. It is our duty to be continually living in such a way that we are ready for Him and not ashamed when we see Him. Jesus said, "Watch ye therefore: for ye know not when the master of the house cometh, at even, or at midnight, or at the cockcrowing, or in the morning: Lest coming suddenly he find you sleeping" (Mark 13:35–36). And 1 John 3:3, also speaking of the return of Christ, says, "And every man that hath this hope in him purifieth himself, even as he is pure." Knowing Christ is returning gives us hope and motivation to live in readiness for His return.

Today's Growth Principle: Do not let the pressures of life distract you from the wonderful promise that Jesus is coming again.

The Slavery of Sin

*Put them in mind to be subject to principalities and powers, to obey magistrates, to be ready to every good work, To speak evil of no man, to be no brawlers, but gentle, shewing all meekness unto all men. For we ourselves also were sometimes foolish, disobedient, deceived, serving divers lusts and pleasures, living in malice and envy, hateful, and hating one another.—*TITUS 3:1-3

Before his conversion, John Newton was a profane and violent slave trader. After a confrontation with fellow crew members in 1745, Newton was abandoned in Africa and spent three years as a slave himself—a period which he called being "a servant of slaves." It was after his rescue in 1748 that Newton was converted. He eventually became a powerful preacher and an advocate for the abolition of the slave trade. Newton never forgot his own time in chains.

The Bible describes sin as enslavement. When we read about the horror of slavery, which is not just a relic of the past, but still practiced in many places today, we find it hard to picture a worse way to live. A slave does not have the ability to control his or her own life. The master sets the terms. Of course sin does not present that part of the picture during the temptation. It is only afterward that we realize the fetters that follow violating God's law.

The power of sin cannot be broken apart from a stronger power. On the cross, Jesus purchased not just our salvation but our freedom from sin. Yet too often we volunteer to go back to the chains that should have no power over our lives. "Stand fast therefore in the liberty wherewith Christ hath made us free, and be not entangled again with the yoke of bondage" (Galatians 5:1). Before we were saved, we had no choice, but as believers when we sin, it is because we choose to, not because we have to.

Today's Growth Principle: Having been made free by Christ, we must not return again to the slavery of serving sin.

Willing Workers

So built we the wall; and all the wall was joined together unto the half thereof: for the people had a mind to work. But it came to pass, that when Sanballat, and Tobiah, and the Arabians, and the Ammonites, and the Ashdodites, heard that the walls of Jerusalem were made up, and that the breaches began to be stopped, then they were very wroth, And conspired all of them together to come and to fight against Jerusalem, and to hinder it. Nevertheless we made our prayer unto our God, and set a watch against them day and night, because of them.—NEHEMIAH 4:6–9

Jack Barrymore, an early member of the noted acting dynasty, was a gifted performer, but he was known for being extremely lazy even to the point of not caring for his personal hygiene or appearance. Barrymore was in San Francisco in 1906 when the great earthquake hit, and he took shelter in his hotel room bathtub from the aftershocks. When he finally went outside he was forced into a recovery crew by soldiers sent to help with the disaster recovery effort. After his safe return to New York City, a friend made this rather cutting observation: "It took a convulsion of nature to make Jack take a bath and the United States Army to make him go to work."

The value of hard work may be disappearing from the culture around us, but it is no less important now than it always has been. The Christian who mopes and complains through his job is a poor testimony indeed. Instead we should view work as an opportunity for service to the King. No matter what the task assigned to us may be, it is worthy of our cheerful and diligent labor. It is only when God's people join together and work with willing hearts and minds that we see truly great things accomplished for Him. Our attitude toward work matters a great deal.

Today's Growth Principle: The labor that we do is ultimately for God, not for man, and deserves our cheerful and willing work.

What Are You Worth?

And he bearing his cross went forth into a place called the place of a skull, which is called in the Hebrew Golgotha: Where they crucified him, and two other with him, on either side one, and Jesus in the midst. And Pilate wrote a title, and put it on the cross. And the writing was, JESUS OF NAZARETH THE KING OF THE JEWS.—John 19:17-19

The Romans refined their systems of punishment and execution with an eye toward inflicting maximum pain on the victims. The pinnacle of their work was death by crucifixion, which the historian Josephus called "the most wretched of deaths." It was not uncommon for healthy prisoners to live for two or even three days on the cross in agonizing pain. In fact, the word *excruciating* that we use to describe awful pain literally means "from the cross."

Many people struggle with feelings of worthlessness and inadequacy. But when we properly understand the meaning and purpose of the cross, we understand that we have incredible value. Jesus paid an amazing price for our redemption. The cost of the cross becomes even more astonishing when we reflect that it was part of God's plan before He ever created the world. Revelation 13:8 refers to Jesus as "the Lamb slain from the foundation of the world."

Others may hold us in contempt and think us of no value. (They did with Jesus.) We ourselves may struggle to believe that God loves us. But as long as the cross stands in history and memory, we have a vivid reminder of how God views us. God views us as worthy of a supreme sacrifice. There is no limit to His love, and in the light of that love, we find a value that can never be taken away from us. "Hereby perceive we the love of God, because he laid down his life for us..." (1 John 3:16).

Today's Growth Principle: The cross is a powerful reminder of the depth and meaning of God's love for us.

The God Who Knows You

*O LORD, thou hast searched me, and known me. Thou knowest my downsitting and mine uprising, thou understandest my thought afar off. Thou compassest my path and my lying down, and art acquainted with all my ways. For there is not a word in my tongue, but, lo, O LORD, thou knowest it altogether. Thou hast beset me behind and before, and laid thine hand upon me.—*PSALM 139:1-5

Colton, just four years old, had been working on memorizing the Lord's Prayer. Week after week he heard it in church and said the words along with the adults. But as often happens, he didn't quite grasp all the words. So one Sunday he joined in, saying, "Our Father which art in Heaven, I know You know my name."

God does know our names. He knows everything about us down to the smallest details. Jesus said, "But even the very hairs of your head are all numbered. Fear not therefore: ye are of more value than many sparrows" (Luke 12:7). The intimate knowledge that God has of us is a source of strength and comfort. It frees us from the fear that we have to make our way through this world alone. The same God who has the power to create all things has the knowledge of who we are and where we are and what we need.

There are more than seven billion people living on the Earth today. But that vast number is made up of individuals, each of whom is personally known to God by name. The Bible tells us, "He healeth the broken in heart, and bindeth up their wounds" (Psalm 147:3). He does not look at us as a part of a mass of people, but as a single person worthy of His love and care. Only an infinite God is capable of such a deep level of involvement in the lives of so many people. That is the God we have—a God who knows and calls us by name.

Today's Growth Principle: God is a loving Father who will never abandon, forsake, or forget His children.

When God Has All

And now, Israel, what doth the LORD thy God require of thee, but to fear the LORD thy God, to walk in all his ways, and to love him, and to serve the LORD thy God with all thy heart and with all thy soul, To keep the commandments of the LORD, and his statutes, which I command thee this day for thy good?—DEUTERONOMY 10:12–13

When his evangelistic ministry took him to England, J. Wilbur Chapman was eager to meet with William Booth, the founder of the Salvation Army. Chapman sat and talked with the elderly man about his life and ministry, and then asked Booth why he had been able to accomplish so much for God's kingdom. Booth replied, "I will tell you the secret. God has had all there was of me to have. There have been men with greater opportunities; but from the day I got the poor of London on my heart, and a vision of what Jesus Christ could do, I made up my mind that God would have all there was of William Booth. And if there is anything of power in the Salvation Army today, it is because God has had all the adoration of my heart, all the power of my will, and all the influence of my life."

The Christian who loves God with only part of his heart will never be willing to make the sacrifices and commitment necessary to do great things for Him. When Jesus met Peter after the resurrection, He did not berate the brash disciple for his denial. Instead He focused on the condition of Peter's heart. "So when they had dined, Jesus saith to Simon Peter, Simon, son of Jonas, lovest thou me more than these? He saith unto him, Yea, Lord; thou knowest that I love thee. He saith unto him, Feed my lambs" (John 21:15).

When God has only part of our hearts, we try to "fit Him in" as we can—giving occasional bits of service. But when God has all of our hearts and our wills, then we live all of our lives as a sacrifice for Him.

Today's Growth Principle: If you love God as you should, no sacrifice will be too great to make for His service.

Faith and Worry

Let not your heart be troubled: ye believe in God, believe also in me. In my Father's house are many mansions: if it were not so, I would have told you. I go to prepare a place for you. And if I go and prepare a place for you, I will come again, and receive you unto myself; that where I am, there ye may be also. And whither I go ye know, and the way ye know.
—JOHN 14:1-4

Toward the end of 1943, President Roosevelt, Prime Minister Churchill, and Joseph Stalin were scheduled to meet in Tehran, Iran, to discuss strategy in the war against Germany. As the three leaders prepared for the trip, made even more dangerous by the ongoing war, Roosevelt wrote to Churchill and expressed some concern over the meeting location. He feared that Tehran was in range of German bombers, and they could be subject to attack. Churchill sent back this message: "See St. John chapter 14, verses 1 to 4."

Those nine words, and the truth of the verses Churchill referenced, contain the cure for worry in any situation of life. Our faith is not that nothing will ever go wrong—Jesus spoke these words just hours before He was put to death on the cross—but that God is in control, and our eternal destiny is secure in Him. The more that we believe in God, the less we worry. Troubled hearts reveal that we are not trusting Him as we should.

The reminder that Jesus gave to His disciples just before the crucifixion was that there is more than this world in our future. The burdens and troubles and trials of life are real, but they are temporary. And the God who sees us through them has an eternity prepared for us. Nothing that anyone or anything in this world can do will change that. It is settled and secure according to the unfailing promise of Almighty God.

Today's Growth Principle: Worry vanishes when we remember that God is in control and that we can trust Him.

Every Part Is Needed

Nay, much more those members of the body, which seem to be more feeble, are necessary: And those members of the body, which we think to be less honourable, upon these we bestow more abundant honour; and our uncomely parts have more abundant comeliness. For our comely parts have no need: but God hath tempered the body together, having given more abundant honour to that part which lacked: That there should be no schism in the body; but that the members should have the same care one for another.—1 CORINTHIANS 12:22–25

Michael Costa immigrated to England from Italy in the 1800s and became a noted musician, eventually being knighted by Queen Victoria. Though Costa composed a number of pieces, he became best known as a conductor. In a time when it was common for music to be approached somewhat casually, Costa was noted for his ferocious attention to detail. According to one famous story, as he was conducting an orchestra and choral performance, and the sound of dozens of instruments and voices filled the cathedral, Costa stopped everyone cold. "Where is the piccolo?" he asked. The player had stopped, and the conductor could tell the difference.

Every one of us has a vital role to play in the work of God, and every one of those roles, no matter how large or how small it may appear to be, is important. We live in a society that glorifies the things that are most noticeable, but in truth, without each of the parts, the whole will not be complete. When we are tempted to think that no one will notice if we slack off because our job isn't that important, we must remember that God has designed and equipped each of us for a role no one else can fully play. God's plan for His work calls for us to be faithful to carry out our assigned responsibilities.

Today's Growth Principle: God is looking for people who are faithful to play the role in which He has placed them.

Faith that Makes a Difference

Thou, O king, hast made a decree, that every man that shall hear the sound of the cornet, flute, harp, sackbut, psaltery, and dulcimer, and all kinds of music, shall fall down and worship the golden image: And whoso falleth not down and worshippeth, that he should be cast into the midst of a burning fiery furnace. There are certain Jews whom thou hast set over the affairs of the province of Babylon, Shadrach, Meshach, and Abednego; these men, O king, have not regarded thee: they serve not thy gods, nor worship the golden image which thou hast set up.
—DANIEL 3:10–12

According to a recent Barna Research Group study of people born between 1965 and 2002, most (84 percent) of the people who said they were not Christians knew at least one person who they described as a committed Christian. That seems like a good thing, but the follow-up question revealed that only 15 percent of those people felt like the lifestyle of those they described as Christians was significantly different from anyone else.

That is not the way the Christian life is supposed to work. Someone said that too many Christians today are part of the "secret service." Identifying publicly with Jesus can be dangerous in some countries, and it is increasingly unacceptable in polite society to be a committed Christian. But it is only when we become truly committed to Christ that we can accomplish something meaningful. "And after this Joseph of Arimathaea, being a disciple of Jesus, but secretly for fear of the Jews, besought Pilate that he might take away the body of Jesus: and Pilate gave him leave. He came therefore, and took the body of Jesus" (John 19:38).

The approval that should matter most to us is not that of our peers or contemporaries, but that of God. He sees each time we take a stand for Him. He knows if our faith is making a real difference.

Today's Growth Principle: Taking a stand for Jesus is worth it, no matter what the cost may be.

Psalms 40–42   //   Acts 27:1–26   217

Using Whatever We Have

And Jesus said, Let her alone; why trouble ye her? she hath wrought a good work on me. For ye have the poor with you always, and whensoever ye will ye may do them good: but me ye have not always. She hath done what she could: she is come aforehand to anoint my body to the burying. Verily I say unto you, Wheresoever this gospel shall be preached throughout the whole world, this also that she hath done shall be spoken of for a memorial of her.—MARK 14:6–9

Critics of D. L. Moody were quick to point out that his messages, while biblical and passionate, were hardly models of proper use of the English language. The story goes that after one sermon, a man came up to Moody and said, "By the way, I noticed that you made eleven mistakes in grammar in your sermon tonight."

"That is very likely," replied Mr. Moody. "I don't doubt it for a minute. My early education was faulty. I often wish that I had received more schooling. But I am using all the grammar I know in the service of Christ. How is it with you?"

It is easy for us to criticize others for perceived flaws in the way they live for and serve God, but that is the wrong focus. "Who art thou that judgest another man's servant? to his own master he standeth or falleth. Yea, he shall be holden up: for God is able to make him stand" (Romans 14:4). Rather than condemning those who we feel do not measure up, we *should* be concerned with whether we are maximizing the gifts God has given to us to accomplish the most for Him.

The measure God uses to evaluate our work is whether we have done all that we could, not how much we are capable of doing. It is a sin to waste the talents we have been given.

Today's Growth Principle: There may be people more talented than you, but there do not have to be people more committed than you.

God Uses People

Come now therefore, and I will send thee unto Pharaoh, that thou mayest bring forth my people the children of Israel out of Egypt. And Moses said unto God, Who am I, that I should go unto Pharaoh, and that I should bring forth the children of Israel out of Egypt? And he said, Certainly I will be with thee; and this shall be a token unto thee, that I have sent thee: When thou hast brought forth the people out of Egypt, ye shall serve God upon this mountain.—EXODUS 3:10–12

When the time came for God to deliver Israel from bondage in Egypt and take them back to the land He had promised to Abraham, He appeared to Moses in the bush that burned but was not destroyed.

Forty years earlier, Moses had expected to be recognized and accepted as the leader of the Israelites but instead had to flee for his life and had then spent four decades in the desert tending to sheep. That was a far cry from the luxury he had enjoyed in the palace of Pharaoh. It was this now-humbled man whom God chose to bring about a great deliverance.

God did not need Moses' help. He could have sent a single angel to overthrow all the armies of Egypt. He could have appeared in His glory and escorted Israel to the Promised Land. But God always uses people for His work in the world. He doesn't use perfect people, because there aren't any of those. Dr. Bob Jones, Sr. liked to say, "God can hit mighty straight licks with crooked sticks."

When we accept God's calling and undertake His work, He equips us and goes with us so that we have all that we need to do whatever He asks. It is a privilege and an honor to be commissioned by God. He doesn't need us, but He graciously uses us—and then rewards our faithful obedience, which He enabled.

Today's Growth Principle: Never shrink from taking on an assignment God places before you—He will enable you to do it.

The Great Hope of Our Future

And he took up his parable, and said, Balaam the son of Beor hath said, and the man whose eyes are open hath said: He hath said, which heard the words of God, and knew the knowledge of the most High, which saw the vision of the Almighty, falling into a trance, but having his eyes open: I shall see him, but not now: I shall behold him, but not nigh: there shall come a Star out of Jacob, and a Sceptre shall rise out of Israel, and shall smite the corners of Moab, and destroy all the children of Sheth.
—NUMBERS 24:15–17

After recovering from a serious illness on a sea voyage late in his life, the famed poet Alfred, Lord Tennyson began to think more and more about eternity. Reflecting on the future he penned these lines:

> Sunset and evening star,
> And one clear call for me!
> And may there be no moaning of the bar,
> When I put out to sea.
> For though from out our bourne of Time and Place
> The flood may bear me far,
> I hope to see my Pilot face to face
> When I have crossed the bar.

This world is temporary and fleeting. There are many sorrows and pains that accompany life. And at the end looms the darkness of death. But for the Christian there is more—there is the promise that Jesus is waiting, and that we will see His face when this life has ended. For the Christian, death still may bring pain and sorrow, but it is different than that which is experienced by the world. "But I would not have you to be ignorant, brethren, concerning them which are asleep, that ye sorrow not, even as others which have no hope" (1 Thessalonians 4:13).

Today's Growth Principle: The promise of entering Jesus' presence takes away all fear of death for the believer.

Godly Determination

And he said, Take the arrows. And he took them. And he said unto the king of Israel, Smite upon the ground. And he smote thrice, and stayed. And the man of God was wroth with him, and said, Thou shouldest have smitten five or six times; then hadst thou smitten Syria till thou hadst consumed it: whereas now thou shalt smite Syria but thrice.
—2 KINGS 13:18–19

Some years ago, the Wall Street Journal ran a story in the humor column that was something like this: A man sitting on his porch noticed his teenage son leaving the house carrying a guitar, a pick, and a shovel. Somewhat taken aback, he asked, "What are you doing, son?" The young man replied, "My girlfriend asked me to come over and serenade her." His father said, "That's a nice thing to do. What are the pick and shovel for?" "Oh," the teen said, "She wanted me to sing to her from underneath her window, and her family lives in the basement!"

Commitment can overcome obstacles. When we *want* to do what is right, not as a convenience or a whim, but as a commitment, we do not worry about the obstacles. We don't care if others refuse to join in. We don't mind if the results are slow in coming. We just keep on until we have reached the goal and achieved what God has called us to do. Many people start out well, but only do part of the task before becoming discouraged or distracted.

The only way to accomplish great things for God is to stay at the work. No matter how long it takes or how hard it is, if we are doing what is right, we must remain faithful. Most great achievements are not the result of a few spectacular moments of public effort, but instead come from patient and diligent work that continued on and on in the face of obstacles and opposition.

Today's Growth Principle: God is looking for people who are fully committed and will not quit until the job is done.

God's Way or Our Own?

Unto thee, O LORD, do I lift up my soul. O my God, I trust in thee: let me not be ashamed, let not mine enemies triumph over me. Yea, let none that wait on thee be ashamed: let them be ashamed which transgress without cause. Shew me thy ways, O LORD; teach me thy paths. Lead me in thy truth, and teach me: for thou art the God of my salvation; on thee do I wait all the day.—PSALM 25:1–5

We live in a society that glorifies self-guidance. Those who go their own way are often held up as heroes, despite the fact that such a path often leads to pain if not complete destruction. Christians are just as subject to this temptation as those around us. We look for "loopholes" and ways to make the Bible say what we want it to say so that we can do what we want to do. All kinds of sin are justified from verses taken out of context and doctrines constructed out of thin air.

Rather than trying to force our will on the Word of God, we should take it as is and ask the Holy Spirit to help us rightly understand and apply it to our lives. Charles Spurgeon wrote, "It were well for many professors if instead of following their own devices, and cutting out new paths of thought for themselves, they would enquire for the good old ways of God's own truth, and beseech the Holy Ghost to give them… teachable spirits."

There are only two ways available—our own way and God's way. Those who insist on setting their own course in opposition to God's plan and wise advice from others can have it, but only at great cost. This is why Proverbs 5:11–13 warns us to listen to God's instructions so that we don't come to the place where we "…mourn at the last, when thy flesh and thy body are consumed, And say, How have I hated instruction, and my heart despised reproof; And have not obeyed the voice of my teachers, nor inclined mine ear to them that instructed me!"

Today's Growth Principle: Wisdom seeks to learn and apply the truths of Scripture rather than getting its own way.

AUGUST

The Doors God Closes

Now when they had gone throughout Phrygia and the region of Galatia,
and were forbidden of the Holy Ghost to preach the word in Asia, After
they were come to Mysia, they assayed to go into Bithynia: but the Spirit
suffered them not. And they passing by Mysia came down to Troas. And
a vision appeared to Paul in the night; There stood a man of Macedonia,
and prayed him, saying, Come over into Macedonia, and help us.
—ACTS 16:6–9

Frederick Robertson had his life planned out. He expected to enter the British Army and become an officer just as his father had been. He grew up in forts and army headquarters and loved watching the soldiers drill and prepare for battle. But his hopes were bitterly dashed when, despite an excellent academic record, he was left off the list for commissioning of new officers. Instead Robertson went to Oxford and trained for the ministry. He became a pastor in Brighton, England, for many years, and he touched the lives of many. God had a different position in mind for Frederick Robertson.

Often our plans do not coincide with what God has in mind, and He steps in to direct us toward a different path. It is vital that we view these setbacks properly. Some people become bitter and disillusioned when God closes a door that they wanted opened. Yet His wisdom and knowledge far exceed our own, and He knows what is best both for our lives and for His work. We must be willingly submitted to the direction of God, even when it is not what we would prefer.

It is easy for us to trust God when things are going well. And it is not difficult to accept a closed door if we readily see an alternate path before us. Real faith trusts God even when the closed door seems final and no other open door seems helpful. He knows what is best, and we must trust His plan.

Today's Growth Principle: Trusting God even when we do not understand His plan is the essence of faith.

Don't Go Too Far

*And Moses said, It is not meet so to do; for we shall sacrifice the abomination of the Egyptians to the LORD our God: lo, shall we sacrifice the abomination of the Egyptians before their eyes, and will they not stone us? We will go three days' journey into the wilderness, and sacrifice to the LORD our God, as he shall command us. And Pharaoh said, I will let you go, that ye may sacrifice to the LORD your God in the wilderness; only ye shall not go very far away: intreat for me.—*EXODUS 8:26–28

When the plagues God sent to Pharaoh began to inflict serious hardship on Egypt, Pharaoh tried to bargain with Moses. He would let the Israelites worship God, but he didn't want them to leave the land. He offered Moses a compromise, insisting that the people "shall not go very far away." This is an offer that Satan makes time and again to God's people to try to derail them from effective service. He counsels us to serve God, but not to take things too far.

Christians who are on fire for God and are willing to commit their lives to His service will certainly be viewed as strange. If we truly believe what God says and act upon it with our whole hearts, it should not be surprising if the world thinks we have lost our minds. This was the experience Paul had when he was offered the opportunity to defend himself before a Roman governor and shared his testimony as well as God's plan of salvation. "And as he thus spake for himself, Festus said with a loud voice, Paul, thou art beside thyself; much learning doth make thee mad" (Acts 26:24).

God is worthy of our complete and total devotion and obedience. We are commanded to love Him above all else. We are called to give ourselves to His service, even to the point of laying down our lives if necessary. What God commands is never "too far."

Today's Growth Principle: Do not listen to the voices that tempt you to offer half-hearted or partial service to God.

Change the Seeds to Change the Harvest

Sow to yourselves in righteousness, reap in mercy; break up your fallow ground: for it is time to seek the LORD, till he come and rain righteousness upon you. Ye have plowed wickedness, ye have reaped iniquity; ye have eaten the fruit of lies: because thou didst trust in thy way, in the multitude of thy mighty men. Therefore shall a tumult arise among thy people, and all thy fortresses shall be spoiled, as Shalman spoiled Betharbel in the day of battle: the mother was dashed in pieces upon her children.
—HOSEA 10:12–14

California is one of the great agricultural regions of the world. Billions of dollars worth of fruit and vegetables that are grown in our state are shipped across the country and around the world, feeding millions of people. Every farmer knows exactly what crop he is going to harvest. Although he does not know how much rain will fall, how hot the sun will be, or whether his harvest will be excellent, average, or poor, he does know what he will be harvesting, because he knows what he planted.

God has ordered and established the world from creation with the principle of sowing. "And God said, Let the earth bring forth grass, the herb yielding seed, and the fruit tree yielding fruit after his kind, whose seed is in itself, upon the earth: and it was so" (Genesis 1:11). Every harvest is determined by the seed.

Many people do not like the painful harvest that follows sin and disobedience, but they are unwilling to plant righteousness. There is no alternative plan available. You will reap whatever you choose to sow. Every person who laments the bitter harvest of evil consequences that follows wicked living has only himself to blame. Likewise those who plant obedience can confidently expect blessing to follow.

Today's Growth Principle: The only place we can make an effective choice of what we will harvest is when we choose what seeds we will plant.

The Blessing of Brokenness

When thou criest, let thy companies deliver thee; but the wind shall carry them all away; vanity shall take them: but he that putteth his trust in me shall possess the land, and shall inherit my holy mountain; And shall say, Cast ye up, cast ye up, prepare the way, take up the stumblingblock out of the way of my people. For thus saith the high and lofty One that inhabiteth eternity, whose name is Holy; I dwell in the high and holy place, with him also that is of a contrite and humble spirit, to revive the spirit of the humble, and to revive the heart of the contrite ones.
—ISAIAH 57:13–15

By nature we want to be lifted up. It has been that way ever since the Fall of man. We want to be admired and respected and self-sufficient. But while we certainly should live in a way that is respectable, if our focus and motivation is the praise and applause of men, we will forfeit the power and blessing of God. "But he giveth more grace. Wherefore he saith, God resisteth the proud, but giveth grace unto the humble" (James 4:6).

When we reach the end of ourselves, we have the opportunity to go to our Lord in humility and seek His grace and help. Andrew Murray said, "Just as water ever seeks and fills the lowest place, so the moment God finds you abased and empty, His glory and power flow in." The things that create empty places in our lives—defeats, disappointments, losses, setbacks, and brokenness—are an enormous opportunity if we use them properly.

Sometimes people respond with anger or bitterness, but other times they turn to God. It is in those moments when we are least filled with self that we can see His power fully revealed. Scripture and church history are filled with people who did great things for God in the midst of great pain and hardship because they took their brokenness to God.

Today's Growth Principle: We must be emptied of self before we can be filled with God's grace and power.

The Real Choice We Face

Know ye not, that to whom ye yield yourselves servants to obey, his servants ye are to whom ye obey; whether of sin unto death, or of obedience unto righteousness? But God be thanked, that ye were the servants of sin, but ye have obeyed from the heart that form of doctrine which was delivered you. Being then made free from sin, ye became the servants of righteousness.—ROMANS 6:16–18

One of the most effective deceptions practiced by Satan is to convince people that they have a choice to be completely free in the world—making their own decisions and going their own way. This lie has led countless people to destruction. The truth is that every person born into this world is a servant to something. The only freedom we have is in the choice of what we will serve. By the power of God through the gospel, we are offered the choice to serve righteousness rather than sin. But if we do not exercise that choice, even as believers, we will live in bondage to sin.

The illusion of freedom is quickly shattered once the consequences of sin begin to appear. The fleeting pleasures of sin are quickly replaced by chains and bondage. The harvest of the seeds that we sow cannot be avoided. The choice that leads to freedom from God's service inevitably leads to bondage to Satan. The choice that leads to freedom from sin places us in binding service to God.

Consider the Prodigal Son. When he left his home for the far country, he thought he was moving toward freedom. He would leave behind his father's rules and live as he chose. Instead he found himself with the dirty job of feeding pigs—and being so hungry he was coveting what they ate. That is the path we choose when we decide to pursue freedom by throwing off the "shackles" of God's requirements. It only leads to slavery and suffering.

Today's Growth Principle: There is no true freedom apart from choosing to serve God and righteousness in this world.

Guard Who Influences You

Blessed is the man that walketh not in the counsel of the ungodly, nor standeth in the way of sinners, nor sitteth in the seat of the scornful. But his delight is in the law of the LORD; and in his law doth he meditate day and night. And he shall be like a tree planted by the rivers of water, that bringeth forth his fruit in his season; his leaf also shall not wither; and whatsoever he doeth shall prosper.—PSALM 1:1-3

It is no surprise when liberal professors of religion deny the truth of God's Word. We have come to expect it from what are regarded as the leading educational institutions in our country, despite the fact that some of those very schools were founded with the primary purpose to train preachers for the ministry. So when someone like Bart Ehrman, who teaches at the University of North Carolina said, "God, if He exists, cannot be Jesus Christ, or the God of the Bible" Christians are not shocked. What is shocking is that Ehrman grew up in church and described himself as a "born-again fundamentalist" at one point in his life. Whether or not he had been truly born again, I cannot know. But I do know that during his college and graduate training that his faith was undermined by the attacks of his professors, and today Ehrman calls himself an agnostic atheist.

There is no faith so strong that it cannot be overwhelmed if the influences in our lives all work to undermine that faith. We can keep faith in hostile cultures that speak out and work against it—just as men like Joseph and Daniel did—but we cannot keep faith if we allow those negative influences to direct our lives. No matter how gifted a teacher may be, if he does not believe the truth, he will not influence you toward God. As our society becomes more anti-Christian than ever, it is vitally important that we listen most to those who believe and speak the truth.

Today's Growth Principle: Be extremely careful about those you allow to influence your heart and your mind.

How to Find the Truth

Then on that day David delivered first this psalm to thank the LORD into the hand of Asaph and his brethren. Give thanks unto the LORD, call upon his name, make known his deeds among the people. Sing unto him, sing psalms unto him, talk ye of all his wondrous works. Glory ye in his holy name: let the heart of them rejoice that seek the LORD. Seek the LORD and his strength, seek his face continually.—1 CHRONICLES 16:7-11

One of the noted early philosophers of ancient Greece was Diogenes, who was a founder of the Cynics. Diogenes delighted in challenging the assumptions and sloppy thinking of others. When Plato's famous Academy defined humans as "featherless bipeds," Diogenes took them a plucked chicken and argued they should consider it a man. Perhaps his most famous act was carrying a lighted lantern through the streets and markets of Athens during the daytime. When asked what he was doing, Diogenes is said to have replied, "I am looking for an honest man."

Most people are looking for truth and honesty in others, but we recognize it as a rare commodity in our world. Many of us know what it is like to be disappointed by someone we trusted, when it turned out the faith we placed in what we were told did not have a solid foundation. The proper response to these disappointments is not to become cynical, but to seek God more.

David knew what it was like to be falsely accused, betrayed, and lied about. He knew what it was like to have the very people he had delivered from certain death turn against him. He also knew that God is an unfailing source of truth. So David focused on seeking help and hope from God. He knew God's faithfulness could always be trusted. God is complete truth, and there is no deceit within His nature.

Today's Growth Principle: Those who trust in God and seek His face are never abandoned and never let down.

Only One Door to Heaven

Verily, verily, I say unto you, He that entereth not by the door into the sheepfold, but climbeth up some other way, the same is a thief and a robber. But he that entereth in by the door is the shepherd of the sheep. To him the porter openeth; and the sheep hear his voice: and he calleth his own sheep by name, and leadeth them out.—JOHN 10:1-3

The most important question every individual must answer is the question that determines his or her eternal destiny. Despite what many in our day teach and promote, God has clearly declared that there is only one way to Heaven. There are not many paths all leading in the same general direction that eventually get everyone to the right destination. The only way that we can be justified in the sight of God and be cleansed of the sin that separates us from God is to accept in faith the sacrifice of Jesus Christ on the cross on our behalf. Many people fail to receive salvation because, while they believe that Jesus is important, they also wrongly think that they have to be part of the process by doing something to deserve or earn their salvation. They think perhaps Jesus opened the way to Heaven and now it is up to them to take all the steps to get there. But Scripture teaches us that Jesus *is* the door—not that He merely opened the door.

Dr. Curtis Hutson put it this way: "I am a church member. I have been baptized. I try to live right. I have been preaching since I was twenty years old. I travel every week of my life going from church to church throughout this country to preach the gospel. But I do none of these things to be saved. My only hope of Heaven is the fact that Jesus Christ died for me. He paid my sin debt. I am trusting Him alone for salvation. I am not trusting my good works, my church membership, my baptism, or anything else. When we stand before God, the only thing that He will count is what His Son did at Calvary."

Today's Growth Principle: Salvation is only found in Christ alone, and anything we try to add to His gift keeps us from truly receiving it.

Getting Serious about God

Then shall ye call upon me, and ye shall go and pray unto me, and I will hearken unto you. And ye shall seek me, and find me, when ye shall search for me with all your heart. And I will be found of you, saith the LORD: *and I will turn away your captivity, and I will gather you from all the nations, and from all the places whither I have driven you, saith the* LORD; *and I will bring you again into the place whence I caused you to be carried away captive.*—JEREMIAH 29:12–14

There are many resources and teachings available for Christians on the subjects of growing in grace and becoming closer to God. I'm thankful for all the ones that are faithful to the Bible and encourage good habits and correct doctrine. But in truth this is not a difficult subject to understand—the difficulty is in the execution, not the education. The bottom line of our Christian life is determined by the direction in which our hearts are pointed. If the heart is not fixed on God, other things will intervene to draw us away from Him.

A. W. Tozer said, "Come near to the holy men and women of the past, and you will soon feel the heat of their desire after God. They mourned for Him, they prayed and wrestled and sought for Him day and night, in season and out; and when they had found Him, the finding was all the sweeter for the long seeking...Complacency is a deadly foe of all spiritual growth."

We do not have to rely on our own strength to fix our hearts on God. He enables and equips us to seek Him as He commands. "A new heart also will I give you, and a new spirit will I put within you: and I will take away the stony heart out of your flesh, and I will give you an heart of flesh" (Ezekiel 36:26).

Today's Growth Principle: Seeking to follow God partially is doomed to failure—complacency never brings you close to God.

Saved Already

Be not thou therefore ashamed of the testimony of our Lord, nor of me his prisoner: but be thou partaker of the afflictions of the gospel according to the power of God; Who hath saved us, and called us with an holy calling, not according to our works, but according to his own purpose and grace, which was given us in Christ Jesus before the world began, But is now made manifest by the appearing of our Saviour Jesus Christ, who hath abolished death, and hath brought life and immortality to light through the gospel:—2 TIMOTHY 1:8-10

Salvation is not something that we will get when we die or when the Lord returns—it is already ours from the moment that we place our faith in Christ as our Saviour. Charles Spurgeon wrote, "Believers in Christ Jesus are saved. They are not looked upon as persons who are in a hopeful state, and may ultimately be saved, but they are already saved. Salvation is not a blessing to be enjoyed upon the dying bed, and to be sung of in a future state above, but a matter to be obtained, received, promised, and enjoyed now."

So many people live with doubts and uncertainty concerning their salvation. They worry about whether or not they are truly saved, or wonder if they might lose their salvation. God does not want us to live beset by doubt and fear. He not only saves us, but He wants us to know it for certain. "These things have I written unto you that believe on the name of the Son of God; that ye may know that ye have eternal life, and that ye may believe on the name of the Son of God" (1 John 5:13). The Christian who lives without confidence in his salvation will not be an effective worker and witness for the Lord. The devil delights in doubt, but He cannot take away what God has already given.

Today's Growth Principle: If you have put your faith in Christ as your Saviour, live in the glorious assurance and confidence offered to you as a child of God saved by His grace.

The Importance of Walls

The words of Nehemiah the son of Hachaliah. And it came to pass in the month Chisleu, in the twentieth year, as I was in Shushan the palace, That Hanani, one of my brethren, came, he and certain men of Judah; and I asked them concerning the Jews that had escaped, which were left of the captivity, and concerning Jerusalem. And they said unto me, The remnant that are left of the captivity there in the province are in great affliction and reproach: the wall of Jerusalem also is broken down, and the gates thereof are burned with fire.—NEHEMIAH 1:1–3

In ancient times, before airplanes and artillery, a city's greatest defense against attacking invaders was the height and thickness of its walls. The walls that the great king Nebuchadnezzar had built around his capital city of Babylon were massive. The ancient Greek historian Herotodus said they were eighty feet thick and that chariot races were held on the top of the walls where everyone could watch the competitors from the city below. A city that had no walls had little hope of holding off an enemy army that came against them.

Though such walls no longer offer defense against modern military technology, they are a wonderful metaphor for the Christian life. We need guards and barriers to keep us safe from the attacks of Satan. These walls are not primarily external, but internal. The greatest damage done to our lives and character comes from within. This is why Scripture emphasizes guarding our *hearts*. "Keep thy heart with all diligence; for out of it are the issues of life" (Proverbs 4:23).

The old saying goes, "Eternal vigilance is the price of liberty." This is just as true in the spiritual realm as it is in the physical realm. The devil doesn't take days off. We must maintain our diligence and caution to avoid sin.

Today's Growth Principle: Maintaining our purity and our testimony requires diligent and careful guarding of the walls of our hearts.

Serious Praying

In the third year of Cyrus king of Persia a thing was revealed unto Daniel, whose name was called Belteshazzar; and the thing was true, but the time appointed was long: and he understood the thing, and had understanding of the vision. In those days I Daniel was mourning three full weeks. I ate no pleasant bread, neither came flesh nor wine in my mouth, neither did I anoint myself at all, till three whole weeks were fulfilled. —DANIEL 10:1–3

If we are honest, we must admit that a vast majority of the prayers offered, both in our churches and in private are surface prayers. They follow the accepted forms and use the language to which we have grown accustomed, but there is little fervent intensity in praying. We are greatly blessed, especially here in America, with both more freedom than Christians have enjoyed through the centuries and more material blessings. As a result, we sometimes fail to depend on God and become self-reliant. This has a definite impact on the way we pray.

If we recognized that even with prosperity and freedom abounding we are still utterly reliant on God's help for every part of life, our prayers would change. Rather than casually going down a prayer list, we would pour out our hearts to God, pleading for His help and asking Him to work in and through our lives in a mighty way. That kind of praying doesn't just change us—it changes everything around us. "And when they had prayed, the place was shaken where they were assembled together; and they were all filled with the Holy Ghost, and they spake the word of God with boldness" (Acts 4:31).

We have been given access to a resource beyond human limits or even human understanding. God's power and resources have been offered to us to do His work if we will but ask for them. Yet too often we do not pray seriously.

Today's Growth Principle: The more seriously we regard and practice prayer, the more powerfully we see God work.

Busy or Productive?

Now when he had left speaking, he said unto Simon, Launch out into the deep, and let down your nets for a draught. And Simon answering said unto him, Master, we have toiled all the night, and have taken nothing: nevertheless at thy word I will let down the net. And when they had this done, they inclosed a great multitude of fishes: and their net brake.
—LUKE 5:4–6

Because of the huge crowd that came to hear Jesus preach, He borrowed Peter's boat and stood in it while the people gathered on the shore. The water naturally carried the sound of His voice and ensured that the people could hear what Jesus said. When He was done with His message, Jesus had a plan to repay Peter, a commercial fisherman, for the use of his boat—a great haul of fish. Peter pointed out that despite working the entire night, he and his brother had nothing to show for it. This was not merely a frustration of a hobby, but rather it was a major problem for a man who made his living catching fish. Peter needed results, not just activity.

Most of us know the feeling of working all day without getting anything done. There is no benefit in being busy alone. The answer for productivity in our lives is the same as it was for Peter—when God steps in, everything changes.

Too many times we labor in our own strength, attempting to accomplish that which can only be done through divine enabling. R. A. Torrey said, "We are too busy to pray, and so we are too busy to have power. We have a great deal of activity but accomplish little. We have many services but few results." God wants us to work hard, but He expects us to do that work in dependence on Him. He is the one who transforms our work into a harvest.

Today's Growth Principle: Before we labor, we must seek God's face and God's power so that our work will be productive.

The Promise of Power

And he said unto them, It is not for you to know the times or the seasons, which the Father hath put in his own power. But ye shall receive power, after that the Holy Ghost is come upon you: and ye shall be witnesses unto me both in Jerusalem, and in all Judaea, and in Samaria, and unto the uttermost part of the earth.—ACTS 1:7–8

One of the biggest trade shows in the world is the annual Consumer Electronics Show hosted by the Consumer Technology Association each year in Las Vegas. More than 180,000 people browse booths filled with the latest gadgets, tools, and toys put on display by hundreds of vendors. The show in January of 2018 featured an unusual and unwelcome interruption—the electricity went out for more than two hours. Without power, none of the devices worked, no matter how advanced and how cutting edge they were.

The Christian life and our work for God depend on power, and that power does not come from us. The instruction that Jesus gave to His disciples was to not attempt to begin their work until they had received the promised power. "And, being assembled together with them, commanded them that they should not depart from Jerusalem, but wait for the promise of the Father, which, saith he, ye have heard of me" (Acts 1:4). There are many sincere, dedicated, and devoted people who are not seeing fruit in their lives or service because they are not operating in God's power.

The Holy Spirit is given to every believer at the moment of salvation. But there is an ongoing process of allowing His power to flow through us: "And be not drunk with wine, wherein is excess; but be filled with the Spirit" (Ephesians 5:18). There is no shortage of power on God's end. His "transmission lines" never go down.

Today's Growth Principle: Effective work and ministry can only be accomplished through the power of the Holy Spirit on our lives.

Being Shocked at Sin

Then were assembled unto me every one that trembled at the words of the God of Israel, because of the transgression of those that had been carried away; and I sat astonied until the evening sacrifice. And at the evening sacrifice I arose up from my heaviness; and having rent my garment and my mantle, I fell upon my knees, and spread out my hands unto the LORD my God, And said, O my God, I am ashamed and blush to lift up my face to thee, my God: for our iniquities are increased over our head, and our trespass is grown up unto the heavens.—EZRA 9:4–6

One of the greatest dangers of sin is the way in which we slowly and subtly become accustomed to it. When there is sin all around us, as is true in our day, it is easy for us to stop thinking that it is shocking and horrible. Alexander Pope wrote:

> Vice is a monster of so frightful mien
> As to be hated needs but to be seen;
> Yet seen too oft, familiar with her face,
> We first endure, then pity, then embrace.

Sin is still just as wicked as ever, no matter how much of it there is or how accepted it may become by society. When Ezra returned from Babylon to teach the Jewish people the law of God, he found that they had ignored the commandments God had given Israel concerning marrying those who worshipped false gods. This practice was widespread and had become culturally acceptable. But it was shocking to Ezra who had committed his life to live by God's law and to teach that law to others.

Because he refused to accept or downplay or normalize sin, Ezra was able to lead the people to repentance and revival. One of the great needs of our day is Christians who are shocked and appalled by sin.

Today's Growth Principle: If we find sin acceptable in the lives of others, it will not be long before we find it acceptable in ourselves as well.

Letting Go of Sin

And this was known to all the Jews and Greeks also dwelling at Ephesus; and fear fell on them all, and the name of the Lord Jesus was magnified. And many that believed came, and confessed, and shewed their deeds. Many of them also which used curious arts brought their books together, and burned them before all men: and they counted the price of them, and found it fifty thousand pieces of silver. So mightily grew the word of God and prevailed.—ACTS 19:17–20

One of the most effective churches established by Paul on his missionary travels was the church at Ephesus. Though the city was a center of idolatry and the worship of Diana, the power of God touched many hearts, and Jews and Gentiles alike responded to the gospel message. According to some historical records, among the pastors of this great church were the Apostle John, Timothy, and Onesimus, the runaway slave Paul led to Christ while imprisoned in Rome.

Part of the effectiveness of the church in Ephesus was their commitment to addressing their own sin completely. When the believers came together there, they did not downplay their past lives. They identified their sins and confessed them. Then they took the remnants of their past lives—the books that contained information about the demonic worship of idols—and publicly burned them. They left no trace behind of the former things. They did not try to hold on to the parts that "weren't so bad" but rather completely gave them up.

The belief that we can leave a little bit of sin in a few hidden corners of our lives without it impacting the rest is a deadly lie from Satan. The only cure for sin is complete eradication of the practices, habits, and tools that facilitated it in our lives. The power of God offers us freedom from sin, but we must completely leave sin behind to live in that freedom.

Today's Growth Principle: Like the roots of a weed, any tiny vestige of sin we leave in our hearts will sprout new growth.

The Reasonable Service of Sacrifice

I beseech you therefore, brethren, by the mercies of God, that ye present your bodies a living sacrifice, holy, acceptable unto God, which is your reasonable service. And be not conformed to this world: but be ye transformed by the renewing of your mind, that ye may prove what is that good, and acceptable, and perfect, will of God.—ROMANS 12:1-2

I read about a missionary in Central America who was preparing to retire after many years of fruitful service in the poor mountain villages. Those whose lives she had touched wanted to hold a celebration to honor her, so word went from town to town to come together on a certain day for a farewell event. When the missionary arrived, she saw an elderly man who had walked four days from his remote home to get there, bringing the only gift he could afford—two coconuts. When she expressed her surprise that he had traveled so far, the man replied, "The long walk was part of the gift."

The right attitude toward serving God should never be frustration or the feeling that the cost of service is too high. What was the cost of our salvation? Nothing less than the precious blood of the very Son of God. In light of the incredible mercy we have received, it cannot be unreasonable for us to make any sacrifice God calls on us to make for Him. The reality is that God does not need our help to accomplish His purposes—He graciously allows us to be part of His work, using the gifts and power He provides. There are some who resent or complain about the cost of serving God. This reveals a lack of understanding and gratitude for the grace and mercy received from our loving Father in Heaven. If we truly recognize and appreciate what we have been given, it will be easy for us to sacrificially serve the Lord.

Today's Growth Principle: Because of His grace freely given, nothing that God asks of us for His service is too much to be reasonable.

Breathing Underwater

Knowing that he which raised up the Lord Jesus shall raise up us also by Jesus, and shall present us with you. For all things are for your sakes, that the abundant grace might through the thanksgiving of many redound to the glory of God. For which cause we faint not; but though our outward man perish, yet the inward man is renewed day by day.
—2 CORINTHIANS 4:14–16

Fish have gills which allow them to separate the oxygen from the water in which they swim, but humans have no such apparatus and can only stay underwater for short periods of time. In the late 1800s, large bulky systems to provide oxygen for divers began to be used, mostly for salvage and underwater construction operations. The modern idea of diving for pleasure took longer to develop. In 1952, a Major in the United States Army, Christian Lambertsen, received a patent for an idea for a re-breathing system he had developed for use during World War II. The name which we still use today, scuba, is an acronym for the description of the device: self contained underwater breathing apparatus.

The reason that a diver can stay underwater for lengthy periods of time is that he takes an air supply with him. As Christians we are surrounded by a hostile environment in the world. We cannot "breathe" in those surroundings. But we have been given a source of strength and power within that allows us to function with power and victory even though we are operating in enemy territory. "For whatsoever is born of God overcometh the world: and this is the victory that overcometh the world, even our faith" (1 John 5:4). The ocean outside a diver's face plate is hostile but unable to harm him as long as the system works properly and he does not allow water inside. The air flows freely from the tank into his lungs. We have the Holy Spirit of God to give us victory over the world. We live in the world, but should remember that it is not our home.

Today's Growth Principle: The world outside our hearts cannot derail us unless we let it inside our hearts.

Clinging to Temporary Things

Love not the world, neither the things that are in the world. If any man love the world, the love of the Father is not in him. For all that is in the world, the lust of the flesh, and the lust of the eyes, and the pride of life, is not of the Father, but is of the world. And the world passeth away, and the lust thereof: but he that doeth the will of God abideth for ever.
—1 JOHN 2:15–17

Lot should never have been in Sodom in the first place, and the only reason he survived God's judgment on that sinful city was because of Abraham's intercession and God's mercy. In the end, the angels took Lot, his wife, and their two unmarried daughters out of the town before the brimstone fell. But though their physical bodies may have changed locations, that did not change the things they loved and valued. Lot's wife left only with the greatest reluctance, because she loved what she was leaving behind, sinful though it was—and it cost her everything. "But his wife looked back from behind him, and she became a pillar of salt" (Genesis 19:26).

The world attempts to draw our attention and allure our hearts away from God. It is filled with temptations that draw us toward sin and appeal to our fallen appetites. Yet even though we know this is true, it is hard for us to not be drawn into evil. Too many Christians sin because they are in love with the things of the world, so they rationalize bad behavior and cling to evil when they should instead be clinging to God and what is right and good. Author David Wells wrote, "Worldliness is what any particular culture does to make sin look normal and righteousness look strange." The snares placed around us have no power if we love our Father in Heaven and focus on what is eternal instead.

Today's Growth Principle: Because this world is temporary, falling for the lies of sin leads to destruction rather than lasting joy.

Making Much of the Bible

Blessed is the man that walketh not in the counsel of the ungodly, nor standeth in the way of sinners, nor sitteth in the seat of the scornful. But his delight is in the law of the LORD; and in his law doth he meditate day and night. And he shall be like a tree planted by the rivers of water, that bringeth forth his fruit in his season; his leaf also shall not wither; and whatsoever he doeth shall prosper.—PSALM 1:1–3

I read about a man in India writing to a friend and giving a report on a mighty work God was doing in his church and his community by saying, "We are having a great rebible here." His second-language vocabulary may not have been quite right, but the sentiment is exactly right. What we need is not better methods or new doctrines or cutting edge techniques. What we need is to be "rebibled"—to have the Word of God fill our hearts and minds and to change the way we live.

Thousands of years have passed since the first part of the Bible was recorded. The individual books were penned by a variety of human authors in different countries and different languages. Any human product thus created would be riddled with inconsistencies and contradictions and errors. The Bible, however, is not because each author was inspired by the Holy Spirit so that the words God meant for us to have were faithfully recorded. "For the prophecy came not in old time by the will of man: but holy men of God spake as they were moved by the Holy Ghost" (2 Peter 1:21).

The Bible is constantly under attack, both by those who deny it and by those who wish to alter it to fit their beliefs and practices. When we set ourselves up to judge what God has said, we destroy our ability to receive His guidance and direction and truth. Exercising faith in God's Word means more than simply accepting what it says. It is also following it in obedience day by day.

Today's Growth Principle: God has given us an incredible treasure and resource in His Word; make use of it today.

God Sees Us All the Same

With good will doing service, as to the Lord, and not to men: Knowing that whatsoever good thing any man doeth, the same shall he receive of the Lord, whether he be bond or free. And, ye masters, do the same things unto them, forbearing threatening: knowing that your Master also is in heaven; neither is there respect of persons with him.—EPHESIANS 6:7–9

Among the most unlikely relics recovered after the sinking of the Titanic was a letter written by first class passenger Alexander Holverson to his mother. Holverson apparently intended to mail it when the great ship reached New York City. But the fateful encounter with the iceberg ended that plan, and the letter was found when Holverson's body was recovered. The letter was sold in 2017 at auction, fetching a record price of more than $165,000. In the three-page letter, Holverson described the ship and his fellow passengers, writing, "Mr. and Mrs. John Jacob Astor is [sic] on this ship. He looks like any other human being, even tho he has millions of money. They sit out on the deck with the rest of us."

At the time, Astor was one of the richest men in the world. But after placing his expectant wife on the final lifeboat that left the doomed ocean liner, Astor stayed on the deck with most of the other men in first class and perished in the icy waters of the ocean. In the end, despite his great wealth, Astor died just as every person does.

No matter how much we achieve or accomplish, God views us through the same lens—equal in His sight. He does not play favorites or regard some above others. Each person is a fallen sinner in need of His freely-offered grace. Great fame or wealth may gain status in the eyes of the world, but God sees us all the same.

Today's Growth Principle: We are commanded to treat all people justly and lovingly, without respect of persons, just as God treats us.

Avoiding the Stain of the World

Wherefore come out from among them, and be ye separate, saith the Lord, and touch not the unclean thing; and I will receive you, And will be a Father unto you, and ye shall be my sons and daughters, saith the Lord Almighty. Having therefore these promises, dearly beloved, let us cleanse ourselves from all filthiness of the flesh and spirit, perfecting holiness in the fear of God.—2 CORINTHIANS 6:17–7:1

I came across a story from the late 1800s of a group of society young people who decided to tour a nearby coal mine. On the appointed day they showed up and met their guide. While most of them had dressed appropriately for the occasion, one of the young ladies had worn a lovely white tea dress. Her friends questioned her choice of apparel, but she appealed to their tour guide. "Can't I wear a white dress into the coal mine?" After a moment he replied, "There's nothing to keep you from wearing a white frock into the mine, but there's a considerable amount there that will keep you from wearing a white frock out."

The thought that we can walk deeply into the things of the world without it having an impact on us is folly. While we are not meant to withdraw from the world and become hermits, we also must not yield to the temptation to get as close to sinful things as we can. Those who think that they have reached a point in their sanctification and growth that they can allow themselves some "small" sins without damage are falling right into Satan's trap. He loves the self-confident Christian, because the devil knows that it will not be long until sin gains control. "Pure religion and undefiled before God and the Father is this, To visit the fatherless and widows in their affliction, and to keep himself unspotted from the world" (James 1:27).

Today's Growth Principle: If we want a close relationship with God, we must cleanse our hearts of the things of the world.

A Proper Sense of Self

The king spake, and said, Is not this great Babylon, that I have built for the house of the kingdom by the might of my power, and for the honour of my majesty? While the word was in the king's mouth, there fell a voice from heaven, saying, O king Nebuchadnezzar, to thee it is spoken; The kingdom is departed from thee. And they shall drive thee from men, and thy dwelling shall be with the beasts of the field: they shall make thee to eat grass as oxen, and seven times shall pass over thee, until thou know that the most High ruleth in the kingdom of men, and giveth it to whomsoever he will. —DANIEL 4:30–32

The great basketball coach John Wooden won a record ten NCAA championships at the University of California, Los Angeles (UCLA). Over the years, he worked with many talented young men, but not all of them reached their potential. In time, he came to realize that the way they viewed themselves determined how they approached both practice and games—and that determined their results. Eventually Wooden developed the following aphorism he would share with each new team: "Talent is God given. Be humble. Fame is man-given. Be grateful. Conceit is self-given. Be careful."

The devil has taken down many through the snare of pride. It's easy for us to listen to the voices that tell us we are special and deserve applause and credit. But as the great king Nebuchadnezzar found out when he boasted of his empire, God alone deserves glory and honor. It took Nebuchadnezzar seven years living like an animal to learn his lesson. Pride is a direct attack on God's greatness. God hates pride just as much today as He always has. Though He shares good things with us because of His gracious love for us, He will not share His glory. He calls us to praise Him rather than lifting ourselves up in pride.

Today's Growth Principle: Instead of lifting ourselves in pride, we should lift our hearts and our voices in praise to God.

No Reason to Fear

He will not suffer thy foot to be moved: he that keepeth thee will not slumber. Behold, he that keepeth Israel shall neither slumber nor sleep. The Lord is thy keeper: the Lord is thy shade upon thy right hand. The sun shall not smite thee by day, nor the moon by night. The Lord shall preserve thee from all evil: he shall preserve thy soul.—PSALM 121:3-7

Young Amy was making the transition to sleeping in her own room at night and was struggling with her fear of the dark. She didn't like being on her own when she wasn't able to see. When her mother came to tuck her in, the four-year-old pointed to the moon shining outside her window. "Mother," she asked, "is the moon God's light?" "Yes," said her mother. Amy's next question was, "Will God blow out His light and go to sleep?" Her mother replied, "No, my child. God never goes to sleep." Then with the simplicity of a child's faith she said, "Well, so long as God is awake, I am not afraid."

The basis for our confidence is not a belief that nothing will ever go wrong. The idea that God's children never suffer the consequences of living in a fallen world sounds attractive, but it is not true. He does not promise to make us comfortable, but to make us like His Son. "And we know that all things work together for good to them that love God, to them who are the called according to his purpose. For whom he did foreknow, he also did predestinate to be conformed to the image of his Son…" (Romans 8:28–29).

But God also promises to keep us in His care and only allow us to be touched by those things that are a part of His plan for us. He never takes a day off, and He never leaves us to face trouble on our own. "Let your conversation be without covetousness; and be content with such things as ye have: for he hath said, I will never leave thee, nor forsake thee" (Hebrews 13:5).

Today's Growth Principle: God's unfailing love and care for us give us the basis to trust Him even when we cannot see His plan.

Prayer and Overcoming Sin

And he cometh, and findeth them sleeping, and saith unto Peter, Simon, sleepest thou? couldest not thou watch one hour? Watch ye and pray, lest ye enter into temptation. The spirit truly is ready, but the flesh is weak. And again he went away, and prayed, and spake the same words. And when he returned, he found them asleep again, (for their eyes were heavy,) neither wist they what to answer him.—MARK 14:37-40

There was a marked difference between Jesus and His disciples the night before the crucifixion. He knew what was coming, but though He had given them warning, the disciples did not recognize the seriousness of what was about to happen. As a result, when it was time to pray, they fell asleep instead. Even after Jesus came back and asked them why they could not pray for just one hour, Peter, James, and John went right back to sleep as soon as Jesus went to pray alone again. Later that very night, because Peter had not fortified himself with prayer, he was vulnerable, and failed when the moment of temptation came.

So many times we fill our days and hours with activity—good activity carried out with good intentions—but we neglect to pray. Like Peter, we leave ourselves open to temptation when we fail to seek God's face. We must be people of prayer, not just in church or at meals or at bedtime, but on a regular and consistent basis throughout the day. David Brainard said, "Oh! One hour with God infinitely exceeds all the pleasures and delights of this lower world."

When we do not pray, we are restricted to our own strength. We lose access to the power of God that equips and enables us to overcome the temptations of the devil. Prayer is our protection, and that is why Jesus taught us to pray, "And lead us not into temptation, but deliver us from evil: For thine is the kingdom, and the power, and the glory, for ever. Amen" (Matthew 6:13).

Today's Growth Principle: A Christian who does not pray forfeits the power and protection God offers to overcome temptation.

How to Glorify God

*These things hast thou done, and I kept silence; thou thoughtest that I was altogether such an one as thyself: but I will reprove thee, and set them in order before thine eyes. Now consider this, ye that forget God, lest I tear you in pieces, and there be none to deliver. Whoso offereth praise glorifieth me: and to him that ordereth his conversation aright will I shew the salvation of God.—*PSALM 50:21–23

Billy Bray, the noted English evangelist and preacher of the early 1800s, was saved from a life of drunkenness and sin. In response to the dramatic effect of his conversion, he went everywhere praising God. Bray said, "I can't help praising God. As I go along the street I lift one foot and it seems to say, 'Glory!' and I lift the other, and it seems to say, 'Amen!' And they keep on like that all the time I'm walking."

God delights in hearing the praises and worship of His people. There is nothing that He needs—He is complete in and of Himself, and we cannot add to His wealth or wisdom by anything that we do. Yet He graciously allows us to take our praise to Him and accepts it as an offering. There are many different ways in which we can glorify God with our lives, but one of the most powerful and most important is to praise Him.

Our praise is important to our own lives, but it also has a powerful impact on those around us. "When the LORD turned again the captivity of Zion, we were like them that dream. Then was our mouth filled with laughter, and our tongue with singing: then said they among the heathen, The LORD hath done great things for them" (Psalm 126:1–2). When we joyfully declare what God has done for us, we create an eagerness in the hearts of others to learn more about Him.

Today's Growth Principle: Our culture presents a twisted view of God which we can counter with our honest and heartfelt praise.

Chosen People and God's Promises

For thou art an holy people unto the LORD thy God: the LORD thy God hath chosen thee to be a special people unto himself, above all people that are upon the face of the earth. The LORD did not set his love upon you, nor choose you, because ye were more in number than any people; for ye were the fewest of all people: But because the LORD loved you, and because he would keep the oath which he had sworn unto your fathers, hath the LORD brought you out with a mighty hand, and redeemed you out of the house of bondmen, from the hand of Pharaoh king of Egypt.
—DEUTERONOMY 7:6–8

We often speak of the Israelites as God's chosen people because that is the way that He referred to them. Long before there was a nation at all, God called Abraham to leave his home and country and journey to a new land. It would be hundreds of years before Israel could truly be called a nation, but God was faithful to keep that promise. When He chooses a people, He follows through with His promises to them.

But the nation of Israel is not the only chosen people referred to in Scripture. The New Testament uses the same language to describe Christians. We are not a random group, but rather a specific and identified body of followers of Jesus Christ. "But ye are a chosen generation, a royal priesthood, an holy nation, a peculiar people; that ye should shew forth the praises of him who hath called you out of darkness into his marvellous light" (1 Peter 2:9).

Like the Israelites, there is much we have been promised that we have not yet received. But every promise of God is faithful and true, and we can count on it coming to pass, no matter how long it may take.

Today's Growth Principle: Remember the promises God has made in His Word, and confidently believe that He will fulfill them.

Silent Christians

By the rivers of Babylon, there we sat down, yea, we wept, when we remembered Zion. We hanged our harps upon the willows in the midst thereof. For there they that carried us away captive required of us a song; and they that wasted us required of us mirth, saying, Sing us one of the songs of Zion. How shall we sing the LORD's song in a strange land?—
PSALM 137:1–4

For God's people to be surrounded by enemies is not new—it has happened over and over again throughout the centuries. Sadly, however, one of the common responses to hardship and enmity is silence. Instead of publicly declaring our praise of God and our allegiance to Him, we are tempted to put our heads down and try to avoid making waves. At a time when a business or even a church can be sued for trying to practice the faith taught in the Scriptures, it is tempting to avoid taking a firm stand. But it is in the moments of challenge that our voices are most important.

The opening of our mouths in praise and worship to God is not optional in the Christian life. It is not something to practice sporadically or only at certain times. Instead it is to be part of our daily existence, so that all who know us recognize our gratitude toward the God we serve. The silent Christian is a disobedient Christian.

Charles Spurgeon said, "Doth not all nature around me praise God? If I were silent, I should be an exception to the universe. Doth not the thunder praise Him as it rolls like drums in the march of the God of armies? Do not the mountains praise Him when the woods upon their summits wave in adoration? Doth not the lightning write His name in letters of fire? Hath not the whole earth a voice? And shall I, can I, silent be?"

Today's Growth Principle: God created us to praise Him, and this is just as true in difficult times as in times of blessing.

When Only Prayer Will Do

Then came the disciples to Jesus apart, and said, Why could not we cast him out? And Jesus said unto them, Because of your unbelief: for verily I say unto you, If ye have faith as a grain of mustard seed, ye shall say unto this mountain, Remove hence to yonder place; and it shall remove; and nothing shall be impossible unto you. Howbeit this kind goeth not out but by prayer and fasting.—MATTHEW 17:19–21

While Jesus was on the Mount of Transfiguration with Peter, James and John, a desperate father brought his demon-possessed son to the other disciples and sought for help. Despite the fact that they had cast demons out of other people, they could do nothing with this one. It was not until Jesus returned, that the young man's father's prayers were answered and the boy was delivered. When the disciples asked the Lord what made the difference, He told them it was a lack of prayer on their part.

Dr. John Rice said, "My greatest sin, and yours, is prayerlessness. My indecision, my lack of wisdom, my lack of guidance come directly out of my prayerlessness. All the times I have fallen into sin, have failed in my duties, have been bereft of power, or disconsolate for lack of comfort, I can charge to the sin of prayerlessness. Oh! Horrible sin, the lack of prayer!"

So many Christians are frustrated because they are trying to do in their own strength what can only be accomplished through the power of God. And the means by which God has ordained to release that power in our lives is prayer. Yet despite the fact that we are told this again and again in the Bible, how often we fail to pray? Intense, serious, passionate prayer, even to the point of fasting, is required to deal with the issues that life throws at us. Without prayer we will falter and fail.

Today's Growth Principle: God's work will not have the power to succeed in our lives unless we are truly people of prayer.

The Importance of Intercession

I exhort therefore, that, first of all, supplications, prayers, intercessions, and giving of thanks, be made for all men; For kings, and for all that are in authority; that we may lead a quiet and peaceable life in all godliness and honesty. For this is good and acceptable in the sight of God our Saviour; Who will have all men to be saved, and to come unto the knowledge of the truth.—1 TIMOTHY 2:1-4

If we kept careful record of our requests during the time we spend in prayer, most Christians would find that a great majority of our praying is self-focused. Yet while we are invited and encouraged to pray for our needs to be met, and we do so, there are many commands given to us in Scripture to pray for the needs of others. If there is one single missing ingredient in the prayer life of the modern church that keeps us from seeing God work as we long to see, it is no doubt the lack of intercession. E. M. Bounds wrote, "Prayer must be broad in its scope—it must plead for others. Intercession for others is the hallmark of all true prayer. Prayer is the soul of a man stirred to plead with God for men."

A Christian who prays only for himself is not only self-focused, but he is self-limiting. At his disposal is the incredible opportunity for prayer to impact the lives of others, yet he is using prayer only for his own needs. We need Christians today who will pray beyond the confines of their homes, their families, their jobs, and their health.

The night before His death on the cross, Jesus certainly spent time praying for His own strength and the coming trial. But first He prayed, not just for His disciples, but for us as well. "Neither pray I for these alone, but for them also which shall believe on me through their word;" (John 17:20). The Apostle Paul, likewise, prayed regularly and fervently for others. He began almost each epistle sharing that he was giving thanks and praying for the spiritual growth of those to whom he wrote.

Today's Growth Principle: The impact of our lives on others will be strongest through prayer.

Being One of the Righteous

Peradventure there be fifty righteous within the city: wilt thou also destroy and not spare the place for the fifty righteous that are therein? That be far from thee to do after this manner, to slay the righteous with the wicked: and that the righteous should be as the wicked, that be far from thee: Shall not the Judge of all the earth do right? And the LORD said, If I find in Sodom fifty righteous within the city, then I will spare all the place for their sakes.—GENESIS 18:24–26

It is easy to discern that we are living in an increasingly wicked society. Things that once were against the law of both God and man are now not just accepted or tolerated, but praised and held up as something good. The open flaunting of immorality in ancient Sodom was deserving of the judgment of God, and sadly, America is hurtling down the same path. But while we rightly say Sodom was judged for its great evil, if the righteous people who lived there had been doing what they should, the judgment would have been averted. It was the failure of the righteous people that sealed the fate of Sodom.

In answer to Abraham's earnest prayers, God agreed not to destroy the city if He found fifty righteous people there. Abraham kept lowering the number needed until he got to ten, and God promised He would spare the city for just ten righteous people. But even that low bar could not be cleared, as it seems that Lot, a righteous man living in Sodom, had not influenced even a handful of people for God and righteousness. Sodom was evil, but it was not without hope. There are examples of entire cities and even countries repenting of great wickedness and turning to God, and who knows but that Sodom would have been one of those had Lot cared to direct the hearts of those around him to God.

Today's Growth Principle: We have a huge responsibility to be the righteous people whose faith spreads to others in an evil world.

SEPTEMBER

When You Trust God and Things Go Wrong

And they said unto them, The Lord look upon you, and judge; because ye have made our savour to be abhorred in the eyes of Pharaoh, and in the eyes of his servants, to put a sword in their hand to slay us. And Moses returned unto the Lord, and said, Lord, wherefore hast thou so evil entreated this people? why is it that thou hast sent me? For since I came to Pharaoh to speak in thy name, he hath done evil to this people; neither hast thou delivered thy people at all.—EXODUS 5:21–23

Sometimes the difficulties of life are the natural consequence of sins and mistakes. Sometimes they are God's chastisement to encourage us to repent and return to Him. But there are times when we are doing right to the best of our ability and walking by faith when it seems like things just keep getting worse. The more we try to follow God, the harder our pathway becomes. This should not come as a surprise to us, for we have an active enemy who is committed to hindering us in our spiritual walk and work for God.

The critical thing for us to remember is that difficulty does not equal God's displeasure. Sometimes the things which are most painful to us are in our lives because God is using them to work in a greater way than we can see. Paul faced this with the "thorn in the flesh" that came into his life. After his repeated prayers for its removal were not answered, Paul accepted his suffering as a gift, and gloried in God's sufficient grace. "Therefore I take pleasure in infirmities, in reproaches, in necessities, in persecutions, in distresses for Christ's sake: for when I am weak, then am I strong" (2 Corinthians 12:10). The Lord does not promise us ease and comfort, but He does promise us His grace.

Today's Growth Principle: When you do right and things go wrong, keep trusting God and doing right.

How to Get Things Done

Six days shalt thou labour, and do all thy work: But the seventh day is the sabbath of the LORD thy God: in it thou shalt not do any work, thou, nor thy son, nor thy daughter, thy manservant, nor thy maidservant, nor thy cattle, nor thy stranger that is within thy gates: For in six days the LORD made heaven and earth, the sea, and all that in them is, and rested the seventh day: wherefore the LORD blessed the sabbath day, and hallowed it.—EXODUS 20:9–11

Adam Clarke, the English theologian of the early 1800s, wrote one of the most influential Bible commentaries ever produced. He was not a fast writer or reader, but he was very diligent. It took him forty years of laborious effort to complete his six-volume work, with the last book published in 1826 just six years before his death. In order to have time for his writing in addition to his ministerial duties, Clarke got up early each morning. The story goes that a young preacher visiting him inquired about his routine. "Do you pray about getting up so early?" he asked. "No," Clarke replied. "I just get up."

The best way to get things done is to simply begin working. Looking for the perfect time and circumstances to begin work usually ends with doing nothing at all. Solomon warned, "He that observeth the wind shall not sow; and he that regardeth the clouds shall not reap" (Ecclesiastes 11:4). The difference in the level of accomplishment reached is not usually a matter of extreme talent or resources, but rather a matter of dedication and effort. The more seriously we take our work, realizing that God created us for specific opportunities to serve Him, the more devoted and diligent we'll be. Ephesians 2:10 tells us, "For we are his workmanship, created in Christ Jesus unto good works, which God hath before ordained that we should walk in them."

Today's Growth Principle: Work is important, and the more diligently we labor, the more we will accomplish for God.

How God Shows His Love to Us

For every one that asketh receiveth; and he that seeketh findeth; and to him that knocketh it shall be opened. Or what man is there of you, whom if his son ask bread, will he give him a stone? Or if he ask a fish, will he give him a serpent? If ye then, being evil, know how to give good gifts unto your children, how much more shall your Father which is in heaven give good things to them that ask him?—MATTHEW 7:8–11

Because our culture has such a distorted view of God, it is hard for us to overcome the constant barrage of misinformation about Him that we receive. Even some religious groups describe a God who is almost unrecognizable from the God of the pages of Scripture. We must have a proper view of God to live as He commands. And that view can only come to us from the Bible. In its pages is the only true description of His nature and character, and these truths should be the foundation for our attitude toward God.

One of the purposes of Jesus' life and ministry was to reveal the true nature of God. "And I have declared unto them thy name, and will declare it: that the love wherewith thou hast loved me may be in them, and I in them" (John 17:26). At a time when most of the world's religions featured a god or many gods who were distant and aloof, requiring appeasement for their wrath, Jesus described a loving Father who Himself provided a way for man to come into His presence.

This truth is reinforced in the teaching of Jesus on the subject of prayer. He contrasts God to earthly fathers who, despite their limitations, do their best to provide for their children. God is much more able and willing to respond to our prayers than any human could be. He delights in hearing from us.

Today's Growth Principle: If we do not properly view God as our loving Father, we will not seek His face in prayer as we should.

The Importance of Integrity

Moreover thou shalt provide out of all the people able men, such as fear God, men of truth, hating covetousness; and place such over them, to be rulers of thousands, and rulers of hundreds, rulers of fifties, and rulers of tens: And let them judge the people at all seasons: and it shall be, that every great matter they shall bring unto thee, but every small matter they shall judge: so shall it be easier for thyself, and they shall bear the burden with thee.—EXODUS 18:21-22

Jacques Necker is little remembered now, but in the period leading up to the French Revolution, he was one of the most important people in all of France. He served Louis XVI as Finance Minister, and was basically in control of most of the French economy. It was a turbulent time during which many government officials were using their positions to line their own pockets. This corruption helped lead to the overthrow of the government. But Necker was an exception to that trend. He was so honest that when his estate burned, he ensured that the tax receipts collected for the government were rescued first. And even though he lost all of his personal possessions as a result, Necker still turned in the full amount of the taxes.

There are few things that tempt more people than does money. The temptation to cut corners to get a little more has been around for a long time. When Moses' father-in-law encouraged him to appoint men to help judge the Israelites, one of the most important characteristics they needed to have was that they were not possessed with a spirit of covetousness. The culture around us is geared toward creating dissatisfaction and encouraging people to want more and more. Yet we must be cautious, because it is only a short step from desiring to make our lives better, which is not wrong, to coveting what others have, which is wrong.

Today's Growth Principle: There are very few things that do more to reveal our true integrity than the way we manage money.

Fighting in the Face of Fear

And Jonathan said to the young man that bare his armour, Come, and let us go over unto the garrison of these uncircumcised: it may be that the LORD will work for us: for there is no restraint to the LORD to save by many or by few. And his armourbearer said unto him, Do all that is in thine heart: turn thee; behold, I am with thee according to thy heart. Then said Jonathan, Behold, we will pass over unto these men, and we will discover ourselves unto them.—1 SAMUEL 14:6–8

The Philistines were a huge problem for Israel during the time of the judges and the reign of Saul. They had greater military strength than the Israelites and better technology to produce weapons of war. As a result, the Jews were facing an enemy they had little hope of defeating in battle. But Saul's son Jonathan was not content to cower in fear, even in the face of a superior foe. Instead he decided to step out in faith and take the battle to the enemy. And God used Jonathan to bring about a mighty victory.

We are not told whether or not Jonathan felt fear. He does not appear to have known with certainty that God would indeed give a victory, for he said, "it *may* be that the LORD will work for us" (emphasis mine). The important lesson for us in this story is that despite whatever doubts Jonathan may have had, he and his armor bearer stepped out of hiding and confronted the enemy.

God does strengthen us for the challenges and battles we face, but we will still sometimes face doubts and fears as we head into a conflict. As missionary Elisabeth Elliot said, "Sometimes fear does not subside and you must do it afraid." The call of faith is not to be completely without fear, but rather to do what is right regardless of our fear.

Today's Growth Principle: Even when we are afraid, we can still move forward in what God has called us to do.

No One Turned Away

*And Jesus said unto them, I am the bread of life: he that cometh to me shall never hunger; and he that believeth on me shall never thirst. But I said unto you, That ye also have seen me, and believe not. All that the Father giveth me shall come to me; and him that cometh to me I will in no wise cast out. For I came down from heaven, not to do mine own will, but the will of him that sent me.—*JOHN 6:35–38

One Sunday morning the great evangelist George Whitefield filled the pulpit of one of London's more elegant and upscale churches. Yet his message there was the same as he preached everywhere—that God saves sinners. Whitefield declared, "The Lord Jesus will take the devil's castaways." After the service ended, Whitefield went to eat with some of the leading members of the congregation. Over the meal, someone challenged him regarding his bold declaration that salvation was offered to all who believe.

In response, Whitefield pulled out of his pocket a note that he had received before leaving the church. He asked the critic to read it aloud to the group. It said, "Two poor, lost women stood outside your tabernacle today and heard you say that the Lord would take the devil's castaways. We seized upon this as our last hope, and we write you this to tell you that we rejoice now in believing in Him, and from this good hour we shall endeavor to serve Him who has done so much for us."

No sinner is beyond God's saving. No matter what someone has done or failed to do, the sacrifice of Jesus Christ on the cross is sufficient atonement for their sin. The problem is not that God cannot or will not save, but that each individual must be willing to accept the free offer of salvation provided for them.

Today's Growth Principle: No one who comes to Jesus in faith asking for salvation has ever been turned away.

"Bear His Cross on His Back"

Then said Jesus unto his disciples, If any man will come after me, let him deny himself, and take up his cross, and follow me. For whosoever will save his life shall lose it: and whosoever will lose his life for my sake shall find it. For what is a man profited, if he shall gain the whole world, and lose his own soul? or what shall a man give in exchange for his soul?
—MATTHEW 16:24–26

Jonathan Goforth, who spent many years as a missionary in China, recounted the story of two young Chinese men who lived in a neighboring province. They purchased copies of the New Testament from a bookseller and began to read the Word of God in their own language. When they came to the instruction of Jesus to take up their cross, they were not clear on what it meant. So, following the instruction literally, they made crosses out of bamboo. The Chinese translation said to "bear his cross on his back," and so they tied the crosses to their shoulders and carried them everywhere they went. Soon, they were directed to the mission outpost in Liuchow where they were presented the gospel. When they understood that Christ had already taken the punishment for their sins on His back as He died on the cross, they trusted Him as their Saviour. Then they returned to their village to tell others the Good News.

The cross bearing that God commands for us is not usually a literal demand, but it is a symbol of sacrifice. Those who are not willing to give up what they hold most dear cannot follow Jesus, because that is what He did, even before His death on the cross. "For ye know the grace of our Lord Jesus Christ, that, though he was rich, yet for your sakes he became poor, that ye through his poverty might be rich" (2 Corinthians 8:9). Anything we cling to more than Jesus will prevent us from walking in His footsteps.

Today's Growth Principle: It is impossible to follow Jesus without dying to self.

The Most Valuable Legacy

Blessed is every one that feareth the LORD; that walketh in his ways. For thou shalt eat the labour of thine hands: happy shalt thou be, and it shall be well with thee. Thy wife shall be as a fruitful vine by the sides of thine house: thy children like olive plants round about thy table. Behold, that thus shall the man be blessed that feareth the LORD.—PSALM 128:1-4

At the time of his death in 1913, John Pierpont Morgan was one of the richest men in the world. He was renowned in the world of finance for his ability to put together corporate deals, like his pivotal role in the creation of General Electric and U. S. Steel. Morgan almost single-handedly ended the financial crisis known as the Panic of 1907 by supporting the banks that were on the verge of failing and working with others to prop up companies that would otherwise have gone bankrupt.

Morgan was renowned for his philanthropy, supporting museums and hospitals, and was a major contributor to his church. His priorities and goals for the future were revealed in his will, which began with these words: "I commit my soul into the hands of my Saviour in full confidence that having redeemed it and washed it in His most precious blood, He will present it faultless before the throne of my Heavenly Father, and I entreat my children to maintain and defend at any cost of personal sacrifice the blessed doctrine of the complete Atonement for sin through the blood of Jesus Christ once offered, and through that alone."

Most of us will not leave billions of dollars to our descendants. But all of us can leave them a heritage of faith and love for God and a knowledge of His salvation. There is no greater inheritance than the testimony of a faithful life spent in service to God and a faith that reaches across the generations.

Today's Growth Principle: There is no financial legacy we can leave behind that compares to the legacy of faith in God.

A Call to Holiness

Wherefore gird up the loins of your mind, be sober, and hope to the end for the grace that is to be brought unto you at the revelation of Jesus Christ; As obedient children, not fashioning yourselves according to the former lusts in your ignorance: But as he which hath called you is holy, so be ye holy in all manner of conversation; Because it is written, Be ye holy; for I am holy.—1 PETER 1:13–16

William Longstaff inherited a successful shipping business from his father and resolved to use his resources to further God's work. When D. L. Moody's evangelistic campaign in England was put in doubt because of the death of the main financial backer, Longstaff stepped forward to ensure the needs were met so the meetings could continue. During that campaign, Longstaff shared with Ira Sankey, Moody's songleader, a poem he had written after hearing a sermon on holiness. Later his words were set to music, and the hymn is still being sung today.

> Take time to be holy, speak oft with thy Lord;
> Abide in Him always, and feed on His Word.
> Make friends of God's children, help those who are weak,
> Forgetting in nothing His blessing to seek.
>
> Take time to be holy, the world rushes on;
> Spend much time in secret, with Jesus alone.
> By looking to Jesus, like Him thou shalt be;
> Thy friends in thy conduct His likeness shall see.

We know that we will become like the people with whom we spend the most time. The question for us then is, "Am I becoming like Christ by spending time with Him?"

Today's Growth Principle: The time we spend in God's presence will change our lives and let His holiness be more clearly seen in us.

Proverbs 6–7 // 2 Corinthians 2

No Room for God

*I am the door: by me if any man enter in, he shall be saved, and shall go in and out, and find pasture. The thief cometh not, but for to steal, and to kill, and to destroy: I am come that they might have life, and that they might have it more abundantly. I am the good shepherd: the good shepherd giveth his life for the sheep.—*JOHN 10:9–11

Phillips Brooks, who is best remembered as the author of the Christmas carol "O Little Town of Bethlehem," told of a man who came to him and said, "I have not time or room in my life for Christianity. If it were not so full! You don't know how hard I work from morning till night. When have I time, where have I room for Christianity in such a life as mine?"

Recounting that story Brooks wrote, "It is as if the engine had said it had no room for the steam. It is as if the tree said it had no room for the sap. It is as if the ocean said it had no room for the tide. It is as if the man had said he had no room for his soul. It is as if the life had said it had no time to live, when it is life. It is not something added to life; it is life. A man is not living without it."

It is so easy for us to become caught up in the things of life that we find our relationship with God relegated to an afterthought. Many people substitute a busy life for an abundant life. Jesus said, "…I am come that they might have life, and that they might have it more abundantly" (John 10:10). Yet, even those of us who know the Lord can get caught up in busyness and have no time for personal, intimate fellowship with God as they rush from task to objective to project. It makes no difference what these tasks that keep us from spending time with God are—whether they are secular or religious—if we allow them to fill our days so there is no time left to cultivate our relationship with God.

Today's Growth Principle: Only through Jesus can we have eternal life; and only through cultivating our relationship with Jesus can we enjoy abundant life.

How a People Turn from God

My people are destroyed for lack of knowledge: because thou hast rejected knowledge, I will also reject thee, that thou shalt be no priest to me: seeing thou hast forgotten the law of thy God, I will also forget thy children. As they were increased, so they sinned against me: therefore will I change their glory into shame. They eat up the sin of my people, and they set their heart on their iniquity.—HOSEA 4:6–8

No nation turns away from God in a moment. It is the process of a generation failing to pass on their faith to their children and failing to reach others with the gospel. It is easy to see the evidence of a marked shift in American society today. The number of people who go to church declines, and the rising tide of abortion, divorce, immorality, addiction, and more is clear evidence of a negative shift. Yet despite the abundant proofs of a downturn, more and more people, 56 percent according to a recent Pew Research poll, say that people do not need to believe in God in order to be good and moral.

Daniel Webster, one of America's great statesmen, left this solemn warning, "If we abide by the principles taught in the Bible, our country will go on prospering; but if we and our posterity neglect its instructions and authority, no man can tell how sudden a catastrophe may overwhelm us and bury all our glory in profound obscurity."

God has no grandchildren. Each new generation must have the faith we share taught, explained, and demonstrated to them so it can become their own. When we turn away from following God with our whole hearts, we should not be surprised if our children, grandchildren, friends, co-workers, and neighbors go even further away from Him. There are many consequences for sin, and they are not all immediate. Some of them impact future generations in families and societies.

Today's Growth Principle: If we do not share our faith with our own families and with others, it will be lost.

Power and Praying

*And at even, when the sun did set, they brought unto him all that were diseased, and them that were possessed with devils. And all the city was gathered together at the door. And he healed many that were sick of divers diseases, and cast out many devils; and suffered not the devils to speak, because they knew him. And in the morning, rising up a great while before day, he went out, and departed into a solitary place, and there prayed.—*MARK 1:32–35

Though Jesus was fully and completely God, He was also fully human. He voluntarily took on the limits of a body. He got tired and hungry just like we do. After a full day of ministry that began with teaching in the synagogue at Capernaum, casting out a demon, and healing Peter's mother-in-law, a huge crowd came as soon as the Sabbath was ended. They wanted Jesus to heal and touch those in need. We do not know how long it was before Jesus finished with the multitude, but it must have been long after dark. Yet very early the next morning, we find Jesus getting up to go apart alone and pray.

Prayer is not an adjunct or an accessory to ministry and life. It is an essential ingredient. It is in prayer that we, just as Jesus did, find the strength and power to accomplish what God has set before us. John Wesley said, "I have so much to do, that I must spend several hours in prayer before I am able to do it." The Apostle Paul, undoubtedly an incredibly busy leader, wrote, "Praying always with all prayer and supplication in the Spirit, and watching thereunto with all perseverance and supplication for all saints" (Ephesians 6:18).

Too often we try to work and live in our own power, but if we take that route, we only get what we are able to do. God calls us to tasks that are beyond our natural abilities and strength. To succeed we must have His help, and that help comes to us when we pray.

Today's Growth Principle: The Christian who is too busy to pray will not be able to accomplish what only God can do.

Our Walk and the Word

And he humbled thee, and suffered thee to hunger, and fed thee with manna, which thou knewest not, neither did thy fathers know; that he might make thee know that man doth not live by bread only, but by every word that proceedeth out of the mouth of the LORD doth man live.
—DEUTERONOMY 8:3

When Satan tempted Jesus after He had been fasting and praying for forty days in the wilderness, he used the same techniques he has been using on men and women with great success for centuries. Yet against Jesus, they did not work at all. While Jesus was fully God, He was fully man as well, and He felt the full weight of the temptations. In His response, Jesus gave us a pattern we can follow: He used the Word of God in answer to every offer from the devil. "But he answered and said, It is written, Man shall not live by bread alone, but by every word that proceedeth out of the mouth of God" (Matthew 4:4).

It is impossible to live a victorious and productive Christian life apart from regular, consistent, habitual reading and meditating on the Scriptures. Just as food is the source of our physical strength, God's Word is the source of our spiritual strength. It is instructive that the story of the manna God provided for the children of Israel is used to highlight the importance of the Bible.

The food that God sent from Heaven in response to the Israelites' need was unlike anything they had seen before. It was only available early in the morning. If the people waited too long to gather it, it would melt away in the sun. And it could not be stored up against the future. Except on the Sabbath, the manna had to be gathered each day. The principle for us is the same—we need to gather strength from the Word daily to walk in victory.

Today's Growth Principle: Keep the Word of God central to your thoughts and decisions on a daily basis, and you will see victory over temptation.

God Already Has a Plan

And the passover, a feast of the Jews, was nigh. When Jesus then lifted up his eyes, and saw a great company come unto him, he saith unto Philip, Whence shall we buy bread, that these may eat? And this he said to prove him: for he himself knew what he would do. Philip answered him, Two hundred pennyworth of bread is not sufficient for them, that every one of them may take a little.—JOHN 6:4–7

Almost every day something happens that we do not expect. It may be large or small, and the surprise may be pleasant or unpleasant, but events occur that are not on our schedules or part of our plans. That never happens to God. The problem that seems to us to be overwhelming, like a crowd of thousands of people who need food but there is nowhere to buy it and no money to buy it with, already has a solution in the mind and plan of God. He wants us to trust Him, no matter what circumstances we may face.

The miracle we call the feeding of the five thousand (even though that is just the number of men and the actual crowd was much larger) is recorded in all four Gospels. This is not filler or repetition—it is an important story designed to strengthen our faith. We must remember who God is and what He is willing and able to do when we are tested by the unexpected.

Charles Spurgeon said, "Alterations and afterthoughts belong to short-sighted beings who meet with unexpected events which operate upon them to change their minds, but the Lord who sees everything from the beginning has no such reason for shifting his ground." Our faith cannot be in ourselves, for we have neither the wisdom nor the resources to respond to the unexpected. When things catch us off guard, we must remember to run to God and seek His help.

Today's Growth Principle: When the things we face humanly speaking are beyond our ability and plans, God is able to deliver.

Seeing Through Satan's Schemes

Wherefore I beseech you that ye would confirm your love toward him. For to this end also did I write, that I might know the proof of you, whether ye be obedient in all things. To whom ye forgive any thing, I forgive also: for if I forgave any thing, to whom I forgave it, for your sakes forgave I it in the person of Christ; Lest Satan should get an advantage of us: for we are not ignorant of his devices.—2 CORINTHIANS 2:8–11

There is an old Russian story that following a wave of thefts from a construction site in the Soviet Union, special guards were put in place at each exit to stop the robbers. The first day, the guard noticed a worker with a wheelbarrow filled with bags. "What's in the bags?" he asked suspiciously. "Just sawdust," the worker replied. Refusing to believe him, the guard made him dump the bags and open them. But there were no tools or other materials inside—just sawdust. This happened every day for a week. The guard was convinced something was going on, but he couldn't figure out what it was. Finally he asked, "I know you're up to something, and I promise we won't arrest you for it. But the curiosity is killing me. What are you doing?" "Stealing wheelbarrows," the worker replied.

Satan has been deceiving men and women for thousands of years, not because he keeps coming up with new and more elaborate schemes, but because we keep falling for the same lies and temptations. God calls us to be on guard by paying attention and not allowing the enemy to slip inside our guard. "Be sober, be vigilant; because your adversary the devil, as a roaring lion, walketh about, seeking whom he may devour" (1 Peter 5:8). Since the devil continually attempts to deceive and entrap us, we must be continually watchful and alert to his attempts to lead us astray.

Today's Growth Principle: Be alert to the to hidden temptations of Satan so you see through his deceit.

The Potter's Prerogative

Then I went down to the potter's house, and, behold, he wrought a work on the wheels. And the vessel that he made of clay was marred in the hand of the potter: so he made it again another vessel, as seemed good to the potter to make it. Then the word of the LORD came to me, saying, O house of Israel, cannot I do with you as this potter? saith the LORD. Behold, as the clay is in the potter's hand, so are ye in mine hand, O house of Israel.
—JEREMIAH 18:3–6

God frequently used gripping images from everyday life to illustrate deep spiritual truths to His people. That was the case when He sent the prophet Jeremiah to visit a craftsman making clay pots. Jeremiah was called to minister to a nation that did not want to hear from God. They were perfectly happy to join the worship of Jehovah in small measure with the false religions of their neighbors, but they had no interest in obeying His commandments.

The culture of Jeremiah's day was very much like our own. Today many people claim to follow some form of Christianity, but it is mixed with all sorts of false religion. Calling for obedience to divine commands is considered to be at the least old fashioned, if not outright bigotry. Yet God is the Potter, and we are the clay. He made us, He owns us, and He has the absolute and complete right to full authority in our lives.

As long as we insist on our rights and our way, we will not obey God's commands, and we will not experience the joy of surrender to the One who made us and knows us best. We must remember that we are not in charge of our lives and live according to the precepts of the Word of God. "What? know ye not that your body is the temple of the Holy Ghost which is in you, which ye have of God, and ye are not your own?" (1 Corinthians 6:19).

Today's Growth Principle: Recognizing God's total right of control over our lives should motivate us to joyful obedience.

Wait Until it Dries

Wherefore, my beloved brethren, let every man be swift to hear, slow to speak, slow to wrath: For the wrath of man worketh not the righteousness of God. Wherefore lay apart all filthiness and superfluity of naughtiness, and receive with meekness the engrafted word, which is able to save your souls. —JAMES 1:19–21

The story goes that in a small English village many years ago, a young man was told that he had been insulted by someone he thought was a friend. He rushed out indignantly, planning to demand an apology or have a fight. An elderly man sitting nearby stopped him and asked what his rush was. When the young man explained his purpose, the older man offered some wise counsel: "My dear boy, take a word of advice from an old man who loves peace. An insult is like mud; it will brush off much better when it is dry. Wait a little, till he and you are both cool, and the thing will be easily mended. If you go now, it will only be to quarrel." The angry young man listened and waited rather than confronting the one who had offended him, and soon the friend who had given the insult came and asked forgiveness.

While there may be times when we need to make sure our testimony is not damaged by false accusations, we do not have to fly off the handle and insist on speaking our minds immediately. It is far better to wait until we know for sure exactly what happened or what was said, for many times the early reports are not correct in some or even all their details. And it is better to wait until our temper has cooled before confronting someone who has offended us. This is not to say that we should nurse a grudge, but the passage of a few hours or days may make dealing with a conflict much easier.

Today's Growth Principle: Patience and carefully planned responses have guarded many relationships from being badly damaged.

Catching the Vision

And Samuel said to all the people, See ye him whom the LORD hath chosen, that there is none like him among all the people? And all the people shouted, and said, God save the king. Then Samuel told the people the manner of the kingdom, and wrote it in a book, and laid it up before the LORD. And Samuel sent all the people away, every man to his house. And Saul also went home to Gibeah; and there went with him a band of men, whose hearts God had touched.—1 SAMUEL 10:24–26

When the Israelites insisted on having a king, God instructed Samuel to choose Saul to rule over His people. Though Saul did not end his life well, he was chosen by God as the best available candidate. And, for a time, he did follow God as he led the nation. At the beginning of his reign, Saul was supported by a group of people who had caught the vision for what God intended and wanted to be a part of it. At a time when the people were scattering back across Israel, these men stayed with Saul so they could join him in the work. Our verses above describe these as "a band of men, whose hearts God had touched." Undoubtedly, the friendship and support of these men was invaluable to the new king.

Every great work for God is made possible, at least humanly speaking, because some of God's people are not content with the status quo. Instead they see the vision of what could be done if believers acted in faith and courage. Often, it is a leader who is walking with God who first develops such a vision of faith and casts it to others. But unless others are willing to embrace that vision and follow their leader as a team, the great works of God may not be realized. At one of her public events, Helen Keller was asked what would be worse than being born without being able to see. She replied, "Being born with sight but having no vision." There should be something in our hearts that longs to see God work and to be part of it.

Today's Growth Principle: When we are alert and aware to what God is doing, it is easy for that vision to take deep root in our hearts.

Real Generosity

Moreover, because I have set my affection to the house of my God, I have of mine own proper good, of gold and silver, which I have given to the house of my God, over and above all that I have prepared for the holy house, Even three thousand talents of gold, of the gold of Ophir, and seven thousand talents of refined silver, to overlay the walls of the houses withal: The gold for things of gold, and the silver for things of silver, and for all manner of work to be made by the hands of artificers. And who then is willing to consecrate his service this day unto the Lord?—1 Chronicles 29:3–5

When God sent Nathan the prophet to tell David that He wanted Solomon to build the Temple rather than allowing David to do so, David set out to prepare for his son to complete the task that was in his own heart. He began gathering materials and resources for Solomon to use. In his position as king over Israel, David had access to and ultimate control over all of the nation's wealth. And, while he did use his power as king to begin the preparations, David was not just generous with other people's money. Instead he made a massive contribution from his own wealth so that there would be plenty of gold and silver for the magnificent Temple in Jerusalem. David loved God, and as a result, his affection determined how he spent his resources. This wasn't just a project to him; it was a personal opportunity to worship God by giving of his own treasure.

There is nothing that is more revealing regarding what we really value than the uses to which we put our money. When we invest in the eternal, it speaks volumes concerning the state of our hearts. Jesus said, "But lay up for yourselves treasures in heaven, where neither moth nor rust doth corrupt, and where thieves do not break through nor steal: For where your treasure is, there will your heart be also" (Matthew 6:20–21). Generosity toward God's work shows where our affections are set.

Today's Growth Principle: Real generosity requires real sacrifice of our own personal assets.

A Question of Values

For which cause we faint not; but though our outward man perish, yet the inward man is renewed day by day. For our light affliction, which is but for a moment, worketh for us a far more exceeding and eternal weight of glory; While we look not at the things which are seen, but at the things which are not seen: for the things which are seen are temporal; but the things which are not seen are eternal.—2 CORINTHIANS 4:16–18

When David Livingstone went to Africa, he left behind most of the comforts he could have enjoyed. A medical doctor's salary would have provided him a lovely home and many luxuries and comforts. Instead he spent most of his adult life in harsh and primitive conditions.

After he had been in Africa for some time, he constructed a house with a lovely garden at the mission station in Mabotsa. But when Livingstone heard that other missionaries were criticizing the expense, he gave the house away and moved further into the jungle to ensure that the work was not hindered. Later Livingstone wrote, "I do like a garden, but Paradise will make amends for all our privations here."

The devil tries to get us to focus on the things of this world. He encourages us to strive to accumulate possessions, and he tempts us to judge our value by what we have and do not have. God instead provides things that are lasting and eternal—that do not lose value or fade away. When we value what matters to Him, we will not hold tightly to our earthly possessions. While we should be grateful for every material blessing we receive, we must never forget that this world is not our home. "And the world passeth away, and the lust thereof: but he that doeth the will of God abideth for ever" (1 John 2:17). Our hearts must be fixed on the things that truly matter.

Today's Growth Principle: Nothing that exists in this world can compare to what is waiting for those who have trusted Christ.

"I Will Have My Rights"

To wit, that God was in Christ, reconciling the world unto himself, not imputing their trespasses unto them; and hath committed unto us the word of reconciliation. Now then we are ambassadors for Christ, as though God did beseech you by us: we pray you in Christ's stead, be ye reconciled to God. For he hath made him to be sin for us, who knew no sin; that we might be made the righteousness of God in him.
—2 Corinthians 5:19–21

Dr. H. A. Ironside told of a church business meeting where a bitter dispute arose between members of the board. Ironside said, "I can remember one man springing to his feet and with clenched fists saying, 'I will put up with a good deal, but one thing I will not put up with, I will not allow you to put anything over on me; I will have my rights!' An old Christian responded, 'You did not mean that; did you? If you had your rights, you would be in Hell. And you are forgetting that Jesus did not come to get His rights; He came to get His wrongs, and He got them.' I can still see that man standing there for a moment like one transfixed, and then the tears broke from his eyes and he said, 'Brethren, I have been all wrong. Handle the matter however you think best.'"

Before we insist on getting what we deserve, we would be wise to stop and reflect on exactly what that would mean. So often we insist on getting our own way, forgetting that Jesus did exactly the opposite. "Let this mind be in you, which was also in Christ Jesus: Who, being in the form of God, thought it not robbery to be equal with God: but made himself of no reputation, and took upon him the form of a servant, and was made in the likeness of men" (Philippians 2:5–7). If Jesus had insisted on clinging to and receiving His rights, we would have no hope of salvation.

Today's Growth Principle: Rather than insisting on our rights, we should give thanks for God's mercy.

The Fruit of Not Forgiving

And Joab fell to the ground on his face, and bowed himself, and thanked the king: and Joab said, To day thy servant knoweth that I have found grace in thy sight, my lord, O king, in that the king hath fulfilled the request of his servant. So Joab arose and went to Geshur, and brought Absalom to Jerusalem. And the king said, Let him turn to his own house, and let him not see my face. So Absalom returned to his own house, and saw not the king's face.—2 SAMUEL 14:22–24

David's failure to correct his children when they did wrong brought great trouble to his family. Absalom killed his own brother Amnon when David refused to deal with his horrible sin, then fled for his life, fearing that David would kill him for taking the life of the heir to the throne. Years passed, and it took a trick by David's general, Joab, to get David to extend permission for Absalom to return to Israel. But even then, David did not really forgive his son and refused to allow Absalom into his presence. It was not right for Absalom to later lead a rebellion against his father, but we can certainly see that David's lack of forgiveness made Absalom vulnerable to temptation.

When we do not forgive others, it does not just damage our relationships with them, but it hinders our relationship with God and makes them vulnerable to other temptations as well. Evangelist R. A. Torrey said, "That is the trouble with some of you. Someone has done you an injury, or you think he has, and you will not come [close to God] because you want to cherish this bitter grudge in your heart." Too many people are still in bondage to hurts of the past because they simply will not let things go. But we cannot be right with God or with others unless we are willing to forgive those who wrong us, just as God forgives us.

Today's Growth Principle: When we are wronged, we must be willing to forgive, or those we love may suffer the consequences of our bitterness.

Revealing Jesus

And I, brethren, when I came to you, came not with excellency of speech or of wisdom, declaring unto you the testimony of God. For I determined not to know any thing among you, save Jesus Christ, and him crucified. And I was with you in weakness, and in fear, and in much trembling. And my speech and my preaching was not with enticing words of man's wisdom, but in demonstration of the Spirit and of power:—1 CORINTHIANS 2:1-4

On a mission trip to India, Dr. George Truett was invited to address the students at a university. Before he spoke, he was warned to expect a hostile response because of the strong influence of Hinduism among the students. One official warned him, "When you are through preaching, people in the audience will ask you questions that are difficult to answer. They will contradict everything that you say." Dr. Truett prayed earnestly and then stood and preached a clear gospel message about salvation through faith in Jesus alone. When he finished, there was a long silence. Finally one of the leading Hindu students stood and said, "Sir, we have nothing against the Christ this man has preached."

The lost world around us wants many things, but what it needs most of all is a clear presentation of Jesus Christ, the only hope of salvation. Just as the foreigners from Greece who came to Jerusalem during the ministry of the Lord, the people around us have a pressing need. "The same came therefore to Philip, which was of Bethsaida of Galilee, and desired him, saying, Sir, we would see Jesus" (John 12:21). It is not our eloquence or our gifting that makes a difference to people, but the Jesus we talk about and reflect in our actions. His name and His righteousness must be lifted up and presented to the world. This is our purpose and calling in Him.

Today's Growth Principle: If we faithfully present the message of Jesus and live as He did, those around us will be touched.

Hiding the Gospel

But if our gospel be hid, it is hid to them that are lost: In whom the god of this world hath blinded the minds of them which believe not, lest the light of the glorious gospel of Christ, who is the image of God, should shine unto them. For we preach not ourselves, but Christ Jesus the Lord; and ourselves your servants for Jesus' sake. For God, who commanded the light to shine out of darkness, hath shined in our hearts, to give the light of the knowledge of the glory of God in the face of Jesus Christ.
—2 CORINTHIANS 4:3–6

Perhaps the best-known and most widely-distributed gospel tract of the 1800s was called "Come to Jesus." Written by a British pastor named Newman Hall, the tract was handed out to hundreds of thousands of soldiers during the American Civil War. After the war, Hall became embroiled in a theological dispute that grew heated. He used his literary ability to write a response which dissected, not just the opposing point of view, but those who held and promoted it.

After he was done writing, Hall asked a friend to read it before he had it printed and distributed. The friend agreed that it was a powerful and pointed piece and asked if Hall had a title for it yet. When Hall replied that he did not and was looking for ideas, the friend said, "Why don't you call it 'Go to the Devil' by the author of 'Come to Jesus'?"

The way that we act, talk to, and treat other people should be a reflection of the grace that God extended to us in allowing us to become part of His family. First John 3:1 tells us that God bestowed His love on us and reminds us that we are "called the sons of God." We have a responsibility as His children to not bring dishonor on the family name. One of the reasons the world is not being reached is because of the failure of Christians to live up to their faith.

Today's Growth Principle: We should never treat others in such a way that the hope of the gospel message is obscured by our actions.

All Things Made New

And that he died for all, that they which live should not henceforth live unto themselves, but unto him which died for them, and rose again. Wherefore henceforth know we no man after the flesh: yea, though we have known Christ after the flesh, yet now henceforth know we him no more. Therefore if any man be in Christ, he is a new creature: old things are passed away; behold, all things are become new.
—2 CORINTHIANS 5:15–17

Evangelist Harry Rimmer told the story of a man who was saved on a Sunday night in one of his meetings. On Tuesday the man came to the church and asked for his help. Rimmer said, "He had some trouble starting, but finally informed me that he had deserted his wife and baby daughter six months before. The poor fellow wept like a child as he unfolded his tale. He offered no excuses, asked for no favor, just begged for forgiveness. I somehow phrased his pitiful pleas, and we mailed it together. Two weeks later he came in accompanied by his wife and wee daughter. I never saw a happier man in all my life. When his wife got his letter she wasted no time writing; she answered it in person!"

Those of us who have been saved for a number of years must be careful not to forget the transformation that the new birth brought to our lives. We must continue to walk according to the new nature we have been given. "Therefore we are buried with him by baptism into death: that like as Christ was raised up from the dead by the glory of the Father, even so we also should walk in newness of life" (Romans 6:4).

God's plan is not for our salvation to be an event that takes place in the past and then is left behind. We are to be living in the new nature in the present as well.

Today's Growth Principle: The impact of salvation should be clearly visible in our lives every day.

Carrying on the Work

And therefore did the Jews persecute Jesus, and sought to slay him, because he had done these things on the sabbath day. But Jesus answered them, My Father worketh hitherto, and I work. Therefore the Jews sought the more to kill him, because he not only had broken the sabbath, but said also that God was his Father, making himself equal with God.
—JOHN 5:16–18

In 1852 an engineer named John Augustus Roebling began promoting the idea of a suspension bridge to cross the East River between Manhattan and Brooklyn in New York City. It took him nearly fifteen years to convince government leaders of the practicality of his design and secure the funding. Not long before the work was to begin, Roebling died from complications and infection after an accident during his survey work. Before he died, he placed the project in the hands of his son Washington Roebling who supervised the construction. After fourteen years of labor, the Brooklyn Bridge opened and has been in use ever since. The work continued because someone was willing to carry it on.

Jesus returned to Heaven almost two thousand years ago but the work that He began must continue. The only way that can happen is if we as His followers take up the mission and carry out the tasks that He left for us to do. This is the purpose and plan of God for reaching the world. We were not just saved to so we can enjoy Heaven in years to come. We have a calling and a mission to fulfill as long as we are on Earth. Jesus said, "Verily, verily, I say unto you, He that believeth on me, the works that I do shall he do also; and greater works than these shall he do; because I go unto my Father" (John 14:12). We do not need a new plan for our age, but rather a new commitment from God's people to obey His command to live and work as Jesus did.

Today's Growth Principle: God's purpose for our world will be accomplished as His children work to carry it out.

Recognize the Danger

And have no fellowship with the unfruitful works of darkness, but rather reprove them. For it is a shame even to speak of those things which are done of them in secret. But all things that are reproved are made manifest by the light: for whatsoever doth make manifest is light. Wherefore he saith, Awake thou that sleepest, and arise from the dead, and Christ shall give thee light.—EPHESIANS 5:11-14

When Hurricane Katrina flooded much of New Orleans, Coast Guard helicopter pilot Lt. Iain McConnell was sent from his base in Florida to help rescue those who had been stranded in their homes by the rising water. He and his crew were able to save dozens of people, but the thing he remembers most is not the people they rescued, but those who refused help. McConnell later wrote about one mission he'll never forget: "On the fourth mission, to our great frustration, we saved no one—but not for lack of trying. The dozens we attempted to rescue refused pickup! Some people told us to simply bring them food and water. 'You are trying to live in unhealthy conditions and the [flood]water will stay high for a long time,' we warned them. Still, they refused. I felt frustrated and angry, since we had used up precious time and fuel, and put ourselves at risk during each rescue attempt. I felt like they were ungrateful. But, in truth, they did not know how desperate their situation was."

The world around us is filled with dangers, although most of them are not as visible as quickly rising floodwaters. Yet too many people, including Christians, are living carelessly, without an appreciation for the peril they face. We have an enemy who is actively trying to destroy our lives every day, and we must be aware of the danger if we are to avoid it. "Be sober, be vigilant; because your adversary the devil, as a roaring lion, walketh about, seeking whom he may devour" (1 Peter 5:8).

Today's Growth Principle: The church and our world need more Christians who are aware of the urgency of what we face.

Who Sees God Work?

And shall say, Cast ye up, cast ye up, prepare the way, take up the stumblingblock out of the way of my people. For thus saith the high and lofty One that inhabiteth eternity, whose name is Holy; I dwell in the high and holy place, with him also that is of a contrite and humble spirit, to revive the spirit of the humble, and to revive the heart of the contrite ones. For I will not contend for ever, neither will I be always wroth: for the spirit should fail before me, and the souls which I have made.—ISAIAH 57:14–16

As we read the Bible and church history, we see God working in mighty ways. We sometimes fall into the trap of thinking that it was only because certain people had such amazing faith that they saw powerful works of God. Yet the pattern of God's work in our world is not so much about great people, but about humble ones. It is only when we recognize and acknowledge our own inability that we seek God's help.

When the disciples asked Jesus to teach them to pray, He gave them the model prayer, frequently referred to as "the Lord's prayer." Then He went on to give them an illustration of a man asking a friend for food to share with an unexpected guest. "And he said unto them, Which of you shall have a friend, and shall go unto him at midnight, and say unto him, Friend, lend me three loaves; For a friend of mine in his journey is come to me, and I have nothing to set before him?" (Luke 11:5–6).

We forget sometimes how much we need the Lord. If we think that we are sufficient in our own strength, ability, or resources, we will not urgently seek the help of God. And because He has ordained prayer as the means by which we receive His help, if we do not ask, we will not receive. "Hitherto have ye asked nothing in my name: ask, and ye shall receive, that your joy may be full" (John 16:24).

Today's Growth Principle: The only way to see God work in great power is to recognize our complete dependence on Him.

What Happens When We Pray?

Confess your faults one to another, and pray one for another, that ye may be healed. The effectual fervent prayer of a righteous man availeth much. Elias was a man subject to like passions as we are, and he prayed earnestly that it might not rain: and it rained not on the earth by the space of three years and six months. And he prayed again, and the heaven gave rain, and the earth brought forth her fruit.—JAMES 5:16–18

There is a great deal of attention paid to prayer in the church today, but many times it is only theoretical. We tend to talk about prayer more than we actually practice it. If we are not careful, we can become what Dr. Curtis Hutson called "practical atheists." We believe there is a God, but we live as if we do not. And when we do not pray, we rob both ourselves and God's work of the power and resources that are needed.

Prayer is not a relic. It is not something reserved for great saints of the past but out of date in the modern era. Prayer works just as surely now as it has for thousands of years. We must never forget the privilege God has offered us to boldly enter His presence and make our requests, confident in His ability to respond. Charles Spurgeon wrote, "Prayer moves the arm that moves the world."

Our society glorifies the myth of those who do it on their own, people who pull themselves up by their own bootstraps without any help. But God honors and rewards those who live in dependence on His strength and claim His promised resources to accomplish His purposes.

Sometimes we have a tendency to think of people who are consistent in prayer and often see God's answers to prayer as some kind of super Christians. Elijah's example, however, shows us that this is not the case at all. Elijah was just a man, and one who faced similar struggles as we do. The reason Elijah saw his prayers answered, however, is simply because he prayed.

Today's Growth Principle: A Christian who does not pray will not have a positive impact for Christ in the world.

Seeing God's Purpose

Behold, I go forward, but he is not there; and backward, but I cannot perceive him: On the left hand, where he doth work, but I cannot behold him: he hideth himself on the right hand, that I cannot see him: But he knoweth the way that I take: when he hath tried me, I shall come forth as gold. My foot hath held his steps, his way have I kept, and not declined.
—JOB 23:8–11

Very few people have suffered the number and intensity of the trials that Job faced. His story is so familiar that even the secular world uses it as a reference guide for tragedy. Yet for all its familiarity, too many times the point of the story gets lost. All of us endure hardship and affliction from time to time. Thankfully most of these trials are not on such a life-altering scale, but that does not mean that they are not painful and difficult to endure. The underlying truth we must remember is the one that Job kept coming back to: God is always faithful, and we can trust His purposes even when we cannot see what He is doing.

Alan Redpath wrote, "There is nothing—no circumstance, no trouble, no testing—that can ever touch me until, first of all, it has gone past God and past Christ right through to me. If it has come that far, it has come with a great purpose, which I may not understand at the moment. But as I refuse to become panicky, as I lift up my eyes to Him and accept it as coming from the throne of God for some great purpose of blessing to my own heart, no sorrow will ever disturb me, no trial will ever disarm me, no circumstance will cause me to fret—for I shall rest in the joy of what my Lord is! That is the rest of victory!"

In Romans 8:28 God assures us that His purposes for us are good and that He will make "…all things work together for good to them that love God, to them who are the called according to his purpose."

Today's Growth Principle: Victory is not found in the absence of trials, but in trusting God's purposes through them.

OCTOBER

Walking with a Renewed Mind

If so be that ye have heard him, and have been taught by him, as the truth is in Jesus: That ye put off concerning the former conversation the old man, which is corrupt according to the deceitful lusts; And be renewed in the spirit of your mind; And that ye put on the new man, which after God is created in righteousness and true holiness.—EPHESIANS 4:21–24

One of the earliest known teachers of painting in Italy was Cennino d'Andrea Cennini. Sometime in the late 1300s or early 1400s he wrote a book called *Il libro dell'arte: The Craftsman's Handbook*. It was an early "how to" book that covered everything from brushes and paints to detailed instruction on different painting techniques. Cennini recommended a course of study that lasted thirteen years, beginning with long sessions of copying the works of master artists to prepare the painter. He believed that by learning what greatly skilled artists had done, a young painter would develop proper habits and techniques.

There is a reason that Paul instructs us, "Let this mind be in you, which was also in Christ Jesus" (Philippians 2:5). When we view things as Christ does and think as He thinks, we will act as He acted. Proper behavior on the outside begins with proper thinking on the inside. Because of the fallen nature of man, our normal thought process is corrupted and cannot be trusted.

Instead, we must learn through the pages of Scripture and the illumination of the Holy Spirit to think with the mind of Christ. The disciples learned this lesson during their time with Jesus, and after He returned to Heaven, their conduct demonstrated their commitment to His way of thinking: "Now when they saw the boldness of Peter and John, and perceived that they were unlearned and ignorant men, they marvelled; and they took knowledge of them, that they had been with Jesus" (Acts 4:13).

Today's Growth Principle: Christ-like conduct in daily life begins when our minds are renewed to Christ-like thinking.

It Is Finished

For Christ is not entered into the holy places made with hands, which are the figures of the true; but into heaven itself, now to appear in the presence of God for us: Nor yet that he should offer himself often, as the high priest entereth into the holy place every year with blood of others; For then must he often have suffered since the foundation of the world: but now once in the end of the world hath he appeared to put away sin by the sacrifice of himself.—HEBREWS 9:24–26

In the 1980s, archaeologists discovered an ancient papyrus dating back to around 170 BC. The document is a receipt for payments over the course of several months. Because the papyrus is only a fragment, it is not clear to whom these payments were made, but one thing is very clear. Written at the top is the Greek word *tetelestai*, indicating that the accounts listed had been paid in full. This is the same word Jesus used on the cross, translated in English, "It is finished."

The work of salvation is done—once and for all. It does not need to be repeated, expanded, or improved. It only needs to be received by grace through faith. Most of the religious systems invented by people throughout history have focused on what man must do or not do in order to be accepted by God. But the plan of salvation God has given is different. It rests entirely upon the work Jesus did. False religion says "do," but Christ says, "done!" Salvation is a gift, received by faith in Christ's finished work.

It is true that Christians are commanded to be diligent in their work for the Lord, but that has nothing to do with receiving our redemption. Service is a matter of obedience, not of adding up points to "deserve" salvation. Nothing we can do could add to what Jesus completed, and any attempt to do so demonstrates a lack of understanding of salvation.

Today's Growth Principle: The sacrifice of Christ is sufficient for your salvation. If you have received Him as your Saviour, your sin debt is paid in full.

A Certain Eternal Destination

Wherefore Jesus also, that he might sanctify the people with his own blood, suffered without the gate. Let us go forth therefore unto him without the camp, bearing his reproach. For here have we no continuing city, but we seek one to come. By him therefore let us offer the sacrifice of praise to God continually, that is, the fruit of our lips giving thanks to his name.
—HEBREWS 13:12–15

If you have the opportunity to visit Israel, there are numerous amazing archaeological sites you can see. One of the most revealing is Tel Megiddo. This ancient city predates Israel's arrival in the land of Canaan, and is located near where the Battle of Armageddon will one day take place. A series of excavations has revealed no less than twenty-six distinct cities built on the site, each one on top of the ruins of the preceding city. It is a stark illustration of the transient nature of things here on Earth. Nothing truly lasts in this world.

Yet as Christians, we have the hope of a "continuing city." We are promised a permanent, abiding, unending dwelling in Heaven in a place where there is no sin, no sickness, no night and no tears. Not only is Heaven perfect now, but it always will be: "And there shall in no wise enter into it any thing that defileth, neither whatsoever worketh abomination, or maketh a lie: but they which are written in the Lamb's book of life" (Revelation 21:27).

The human mind with its finite understanding cannot grasp the full wonders of Heaven, but we do know that it will not only be perfect, but enduring. This life may be filled with things that do not last, but eternity with God, rejoicing in His presence, and praising and glorifying Him with perfect love will never end. The great glory of Heaven is that it will truly last forever.

Today's Growth Principle: The only sure and certain hope is not found in the things of this world, but in the promise of eternity.

Faithful unto Death

These things have I spoken unto you, that ye should not be offended. They shall put you out of the synagogues: yea, the time cometh, that whosoever killeth you will think that he doeth God service. And these things will they do unto you, because they have not known the Father, nor me. But these things have I told you, that when the time shall come, ye may remember that I told you of them. And these things I said not unto you at the beginning, because I was with you.—John 16:1–4

According to one recent report, more than ten Christians on average are killed every single day because of their faith. In country after country around the world, those who express faith in Jesus Christ put a target on themselves and their families because opposition to Christianity there is not limited to verbal objections. While we are thankful that in America we've been able to worship and witness without fear of being killed, that right is rare and not guaranteed to continue in the future.

Throughout the history of the church, men and women have faced a choice between being true to God and the risk of death. Though some have failed that challenge and renounced their faith, there is a glorious tradition of those who were faithful even unto death. While we certainly hope to never be placed in that position, we are not promised ease and safety as followers of the Lord who gave His life on a cross.

The only way we can pass the most critical tests of faith is for our faith to be strengthened before those moments come. Daniel did not decide whether or not to pray when the law forbidding it was passed. He had already made his decision and was praying long before (Daniel 6:10). The choices that we make today determine the choice we would make if we faced a life and death struggle of faith.

Today's Growth Principle: Our faith must be developed in times of calm in order to stand in the times of storm.

Addressing the Real Problem

And the LORD said unto Joshua, Get thee up; wherefore liest thou thus upon thy face? Israel hath sinned, and they have also transgressed my covenant which I commanded them: for they have even taken of the accursed thing, and have also stolen, and dissembled also, and they have put it even among their own stuff. Therefore the children of Israel could not stand before their enemies, but turned their backs before their enemies, because they were accursed: neither will I be with you any more, except ye destroy the accursed from among you.—JOSHUA 7:10–12

I heard about an irate woman who entered a bakery to register her complaint. "I sent my son in this morning to buy two pounds of cookies," she said. "But I just weighed them, and there is only one pound. I think you should check your scale." The manager looked at her for a moment and then replied, "Your son carried the cookies? Maybe you should weigh your son instead of the cookies."

We tend to look in the wrong places for the solutions to our problems. When the Children of Israel were defeated in the battle at Ai, Joshua turned to pray. While that may seem like the right place to look for the solution, God told him to get up and deal with the sin in the camp. The root of the problem was Achan's sin in taking spoils of war from Jericho which God had reserved for Himself. Until that problem was addressed, no progress could be made. The reality is that many times we would rather pray or perform a religious activity instead of confronting a sin, especially in our own lives. Too often we try to "make up" for our sins, not by confessing and forsaking them, but by service in some other area. God does not work on the barter system. He freely forgives our sin and by grace draws our hearts back into right fellowship with Him. But pretending as if sin does not exist is not a valid option if we want a close relationship with God and His power on our lives.

Today's Growth Principle: Guard against going through religious motions while avoiding confessing and forsaking sin.

An Unfailing Support

*Let your conversation be without covetousness; and be content with such things as ye have: for he hath said, I will never leave thee, nor forsake thee. So that we may boldly say, The Lord is my helper, and I will not fear what man shall do unto me.—*HEBREWS 13:5-6

Challenged by the pioneer missionary Robert Moffat, David Livingstone dedicated his life to taking the gospel to Africa. He labored for years, enduring great physical hardship. On a rare trip back to his homeland, Livingstone was asked to speak about his work. Standing with his left arm hanging useless after it had been crushed by a lion, with his gaunt body wracked with malaria, Livingstone said, "Would you like me to tell you what supported me through all the years of exile among a people whose language I could not understand, and whose attitude toward me was always uncertain and often hostile? It was this, '…Lo, I am with you alway, even unto the end of the world' [Matthew 28:20]. On these words I staked everything, and they never failed."

Through the centuries, the people of God have relied on the promises of God, and none of those promises have ever failed. The presence of God in our lives is certain and unchanging. He does not go away or abandon us or even rest. "Behold, he that keepeth Israel shall neither slumber nor sleep" (Psalm 121:4). The world is filled with obstacles, challenges, and difficulty. But as Christians, we never face any of them alone. Though we can ignore the resources and help God offers and insist on going our own way, we always have the option of fleeing to the throne of grace to seek God's grace and help (Hebrews 4:16). There is no reason for us to fear what we may face, because God's presence extends beyond this life. At the moment we die, we will be in Heaven with Him forever.

Today's Growth Principle: The Holy Spirit lives within every believer, and He is God's promise that we will never be forsaken.

Clean Living, Clean Lights

No man, when he hath lighted a candle, putteth it in a secret place, neither under a bushel, but on a candlestick, that they which come in may see the light. The light of the body is the eye: therefore when thine eye is single, thy whole body also is full of light; but when thine eye is evil, thy body also is full of darkness. Take heed therefore that the light which is in thee be not darkness.—LUKE 11:33–35

Before the spread of electricity, most homes in America used lanterns filled with kerosene or whale oil for light. The majority of these lanterns used a glass container to keep the flame from getting either blown out by gusts of wind or from starting a fire. Over time, the glass would be smudged by the soot from the burning wick, and the light would become less and less bright until the glass was cleaned. Without that important step, the light would not have the impact on the darkness that was needed.

The Bible uses a metaphor of Christians as lights in several places. Of course we understand that we do not produce the light—that is God's job, for light is part of His very nature and essence (1 John 1:5). But we are commanded to be lights as we live in a world of darkness. That requires a commitment on our part to live according to the Word of God. Pastor Bobby Roberson said, "I don't have to keep the light shining, I just have to keep the globe clean!"

It is a tragic error to suppose that by becoming more and more like the world we will gain a greater influence on others. Instead the accumulation of sinfulness and worldly living dims our light until it reaches the point where it can hardly be seen. Instead of conforming to the world, we need to be continually cleansed and forgiven so that our lights will shine brightly.

Today's Growth Principle: If our lives are not clean, the impact we have on those around us will be diminished.

The Greatest Rejoicing

But the father said to his servants, Bring forth the best robe, and put it on him; and put a ring on his hand, and shoes on his feet: And bring hither the fatted calf, and kill it; and let us eat, and be merry: For this my son was dead, and is alive again; he was lost, and is found. And they began to be merry.—LUKE 15:22-24

In his classic book, *Tom Sawyer*, Mark Twain recounts the decision of Tom, Huckleberry Finn, and another of their friends named Joe to run away and become pirates. The boys are having a wonderful time living on an island in the Mississippi River when they realize that their families and the people in the town believe that they have drowned. Tom gets the idea that they will wait until their funeral before revealing that they are still alive.

At the conclusion of the memorial service, the boys file into the back of the church, to the amazement of the people who have gathered to mourn. Twain wrote, "Suddenly the minister shouted at the top of his voice: 'Praise God from whom all blessings flow—SING!—and put your hearts in it!' And they did." The congregation, "Swelled up with a triumphant burst, and…it shook the rafters. As the 'sold' congregation trooped out they said they would almost be willing to be made ridiculous again," if it meant they could sing with such enthusiasm.

There is no joy like the joy of the lost who are found. This is true in the physical world, but it is even more true in the spiritual. The greatest need of every person is salvation, and when that need is met, there is great joy. Jesus said, "I say unto you, that likewise joy shall be in heaven over one sinner that repenteth, more than over ninety and nine just persons, which need no repentance" (Luke 15:7).

Today's Growth Principle: When we are faithful to witness and the lost are saved, there is great joy in both Heaven and Earth.

Praying for the Harvest

But when he saw the multitudes, he was moved with compassion on them, because they fainted, and were scattered abroad, as sheep having no shepherd. Then saith he unto his disciples, The harvest truly is plenteous, but the labourers are few; Pray ye therefore the Lord of the harvest, that he will send forth labourers into his harvest.—MATTHEW 9:36–38

During the Iranian hostage crisis in 1980, a missionary was invited to address a large church here in the States for their "missions minute" during one of their services. Since he had only been given a minute, he wanted to do something that would make an impact. He decided to ask the audience two revealing questions. He started with, "How many of you are praying for the fifty-two American hostages being held in Iran?" Hands went up all over the auditorium. "Praise the Lord," he said. "Now let me ask you another question. How many of you are praying for the forty-two million Iranians being held hostage by Islam?" Not one hand was raised.

There are many things each of us should be doing to promote and support the cause of reaching the lost, both at home and around the world. We should be involved with encouraging missionaries, giving to the cause, and if the opportunity is available, going to different mission fields. We should be active in the soulwinning program of the local church. We should keep up with what is going on regarding missions. But nothing we can do is more important than prayer.

The work of reaching the lost is not accomplished through human strength, ingenuity, programs, personalities, or methods. The work of reaching the lost is only accomplished through the power of God. And that power is only available through prayer. We should be regularly and diligently praying for the health, protection, and effectiveness of missionaries, and for more to join them in the work.

Today's Growth Principle: Not a single day should pass without your prayers for the work of evangelism all across the globe.

Beware of Biting

For, brethren, ye have been called unto liberty; only use not liberty for an occasion to the flesh, but by love serve one another. For all the law is fulfilled in one word, even in this; Thou shalt love thy neighbour as thyself. But if ye bite and devour one another, take heed that ye be not consumed one of another. This I say then, Walk in the Spirit, and ye shall not fulfil the lust of the flesh.—GALATIANS 5:13–16

In November of 2014, an Australian homeowner found an unpleasant surprise on her front porch—a poisonous brown tree snake nearly five feet long. The animal control expert who responded to her call for help determined that the snake was dead. The unusual thing was that its fangs were buried in its own back. A veterinarian who examined the snake reported that it appeared to have died from its own poison.

There are few things more damaging to the body of Christ than bitter and unloving words. Whether these are spoken to the individual directly, or whispered against them behind closed doors, words matter. They carry great weight, and can cause great harm. Solomon pointed out this enormous responsibility when he wrote, "Death and life are in the power of the tongue: and they that love it shall eat the fruit thereof" (Proverbs 18:21).

And many times, like the Australian brown snake, if we are not careful about our speech toward others, we will find ourselves the victim of our own poisonous words. The problem is that if our tongues are guided by our flesh rather than by the Holy Spirit, our words will not encourage and edify others. Left unchecked, negative words bring death and destruction. While we may only intend for that harm to come to others, if we plant a crop of criticism, gossip, and slander, we should not be surprised to receive the same in return.

Today's Growth Principle: The power of the tongue makes it essential that we choose our words to and about others with great care.

The Importance of Encouragement

For we can do nothing against the truth, but for the truth. For we are glad, when we are weak, and ye are strong: and this also we wish, even your perfection. Therefore I write these things being absent, lest being present I should use sharpness, according to the power which the Lord hath given me to edification, and not to destruction.—2 CORINTHIANS 13:8–10

I heard a story about a young lady named Mary who had a tough day at school. As soon as she got home, she started commiserating about it. She moaned, "Nobody loves me. the whole school hates me. In fact, the whole world hates me!" Her little brother quickly responded, "That's not true, Mary. Some people don't even *know* you." There are many times when those around us fail to provide the help and encouragement that we could use in a difficult moment.

In truth, all of us have the opportunity to edify and encourage others, and that is God's plan for our lives. God's creation was perfect before sin entered the world, yet God still said it was "not good" for man to be alone. While that specifically referred to marriage, it is true in every area of life. We are not designed to live in isolation. Solomon wrote, "Two are better than one; because they have a good reward for their labour. For if they fall, the one will lift up his fellow: but woe to him that is alone when he falleth; for he hath not another to help him up" (Ecclesiastes 4:9–10).

While we cannot guarantee we will always receive words of encouragement from others, we do have full control over what others hear from us. We always have the ability to speak kindly. As someone once said, "Nice is free." There's no shortage of people around us who would be thrilled to hear a word of comfort and hope from someone who cares.

Today's Growth Principle: A few kind words of encouragement cost us nothing, but they mean so very much to the hearer.

Christ-Like Service

But Jesus called them to him, and saith unto them, Ye know that they which are accounted to rule over the Gentiles exercise lordship over them; and their great ones exercise authority upon them. But so shall it not be among you: but whosoever will be great among you, shall be your minister: And whosoever of you will be the chiefest, shall be servant of all. For even the Son of man came not to be ministered unto, but to minister, and to give his life a ransom for many.—MARK 10:42–45

On their last trip to Jerusalem, where Jesus would be crucified, the disciples had a falling out. The conflict was not the result of a doctrinal disagreement or a difference over strategy to effectively reach the world. Instead, it was a fight over who would have the position of greatest prominence and power among them. Sadly, things have not changed much over two thousand years—there is still great desire among the people of God to be exalted and praised and to have authority over others. Yet the call of Christ remains clear: if we are to truly follow Him, we must serve others instead of trying to be seen as the greatest.

A major cause of conflict in the church today is that not enough Christians are willing to be humble servants. While many are willing to serve in positions of leadership or prominence, not as many are willing to serve simply to fill unnoticed needs. Those who gladly devote themselves to ministering to others, however, do not create strife. "Only by pride cometh contention: but with the well advised is wisdom" (Proverbs 13:10).

In the Upper Room the night before He died, Jesus took a towel and washed the feet of His disciples. This dirty and demeaning task was considered beneath the dignity of any self-respecting Jewish man, but the Lord of all creation willingly humbled Himself to perform it. Whether or not we are willing to make the sacrifices required to serve others speaks directly to our depth of commitment to live as Jesus commands.

Today's Growth Principle: There is little competition for the role of servant, but there is great praise from God for those who take it.

Putting Truth into Practice

If we assay to commune with thee, wilt thou be grieved? but who can withhold himself from speaking? Behold, thou hast instructed many, and thou hast strengthened the weak hands. Thy words have upholden him that was falling, and thou hast strengthened the feeble knees. But now it is come upon thee, and thou faintest; it toucheth thee, and thou art troubled.—JOB 4:2-5

When God allowed Satan to take away everything Job had, three friends came to commiserate with Job. They proved to be poor comforters because they did not understand the real reason for what was going on. Instead, they accused Job of harboring secret sins and somehow bringing his misfortune upon himself. Interestingly, however, Job's friend Eliphaz began his condemnation with words of praise. The description he provided of Job's life is one that any of us would be pleased to have said of our lives. He described how Job had been a help and source of comfort to many who had suffered greatly.

Yet, Eliphaz followed these words by insisting that in the moment of crisis, Job was failing the test he had encouraged others to pass. Now we know from the Bible account what was actually happening, and that Job's faith in God did not waver. He said, "Though he slay me, yet will I trust in him: but I will maintain mine own ways before him" (Job 13:15). All of us face moments when the things we have believed and taught and shared with others are tested. It is in those moments that the reality of our belief is revealed.

Given a choice, we would not select great tragedy for our lives or for those we love. However, God is at work in every situation, whether we can see His hand or not. Our responsibility is to maintain our faith and put into practice in our lives the truths we have believed and shared with others.

Today's Growth Principle: It is in the moments when our faith is tested most that we can truly assess its worth.

No Prayer, No Peace

Rejoice in the Lord alway: and again I say, Rejoice. Let your moderation be known unto all men. The Lord is at hand. Be careful for nothing; but in every thing by prayer and supplication with thanksgiving let your requests be made known unto God. And the peace of God, which passeth all understanding, shall keep your hearts and minds through Christ Jesus.—PHILIPPIANS 4:4–7

I read a parable about two women who had gotten together to do laundry and some clothing repair work. As they talked about their lives, one said, "My husband is so miserable. Nothing goes right at work, and he can't find anything good on television. Our home is a place of despair. When we go to church, the song leader is terrible and the pastor is dumb." The other replied, "My husband is so excited. He can't wait to go to church. He loves the sermons and enjoys his job. We laugh all the time and enjoy our family time together." Quiet descended on the room as the women continued working on their repairs. Then, at the same time, they both noticed which part of the garments they were repairing—the first woman was patching the seat of her husband's pants, while the other was patching the knees.

There is a powerful lesson in that story. The difference between those who are joyful and live lives of peace and those who do not, is not found in circumstances. All of us face troubles and trials as we go through this life in a fallen, sin-filled world. The difference is internal—whether we gripe and complain and feel sorry for ourselves, or whether we turn to God, praying in faith for His grace to face our trials. The peace of God is not a random feeling that comes and goes. It is a conscious awareness of His presence found as we spend time in His Word and in prayer. Too often, prayer is a last resort rather than our first response to a challenge or trial.

Today's Growth Principle: No matter the troubles we face, there is peace for those who pour out their hearts to God.

The Impact of the Bible

I have given them thy word; and the world hath hated them, because they are not of the world, even as I am not of the world. I pray not that thou shouldest take them out of the world, but that thou shouldest keep them from the evil. They are not of the world, even as I am not of the world. Sanctify them through thy truth: thy word is truth.—JOHN 17:14–17

Those of us who love the Word of God know that it is a source of peace, hope, inspiration, guidance, instruction, and doctrine. But to much of the world, the Bible is simply a collection of fables, unworthy of attention or respect. If we hold a high and proper opinion of the Scriptures, we should not be surprised to find that the world will reject our beliefs as a source of conflict and strife. As Christians in America, we have enjoyed great religious freedom, but that is not promised to us. We need to know what we believe and why we believe it, and be ready to stand for it no matter what. First Peter 3:15 admonishes us, "But sanctify the Lord God in your hearts: and be ready always to give an answer to every man that asketh you a reason of the hope that is in you with meekness and fear."

The preparation of the Christian for living in days of persecution and opposition begins with our relationship with the Bible. If we do not have a deep personal commitment to the Word of God before the trouble starts, it will be too late to develop it afterwards. Yet too often, we treat the Bible casually and pick and choose what to focus on rather than taking all that God has given us seriously. This especially applies to the parts that convict us of sin and call us to repentance. Charles Spurgeon said, "If any text has a quarrel with you, quarrel with yourself; but yield wholly to the Word of God." Our opinions and traditions are not strong enough to overcome the world, but the Bible is.

Today's Growth Principle: When we love and follow the Bible, the world may hate us, but God will sanctify and empower us.

The Key to Effective Ministry

But we were gentle among you, even as a nurse cherisheth her children: So being affectionately desirous of you, we were willing to have imparted unto you, not the gospel of God only, but also our own souls, because ye were dear unto us. For ye remember, brethren, our labour and travail: for labouring night and day, because we would not be chargeable unto any of you, we preached unto you the gospel of God.—1 THESSALONIANS 2:7–9

At a time without any of the modern communication tools or travel comforts that we take for granted, the Apostle Paul journeyed thousands of miles, enduring great physical suffering to preach the gospel to multitudes of people. He planted churches across the Roman Empire, preaching with power and teaching the new converts. Young believers who he trained, like Timothy and Titus, carried on the work of the gospel ministry as they led churches in places like Ephesus and Crete, continuing what Paul had begun. There is no question that Paul's ministry was effective. But why did he accomplish so much?

We tend to look at Paul as a giant of the faith, but while he was a great pattern and model of ministry, Paul was not without his faults and his detractors. It was not so much his talent or gifts as a speaker that produced the results as it was the power of the Spirit poured out through Paul's heart for those to whom he ministered. In fact, Paul's speaking was sometimes critiqued as ineffective. "For his letters, say they, are weighty and powerful; but his bodily presence is weak, and his speech contemptible" (2 Corinthians 10:10).

But no one could deny the compassion and fervor with which Paul labored to reach the lost and train the saints. He cared about people. As a result, he was patient, gentle, dedicated, and loving in his approach. Paul shook the world, not by his gifts, but by his compassion.

Today's Growth Principle: Effective ministry to others is not a matter of talent, skill, and gifts, but of obedience and heart.

Get to Work

Remember therefore from whence thou art fallen, and repent, and do the first works; or else I will come unto thee quickly, and will remove thy candlestick out of his place, except thou repent. But this thou hast, that thou hatest the deeds of the Nicolaitans, which I also hate. He that hath an ear, let him hear what the Spirit saith unto the churches; To him that overcometh will I give to eat of the tree of life, which is in the midst of the paradise of God.—REVELATION 2:5-7

There is an old story about a father whose son was somewhat stubborn and required a great deal of persuading to obey the instructions he was given. After he graduated from high school, he decided to join the Marines. On his first trip home after boot camp, he was noticeably changed. He said to his father, "You know, my life makes sense now, Dad. Everything you said and did when I was growing up now makes sense. I really, really understand." Somewhat surprised, but very pleased, his father expressed his pride and appreciation. Then he asked his son, "What is the biggest lesson you have learned?" Without hesitation the young man replied, "I learned what *now* means."

The Lord does not just expect us to do what He commands, but to do it without delay. There is a marked human tendency to procrastination, even in situations in which speedy action seems the best course. When the plague of frogs descended on Egypt, rendering the land nearly unlivable, Pharaoh begged Moses to pray that they would be taken away. When Moses agreed, he asked when Pharaoh wanted that to happen. "And he said, To morrow. And he said, Be it according to thy word: that thou mayest know that there is none like unto the LORD our God" (Exodus 8:10).

If we know what is right, there is no reason for delay in doing it. We honor God when we quickly respond to Him.

Today's Growth Principle: There is no substitute for quick obedience to whatever God places in front of us to do.

When the Air Conditioner Fails

And now, behold, the children of Ammon and Moab and mount Seir, whom thou wouldest not let Israel invade, when they came out of the land of Egypt, but they turned from them, and destroyed them not; Behold, I say, how they reward us, to come to cast us out of thy possession, which thou hast given us to inherit. O our God, wilt thou not judge them? for we have no might against this great company that cometh against us; neither know we what to do: but our eyes are upon thee.
—2 CHRONICLES 20:10–12

I read about a veteran military pilot who was teaching a group of trainees. At one point in his talk, he referred to the plane's jet engine as an air conditioner. One of the new pilots raised his hand and asked why he called the engine that. With a grin the veteran replied, "Because if it stops working, you start sweating real quick!" All of us face moments when something we're counting on suddenly falls away. Perhaps it is a serious medical diagnosis, a car accident, a family relationship torn apart, or a job that unexpectedly goes away. How should we respond in those moments when the "air conditioner" fails?

King Jehoshaphat had one of those moments when the Ammonites and Moabites joined forces to fight against him. His army was greatly outnumbered, and there seemed to be no chance of survival, let alone victory. But in that moment he cried out to God in faith, and God heard and answered his prayers. Not only did God bring deliverance, but Jehoshaphat didn't even have to fight. God turned the alliance of enemies against each other, and they destroyed their own armies.

God is able to deliver us from trials and troubles today. But we must keep our faith and focus on Him, rather than giving in to despair or trying to take matters into our own hands.

Today's Growth Principle: Those who keep their eyes on God in times of trouble will find His help and deliverance.

Reasons to Refrain from Wrath

Every good gift and every perfect gift is from above, and cometh down from the Father of lights, with whom is no variableness, neither shadow of turning. Of his own will begat he us with the word of truth, that we should be a kind of firstfruits of his creatures. Wherefore, my beloved brethren, let every man be swift to hear, slow to speak, slow to wrath: For the wrath of man worketh not the righteousness of God.—JAMES 1:17–20

There are not any new problems in our day. There may be new forms and methods of doing wrong, but the basic underlying temptations and sins are the same as they have been for thousands of years. The same sins of the heart—envy, lust, bitterness, and anger—that spurred the evil in the days of Noah that resulted in the destruction of the world by the Flood are still with us today. And of all the sins that bring destruction and damage to the world, few have a deeper impact than anger. This was just as true in the first century when James penned the words in the verses above as it is today.

James gives us two powerful reasons to refrain from wrath: First, James points out the purpose of God for our lives—that our salvation produces fruitful lives. God is not just interested in our eternal destiny, but in how we live here on Earth. Being quick to anger, "flying off the handle," and losing our temper hinders fruit bearing. If we are known as angry and wrathful people, who will want to listen to us proclaim a message of peace and hope?

Second, we see that anger left unchecked always leads to further sin. Those who have wrath in their hearts will soon have evil in their deeds. We cannot be the righteous children of God we are called to be if we are angry all the time.

Today's Growth Principle: If we long to be like Jesus, we cannot allow anger to rule unchecked in our hearts.

A Passion for People

Say not ye, There are yet four months, and then cometh harvest? behold, I say unto you, Lift up your eyes, and look on the fields; for they are white already to harvest. And he that reapeth receiveth wages, and gathereth fruit unto life eternal: that both he that soweth and he that reapeth may rejoice together. And herein is that saying true, One soweth, and another reapeth. I sent you to reap that whereon ye bestowed no labour: other men laboured, and ye are entered into their labours.—JOHN 4:35–38

After many years of fruitful work with the Salvation Army, the founder, General William Booth, was invited to a personal audience with Queen Victoria. The ruler of England had heard about his work in the slums among the poor, preaching the gospel, and helping those in need. When she asked for the secret of his success, Booth replied, "Your Majesty, some men have a passion for money. Some people have a passion for things. I have a passion for people."

All around us there are people with an eternal destiny who need someone to give them the good news of salvation through the sacrifice of Jesus Christ. Yet many Christians seldom, if ever, think about that most pressing need. Like the disciples who wanted Jesus to send the crowd of people away without any food, we too often view others as an annoyance or a burden, rather than seeing them as precious souls for whom Christ died.

The harvest is not waiting to get ripe. The fields *are* white—ready for harvest. Tens of thousands of people will die today, many of them without ever hearing the gospel. There are no second chances to accept Christ. If no one reaches them in this life, they will spend eternity in Hell apart from God. That sobering truth should motivate us and give us a burning passion for people.

Today's Growth Principle: If our hearts are not broken over those who are lost, we do not have the heart of Jesus.

Off the Hook Forever

Let the wicked forsake his way, and the unrighteous man his thoughts:
and let him return unto the LORD, and he will have mercy upon him;
and to our God, for he will abundantly pardon. For my thoughts are not
your thoughts, neither are your ways my ways, saith the LORD. For as the
heavens are higher than the earth, so are my ways higher than your ways,
and my thoughts than your thoughts.—ISAIAH 55:7–9

Under the United States Constitution, the president has wide ranging power to grant pardons. Article II, Section 1 says that the president "shall have power to grant reprieves and pardons for offences against the United States, except in cases of impeachment." Once the president has issued a pardon, there is no review or recourse for anyone who objects. The law of the land grants presidents the ability to act in all federal cases except for impeachments.

God's power, however, goes significantly further. While the president can give earthly pardon, God is still the final Judge, and all will stand before Him one day, regardless of their earthly verdict. And yet, God is able and willing to fully forgive and pardon all that we have done against Him. No sin is too great to be pardoned if it is confessed and forsaken. With such a wide ranging and unqualified offer of forgiveness on the table, why do so many people fail to take advantage of His abundant pardon? In large measure, it is because we are bound by the limits of our thinking. Because we do not find it easy to freely forgive and forget what has been done to us, we think God will hold grudges and remember our sins. But the Lord is not limited in His ability to wipe the slate clean. He never brings up sins that we have dealt with. Indeed, He forgets them. "For I will be merciful to their unrighteousness, and their sins and their iniquities will I remember no more" (Hebrews 8:12). When we have been forgiven by God, we are cleansed forever.

Today's Growth Principle: Having received a full pardon from God, we should not let guilt for what has been forgiven keep us in chains.

Aligned with God

Therefore if any man be in Christ, he is a new creature: old things are passed away; behold, all things are become new. And all things are of God, who hath reconciled us to himself by Jesus Christ, and hath given to us the ministry of reconciliation; To wit, that God was in Christ, reconciling the world unto himself, not imputing their trespasses unto them; and hath committed unto us the word of reconciliation.—2 Corinthians 5:17–19

All over the world there are people who realize that they need to have a proper relationship with God. While some deny His existence, most recognize the reality of a Deity, even if they do not fully understand who God is. There are many religions and belief systems that attempt to bring us into alignment with God, but there is only one way that works. Only through accepting the payment made for our sins by Christ on the cross, can we be reconciled to God. There are no other options.

No effort on our part can atone for our sins, because the only just and fitting penalty for sin is separation from God forever. "For the wages of sin is death; but the gift of God is eternal life through Jesus Christ our Lord" (Romans 6:23). Yet in His amazing love and mercy, God provided His Son Jesus as the sacrifice for our sins. "Who his own self bare our sins in his own body on the tree, that we, being dead to sins, should live unto righteousness: by whose stripes ye were healed" (1 Peter 2:24). When we, in faith, receive His offer of salvation, our sins are forgiven—completely and forever.

Charles Spurgeon said, "When God pardons a man's sins, he pardons them all; he makes a clean sweep of the whole. God never pardons half a man's sins, and leaves the rest in His book. He has pardon for all sin at once." When we turn to Christ and accept Him as our Saviour, His perfect holiness is credited to our account in place of our sins. There is no other way to be right with God.

Today's Growth Principle: If you claim Christ's offer of salvation, your sins will be forgiven forever and you will receive eternal life.

Ready to Receive God's Blessing

And I will send hornets before thee, which shall drive out the Hivite, the Canaanite, and the Hittite, from before thee. I will not drive them out from before thee in one year; lest the land become desolate, and the beast of the field multiply against thee. By little and little I will drive them out from before thee, until thou be increased, and inherit the land.
—EXODUS 23:28–30

Many of us remember the childhood experience of "driving" the family car while seated on the lap of a parent or relative. We would tightly grip the wheel with both little hands while the adult pushed on the gas pedal and brake. They would be right there to steer for us if we started to get off course.

The reality was that while we might have wanted to drive the car, we simply weren't ready for the responsibility involved and didn't have the skills needed to do so safely. It would take years of physical growth, mental development, and emotional maturity before we were ready to take the wheel.

Often people are frustrated because God is not giving them the things they want—a particular position, a promotion, an opportunity to play a certain role. What they fail to realize is the delay could well be the result of the fact that God knows they are not yet ready to handle that task. We tend to view our strengths, talents, and abilities through a lens that makes us look good, but God knows what is in our hearts.

If rather than viewing delay as a judgment or a failure of God to give us what we have coming, we would view that time as a learning experience, we would probably receive new opportunities and open doors more quickly. It is always safe to trust God's judgment and timing when it comes to our path through life.

Today's Growth Principle: Trust God to give you the responsibilities and privileges for which He knows you are prepared.

Faith in Times of Crisis

*Hear my cry, O God; attend unto my prayer. From the end of the earth will I cry unto thee, when my heart is overwhelmed: lead me to the rock that is higher than I. For thou hast been a shelter for me, and a strong tower from the enemy. I will abide in thy tabernacle for ever: I will trust in the covert of thy wings. Selah.—*PSALM 61:1-4

The idea that a Christian will only receive good things from God and coast through life on a bed of blessings sounds good and draws large crowds and television audiences. But it is not the reality of life presented in Scripture. David, who was known as a man after God's own heart, spent years running for his life. He was the number one target on King Saul's list, singled out for death not because he had done wrong, but because of Saul's jealousy. Yet even on days when it seemed that everyone on Earth had turned against him, David clung to his faith in God.

Faith is not a barrier that prevents trouble from coming; it is a shield that keeps those troubles from conquering us. In the moments that challenge us the most, we sometimes feel that we must be strong. But victory is not found in our strength; it is only found in the power of God. Even the apostle Paul, to whom we look as a great example of the Christian life, knew what it was like to be pushed to the edge. He wrote, "For, when we were come into Macedonia, our flesh had no rest, but we were troubled on every side; without were fightings, within were fears" (2 Corinthians 7:5).

We sometimes think that if our faith were stronger we wouldn't worry at all. But David was overwhelmed and Paul was troubled. We must understand that faith is not the absence of fear, but the continuance of trust and obedience.

Today's Growth Principle: Faith in times of trial provides the strength to trust God until the victory comes.

Doing What Matters Most

And it came to pass, that after three days they found him in the temple, sitting in the midst of the doctors, both hearing them, and asking them questions. And all that heard him were astonished at his understanding and answers. And when they saw him, they were amazed: and his mother said unto him, Son, why hast thou thus dealt with us? behold, thy father and I have sought thee sorrowing. And he said unto them, How is it that ye sought me? wist ye not that I must be about my Father's business?
—LUKE 2:46–49

None of us has enough time, money, or talent to accomplish everything that could be done. Every day we have to make choices about how we will invest what we have been given. Every night there will be things that did not get accomplished. Our task is to work to the best of our ability to see that the most important things are done. This requires that we identify what matters most, and dedicate ourselves to living so that those things are accomplished.

Priorities do not set themselves. You must purposefully set them and then resist the natural drift away from them. This will include saying "no" to some opportunities or activities that don't contribute toward or that prohibit you from doing what matters most. But it is easier to say "no" to something when there is a greater "yes" burning inside. When you start by identifying your God-given priorities, it helps you identify that greater "yes," making your needed "no" more clear.

The excuses that we often hear (or that we use ourselves) for why things that matter don't get done usually reveal that it was what mattered most that was done rather than what was claimed as the goal. Many people lament what they have failed to accomplish without realizing that it was the choices they made that kept them from their goals.

Today's Growth Principle: When our hearts are filled with what matters most to God, we will devote our lives to what is truly important.

The Problem Lies Within

Let no man say when he is tempted, I am tempted of God: for God cannot be tempted with evil, neither tempteth he any man: But every man is tempted, when he is drawn away of his own lust, and enticed. Then when lust hath conceived, it bringeth forth sin: and sin, when it is finished, bringeth forth death.—JAMES 1:13-15

In 1958, a high school guidance counselor wrote a recommendation to Harvard University, urging them to admit one of her students. She said, "I believe Ted has one of the greatest contributions to make to society. He is reflective, sensitive, and deeply conscious of his responsibilities to society." The student she was recommending had an IQ of 167 and was graduating from high school at just sixteen years of age. The young man, who so many expected to do great things was Ted Kaczynski, who became the terrorist murderer known as the "Unabomber."

Dr. Bob Jones, Sr. used to say, "Behind every tragedy in human character lies a long process of wicked thinking." We do not accomplish good things because we are good. Every human born into this world has a sinful nature that is opposed to God. The most brilliant minds and the best education money can buy cannot change the inherent nature of man. Only God can do that through the power of salvation that provides a new nature. The only hope, the only cure, for sin is found in turning to Christ. The Bible tells us, "Therefore if any man be in Christ, he is a new creature: old things are passed away; behold, all things are become new" (2 Corinthians 5:17).

Once we are saved, we still wrestle with fleshly desires that lead us into temptation. Only by recognizing that we have been delivered from sin and relying on the power of God to resist temptation will we be able to experience victory.

Today's Growth Principle: Rather than blaming our circumstances for temptation, we should look to God for His help in overcoming it.

Faith in Lengthy Trials

And her adversary also provoked her sore, for to make her fret, because the LORD had shut up her womb. And as he did so year by year, when she went up to the house of the LORD, so she provoked her; therefore she wept, and did not eat. Then said Elkanah her husband to her, Hannah, why weepest thou? and why eatest thou not? and why is thy heart grieved? am not I better to thee than ten sons?—1 SAMUEL 1:6–8

There have been times in my life when trouble has come, and I've gone to my knees in prayer and seen God work almost immediately to resolve the issue. I've seen Him provide in ways beyond human explanation—ways that could only be Him at work. There have been other times of trouble when my prayers and petitions have been every bit just as sincere and heartfelt, when there is nothing hindering my relationship with God, when I am walking in close fellowship with Him, but there has been no immediate answer.

God does promise to meet our needs, but He does not promise to work in the way that seems best to us. What He expects from us is that we trust just as much when the answer to our prayer is delayed as we do when it comes right away. The natural tendency in those moments is to think that God has failed and that we must take matters into our own hands. But that approach always leads to failure.

In truth, there are times when a delay is a vital part of God's plan to strengthen and build us into what He desires. James 1:3–4 tells us, "Knowing this, that the trying of your faith worketh patience. But let patience have her perfect work, that ye may be perfect and entire, wanting nothing." We must continue to trust and wait for God to work in His time.

Today's Growth Principle: The true measure of our faith can only be taken in times when it is put to the most severe test.

Patterns to Follow, Patterns to Break

Amon was twenty and two years old when he began to reign, and he reigned two years in Jerusalem. And his mother's name was Meshullemeth, the daughter of Haruz of Jotbah. And he did that which was evil in the sight of the LORD, as his father Manasseh did. And he walked in all the way that his father walked in, and served the idols that his father served, and worshipped them: And he forsook the LORD God of his fathers, and walked not in the way of the LORD. —2 KINGS 21:19–22

Some people learn early of God's love and accept His salvation at a young age. They develop the habits of church attendance, Bible reading, prayer, and giving early in life. Others do not have that advantage. Being saved later, there are negative habits from their younger years that they must overcome. Dostoyevsky wrote, "The second half of a man's life is made up of the habits he acquired during the first half."

But all of us, whether we had a head start with a godly family or not, have tendencies and habits of which we must be aware if we want to do what is right and pleasing in God's eyes. It is easy for us to overlook things that we are used to doing. For example, a person who grew up giving quick vent to anger may not recognize the issues their outbursts can cause for themselves and for others. It seems "normal" because it is part of a pattern of living.

We need to be alert and aware as we make our way through life to negative tendencies and patterns that we may have acquired, and be vigilant not to accept them. In the same way, we need to be aware of our good habits and behaviors, and do what we can to reinforce them so that they continue.

Today's Growth Principle: If we do not pay careful attention to our habits and tendencies, we will tolerate sin that should be cast out of our lives.

God Always Cares

And there arose a great storm of wind, and the waves beat into the ship, so that it was now full. And he was in the hinder part of the ship, asleep on a pillow: and they awake him, and say unto him, Master, carest thou not that we perish? And he arose, and rebuked the wind, and said unto the sea, Peace, be still. And the wind ceased, and there was a great calm. And he said unto them, Why are ye so fearful? how is it that ye have no faith?—MARK 4:37–40

After a long day of ministry, Jesus got in a boat with His disciples to cross the Sea of Galilee. Because of the cliff formations that ring much of that small body of water, it is subject to violent storms. The winds sweep down and stir the water, creating massive waves. Such a storm hit their boat that night, and in fear and despair the disciples woke Jesus with a form of the question many of us have asked of God at one time or another: "Don't You care about my trouble?"

It is always a mistake to evaluate how God feels about us by how we feel about our circumstances. His love is unfailing and never changes. That does not mean that we will never experience storms. And while some of the hardships we undergo are a result of the consequences of our choices and actions, many times we are suffering because we are right where God wants us to be. The storm the disciples experienced led them to doubt whether Jesus cared about their needs. Yet by this time they had seen ample evidence of both the power of God and the love Jesus had for them. In the midst of the storm, they forgot that truth, and as a result their faith failed in the moment of challenge.

You can settle it in your heart right now: God loves you, no matter what you are facing. The winds and waves of life are never an indication that God has forsaken us. They are only a reminder that nothing is greater than His power.

Today's Growth Principle: If we listen to our fears rather than our faith, we will doubt God's love and care for us.

Worthy of the Cost

Do all things without murmurings and disputings: That ye may be blameless and harmless, the sons of God, without rebuke, in the midst of a crooked and perverse nation, among whom ye shine as lights in the world; Holding forth the word of life; that I may rejoice in the day of Christ, that I have not run in vain, neither laboured in vain. Yea, and if I be offered upon the sacrifice and service of your faith, I joy, and rejoice with you all.—PHILIPPIANS 2:14–17

The pioneering work of missionary J. Hudson Taylor in China benefited greatly from the help of his wife Maria. She had spent her early years in China, and her knowledge of the language was invaluable to their ministry. In addition to teaching, writing, and witnessing, she gave birth to nine children, only four of whom survived to adulthood. All four adult Taylor children became missionaries with the China Inland Mission. Despite her grief at the loss of her little boys and girls, Maria Taylor remained faithful to the work until her death from cholera in 1871. On her gravestone these words were carved:

AN EARNEST CHRISTIAN AND DEVOTED MISSIONARY,

A FAITHFUL AND AFFECTIONATE WIFE AND TENDER MOTHER,

A SINCERE AND WARM HEARTED FRIEND,

TO HER TO LIVE WAS CHRIST, AND TO DIE WAS GAIN

The things we endure in this life because of our service for God may sometimes be painful, but they do not compare to what God has done for us, nor do they compare to the rewards that He offers those who faithfully serve Him. "And he said unto them, Verily I say unto you, There is no man that hath left house, or parents, or brethren, or wife, or children, for the kingdom of God's sake, Who shall not receive manifold more in this present time, and in the world to come life everlasting" (Luke 18:29–30).

Today's Growth Principle: There is no sacrifice we make for God's work that is greater than He deserves.

The Joy of Answered Prayer

And Hannah prayed, and said, My heart rejoiceth in the LORD, mine horn is exalted in the LORD: my mouth is enlarged over mine enemies; because I rejoice in thy salvation. There is none holy as the LORD: for there is none beside thee: neither is there any rock like our God. Talk no more so exceeding proudly; let not arrogancy come out of your mouth: for the LORD is a God of knowledge, and by him actions are weighed.
—1 SAMUEL 2:1–3

Helen Roseveare, who was a medical missionary in Africa, told the story of a remarkable answer to prayer. A mother had died in childbirth leaving a dangerously premature infant child. There were no advanced facilities, so their normal practice was to keep the baby warm with a hot water bottle. But as they filled the bottle it burst because the rubber had decayed in the African climate. Unfortunately, they had no replacement. Dr. Roseveare doubted the baby would live. But that day they prayed with the other children at the mission.

Dr. Roseveare recounted, "During the prayer time, one ten-year-old girl, Ruth, prayed with the usual blunt consciousness of our African children. 'Please, God,' she prayed, 'send us a water bottle. It'll be no good tomorrow, God, the baby'll be dead; so, please send it this afternoon.'" Dr. Roseveare was stunned at the girl's simple faith, hardly daring to believe the prayer could be answered. But that very day she received a package sent by friends from her home church in England. Not only had the package been five months in the mail, but it was the first package she had received in four years on the field. Among the supplies it included was a new hot water bottle that saved the baby's life.

There is no restriction on God's ability to meet and supply our needs. Yet all too often we fail to receive what God could and would give us simply because we lack the faith to ask Him to work.

Today's Growth Principle: When we do not believe God enough to pray, we miss the joy of seeing Him working in our lives.

NOVEMBER

The Man Who Amazed Jesus

The centurion answered and said, Lord, I am not worthy that thou shouldest come under my roof: but speak the word only, and my servant shall be healed. For I am a man under authority, having soldiers under me: and I say to this man, Go, and he goeth; and to another, Come, and he cometh; and to my servant, Do this, and he doeth it. When Jesus heard it, he marvelled, and said to them that followed, Verily I say unto you, I have not found so great faith, no, not in Israel.—MATTHEW 8:8–10

When it comes to faith, we aren't always clear on what it means. We often talk of faith as an abstract belief, but Bible faith is never seen in the mind. Instead it is demonstrated in the actions taken by those who have it. So it was in the life of a Roman centurion who came to Jesus to ask that his servant be healed.

It is easy for us to brush by the cultural details of this story, but they are relevant to understanding the significance of the passage: Roman centurions in Jesus' day did not attain their position by popularity or connections. A general might owe his job to a rich relative and live above the fray of battle, but the centurions, each of whom commanded one hundred trained soldiers, were in the thick of the fighting. They were hardened men who possessed the power of life and death over those under their command. But what they did understand was authority—the relation between command and obedience.

That is what amazed Jesus. The centurion's faith was expressed in his belief that a word from Jesus would be obeyed without Him ever seeing the servant. He believed that nothing, neither disease nor distance, could stop what Jesus said from happening. That is the faith God is looking for—a belief in His Word that is expressed in our actions relying on what He promised.

Today's Growth Principle: If our faith is to be pleasing to God, then it must be an active, obedient faith.

Be an Encourager

The Lord give mercy unto the house of Onesiphorus; for he oft refreshed me, and was not ashamed of my chain: But, when he was in Rome, he sought me out very diligently, and found me. The Lord grant unto him that he may find mercy of the Lord in that day: and in how many things he ministered unto me at Ephesus, thou knowest very well.
—2 TIMOTHY 1:16–18

On his first preaching trip to England, D. L. Moody had an encounter with a British preacher named Henry Varley that changed the course of his life. Years later, now as the best known evangelist in the world, Moody returned to England and asked to meet with Varley to thank him for the impact of their brief meeting. Varley later wrote: "Mr. Moody asked me to join him in the vestry of the Baptist Church. We were alone, and he recalled the night's meeting at Willow Park and our converse the following morning. 'Do you remember your words?' he said. I replied, 'I well remember our interview, but I do not recall any special utterance.'"

Varley had said to Moody, "The world has yet to see what God will do with a man fully consecrated to Him." Though he didn't recall the words, they made a dramatic impact. Moody said, "Those were the words sent to my soul, through you, from the living God. As I crossed the wide Atlantic, the boards of the deck of the vessel were engraved with them, and when I reached Chicago, the very paving stones seemed marked with [them]. I felt that I must not let more time pass until I let you know how God had used your words to my inmost soul." Few people have heard of Henry Varley, but his words of encouragement and challenge sparked a mighty movement of God. We have the opportunity to encourage others every day—and we should do it.

Today's Growth Principle: The power of our words to help and encourage others in their Christian lives is a mighty responsibility.

Expecting Opposition

And it may be that I will abide, yea, and winter with you, that ye may bring me on my journey whithersoever I go. For I will not see you now by the way; but I trust to tarry a while with you, if the Lord permit. But I will tarry at Ephesus until Pentecost. For a great door and effectual is opened unto me, and there are many adversaries.—1 CORINTHIANS 16:6–9

Although there are some who teach that the Christian life is an uninterrupted succession of blessings followed by happiness that leads to relaxation and enjoyment in great abundance, this is not what we find in God's Word. While God does bless His children, He does not promise us lives of ease. Everyone who has accomplished great things for God's Kingdom has done so in the face of obstacles. In fact if we are not being resisted and opposed by the forces of evil, it is probably an indication that we are not doing what we should for God. If we are doing something meaningful and important for God, we should not expect things to go smoothly.

The night before the crucifixion Jesus told His disciples, "These things I have spoken unto you, that in me ye might have peace. In the world ye shall have tribulation: but be of good cheer; I have overcome the world" (John 16:33). If our perfect Lord was violently and bitterly opposed, why should we expect acceptance and ease?

Rather than looking to the world for comfort, we should expect opposition while knowing the Lord Himself will comfort our hearts. Rather than being discouraged by obstacles, we should be encouraged knowing that Jesus has overcome the world and can give us peace through the difficulties. In fact, sometimes opposition is a sign that we are making a difference for God. Even Paul found that God's open doors of ministry didn't come without spiritual conflict.

Today's Growth Principle: The devil never gives up without a struggle, and if we are working for God, we can expect his opposition.

The God of Deliverance

I acknowledged my sin unto thee, and mine iniquity have I not hid. I said, I will confess my transgressions unto the LORD; and thou forgavest the iniquity of my sin. Selah. For this shall every one that is godly pray unto thee in a time when thou mayest be found: surely in the floods of great waters they shall not come nigh unto him. Thou art my hiding place; thou shalt preserve me from trouble; thou shalt compass me about with songs of deliverance. Selah.—PSALM 32:5-7

While fighting on Long Island in the early part of the Revolutionary War, George Washington found his troops outnumbered by British forces under the command of General Howe by nearly four to one. They were in danger of being surrounded and forced to surrender, a defeat that would have almost surely ended the bid for American independence. Washington's only hope was to evacuate his troops under cover of darkness so that the war could continue.

The audacious plan worked because of three events that each occurred with perfect timing. A severe daytime storm with strong winds kept the British Navy from sailing up behind Washington's position. Then overnight the wind died and the seas calmed so that the small boats could ferry the soldiers to safety. Finally, before dawn the next morning, a dense fog prevented the British from seeing that Washington had fled. God had provided a way of escape. Washington would later write, "The Hand of Providence has been so conspicuous in all this—the course of the war—that he must be worse than an infidel that lacks faith."

God's hand is not shortened in our day. He is still able to work mighty things for those who rely on Him in faith. We have been given the privilege of fleeing to Him for refuge and deliverance, and we should do so in times of trouble.

Today's Growth Principle: Those who keep their trust in God in their darkest days will see His hand work in great ways in their lives.

The Only Cure for Sin

Be it known unto you all, and to all the people of Israel, that by the name of Jesus Christ of Nazareth, whom ye crucified, whom God raised from the dead, even by him doth this man stand here before you whole. This is the stone which was set at nought of you builders, which is become the head of the corner. Neither is there salvation in any other: for there is none other name under heaven given among men, whereby we must be saved.—ACTS 4:10–12

Though many people like to think that they are okay because they are not as bad as some others, the reality is that all of us are sinners. Every person born into this world is born under the curse and penalty of sin. And despite what some people say, there is only one way sin can be forgiven and our relationship with God changed from our natural enmity toward Him to becoming part of His family—through accepting the salvation freely offered through Jesus Christ. No other solution is available, and if someone chooses to follow another path, he is heading toward destruction.

Dr. John R. Rice told of a man who had a sore on his cheek. He said, "The sore seemed incurable. It grew larger and worse. Surely, his friends said, it was cancer. He should have gone at once for treatment or surgery. But no, he read an ad in the paper where a quack doctor offered to sell a salve that would cure cancer. He bought the salve, boasted that he had saved the doctor's expense and the pain of surgery, and applied the salve diligently. The sore healed over on the outside, but went on with its deadly work, and after awhile the man died of cancer. He would not call for help though he desperately needed it." It is a tragedy for people to remain lost because they will not take God's offer.

Today's Growth Principle: The only hope of salvation is when we accept God's offer of Christ's substitutionary payment for sin.

The God Who Is There

*Every place that the sole of your foot shall tread upon, that have I given unto you, as I said unto Moses. From the wilderness and this Lebanon even unto the great river, the river Euphrates, all the land of the Hittites, and unto the great sea toward the going down of the sun, shall be your coast. There shall not any man be able to stand before thee all the days of thy life: as I was with Moses, so I will be with thee: I will not fail thee, nor forsake thee.—*JOSHUA 1:3–5

When we read of the way God has worked in the lives of men and women of faith in the Bible and in history, we often focus on the characteristics of their lives that enabled them to do great things for God—perhaps their faith, courage, prayer life, passion, diligence, or some other notable quality. But while we can learn from the actionable attributes of those whom God has used, we should never allow our primary focus to remain on people. Our vision should be fixed on God instead. When Moses died, the Israelites needed a new leader, but they did not need a new God. They needed their new leader, Joshua, to live and lead with a sense of God's presence.

It is the same for us. Although we believe and teach that God never changes, we do not always live as if He is active and involved in our lives. Too often we settle for what we can accomplish on our own rather than seeking the presence and power of God as a reality in our lives. The Christian life was never meant to be lived apart from God's provision, and indeed it cannot be. The God who sees and judges the heart knows whether or not we are close to Him, even if others may be deceived. The reality is that life is more than we can manage. But we are not alone. "God is our refuge and strength, a very present help in trouble" (Psalm 46:1).

Today's Growth Principle: Unless we learn to rely on God, we will never accomplish His purpose and will for our lives.

The Key to Overcoming Obstacles

And they spake unto all the company of the children of Israel, saying, The land, which we passed through to search it, is an exceeding good land. If the LORD delight in us, then he will bring us into this land, and give it us; a land which floweth with milk and honey. Only rebel not ye against the LORD, neither fear ye the people of the land; for they are bread for us: their defence is departed from them, and the LORD is with us: fear them not.—NUMBERS 14:7-9

There is an old story about a shoe salesman in the days of the British empire who was sent to begin a new branch of the business in an African nation. A few days after he arrived, he sent a telegram home, announcing his resignation. "This place is hopeless for the shoe business. Everyone goes barefoot." Undaunted, the company sent out a replacement. A few days after he arrived, he too cabled a message home. "Send more shoes. The market is unlimited!"

All of us face obstacles and difficulties in the course of daily living. These obstacles and difficulties are not always because of a special attack of Satan (although that sometimes happens) or a judgment on us. Often, it is simply part of living in a broken world. Things are going to go wrong, and there are going to be problems. The question is how we will respond. Will we allow ourselves to be discouraged, or will we realize that God's promises are still in operation and that we can trust Him for victory?

When the ten spies gave a discouraging report, the Children of Israel refused to enter the land, despite the impassioned pleas of Joshua and Caleb. Rather than focusing on the giants and the walled cities, those two faithful men were focused on God. They realized that if God was on their side, there was nothing to fear from any obstacle.

Today's Growth Principle: Do not allow any obstacle to convince you to take your eyes off Jesus, and you will find victory.

The Substance of Faith

Now faith is the substance of things hoped for, the evidence of things not seen. For by it the elders obtained a good report. Through faith we understand that the worlds were framed by the word of God, so that things which are seen were not made of things which do appear.
—HEBREWS 11:1–3

I came across a beautiful story of a little three-year-old boy named Todd who lived in Rhode Island. His father decided to take him to a windy spot on the beach to fly a kite. Never having flown a kite before, Todd had obvious doubts. His father assured him that all was well, and the kite would go up as planned. As Todd unraveled the string, and watched the kite go up into the sky, he was heard to say, "I knew it would fly, Daddy. You said it would."

So many times we fail to trust God because we do not see Him working. Like Peter walking on the water, we make progress for a time, but then the circumstances catch our attention and lead us to doubt— and sink. The tendency of human nature is to want evidence before we believe. But God's plan is for us to not only trust Him, but also to regard our faith as the evidence itself. Faith is not imaginary, just because it is not seen. It is real and it has substance. And when we act in faith, we see God work.

Our faith in action brings honor and glory to God. Writing about the life of Abraham, Paul reminds us that even though he was almost one hundred years old, Abraham still believed God would give him a son. "He staggered not at the promise of God through unbelief; but was strong in faith, giving glory to God" (Romans 4:20). The lack of faith, rather than the circumstances that we face, is what causes us to stagger and fail.

Today's Growth Principle: It is impossible for God's promises to fail— but it is possible for us to miss them because of a lack of faith.

Unclaimed Blessings

And the LORD said unto Abram, after that Lot was separated from him,
Lift up now thine eyes, and look from the place where thou art northward,
and southward, and eastward, and westward: For all the land which
thou seest, to thee will I give it, and to thy seed for ever. And I will make
thy seed as the dust of the earth: so that if a man can number the dust
of the earth, then shall thy seed also be numbered. Arise, walk through
the land in the length of it and in the breadth of it; for I will give it unto
thee.—GENESIS 13:14–17

The size and area of the land that God promised to Abraham was vast. The promise seemed beyond the realm of what was possible. Yet Abraham believed it, even as a childless man nearing one hundred years of age. And in time, a great nation did come from his descendants, just as God had promised.

Yet, four hundred years later, when God delivered Israel from slavery in Egypt and led them across the wilderness miraculously providing for their every need, they refused to enter the Promised Land, doubting that God could give them what He had promised. It took forty years in the wilderness before they finally began to take possession of what God had promised. And even then, they did not do a thorough job. "Now Joshua was old and stricken in years; and the LORD said unto him, Thou art old and stricken in years, and there remaineth yet very much land to be possessed" (Joshua 13:1). Even as the nation's greatest land mass under the reigns of David and Solomon, Israel never reached the boundaries of the land God promised to Abraham. This was not a failure on God's part, but rather a failure of the Israelites to do what was needed to claim what God had offered them. They were greatly blessed and helped by God, but they could have had so much more. He was able to fully give them all He had promised, but they did not claim it.

Today's Growth Principle: The lack of victory we experience comes from our failure to claim what God freely offers.

Unseen Value

*Who hath believed our report? and to whom is the arm of the LORD revealed? For he shall grow up before him as a tender plant, and as a root out of a dry ground: he hath no form nor comeliness; and when we shall see him, there is no beauty that we should desire him. He is despised and rejected of men; a man of sorrows, and acquainted with grief: and we hid as it were our faces from him; he was despised, and we esteemed him not.—*ISAIAH 53:1–3

In 2014, security guards at an art exhibit in southern Italy were stunned when they arrived in the morning and found a modern art display valued at $15,000 gone. Contrary to what one would first assume, however, the loss was not the work of clever thieves. The exhibit, which consisted of newspapers, cardboard, and cookies, had been thrown away by the cleaning crew who thought it was trash left behind by workers setting up exhibits in the gallery.

Most people do not think of artwork when they see pieces of trash. But it is not just in the realm of art appreciation that the tendency to devalue what does not appear to match our conception occurs. The same thing happened when Jesus came. Though Jesus' life and ministry showed Him to be the Messiah, most people did not believe in Him. Some doubted because of where He grew up. "And Nathanael said unto him, Can there any good thing come out of Nazareth? Philip saith unto him, Come and see" (John 1:46). Others viewed His lack of interest in overthrowing the Romans and restoring Jewish independence as grounds for not following Jesus. And so, despite His presence among them and all the good works He did, Jesus was despised and rejected.

Even today, people do not value Jesus for who He is—God who came in the flesh to make a sacrifice for our sin. But we who know Him as our Saviour treasure our relationship with Him.

Today's Growth Principle: We who know Christ have the opportunity to tell others who He really is and how He can change their lives.

A Message that Cannot Be Contained

Then I said, I will not make mention of him, nor speak any more in his name. But his word was in mine heart as a burning fire shut up in my bones, and I was weary with forbearing, and I could not stay. For I heard the defaming of many, fear on every side. Report, say they, and we will report it. All my familiars watched for my halting, saying, Peradventure he will be enticed, and we shall prevail against him, and we shall take our revenge on him.—JEREMIAH 20:9–10

Five-year-old Hannah came to her mother one morning and said, "Mommy, I think Jesus has moved out of my heart." The mother was concerned about her daughter's understanding of salvation and security, so she asked the little girl where she thought Jesus had gone. Hannah replied, "Oh Jesus is still inside me. I think He moved to my throat because all I want to do is tell people about Him!"

There are some places in the world today where witnessing must be done with care and caution to avoid persecution. But that is not why most of us do not witness as we should. We face no serious harassment from sharing the gospel. Someone might say something unkind or even slam a door in our face, and we may face broken relationships for sharing the gospel. We do not usually, however, face the kind of threats and violence that often greeted the early followers of Jesus when they told others about Him.

So why are so many Christians silent when it comes to the most important message we can share with others? While there are many causes, the root is found in the heart. If we have appreciation for our own salvation and an understanding of the fate of those without Christ, we will be motivated to be witnesses for Christ.

Today's Growth Principle: It is not laws that keep us from being faithful witnesses but coldness of the heart.

Clean Inside and Out

Who shall ascend into the hill of the LORD? or who shall stand in his holy place? He that hath clean hands, and a pure heart; who hath not lifted up his soul unto vanity, nor sworn deceitfully. He shall receive the blessing from the LORD, and righteousness from the God of his salvation. This is the generation of them that seek him, that seek thy face, O Jacob. Selah.
—PSALM 24:3–6

Today we look back on the life and ministry of Charles Haddon Spurgeon with great appreciation and respect, but during his lifetime he was frequently the target of bitter attacks. His uncompromising stand for truth never wavered, and many people criticized him for not trimming his message to better fit the prevailing opinions of the day. It is said he was threatened that if he did not stop preaching against certain sins his reputation would be ruined. Spurgeon replied, "Write all you know about me across the heavens."

The only way we can make a statement like that is if we are living in close fellowship with God, not just in public but in private as well. When David wrote of the person who was able to enter God's presence, he highlighted the importance of both inward and outward righteousness in the eyes of the Lord. It is not enough just to adhere to outward standards where our conduct can be seen by others. We must also be right and clean on the inside.

Praise God that the blood of Jesus cleanses us from every sin within, and the righteousness of Jesus is applied to our account before God. To grow in our relationship with God and to keep a right testimony before others, however, we must take care that we are living in such a way that our lives—private and public—are in accordance with the forgiveness God has already given us. We must not hide sin or disobedience within our hearts.

Today's Growth Principle: We will not long remain clean outwardly unless we first carefully guard our purity inwardly.

Seeing Jesus as He Truly Is

When Jesus came into the coasts of Caesarea Philippi, he asked his disciples, saying, Whom do men say that I the Son of man am? And they said, Some say that thou art John the Baptist: some, Elias; and others, Jeremias, or one of the prophets. He saith unto them, But whom say ye that I am? And Simon Peter answered and said, Thou art the Christ, the Son of the living God.—MATTHEW 16:13–16

Most people in our society have some knowledge of Jesus, but the picture they have of Him is often different than the one found in the pages of the Bible. I came across a list someone had put together of some of the ways in which our world views the Lord.

- They have Republican Jesus and Democrat Jesus who favors whichever government policies they happen to prefer.
- They have Therapist Jesus, who helps us cope with life's problems and tells us how valuable we are and not to be so hard on ourselves.
- They have Open-minded Jesus—who loves everyone all the time no matter what (except for people who are not as open-minded as you).
- They have Touchdown Jesus—who helps athletes run faster and jump higher.
- They have Guru Jesus—a wise, inspirational teacher who believes in you and helps you find your center.

The reality is that Jesus is exactly what Peter declared Him to be—the Messiah, and the Son of God. Jesus was not just a teacher, or an example or a prophet. He is God who came as the Saviour for all who believe, and no one who views Him as less than that has any hope of salvation. We need to elevate Jesus in our thinking, and follow Him daily.

Today's Growth Principle: Only when we see Jesus for who He truly is can we experience the salvation and hope He offers.

Fill up on the Word of God

And let the peace of God rule in your hearts, to the which also ye are called in one body; and be ye thankful. Let the word of Christ dwell in you richly in all wisdom; teaching and admonishing one another in psalms and hymns and spiritual songs, singing with grace in your hearts to the Lord. And whatsoever ye do in word or deed, do all in the name of the Lord Jesus, giving thanks to God and the Father by him.—COLOSSIANS 3:15–17

Take a moment to think about the most delicious meal you've ever eaten. Perhaps it was an old family secret recipe that made the food come alive. Perhaps it was a high-class restaurant you visited for a special occasion. But it seemed like every bite was filled with flavor and it was a delight to eat. Did you clean your plate, or did you stop after two or three bites and say, "Well that was really good but I don't want to eat anymore"? Of course, you ate until you were full and probably then some.

If we are to be the people God has called us to be, then a few bites of His Word now and then are not enough. We need to be like diners in front of a delicious meal who eat and eat because they cannot believe how good it tastes. In fact, we should view the Bible as even more important than our daily food. Job said, "Neither have I gone back from the commandment of his lips; I have esteemed the words of his mouth more than my necessary food" (Job 23:12). First Peter 2:2 encourages us, "As newborn babes, desire the sincere milk of the word, that ye may grow thereby."

We have a generation of spiritually malnourished Christians, and it should be no surprise that they are not changing the world. John Jay, the first Chief Justice of the United States Supreme Court said, "The Bible is the best of all books, for it is the word of God and teaches us the way to be happy in this world and in the next."

Today's Growth Principle: If the Bible does not fill our hearts and minds, we will not grow as Christians.

Believing What God Says

And the angel answered and said unto her, The Holy Ghost shall come upon thee, and the power of the Highest shall overshadow thee: therefore also that holy thing which shall be born of thee shall be called the Son of God. And, behold, thy cousin Elisabeth, she hath also conceived a son in her old age: and this is the sixth month with her, who was called barren. For with God nothing shall be impossible. And Mary said, Behold the handmaid of the Lord; be it unto me according to thy word. And the angel departed from her.—LUKE 1:35–38

Mary was presented with a completely unprecedented assignment from God. Never before had a virgin borne a child, and never before had God willingly joined Himself to human nature so that there could be a Saviour for mankind. Though she did not fully understand how God's plan for her would work or what the cost would be, Mary believed that His purpose would be fulfilled in her life. Her expression of faith was that things would happen "according to thy word."

The basis of our faith is the Word of God. That is where we find the promises God has given to us. It's important to understand that not everything people believe is genuine faith based on the Bible. Some people believe that if you speak the words, you will have health, wealth, and any material prosperity you desire. God did not promise that. Real faith is only that which we believe and act on based on what God actually says.

To have that faith, we must be people of the Word. Evangelist D. L. Moody said, "I prayed for faith and it did not come, but when I read the Word of God then faith came." Romans 10:17 tells us, "So then faith cometh by hearing, and hearing by the word of God." There are no victorious, effective Christians who are not men or women of genuine and active faith.

Today's Growth Principle: What we believe or hope may not happen, but we can rest assured that God will fulfill His promises.

Victory over Stress

And the LORD looked upon him, and said, Go in this thy might, and thou shalt save Israel from the hand of the Midianites: have not I sent thee? And he said unto him, Oh my Lord, wherewith shall I save Israel? behold, my family is poor in Manasseh, and I am the least in my father's house. And the LORD said unto him, Surely I will be with thee, and thou shalt smite the Midianites as one man.—JUDGES 6:14–16

Many people in our society struggle with stress. A study by AARP a few years ago identified approximately $300 billion in costs—medical care, lost time from work, etc.—associated with stress. In their survey, four out of ten adults said they had trouble sleeping because of stress, slightly over half had serious worries about their health, and seventy percent worried about their jobs. While some worries are based on what might happen, others are based on real problems. As I once heard someone put it, the leading cause of stress is reality.

The situation Gideon faced when God called him to deliver Israel was certainly stressful. The Midianites had overrun the country, stealing the food that the Israelites grew. Things were so bad that Gideon was hiding just to thresh his wheat so that it too would not be stolen and there would be something to eat. He greeted the news, delivered by an angel, that he had been chosen to lead a great military campaign with amazement. He did not understand how a victory was possible.

But God told Gideon the one thing that would make all the difference—that God would be with him. This is the same promise that Jesus made before He returned to Heaven: "Teaching them to observe all things whatsoever I have commanded you: and, lo, I am with you alway, even unto the end of the world. Amen" (Matthew 28:20). The burdens may be real, but His presence provides peace.

Today's Growth Principle: The promise of God's presence is our hope of victory, not only over obstacles, but over stress and worry as well.

The Torment of Not Forgiving

*Then his lord, after that he had called him, said unto him, O thou wicked servant, I forgave thee all that debt, because thou desiredst me: Shouldest not thou also have had compassion on thy fellowservant, even as I had pity on thee? And his lord was wroth, and delivered him to the tormentors, till he should pay all that was due unto him. So likewise shall my heavenly Father do also unto you, if ye from your hearts forgive not every one his brother their trespasses.—*MATTHEW 18:32–35

When Peter asked how often he had to forgive someone who had wronged him, apparently seeking to limit the extent of forgiveness, Jesus responded with the parable of a king who was owed a massive sum by one of his servants. Instead of demanding the repayment that was rightly his, he freely forgave the debt, giving the man new hope for his future. But the servant who was forgiven was also owed a debt. Rather than extending the same grace he had been shown, he demanded full repayment, grabbing the man by the throat and throwing him into jail.

Forgiveness is one of the issues that many Christians struggle with, because to truly forgive someone from the heart, we have to take our hands away from their throats and give up our right to insist that they get what is coming to them. Many hold grudges for years rather than take this important step.

The problem is that refusing to forgive has far greater consequences for us than for the person who has wronged us. It harms our health both spiritually and physically when we insist on carrying the weight of past offenses. And as severe as the consequences on human relationships are, a failure to forgive destroys our close fellowship with God. "But if ye forgive not men their trespasses, neither will your Father forgive your trespasses" (Matthew 6:15).

Today's Growth Principle: Forgiveness isn't changing the past; it is letting God be the judge of the past and freeing yourself for a brighter future.

A Burden for Others

For I know this, that after my departing shall grievous wolves enter in among you, not sparing the flock. Also of your own selves shall men arise, speaking perverse things, to draw away disciples after them. Therefore watch, and remember, that by the space of three years I ceased not to warn every one night and day with tears.—ACTS 20:29–31

Anyone who is involved with ministering to, caring for, teaching, and reaching others has days when it feels like what we are doing simply isn't making a difference. We try everything we know to help someone, only to see that person refuse to listen. We invest in someone's life, only to see that person stray from God looking for greener pastures. We do all we can for someone only to hear that this person told a friend no one helped him when he was hurting. These circumstances are nothing new to Christian service. Paul encountered this at the church in Corinth, even writing, "And I will very gladly spend and be spent for you; though the more abundantly I love you, the less I be loved" (2 Corinthians 12:15).

How do you respond when things don't go right? How do you continue to minister, work, and pray in the face of what seems like failure? A great part of the answer to those questions is found in the motivation for our service. When we are motivated by God's love and allow His compassion for the needs and condition of others to become our own, we will not be deterred by a lack of apparent success.

One of the greatest needs of the church in our day is a generation of Christian workers and leaders who are gripped by a vision of the desperate spiritual condition of those around us. They may not realize their peril, but we should. We need to care more for their needs and join with the prophet Jeremiah in saying, "Oh that my head were waters, and mine eyes a fountain of tears, that I might weep day and night for the slain of the daughter of my people!" (Jeremiah 9:1).

Today's Growth Principle: If your service is motivated by the love of Christ, you will be able to continue during difficult seasons.

Ezekiel 8–10   //   Hebrews 13   337

A Real Walk with God

And Enoch lived sixty and five years, and begat Methuselah: And Enoch walked with God after he begat Methuselah three hundred years, and begat sons and daughters: And all the days of Enoch were three hundred sixty and five years: And Enoch walked with God: and he was not; for God took him.—GENESIS 5:21–24

The list of the descendants of Adam given to us in Genesis 5 includes several men whose faith is later mentioned in Hebrews 11 in the great review of Old Testament saints. But in Genesis 5, only one, Enoch, is singled out with a description of his relationship with God. When the Bible speaks of walking with God, it is talking about a life that is based on and filled with faith. "By faith Enoch was translated that he should not see death; and was not found, because God had translated him: for before his translation he had this testimony, that he pleased God" (Hebrews 11:5).

If our lives are to please God, we must have Him occupy such a position in our hearts that He is the center of our thoughts and affections. J. Oswald Sanders wrote, "It is impossible for a believer, no matter what his experience, to keep right with God if he will not take the trouble to spend time with God. Spend plenty of time with him; let other things go, but don't neglect Him." Too many Christians fill their days and their lives with everything except God. Often, these things that so fill our days are not even bad things, but taken in totality, they become clutter that keep us from having room for Him.

The Lord is not interested in partial devotion. He does not seek small portions of our time; rather, He demands His rightful place at the center of our lives. When we consistently walk with the Lord, our decisions and choices will reflect His priorities and obedience to His commands.

Today's Growth Principle: One of the greatest ways we can exercise faith is by daily walking with God in a meaningful and deep relationship in which He is the center of our lives.

Saved for Sure

And this is the record, that God hath given to us eternal life, and this life is in his Son. He that hath the Son hath life; and he that hath not the Son of God hath not life. These things have I written unto you that believe on the name of the Son of God; that ye may know that ye have eternal life, and that ye may believe on the name of the Son of God. —1 JOHN 5:11-13

D oubt is one of the most effective weapons in the devil's toolbox to use against God's children. Because our service for God is built on the foundation of our faith in Him, Satan tries every means possible to make us doubt whether we are truly saved. While it is important that people not have a false assurance of a salvation they do not possess, it is also vital that those who have been born again know that their salvation is secure.

Dr. John R. Rice was saved when he was a little boy, but many adults questioned his understanding, and as a result he lived with doubt. He later wrote, "I went on for three sad years not sure I was saved. Then I got to reading the Bible and found John 5:24. ["Verily, verily, I say unto you, He that heareth my word, and believeth on him that sent me, hath everlasting life, and shall not come into condemnation; but is passed from death unto life."] I KNEW that I had heard the Word of God. I KNEW that I had trusted Jesus Christ the best I knew how. So there suddenly, gloriously, came the assurance that I was really saved! I know I am saved because it is written in the Bible."

The Bible is given to us for many purposes, but one of those is to give us a confident assurance that the same God who saved us will keep us secure until we reach Heaven. Since no part of our salvation depends on our work or effort, once we have been saved, there is nothing that can cause us to lose it.

Today's Growth Principle: If you have trusted in Christ's payment for your sin and called on Him to save you, do not let Satan drag you down with doubt.

Does the World Move You?

Now among these were of the children of Judah, Daniel, Hananiah, Mishael, and Azariah: Unto whom the prince of the eunuchs gave names: for he gave unto Daniel the name of Belteshazzar; and to Hananiah, of Shadrach; and to Mishael, of Meshach; and to Azariah, of Abednego. But Daniel purposed in his heart that he would not defile himself with the portion of the king's meat, nor with the wine which he drank: therefore he requested of the prince of the eunuchs that he might not defile himself.
—DANIEL 1:6–8

It's easy to see that we are surrounded by a culture that is increasingly hostile to Christianity. Core truths that were once taken for granted are now challenged. Those who believe and publicly state what the Word of God clearly declares are labeled as hateful and bigoted. Christian businesses and religious organizations are being sued, and often losing, simply because the owners and employees are trying to follow their faith in their daily lives. Great pressure is brought to bear on the followers of Jesus Christ to change our long-held beliefs so they align with the current morally confused beliefs of our society. Many have tragically dipped their sails and abandoned the truth.

The challenge we face is not unprecedented. Throughout history, God's people have been surrounded by hostile voices. Daniel and his friends were taken to Babylon as captives and put into an intensive training program designed to break down their old loyalties and beliefs, and shape their thinking to conform to the values of Babylon. Though many young people from many nations had succumbed to that pressure, Daniel, Hananiah, Mishael, and Azariah did not. As a result, they made a difference for God even in the midst of a heathen culture. Someone well said, "The men and women who have moved the world have been the men and women the world could not move."

Today's Growth Principle: Only by standing firm for what is true and right can we make a positive impact on the world around us.

What Love Looks for Most

Charity suffereth long, and is kind; charity envieth not; charity vaunteth not itself, is not puffed up, Doth not behave itself unseemly, seeketh not her own, is not easily provoked, thinketh no evil; Rejoiceth not in iniquity, but rejoiceth in the truth; Beareth all things, believeth all things, hopeth all things, endureth all things.—1 CORINTHIANS 13:4–7

The first winter the Pilgrims spent in Massachusetts was a time of great hardship and suffering. Though the weather was not especially harsh, they were not prepared for winter. The lack of adequate food and shelter and the spread of disease from cramped living conditions took a dreadful toll. By the time spring arrived, 45 of the 102 who had made the journey from England seeking religious freedom were dead. But the losses were not equally distributed. While only three of the thirteen children perished, thirteen of the eighteen married women died. They were making sure their children ate rather than caring for themselves—because of their love.

Love is not selfish. It does not focus on what it can get, but what it can give. Much of what the world refers to as love in our day is radically different from the Bible standard. God's love, the love which we are to have in our lives as a fruit of the indwelling Holy Spirit, looks out for the welfare and benefit of others rather than self. Genuine love in any relationship does not look for what it can get, but what it can give. Philippians 2:4 instructs us, "Look not every man on his own things, but every man also on the things of others."

If we say we love someone but are not willing to sacrifice and put their interests first, it is at best a very shallow imitation of love. Love gives and gives and gives for the sake of the one who is loved. Jesus said, "As the Father knoweth me, even so know I the Father: and I lay down my life for the sheep" (John 10:15).

Today's Growth Principle: To love as God loves, we must care more about the needs of others than our own.

The Problem of Forgetting

For here have we no continuing city, but we seek one to come. By him therefore let us offer the sacrifice of praise to God continually, that is, the fruit of our lips giving thanks to his name. But to do good and to communicate forget not: for with such sacrifices God is well pleased.
—HEBREWS 13:14–16

In 1985, a gifted English musician and conductor named Clive Wearing suffered a severe viral infection that attacked his brain. Though Wearing survived, he was left with a profound case of anterograde amnesia, which meant he could no longer form new memories. Each time he saw his wife, he thought they had been separated for a lengthy period of time. He kept a journal of his experiences each day, but often found that he could not believe what he himself had written about the previous day. Wearing was, however, able to remember the music he had learned before his illness and continued to play the piano in public and conduct choral concerts.

Wearing's wife, Deborah, conducted a campaign to provide better treatment for people suffering from amnesia and wrote a book called *Forever Today.* In it she detailed the devastating impact of her husband's memory loss on both of them and the way that eventually their relationship became stronger than ever.

Though no one has control over the loss of memory due to disease or injury, we are to exercise our spiritual memory. This is true both of remembering what God has done for us, and of remembering what He has commanded us to do for Him. Over and over in Scripture, we see God's people forgetting what He told them and the tragic consequences that followed. We must heed the warning to remember God no matter what happens. "Then beware lest thou forget the LORD, which brought thee forth out of the land of Egypt, from the house of bondage" (Deuteronomy 6:12).

Today's Growth Principle: Remembering who God is and what He has done in your life enables you to continually offer the sacrifice of praise.

The Importance of Gratitude

And one of them, when he saw that he was healed, turned back, and with a loud voice glorified God, And fell down on his face at his feet, giving him thanks: and he was a Samaritan. And Jesus answering said, Were there not ten cleansed? but where are the nine? There are not found that returned to give glory to God, save this stranger.—LUKE 17:15–18

No matter how much or how little we may have as the world measures resources, all of us have a great deal more than we deserve. The good things we enjoy are gifts from God, not the product of our abilities. "Every good gift and every perfect gift is from above, and cometh down from the Father of lights, with whom is no variableness, neither shadow of turning" (James 1:17). Yet all too often our mouths and our hearts are filled with discontent rather than gratitude.

Rather than praising God for His goodness and mercy, we often take for granted the blessings we receive, even thinking that we deserve them. Evangelist D. L. Moody said, "We have in our churches a great deal of prayer, but I think it would be a good thing if we had a praise meeting occasionally. If we could only get people to praise God for what He has done, it would be a good deal better than asking Him continually for something."

Moses warned the Children of Israel of the dangers of taking blessings for granted when they were preparing to enter the Promised Land: "Then beware lest thou forget the LORD, which brought thee forth out of the land of Egypt, from the house of bondage" (Deuteronomy 6:12). The more God does for us, the more risk we face of assuming His bountiful blessings are because of us instead of an expression of His grace and love. Let us never fail to be thankful for all we have received.

Today's Growth Principle: In light of all the benefits we receive from God, it is a great sin not to be grateful.

Thankful Living

It is a good thing to give thanks unto the LORD, and to sing praises unto thy name, O most High: To shew forth thy lovingkindness in the morning, and thy faithfulness every night, Upon an instrument of ten strings, and upon the psaltery; upon the harp with a solemn sound. For thou, LORD, hast made me glad through thy work: I will triumph in the works of thy hands.—PSALM 92:1-4

The story is told of a pastor in the Midwest during the early 1900s walking down the street of a small town and seeing a little boy with his nose pressed up against the window of a store. Inside were jars of candy, and the boy clearly was longing for what he could not afford. Remembering the joy of a piece of candy in his youth, the preacher took the boy inside the store and bought him a whole bag filled with penny candies. But when the preacher asked the boy to give him a piece, the boy clutched it to his chest. "It's mine!" he exclaimed and dashed out of the store.

Every Christian has many reasons to be thankful every day. No matter how bad things seem to be going, we have received eternal gifts that we did not deserve and can never lose through no merit of our own. These blessings are not just one-time events, but an ongoing shower of God's gracious love. "Blessed be the Lord, who daily loadeth us with benefits, even the God of our salvation. Selah" (Psalm 68:19).

Though we often think of giving thanks in terms of what we say, it is more powerfully expressed in our actions. The lives that we lead should be characterized by giving back to God from what He has given to us rather than selfishly trying to hoard every blessing for ourselves. It is impossible for selfishness and thanksgiving to exist side by side in our hearts.

Today's Growth Principle: Gratitude for what God has given us is better shown by our actions than by our words.

Remember to Be Thankful

Bless the LORD, O my soul, and forget not all his benefits: Who forgiveth all thine iniquities; who healeth all thy diseases; Who redeemeth thy life from destruction; who crowneth thee with lovingkindness and tender mercies; Who satisfieth thy mouth with good things; so that thy youth is renewed like the eagle's.—PSALM 103:2–5

In the classic Peanuts Thanksgiving cartoon, Snoopy gets a regular bowl of dog food rather than a holiday meal. He responds, "This isn't fair. The rest of the world today is eating turkey with all the trimmings, and all I get is dog food." Then Snoopy stood there and stared at his dog food for a moment, and said, "I guess it could be worse. I could be a turkey."

The key to being thankful is in remembrance—not just for what we have been given, but for what we have been spared. In our self-esteem focused society, people do not like to consider the true state of man. We build ourselves up so that we feel better, but the reality is that every person born into the world is born into a desperate situation. "He that believeth on the Son hath everlasting life: and he that believeth not the Son shall not see life; but the wrath of God abideth on him" (John 3:36). We who know Christ as our Saviour have much to be thankful for indeed.

We have been given so much, yet too often our only focus is on what we do not have. Allowing our happiness to be dictated by comparing what we have to what we think we deserve, or to what others have is a recipe for disaster. It quickly leads us not just to be ungrateful for what we have received, but to begin coveting what others have. This path quickly leads to many kinds of sin. There is more than just obedience involved in thankful living. Taking time to remember and give thanks protects us from evil in our own hearts.

Today's Growth Principle: Gratitude and thankful living require conscious effort and a commitment to remember what God has done for us.

Ezekiel 27–29   //   1 Peter 3

The Power of Gratitude

And when he had consulted with the people, he appointed singers unto the Lord, and that should praise the beauty of holiness, as they went out before the army, and to say, Praise the Lord; for his mercy endureth for ever. And when they began to sing and to praise, the Lord set ambushments against the children of Ammon, Moab, and mount Seir, which were come against Judah; and they were smitten.
—2 CHRONICLES 20:21–22

When Jehoshaphat faced the threat of an attack by a vast host of his enemies who had joined forces together against him, he recognized that he had no hope of victory humanly speaking. So he wisely sought help from the Lord. God sent word to the besieged king that not only would he be delivered, but that his army would not have to fight at all. In faith and gratitude, Jehoshaphat selected singers to go out ahead of his troops, praising the Lord all the way to the field of battle. When they arrived, they found that the coalition against them had been broken, and that the enemy armies had destroyed each other. There is so much value in praising God and giving thanks for what He has done for us. It is good for our own hearts and lives, and it has a positive impact on those around us.

In his Thanksgiving Day Proclamation in 1924, President Calvin Coolidge wrote, "In acknowledging the receipt of divine favor, in contemplating the blessings which have been bestowed upon us, we shall reveal the spiritual strength of the nation. We shall do well to accept all these favors and bounties with a becoming humility, and dedicate them to the service of the righteous cause of the Giver of all good and perfect gifts. As the nation has prospered let all the people show that they are worthy to prosper by rededicating America to the service of God and man."

Today's Growth Principle: Every child of God has ample reason to rejoice and give thanks, no matter the circumstances.

An Altar to Give Thanks

And Noah builded an altar unto the LORD; and took of every clean beast, and of every clean fowl, and offered burnt offerings on the altar. And the LORD smelled a sweet savour; and the LORD said in his heart, I will not again curse the ground any more for man's sake; for the imagination of man's heart is evil from his youth; neither will I again smite any more every thing living, as I have done. While the earth remaineth, seedtime and harvest, and cold and heat, and summer and winter, and day and night shall not cease.—GENESIS 8:20-22

Noah had the unique experience of his family being the only survivors spared from the Flood that God sent, to judge the wickedness of man. He and his family did not survive that global catastrophe because of his cleverness or foresight, but because of the grace of God. When Noah was warned of the coming judgment, he responded in faith and built the ark according to God's design and specifications. The ark did exactly what God promised, and after more than a year had passed, Noah and his family emerged safely onto dry ground.

The first thing Noah did upon exiting the ark was build an altar to make an offering to God. Truly he had much for which to be thankful—as do we. Most of us, however, would have to acknowledge that we fall short when it comes to giving God the praise and thanks He deserves. Though there are many reasons for our lack of gratitude, one of the great causes is our desire to think that we make it through on our own strength and effort. When we give thanks to God, we admit that He deserves all the praise and glory rather than us. William Jennings Bryan said, "On Thanksgiving Day, we acknowledge our dependence." Let us lay aside our pride and in humility come before the Lord, giving thanks.

Today's Growth Principle: No offering that we present to God can adequately express our thanks and gratitude for His salvation.

"Neither Were Thankful"

For the invisible things of him from the creation of the world are clearly seen, being understood by the things that are made, even his eternal power and Godhead; so that they are without excuse: Because that, when they knew God, they glorified him not as God, neither were thankful; but became vain in their imaginations, and their foolish heart was darkened. Professing themselves to be wise, they became fools,—ROMANS 1:20-22

The increasingly godless culture that surrounds us is filled with evil, but this is hardly the first time God's people have lived in a sea of wickedness. The same was true in the first century when the early church was setting out to take the gospel to the world. The Roman Empire was filled with violence and immorality and was very hostile to the new religion spreading from Jerusalem across their territory. Yet when the Apostle Paul described the society in which evil reigned, he began by accusing them of one particular sin—ingratitude.

Every person on Earth—the saved and the lost—benefit from the amazing grace that God freely provides. No man is able to make the sun shine, cause the winds to blow, or do any of the other essential things that make life possible. Were it not for the benefits provided by God, we would have nothing. Matthew 5:45 tells us that our Father which is in Heaven "maketh his sun to rise on the evil and on the good, and sendeth rain on the just and on the unjust."

As children of God who receive not just His natural benefits, but also eternal salvation, we have a special responsibility to be thankful. There is no excuse for us not to praise and glorify God, not just once a year, but every single day. Charles Spurgeon said, "When joy and prayer are married, their firstborn child is gratitude."

Today's Growth Principle: Take time today to give thanks and praise God for His goodness to you.

Remember the Meaning

For if these things be in you, and abound, they make you that ye shall neither be barren nor unfruitful in the knowledge of our Lord Jesus Christ. But he that lacketh these things is blind, and cannot see afar off, and hath forgotten that he was purged from his old sins. Wherefore the rather, brethren, give diligence to make your calling and election sure: for if ye do these things, ye shall never fall:—2 PETER 1:8–10

I heard a rather humorous story of a man who was quite surprised to see his neighbor leave the house in full football gear—pads and helmet. He called out, "Jim, I didn't know you played football." Jim replied, "I don't. I'm going to the mall to do my Christmas shopping!"

There are a lot of people who get so caught up in the hustle and bustle of Christmas that they lose out on the joy and meaning that makes the celebration of Christ's birth so meaningful. And while it is true that most of those who miss the purpose of Christmas do so because they have not received the gift the Saviour came to offer, it is very possible for Christians to miss any spiritual value in the holiday.

We are not immune from the peril of forgetting what God has done for us just because we are saved. In fact the longer we have been saved, the more danger we face of taking God's great grace and mercy shown to us so clearly that first Christmas for granted. The stunning story of angels and shepherds, a baby in a manger, and wise men traveling to bring gifts to the newborn king are so familiar to us that we no longer stop to rejoice in what God has done. If our focus is where it should be, the stories we've heard hundreds of times before will still be fresh and new to us. Christmas is an incredible opportunity to remember the depth of God's love for us to humble Himself to be born in a manger, ultimately to die on the cross for our sins. But these reminders are easily lost in the busyness of the season.

Today's Growth Principle: Ask the Lord to help you experience the spiritual truths of this Christmas season as if it were your first.

DECEMBER

The Greatness of Jesus Christ

*And the angel said unto her, Fear not, Mary: for thou hast found favour
with God. And, behold, thou shalt conceive in thy womb, and bring forth
a son, and shalt call his name JESUS. He shall be great, and shall be
called the Son of the Highest: and the Lord God shall give unto him the
throne of his father David: And he shall reign over the house of Jacob for
ever; and of his kingdom there shall be no end.—*LUKE 1:30–33

When Gabriel came to Mary to announce that she had been chosen by
God to give birth to the Messiah, he was bringing news that would
completely upend her life. This young woman, espoused to be married
to Joseph, was going to have a baby even though she was a virgin. She
certainly knew that few people, if any, would believe she had remained
pure. Yet Mary accepted her place in God's plan willingly, despite the
upheaval it would bring to her life. Her focus was in the same place God's
focus was—on the Saviour who would be born through her.

There are a lot of things I love about the Christmas season and the
way we celebrate. I'm sure that like our family, yours has traditions for
shopping, giving gifts, singing carols, attending special church services,
and more. These things are what we expect and enjoy during the
holidays. But nothing should ever be allowed to take the primary focus
of everything we do away from *Jesus.* Just as Christmas for Mary was not
primarily about the hardship or upended plans, it should not be for us
about the busyness or the challenges of this special season.

Years ago a popular bumper sticker said, "Jesus is the reason for the
season." The focus of Gabriel's message to Mary was not on what being
the mother of Jesus would mean to *her,* but on who Jesus *is.* He is both
the Saviour and the ruler of the world. And though He has not yet come
to rule on Earth, that promise is just as sure as His first coming.

Today's Growth Principle: Never let anything that comes along with
Christmas obscure your focus on Jesus, the Saviour.

How to Make an Impact

For I determined not to know any thing among you, save Jesus Christ, and him crucified. And I was with you in weakness, and in fear, and in much trembling. And my speech and my preaching was not with enticing words of man's wisdom, but in demonstration of the Spirit and of power: That your faith should not stand in the wisdom of men, but in the power of God.—1 CORINTHIANS 2:2–5

Cato the Elder, the noted Roman orator and statesman, fought nobly for his country against Carthage in the Second Punic War two hundred years before the birth of Christ. After the defeat of Hannibal and his elephants, the Romans signed a peace treaty with Carthage that gave them large areas of land, but allowed Carthage to remain a potential future threat. Cato feared that the Romans had simply turned a blind eye to the danger posed by Carthage, correctly realizing that one day another war would have to be fought—and if care was not taken it would be fought on terms unfavorable to Rome.

Cato the Elder began ending every speech with the words *Carthago delenda est*— "Carthage must be destroyed." The message was clear, but decades passed and Carthage indeed raised a new army before military action was taken to finally remove Carthage as a threat.

For the words that we speak to others to have a life-changing impact, we need more than just insight and wisdom. It is not enough just to be right. We need power, and that power can only come from the Holy Spirit.

There are many gifted preachers and teachers and soulwinners, but the impact that they have on others is not caused by their gifts, but by their empowering to use those gifts. It is not our wisdom and talent that produces change, but the work of God through us. Nothing less will be effective.

Today's Growth Principle: If we want to truly make a difference, then we must be yielded to and filled with the Holy Spirit.

Ezekiel 42–44   //   1 John 1   353

Six Miles from the Manger

Pilate answered, Am I a Jew? Thine own nation and the chief priests have delivered thee unto me: what hast thou done? Jesus answered, My kingdom is not of this world: if my kingdom were of this world, then would my servants fight, that I should not be delivered to the Jews: but now is my kingdom not from hence. Pilate therefore said unto him, Art thou a king then? Jesus answered, Thou sayest that I am a king. To this end was I born, and for this cause came I into the world, that I should bear witness unto the truth. Every one that is of the truth heareth my voice.—JOHN 18:35-37

Jesus was born in Bethlehem, the city of David, just as the ancient prophets had foretold. "For unto you is born this day in the city of David a Saviour, which is Christ the Lord" (Luke 2:11). Bethlehem is just six miles from Jerusalem. Because of its close location, some Bible scholars believe that the shepherds to whom the angels appeared to announce the birth of Christ were keeping flocks of sheep intended to be used for sacrifices in the Temple. The place of Jesus' birth was very close to the place of His death and resurrection, and if we properly understand the Christmas story, those two cannot be separated.

Jesus did not come primarily to teach or to heal or to perform miracles. He came to be the Saviour, making the sacrifice necessary to pay for our sins. He is the only hope and source of salvation. All of man's efforts to atone for sin fall short. But when we come to Jesus, there is hope. As Peter boldly told the high priest, "Neither is there salvation in any other: for there is none other name under heaven given among men, whereby we must be saved" (Acts 4:12). Those who acknowledge their sin and need of a Saviour and turn to Him in faith, accepting salvation as the free gift that it is, are saved forever.

Today's Growth Principle: A person who does not accept God's offer of salvation through Christ alone has missed the whole meaning of Christmas.

Saved and Knowing It

And this is the record, that God hath given to us eternal life, and this life is in his Son. He that hath the Son hath life; and he that hath not the Son of God hath not life. These things have I written unto you that believe on the name of the Son of God; that ye may know that ye have eternal life, and that ye may believe on the name of the Son of God.—1 JOHN 5:11–13

God does not want our eternal destiny to be in question. He not only offers us salvation, but He reminds us again and again that our salvation is certain. He assures those who have turned to Him in faith and received Him as their Saviour that they should have no fear for the future.

Although there are some Christians who need that reassurance, there are many whose problem is not doubting salvation (that they genuinely possess) but trusting in false hopes and believing themselves to be saved when they are not. The evangelist D. L. Moody told the story of a drunken man who stopped him in the street and said, "Don't you remember me? I'm the man you saved here two years ago." "Well," said Moody, "It must have been me, because the Lord certainly didn't do it!" Being saved isn't a matter of simply saying some words. It is a choice from the heart to receive Christ. And with salvation will come a change of heart.

If you have received Christ as your Saviour, you can have the confidence that you have eternal life. If you have the Son, you have life—it really is that simple. God desires for us to be confident in our standing as His children. When we forget that all of our salvation was His work and that we merely accepted what His grace offered, we lose the fear that we may do something to lose it.

Today's Growth Principle: The genuine Christian who lives without assurance of his salvation will be a weak Christian.

A Neglected Necessity for Service

Then the twelve called the multitude of the disciples unto them, and said, It is not reason that we should leave the word of God, and serve tables. Wherefore, brethren, look ye out among you seven men of honest report, full of the Holy Ghost and wisdom, whom we may appoint over this business. But we will give ourselves continually to prayer, and to the ministry of the word.—ACTS 6:2–4

The church in Jerusalem experienced explosive growth following the Day of Pentecost. With thousands of new believers added to the assembly, there soon arose a need for more help in caring for the church than the apostles could give. In particular, there arose a disagreement over how the widows were being cared for. This led to the appointment of the first deacons who would make sure that the needs of all were adequately met. There are several things we might expect to see on the list of requirements for such a service-oriented position, but the list recorded for us in Scripture contains one trait that we often do not associate with caring for others—Spirit fullness.

The power of the Holy Spirit is something we usually think about in terms of pulpit ministry or teaching, but it is just as needed in the hidden tasks of service to the church as it is in public work. There is not meant to be a divide between the tasks we do for God in His strength and the ones we do in our own power. We need God's power just as surely when we perform acts of service as when we teach, preach, or witness. Charles Spurgeon said, "Without the Spirit of God, we can do nothing. We are as ships without the wind, branches without sap, and like coals without fire, we are useless." All Christians have the indwelling Holy Spirit, but not all are yielded to Him so that they live in His power and fullness.

Today's Growth Principle: Any work that we do for God must have His power if we are to accomplish His purposes.

For All Who Believe

He was in the world, and the world was made by him, and the world knew him not. He came unto his own, and his own received him not. But as many as received him, to them gave he power to become the sons of God, even to them that believe on his name: Which were born, not of blood, nor of the will of the flesh, nor of the will of man, but of God.—JOHN 1:10–13

We live in a divided world. Nations go to war over border disputes, resources, and desire for gain. Countries dissolve into warring factions that can no longer live together. This is not a new thing—it has been with us since sin entered the world. But the process of separating and dividing seems to be accelerating in our era. New countries are being created constantly—thirty-four new nations have been created just since 1990.

In a divided world, what is the hope for unity? It surely cannot be found in government parties or programs, for those have been tried and found wanting. It cannot come from education, for more of the world is spending more time in school, yet the divisions remain. It is not found in advances in technology and communication, for despite their promises of connection, they often divide more than ever. The only hope of peace for a world of sinful men is found in the Prince of Peace, who is the Saviour for all who believe.

George Truett said, "Christ was born in the first century, yet He belongs to all centuries. He was born a Jew, yet He belongs to all races. He was born in Bethlehem, yet He belongs to all countries." There is hope in the message of Christmas—not the consumer-crazed holiday many observe, but in the story of a Saviour who came for all those who receive His offer of salvation in faith.

Today's Growth Principle: When we share the message of Christ coming to save sinners, we are giving hope to a divided world.

The Necessity of Redemption

Neither by the blood of goats and calves, but by his own blood he entered in once into the holy place, having obtained eternal redemption for us. For if the blood of bulls and of goats, and the ashes of an heifer sprinkling the unclean, sanctifieth to the purifying of the flesh: How much more shall the blood of Christ, who through the eternal Spirit offered himself without spot to God, purge your conscience from dead works to serve the living God?—HEBREWS 9:12–14

Perhaps you have heard about the little boy who sat down on the lap of a department store Santa with a rather lengthy list of gift ideas. He asked for a bike, a sled, a cowboy outfit, a train set, a baseball glove and a pair of roller skates. When he stopped to take a breath, Santa said, "That's a pretty long list. I'll have to check and make sure you were a very good boy." The boy quickly replied, "You don't have to go to all the trouble of checking. I'll just take the roller skates!"

All of us fall short of God's standard of perfection. While there are no doubt some people who are much better or much worse than average, no one reaches the mark that God has set. "They are all gone out of the way, they are together become unprofitable; there is none that doeth good, no, not one" (Romans 3:12). That means that all of us are in need of a Saviour—which is why Jesus came.

There are many great blessings conferred on those who receive God's free gift of salvation, but none is more important than having the perfect obedience and righteousness of Jesus Christ placed on the record next to our name. As Christians, we have no fear of the list being inspected, for when God sees us, He does so through the blood of His Son, and finds us holy.

Today's Growth Principle: Rather than relying on our efforts for our standing with God, we have the righteousness of Christ on our account.

Seeing Jesus as He Is

Then the Jews took up stones again to stone him. Jesus answered them, Many good works have I shewed you from my Father; for which of those works do ye stone me? The Jews answered him, saying, For a good work we stone thee not; but for blasphemy; and because that thou, being a man, makest thyself God.—JOHN 10:31–33

One of the great tragedies of the way Christmas is celebrated in our culture is that Jesus in the manger becomes just another decoration along with reindeer, snowmen, and Santa figurines. He was far more than just a baby born in unusual circumstances—He was the very Son of God. The refusal to accept Jesus for who He truly is did not start in our generation. It was the same during His life and ministry.

When Jesus went to the Temple for the celebration of Hanukkah (referred to as "the feast of dedication" in John 10) and taught there, the religious leaders tried to stone Him to death.

According to Jewish tradition, the Holy of Holies was defiled by Antiocus Epiphanes, who erected a statue of Zeus and sacrificed pigs on the altar. The blood of the pigs ran down upon the stones that formed the floor. After the revolt of the Maccabees when the Temple was cleansed, there was a dispute over those stones. The argument was made that since they had been in the presence of God's Shekinah glory, they were holy and could not be discarded. But because they had been defiled, they could also no longer be used. The agreement was made to set the stones aside, and let the Messiah determine what should be done with them when He appeared. It is possible that it was these very stones the Jews grabbed when they wanted to stone Jesus in the Temple for declaring Himself to be God and the Saviour.

The Messiah was in their midst, but they refused to acknowledge who He was.

Today's Growth Principle: Let us never lose sight of the true nature of Jesus Christ, or of the reason for His coming to the world.

The Only Opinion that Matters

I charge thee therefore before God, and the Lord Jesus Christ, who shall judge the quick and the dead at his appearing and his kingdom; Preach the word; be instant in season, out of season; reprove, rebuke, exhort with all longsuffering and doctrine. For the time will come when they will not endure sound doctrine; but after their own lusts shall they heap to themselves teachers, having itching ears; And they shall turn away their ears from the truth, and shall be turned unto fables.—2 TIMOTHY 4:1–4

Henry VIII thought of himself as above correction by religious authorities. The story is told that a sermon preached by Hugh Latimer so angered the king that he commanded Latimer to return the following Sunday to apologize for his offensive message. In the pulpit the following Sunday, Latimer read the same text as the previous week and then said, "Hugh Latimer, dost thou know before whom thou are this day to speak? To the high and mighty monarch, the king's most excellent majesty, who can take away thy life, if thou offendest. Therefore, take heed that thou speakest not a word that may displease. But then consider well, Hugh, dost thou not know from whence thou comest— upon whose message thou are sent? Even by the great and mighty God, Who is all-present and who beholdeth all thy ways…Therefore, take care that thou deliverest thy message faithfully." Latimer then proceeded to preach the exact same message from the previous week, but with more fire and passion.

If we want our lives to be a success by God's standards and be judged faithful, our primary focus must be on pleasing Him rather than men. There has never yet been a true prophet who was popular with everyone. The false prophets speak words of peace rather than repentance and become popular. Those who speak the truth may not be popular, but they are approved by God.

Today's Growth Principle: Our first and foremost concern must always be what God thinks, not what man thinks.

The Prince of Peace

For unto us a child is born, unto us a son is given: and the government shall be upon his shoulder: and his name shall be called Wonderful, Counsellor, The mighty God, The everlasting Father, The Prince of Peace. Of the increase of his government and peace there shall be no end, upon the throne of David, and upon his kingdom, to order it, and to establish it with judgment and with justice from henceforth even for ever. The zeal of the LORD of hosts will perform this.—ISAIAH 9:6–7

As I write, according to latest reports, there are about sixty wars, armed conflicts, revolutions, and skirmishes taking place in our world right now. In Syria alone, the civil war that has raged for years now has left almost half a million people dead and more than two million others have fled their homes to try to avoid the fighting. We live in a world filled with strife and conflict. But this is not new. Division has been a part of human life since sin entered into the world.

The bottom line of human conflict is not resources, borders, tribes, languages, or governments—but sin. Indeed apart from God we have no expectation of anything but warfare and division. "There is no peace, saith the LORD, unto the wicked" (Isaiah 48:22). No matter how diligently we work or how devoutly we wish, the sinful nature lurking in the hearts of mankind constantly works against peace.

But in the person of Jesus, we are offered the solution to every conflict. He is the only ruler who offers hope for a lasting peace, and peace is His promise to those who are His children by virtue of receiving His salvation. "Peace I leave with you, my peace I give unto you: not as the world giveth, give I unto you. Let not your heart be troubled, neither let it be afraid" (John 14:27). One day, Jesus will return to establish a kingdom of peace on Earth. But until that day, we still can live in His peace, and we can share that peace with others through the gospel.

Today's Growth Principle: Our only hope for peace with God, with ourselves, and with others is found in Jesus Christ.

The Sacrifice of Christmas

Therefore, as ye abound in every thing, in faith, and utterance, and knowledge, and in all diligence, and in your love to us, see that ye abound in this grace also. I speak not by commandment, but by occasion of the forwardness of others, and to prove the sincerity of your love. For ye know the grace of our Lord Jesus Christ, that, though he was rich, yet for your sakes he became poor, that ye through his poverty might be rich.
—2 CORINTHIANS 8:7–9

It is impossible for our limited understanding to fully grasp the glory and riches of Heaven. We read about the wonders of our eternal home in Scripture, but they at best paint a dim picture of what we will one day see. That perfect place was home to Jesus before the world was created. When He left everything behind to come to Earth as our Saviour, He gave up wealth and power beyond our imagination. Though anything in our world would have been a massive step down, Jesus could still have chosen to be born into what passes for wealth and luxury here. He could have been born in a palace surrounded by all the comforts available.

Instead He chose an ordinary poor family. We know that Mary and Joseph had very little, for the offering that they took to the Temple was the substitute offering Moses provided for those who could not afford the full sacrifice commanded in the law (Leviticus 12:8). Luke 2:24 tells us that Mary and Joseph took Jesus to the Temple to dedicate Him to the Lord "And to offer a sacrifice according to that which is said in the law of the Lord, A pair of turtledoves, or two young pigeons."

Jesus didn't come to Earth to be comfortable or to be worshipped. He didn't come "…to be ministered unto, but to minister, and to give his life a ransom for many" (Matthew 20:28). The love of God for us is measured by the cost of our salvation. It was not just on the cross but in every part of His life that Jesus sacrificed.

Today's Growth Principle: The story of Christmas cannot be appreciated without understanding the sacrifice Christ made for us.

Working While We Wait

*Let your loins be girded about, and your lights burning; And ye yourselves like unto men that wait for their lord, when he will return from the wedding; that when he cometh and knocketh, they may open unto him immediately. Blessed are those servants, whom the lord when he cometh shall find watching: verily I say unto you, that he shall gird himself, and make them to sit down to meat, and will come forth and serve them.—*LUKE 12:35–37

The last promise that Jesus made here on Earth was to tell His disciples that the Holy Spirit would come on them in power so that they could do the work He was leaving them to accomplish: "For John truly baptized with water; but ye shall be baptized with the Holy Ghost not many days hence" (Acts 1:5). When He was taken up into Heaven, the angels appeared with another promise: "Which also said, Ye men of Galilee, why stand ye gazing up into heaven? this same Jesus, which is taken up from you into heaven, shall so come in like manner as ye have seen him go into heaven" (Acts 1:11).

There is a direct connection between these two promises. The power of the Holy Spirit equips us to witness and work effectively for Jesus until the time He returns. We do not know, indeed we are not meant to know, when that day will be. Our responsibility is to fill our days with service for God, so that when the Lord appears we will not be ashamed.

Charles Spurgeon said, "If I knew that our Lord would come this evening, I should preach just as I mean to preach; and if I knew he would come during this sermon, I would go on preaching until He did...The fact that Jesus Christ is to come again is not a reason for star-gazing, but for working in the power of the Holy Ghost."

Today's Growth Principle: Since we do not know when the Lord will return, we must be busy about His work every day.

The Obedience of Jesus

And he said unto them, How is it that ye sought me? wist ye not that I must be about my Father's business? And they understood not the saying which he spake unto them. And he went down with them, and came to Nazareth, and was subject unto them: but his mother kept all these sayings in her heart. And Jesus increased in wisdom and stature, and in favour with God and man.—LUKE 2:49–52

Though Jesus has always been fully and completely eternal God even before the moment of His conception, when He came to this Earth, He was also fully and completely human. And as a human, He had to go through the stages of growth, development, and learning that all of us do. Jesus was not born knowing how to walk or speak or care for Himself. He learned those things through submission and obedience to Mary and Joseph. In doing so, He set a powerful example for us.

I read recently about the extensive training Arabian horses go through in the deserts. The trainers test to make sure the horses are completely obedient. The final test is forcing the horses to go without water for a couple of days, then turning them loose near an oasis. Just as they get close to the water, the trainer blows his whistle. The horses stop, turn around, and come back. When the trainer is sure that he has their obedience, he then gives them a signal to go back to drink as much as they want.

Many people seem to think that they have "outgrown" the need for obedience. They know what God commands in His Word, but they endeavor to change the meaning of words or explain them away through culture and context to avoid obedience. Nothing could be further from the example of Jesus. He was always obedient, from His birth to His death, and we should follow His example.

Today's Growth Principle: If Jesus, the Lord of Heaven and Earth, was subject to the authorities in His life, we have no excuse for rebellion.

The Gift that Never Disappoints

Art thou greater than our father Jacob, which gave us the well, and drank thereof himself, and his children, and his cattle? Jesus answered and said unto her, Whosoever drinketh of this water shall thirst again: But whosoever drinketh of the water that I shall give him shall never thirst; but the water that I shall give him shall be in him a well of water springing up into everlasting life.—JOHN 4:12–14

I heard about two coworkers who were discussing their holiday celebrations after everyone got back to the office from the Christmas break. Dan asked Bob, "So what did you get for Christmas?" Bob replied, "See that brand new red Ferrari parked out in the parking lot?" Dan was shocked. "Seriously? That's incredible!" But Bob said with a sigh, "I got a tie that's the exact same color as that Ferrari."

Most of us know what it is like to be disappointed with a Christmas present. Maybe it was when we were children with an expectation of something specific we had asked for but instead received a replacement. Maybe it was a style or color that we just didn't like as a teenager. Maybe it was completely different from what we were expecting. But when we finished tearing off the wrapping paper and opening the box, we had to do our best to put a smile on our faces that didn't match how we felt, because we felt let down by what we received.

That never happens when we come to Jesus. He meets every need and satisfies every longing in the human heart. Jesus is the perfect sacrifice for our sins, and the perfect Saviour to answer our desires for love, fulfillment, and meaning in life. No wonder the Apostle Paul declared that Jesus is beyond human ability to describe. "Thanks be unto God for his unspeakable gift" (2 Corinthians 9:15). When we go to Him we are never turned away and never left unsatisfied.

Today's Growth Principle: Christmas is ultimately the celebration of the greatest gift in all of history.

God Keeps His Promises

Even so we, when we were children, were in bondage under the elements of the world: But when the fulness of the time was come, God sent forth his Son, made of a woman, made under the law, To redeem them that were under the law, that we might receive the adoption of sons. And because ye are sons, God hath sent forth the Spirit of his Son into your hearts, crying, Abba, Father.—GALATIANS 4:3–6

Politicians are not always known for keeping the promises they make, but I came across an old news story about one who did. When George Jelinek was running for the Kansas state legislature back in the 1960s, he printed up flyers that read, "I will work for you." According to the article, Jelinek won his election and then had an unexpected request from a constituent. "One farmer," Jelinek said, "told me he voted for me and now he needed some help putting up some alfalfa in the barn. And I did it. But I'm going to have to watch what I say!"

Man may break promises, but God is always faithful. He does not work on our timetable, but everything He says will be done. Thousands of years passed between the time God promised Adam and Eve that there would be a coming Messiah who would defeat Satan (Genesis 3:15) and the birth of Jesus in Bethlehem. But it happened just as God said. In fact there is a large number of Old Testament references to the coming of Jesus—the location, timing, and circumstances are given in great detail—and every one of those prophecies were fulfilled.

The Christmas story is not just a baby in a manger, shepherds, angels, and wise men. It is a vivid reminder that everything God says happens just as He promises. "For all the promises of God in him are yea, and in him Amen, unto the glory of God by us" (2 Corinthians 1:20).

Today's Growth Principle: Christmas is a reminder that we can fully rely on everything that God has promised in His Word.

The Consolation of Christmas

And, behold, there was a man in Jerusalem, whose name was Simeon; and the same man was just and devout, waiting for the consolation of Israel: and the Holy Ghost was upon him. And it was revealed unto him by the Holy Ghost, that he should not see death, before he had seen the Lord's Christ. And he came by the Spirit into the temple: and when the parents brought in the child Jesus, to do for him after the custom of the law,—LUKE 2:25–27

Jesus came into the world with a definite purpose and mission. From the time He was a young boy, He was committed to doing His Father's will and work in the world. And that purpose was to accomplish God's plan of redemption for fallen mankind. Jesus was a great teacher, a miracle worker, a healer, an example, and role model to follow, but none of those were His mission. He came to be the Saviour for all who believe.

The aged man Simeon who had been promised that he would see the Messiah before he died recognized the need of salvation. He understood that the curse of sin could only be overcome by the promised Messiah. That was the hope, the consolation, which he so devoutly desired to see. And that hope of salvation is the true message of this holiday. The Lord said, "Even as the Son of man came not to be ministered unto, but to minister, and to give his life a ransom for many" (Matthew 20:28).

In his Christmas song "Jesus, Baby Jesus" Dr. John Rice wrote:

> Jesus, how the angels with delight the story told,
> Told to Mary, Joseph and the shepherds at their fold,
> Full of light, the heavens, as they chanted "peace on earth."
> Jesus, baby Jesus, what glad news, a Saviour's birth!
> Jesus, baby Jesus, there's a cross along the way,
> Born to die for sinners, born for crucifixion day.

Today's Growth Principle: The hope of Christmas is not seen in a manger, but in a cross and an empty tomb.

Light Has Come into the World

He that believeth on him is not condemned: but he that believeth not is condemned already, because he hath not believed in the name of the only begotten Son of God. And this is the condemnation, that light is come into the world, and men loved darkness rather than light, because their deeds were evil. For every one that doeth evil hateth the light, neither cometh to the light, lest his deeds should be reproved.—JOHN 3:18–20

One of the best known classic Christmas movies is *It's a Wonderful Life.* It tells the story of a man named George Bailey who, after spending his years helping others but never being able to fulfill his own dreams reaches a financial crisis and comes the point where he wishes he had never been born. An angel named Clarence (second class—no wings) shows him what the world would be like without his influence. George comes to realize the impact his life has had on so many others, and finally tells Clarence, "I want to live!" In the end, the townspeople George has helped so much come to his aid and everyone gets a happy ending, even Clarence who finally gets his wings. Of course this is fiction, and things don't work like that in the real world.

But Christmas is a powerful reminder of the impact Jesus Christ made when He was born in Bethlehem so long ago. Our world would be vastly different—hopeless—had He never come. Every part of human life, even down to our calendar, is touched by His arrival to bring light into a world of darkness. This is just as true for those who do not believe in Jesus as it is for those of us who are saved. The darkness may hate the light, but it cannot defeat it. "And the light shineth in darkness; and the darkness comprehended it not" (John 1:5), Those of us who have come to His light have a great responsibility to be faithful reflectors of the light to those around us. This is the way to truly celebrate the birth of Christ.

Today's Growth Principle: Christmas is a celebration of the light of God's love that has come into the darkness of a world filled with sin.

Our Precious Saviour

Wherefore also it is contained in the scripture, Behold, I lay in Sion a chief corner stone, elect, precious: and he that believeth on him shall not be confounded. Unto you therefore which believe he is precious: but unto them which be disobedient, the stone which the builders disallowed, the same is made the head of the corner, And a stone of stumbling, and a rock of offence, even to them which stumble at the word, being disobedient: whereunto also they were appointed.—1 PETER 2:6–8

Probably the most famous set of presents ever given were the Imperial Eggs the house of Faberge made for the Tsars of Russia between 1885 and 1917. Numbering fifty in all, most of these intricate and elaborate eggs are in museum and private collections, but some were lost during the Russian Revolution. A man paid $13,302 at a flea market for a sculpted piece that he originally intended to melt for scrap metal. But he had trouble selling it, and about a decade later, in 2012, he investigated further and found that he had the missing Third Imperial Egg—worth more than $30 million. When we think about things that are precious, there are some that are valuable because of their age and craftsmanship. Others have great value because of the materials that went into making them. Some are prized because of who made them. The Faberge eggs are valuable because of all three.

The worth of Jesus is beyond price. There is no measure by which we could appraise or evaluate just how precious He is. But we can and should remember to be grateful for the amazing sacrifice that brought the Lord into the world, and then took Him to the cross. The measure of the worth of the blood that He shed for our salvation is seen in what it purchased—the eternal souls of all of us who accepted God's salvation through Jesus Christ. No human gift will ever compare to the precious Saviour born in Bethlehem.

Today's Growth Principle: Celebrate the birth, life, and work of our precious Saviour every day throughout this Christmas season.

God with Us

And she shall bring forth a son, and thou shalt call his name JESUS: for he shall save his people from their sins. Now all this was done, that it might be fulfilled which was spoken of the Lord by the prophet, saying, Behold, a virgin shall be with child, and shall bring forth a son, and they shall call his name Emmanuel, which being interpreted is, God with us.
—MATTHEW 1:21–23

Dr. Lee Roberson told the story of a little boy whose mother died unexpectedly. He was too young to understand everything about death and Heaven, but he knew that his mother was gone. After the funeral, the father and son returned with their broken hearts to their empty home. When it was time for bed, the little boy asked to sleep with his father. But even that proved scant comfort when the lights were turned off. Through the darkness his soft voice whispered, "Daddy, is your face turned toward me?"

All of us have an empty place in our hearts that only God can fill. No amount of success, money, fame, accomplishment, or earthly love can supply the need only God can meet. And so often in the darkness when no one else can hear, we ask if God sees us and knows the burdens that we are carrying. *Jesus* is the answer to that question—and the answer is *yes!* God not only sees and knows every burden and heartache that we feel, but He came and experienced our world firsthand. Because of this, He is "… touched with the feeling of our infirmities…" (Hebrews 4:15).

Although there are times when we do not *feel* a real sense of God's presence and care in our lives, He is there. Jesus came into the world to bridge the divide that had existed between God and man since Adam and Eve's sin in the Garden of Eden. We do not serve a distant God who is far off and hard to reach. We serve a God who is present with us, and who accepts us into His family through the blood of His Son Jesus.

Today's Growth Principle: Through the coming of Jesus into the world, the gap between us and God has been bridged.

According to the Plan

For God so loved the world, that he gave his only begotten Son, that whosoever believeth in him should not perish, but have everlasting life. For God sent not his Son into the world to condemn the world; but that the world through him might be saved. He that believeth on him is not condemned: but he that believeth not is condemned already, because he hath not believed on the name of the only begotten Son of God.
—JOHN 3:16–18

Even before the creation of the world and Adam's sin in the Garden of Eden, God's plan for our redemption had already been established. Nothing in the Christmas story happened by accident or coincidence. It was all arranged and ordered ahead of time. John wrote, "And all that dwell upon the earth shall worship him, whose names are not written in the book of life of the Lamb slain from the foundation of the world" (Revelation 13:8). The need for a Saviour did not take God by surprise. He was not caught off guard when man fell and death entered the world. There was no search for a solution to the problem of sin—it was already in place.

Jesus made the necessity of salvation crystal clear when He talked to Nicodemus. Every person is born under the condemnation of sin. Our destiny is not determined by our actions, thoughts, or intentions, but by our nature. We start out as sinners, opposed to God. The Saviour did not come for the good, but for those who are hopelessly lost without Him. Jesus said, "But go ye and learn what that meaneth, I will have mercy, and not sacrifice: for I am not come to call the righteous, but sinners to repentance" (Matthew 9:13). Our most desperate need—salvation from our sins—can only be obtained by faith in Jesus as our substitute and Saviour according to God's plan.

Today's Growth Principle: God's love for us is clearly seen in His plan that brought Jesus into the world at Christmas.

The Practice of Praise

And I beheld, and I heard the voice of many angels round about the throne and the beasts and the elders: and the number of them was ten thousand times ten thousand, and thousands of thousands; Saying with a loud voice, Worthy is the Lamb that was slain to receive power, and riches, and wisdom, and strength, and honour, and glory, and blessing.
—REVELATION 5:11–12

When the first angel appeared to the shepherds in the fields outside Bethlehem, he brought the message for which Israel had been waiting for thousands of years—that the Messiah and Saviour had come into the world. But such good news could not be adequately conveyed by a single angel. Instead, a multitude of angels appeared to give praise and glory to God. This should not be a surprise, because each time the Bible reveals a glimpse of what is happening in Heaven, we see angelic praise being offered to God.

If the angels, who do not receive God's gift of salvation praise Him, how much more should those of us who had no hope of entering His presence apart from the coming of Christ as our Saviour praise Him? We are the recipients of the greatest gift of history when we accept salvation by grace through faith. It is the height of ingratitude not to continually thank and praise God for what we have received.

Yet too often that is not the case. The Psalmist expressed his desire to see praise from those who had benefited from God's blessings. "Oh that men would praise the LORD for his goodness, and for his wonderful works to the children of men!" (Psalm 107:8). There should be a constant stream of praise proceeding from our lips, not just at Christmas but throughout the year. The people of God have been granted that status because of His grace and the gift of His Son, and we should devote our lives to honoring and glorifying Him.

Today's Growth Principle: Those who rightly understand the meaning of Christmas will have hearts and mouths filled with praise.

A Gift in Person

And the Word was made flesh, and dwelt among us, (and we beheld his glory, the glory as of the only begotten of the Father,) full of grace and truth. John bare witness of him, and cried, saying, This was he of whom I spake, He that cometh after me is preferred before me: for he was before me. And of his fulness have all we received, and grace for grace. For the law was given by Moses, but grace and truth came by Jesus Christ.
—JOHN 1:14-17

There are times when circumstances force us to only be able to send presents to people we wish we could be with on Christmas. But there is nothing that can compare to being there in person when the wrapping paper comes off and the gift is revealed. There is a connection that is made when we are together with family and loved ones that cannot be experienced any other way.

In every human heart, there is a longing for something deeper and more meaningful than what this world can provide. Moses expressed his longing for a deep and real connection with God when he was leading the Children of Israel. The tasks which he faced required more than an abstract knowledge of God—Moses needed God with him day after day. "And he said unto him, If thy presence go not with me, carry us not up hence" (Exodus 33:15).

Many try to fill the void with other things, but only Jesus can satisfy the longing of the heart. And to meet that need, He came in person. The Lord did not *send* a present—He *came* into the world and took on human form because of our great need of a Saviour. Christmas is not an impersonal story. It is the story of God's love being manifest in a personal way. It is the story of our value in His eyes.

Today's Growth Principle: Jesus came into this world as a visible expression of the amazing love God has for those who do not love Him in return.

The Cost of Christmas

And Joseph and his mother marvelled at those things which were spoken of him. And Simeon blessed them, and said unto Mary his mother, Behold, this child is set for the fall and rising again of many in Israel; and for a sign which shall be spoken against; (Yea, a sword shall pierce through thy own soul also,) that the thoughts of many hearts may be revealed.
—LUKE 2:33–35

I love the Christmas season and the special joy that it brings to those of us who know the Lord. It is a time when we celebrate with family and friends, exchange presents, sing songs, and spend time together. Yet even as we enjoy this wonderful time of year, we should never forget that the greatest gift of Christmas—the Son of God sent into the world to be our Saviour—came at a very high cost.

Man turned against God, violating the one instruction issued in the Garden of Eden. Even in the only perfect setting the world has known, Adam was unwilling to obey. As a result, death entered the world and is the only future of which all can be certain (Romans 5:12). Yet in mercy and grace, even before the Fall, God had already ordained a plan for our salvation, despite the fact that it would require the death of His sinless Son as a sacrifice for our sins.

It is only the amazing love of God for us that can explain why the high cost of Christmas was paid. And it is that love that should motivate us to follow the example of the Lord.

In explaining his lifetime of devoted service to Jesus, Paul wrote, "For whether we be beside ourselves, it is to God: or whether we be sober, it is for your cause. For the love of Christ constraineth us; because we thus judge, that if one died for all, then were all dead" (2 Corinthians 5:13–14). When the love of Christ fills our hearts, we are willing to pay any cost to demonstrate our love to Him.

Today's Growth Principle: The cost of Christmas should compel us to a lifetime of devoted love and service to Jesus Christ.

Nahum // Revelation 14

So Much to Celebrate

*For unto you is born this day in the city of David a Saviour, which is Christ the Lord. And this shall be a sign unto you; Ye shall find the babe wrapped in swaddling clothes, lying in a manger. And suddenly there was with the angel a multitude of the heavenly host praising God, and saying, Glory to God in the highest, and on earth peace, good will toward men.—*LUKE 2:11–14

From the very first Christmas night, the remembrance of Christ's birth has been a joyful and happy time—a time to celebrate. As the angels told the shepherds of the birth of the Saviour, their words were filled with praise to God as they rejoiced at the working of God's plan. And we rejoice at this wonderful time of year as well.

Yes, this busy season is often pressure-filled and stressful. There are long lines in the stores (and if you're like me and put off your Christmas shopping, you find yourself in these long lines on Christmas Eve). There are presents to find and meals to plan. But we must never lose sight of the purpose and meaning of Christmas. If we remain focused on the amazing gift of God's Son, we will find more peace in our hearts and more praise on our lips.

And as we celebrate, we should never forget that the joyful news of Christmas is not meant to be restricted to those who already understand the true meaning of this holiday. The message of salvation through Jesus Christ is meant for all, and it is our duty and privilege to share it with the world, just as the shepherds told all they met about what had happened: "And when they had seen it, they made known abroad the saying which was told them concerning this child" (Luke 2:17). H. A. Ironside wrote, "There are good tidings of great joy for all people, not just for a limited number, but for all people. All men everywhere are invited to put their trust in the Saviour whom God has sent into the world."

Today's Growth Principle: Remembering what Christmas is truly about gives us ample reason for joyful celebration.

A Message to Share

And it came to pass, as the angels were gone away from them into heaven, the shepherds said one to another, Let us now go even unto Bethlehem, and see this thing which is come to pass, which the Lord hath made known unto us. And they came with haste, and found Mary, and Joseph, and the babe lying in a manger. And when they had seen it, they made known abroad the saying which was told them concerning this child.
—LUKE 2:15–17

John Wesley Work, Jr., led the Fisk Jubilee Singers from 1898 to 1904. During that time they traveled across the country bringing their music, including many of the spirituals from the days of slavery to those who had never heard them before. Work was responsible for writing down the melodies for many of these songs which had only existed orally before. A number of them were published in hymnals, including what was originally called the "Plantation Christmas Song." Work's son recalled how early Christmas morning, before the sun came up, the students would go from building to building on campus singing what we know today as "Go Tell it on the Mountain."

> Go, tell it on the mountain,
> Over the hills and everywhere
> Go, tell it on the mountain,
> That Jesus Christ is born.

The shepherds were the first to share the message of the birth of Jesus with the world, but the task they started is still needed. The world is in darkness, and they will only know that the Light has come if someone shares the Good News with them. Every believer has the privilege and responsibility of telling others about Jesus.

Today's Growth Principle: The message and hope of Christmas is too powerful and important not to share with others.

God's Measure of Success

Now after the death of Moses the servant of the LORD it came to pass, that the LORD spake unto Joshua the son of Nun, Moses' minister, saying, Moses my servant is dead; now therefore arise, go over this Jordan, thou, and all this people, unto the land which I do give to them, even to the children of Israel. Every place that the sole of your foot shall tread upon, that have I given unto you, as I said unto Moses.—JOSHUA 1:1–3

At the end of a year, many people stop to reflect on what has transpired in the last twelve months. There are many different measures of success people use to evaluate their lives. Some focus on career achievement or advancement. Others highlight financial success. Some measure by the accomplishments of their children or grandchildren. Churches might look at their attendance. But the measure of success that should matter most to us is what God thinks of what we have done.

After Moses' life, God referred to him with a single phrase that summed up his life: "Moses the servant of the LORD." It wasn't the parting of the Red Sea or leading Israel through the wilderness that were the most significant measuring sticks of Moses' "success." It was that he served God. Everything else was a by-product. Similarly, when God selected Joshua as the replacement for Moses who would lead the Israelites into the Promised Land, He did not focus on his organizational abilities or military prowess, though both of those were real and had been demonstrated time and again during the forty years of wandering the wilderness. Instead, God looked at the way Joshua had faithfully served Moses.

The world may not value ministering to the needs of others, but God holds it in high regard. "For, brethren, ye have been called unto liberty; only use not liberty for an occasion to the flesh, but by love serve one another" (Galatians 5:13).

Today's Growth Principle: True success is to faithfully serve God and others.

Putting Limits on God

For he remembered that they were but flesh; a wind that passeth away, and cometh not again. How oft did they provoke him in the wilderness, and grieve him in the desert! Yea, they turned back and tempted God, and limited the Holy One of Israel. They remembered not his hand, nor the day when he delivered them from the enemy.—PSALM 78:39–42

When God called Abram to leave Ur and go out to a land that would become his inheritance, the "father of the faithful" responded in faith and obedience. When he finally reached the land that would become Israel, God described to him the borders of the promise—which included some 300,000 square miles of land (Genesis 15:18–21). Though Israel would claim the land under Joshua, and a great kingdom would later be established under David and Solomon, at no point did they ever claim all of the land God had promised. In fact, the greatest extent of their possession was only around 10 percent of what God had described to Abraham.

So many times we fail to see God work as He has promised and decide as a result that the problem is with Him. In reality, the problem is with our turning away from what God offers because we do not obey Him. When we suffer the consequences that come from our disobedience, that is not God letting us down. In reality, it is the life of limitation and lack we have chosen when we fail to believe in God's promises and obey waiting for His blessing—when we do not trust and obey.

The problem of powerless living is not with God but with us. "Behold, the LORD's hand is not shortened, that it cannot save; neither his ear heavy, that it cannot hear: But your iniquities have separated between you and your God, and your sins have hid his face from you, that he will not hear" (Isaiah 59:1–2). Unbelief and disobedience limit the work that God will do through our lives.

Today's Growth Principle: If you want to see God's power and promises in your life, yield to Him in obedience and follow Him in faith.

God's Hand in Opposition

*Thou, even thou, art to be feared: and who may stand in thy sight when once thou art angry? Thou didst cause judgment to be heard from heaven; the earth feared, and was still, When God arose to judgment, to save all the meek of the earth. Selah. Surely the wrath of man shall praise thee: the remainder of wrath shalt thou restrain.—*PSALM 76:7–10

William Tyndale set out with a simple goal—to translate the Bible into English so that the people could read for themselves what God had said. He believed that putting the Bible into the common language would expose error and do much to correct the false doctrine preached from the pulpits of English churches. He was right—and he was hated for it. Tyndale spent much of his adult life on the run from the authorities. The story is told that when his first New Testament was published, the government bought up all the copies they could to keep people from reading them, but those profits provided the resources for Tyndale to continue his work and produce a more complete translation.

God does not promise that no one will oppose us when we set out to do something for Him. What He does promise is to go with us and meet our needs. Often God uses the very opposition we face to accomplish what He has set before us. If we become discouraged and give up when things don't go as we would like or think they should, we will surely never accomplish anything of lasting value. "Thou therefore, my son, be strong in the grace that is in Christ Jesus....Thou therefore endure hardness, as a good soldier of Jesus Christ" (2 Timothy 2:1, 3).

We should look for God's hand in the opposition we face. We must never forget that He is able to turn even the worst circumstances to further His purposes. It was the persecution of the early church that God used to quickly spread the gospel around the world. "Therefore they that were scattered abroad went every where preaching the word" (Acts 8:4).

Today's Growth Principle: Do not shrink from opposition to your work for God; regard it as a sign that you're on the right track.

Finding God in Troubled Times

For I know the thoughts that I think toward you, saith the LORD, thoughts of peace, and not of evil, to give you an expected end. Then shall ye call upon me, and ye shall go and pray unto me, and I will hearken unto you. And ye shall seek me, and find me, when ye shall search for me with all your heart. And I will be found of you, saith the LORD: and I will turn away your captivity, and I will gather you from all the nations, and from all the places whither I have driven you, saith the LORD; and I will bring you again into the place whence I caused you to be carried away captive.
—JEREMIAH 29:11–14

Jeremiah lived in a time of great turmoil. During his ministry, enemy armies came to his homeland and looted the Temple in Jerusalem that was built for the worship of Jehovah. The people had turned against the Lord time and again, worshiping false gods and enjoying the sin that they knew God hated. Yet despite the bitter harvest of consequences they were reaping, God had not forgotten them. God wanted to assure His people that while they had forgotten Him, He still loved them and once their hearts were turned back toward Him, He would restore them in ways they could only imagine.

It is easy for us to look around and think that there is no hope—that things will only get worse. But with God nothing is impossible. The powers of this world are insignificant before His might. The needs of this world are no challenge to His unlimited resources. The evil in this world may be great, but it will not prevail against Him. In fact, though the final victory has not yet been given to us, it has already been won for us by Jesus Christ, and nothing the devil can do will change that. The best tool Satan can use against us is to cause us to doubt God. When we are in difficulty, it is more important than ever that we look to Him and trust His promises.

Today's Growth Principle: God is faithful in every situation and circumstance of life, and you can safely trust your future to His care.

The Likeness of Jesus Christ

Behold, what manner of love the Father hath bestowed upon us, that we should be called the sons of God: therefore the world knoweth us not, because it knew him not. Beloved, now are we the sons of God, and it doth not yet appear what we shall be: but we know that, when he shall appear, we shall be like him; for we shall see him as he is. And every man that hath this hope in him purifieth himself, even as he is pure.—1 JOHN 3:1–3

No one was closer to Jesus while He was on Earth than John. Even among the "inner circle" disciples (Peter, James, and John), John sensed a special place in the Lord's affection. In the Gospel account John recorded, he referred to himself as "the disciple whom Jesus loved." I can't think of a better title or description that any of us could receive—John had a close, personal, meaningful relationship with the Lord that characterized his entire life.

But that's not all, because John walked closely with Jesus, he was easily identified as being like Jesus. Acts 4:13 records, "Now when they saw the boldness of Peter and John, and perceived that they were unlearned and ignorant men, they marvelled; and they took knowledge of them, that they had been with Jesus."

Though none of us will achieve perfect Christlikeness here on Earth, it should be our heart's fervent desire to be becoming increasingly like the Lord. And the way we do that is not mystical or hidden. The more clearly and closely we see Him and the more time we spend in His presence, the more His attributes and nature will show in our lives. The more His Spirit continually fills and empowers us, the more others will see Jesus when they look at us. "But we all, with open face beholding as in a glass the glory of the Lord, are changed into the same image from glory to glory, even as by the Spirit of the Lord" (2 Corinthians 3:18).

Today's Growth Principle: Our world today needs the Christians they see to be more like Jesus.

Our Greatest Need for the Coming Year

A new heart also will I give you, and a new spirit will I put within you: and I will take away the stony heart out of your flesh, and I will give you an heart of flesh. And I will put my spirit within you, and cause you to walk in my statutes, and ye shall keep my judgments, and do them. And ye shall dwell in the land that I gave to your fathers; and ye shall be my people, and I will be your God.—EZEKIEL 36:26–28

So often when I counsel with people, I hear them express a longing for a change in their circumstances. So many people believe that if they just had a better job or a better marriage or better parents or a better church, their lives would be transformed. But the reality is that the biggest change anyone needs, is a change of heart. External changes of relationships or circumstances only provide temporary relief at best, for the problems we have arise from within, not from without.

Repeated studies into the lives of people who win large lottery jackpots reveal a consistent pattern. A great majority of those people are worse off five years later than they were before their windfall. No amount of outward change in circumstances or conditions can fix a problem that has its roots in the heart. Jesus said, "There is nothing from without a man, that entering into him can defile him: but the things which come out of him, those are they that defile the man" (Mark 7:15).

More than anything else in our nation, our churches, and our own lives, we need people who have hearts toward God. The things that we love most dictate how we use our time and invest our resources. If God is first, as He should be, then every decision and action will reflect our love for Him.

Today's Growth Principle: If you want to experience God's blessing and guidance, your heart must be fixed on Him.

PRACTICES
OF EFFECTIVE
CHRISTIANS

The Effective Christian Memorizes Scripture

The following principles for effective Scripture memory are taken from *Homiletics from the Heart*, written by Dr. John Goetsch.

1. **Choose a specific time and a quiet place.**
   What gets scheduled gets accomplished. When memorizing the Word of God, you want to free yourself from all distractions.

2. **Organize by topic.**
   Many people attempt to learn the "Golden Chapters" or whole books of the Bible. While this is a noble attempt, it is not the way the Word of God will be used while teaching or preaching. Choose a topic you would like to study and then memorize every verse that deals with it. The next time you are speaking on that particular subject, your mind will be able to tie these verses together to truly allow you to "preach the Word..."

3. **Work out loud.**
   Even though it may sound odd, your mind memorizes better and faster that which it audibly hears. This is why you should choose a specific time and a quiet place!

4. **Walk while you memorize.**
   Your body has a natural sense of rhythm. This is why we memorize the words of songs so quickly. We will memorize much more quickly (and retain it longer) if we are walking around.

5. **Review, review, review.**
   Repetition is the key to learning. The one who is serious about memorizing Scripture cannot simply keep learning new passages weekly. Rather, he must also make the time to review the previous passages already committed to memory. It becomes readily apparent that memorization will take work, but the rewards are worth it!

6. **Set goals of time.**
If you are not careful, you may ask for disappointment by setting goals of verses per week. The reason why is that some verses are more difficult to learn than others. If you set goals of time spent in memorization, God will honor that.

On the following pages you will find many major Bible doctrines and key verses to memorize. It is time to put into practice these six principles.

The Bible

Psalm 119:160—*Thy word is true from the beginning: and every one of thy righteous judgments endureth for ever.*

Isaiah 40:8—*The grass withereth, the flower fadeth: but the word of our God shall stand for ever.*

2 Timothy 3:16–17—*All scripture is given by inspiration of God, and is profitable for doctrine, for reproof, for correction, for instruction in righteousness: That the man of God may be perfect, throughly furnished unto all good works.*

Hebrews 4:12—*For the word of God is quick, and powerful, and sharper than any twoedged sword, piercing even to the dividing asunder of soul and spirit, and of the joints and marrow, and is a discerner of the thoughts and intents of the heart.*

John 17:17—*Sanctify them through thy truth: thy word is truth.*

Matthew 24:35—*Heaven and earth shall pass away, but my words shall not pass away.*

1 Thessalonians 2:13—*For this cause also thank we God without ceasing, because, when ye received the word of God which ye heard of us, ye received it not as the word of men, but as it is in truth, the word of God, which effectually worketh also in you that believe.*

God

Psalm 111:9—*He sent redemption unto his people: he hath commanded his covenant for ever: holy and reverend is his name.*

Isaiah 57:15—*For thus saith the high and lofty One that inhabiteth eternity, whose name is Holy; I dwell in the high and holy place, with him also that is of a contrite and humble spirit, to revive the spirit of the humble, and to revive the heart of the contrite ones.*

Lamentations 3:22–23—*It is of the LORD's mercies that we are not consumed, because his compassions fail not. They are new every morning: great is thy faithfulness.*

Deuteronomy 32:4—*He is the Rock, his work is perfect: for all his ways are judgment: a God of truth and without iniquity, just and right is he.*

Psalm 138:2—*I will worship toward thy holy temple, and praise thy name for thy lovingkindness and for thy truth: for thou hast magnified thy word above all thy name.*

John 4:24—*God is a Spirit: and they that worship him must worship him in spirit and in truth.*

Psalm 90:2—*Before the mountains were brought forth, or ever thou hadst formed the earth and the world, even from everlasting to everlasting, thou art God.*

Jesus Christ

John 1:1, 14—*In the beginning was the Word, and the Word was with God, and the Word was God. And the Word was made flesh, and dwelt among us, (and we beheld his glory, the glory as of the only begotten of the Father,) full of grace and truth.*

Philippians 2:6–8—*Who, being in the form of God, thought it not robbery to be equal with God: But made himself of no reputation, and took upon him the form of a servant, and was made in the likeness of men: And being found in fashion as a man, he humbled himself, and became obedient unto death, even the death of the cross.*

Colossians 1:16–17—*For by him were all things created, that are in heaven, and that are in earth, visible and invisible, whether they be thrones, or dominions, or principalities, or powers: all things were created by him, and for him: And he is before all things, and by him all things consist.*

1 Timothy 2:5–6—*For there is one God, and one mediator between God and men, the man Christ Jesus; Who gave himself a ransom for all, to be testified in due time.*

Hebrews 1:8—*But unto the Son he saith, Thy throne, O God, is for ever and ever: a sceptre of righteousness is the sceptre of thy kingdom.*

Luke 19:10—*For the Son of man is come to seek and to save that which was lost.*

Holy Spirit

John 14:16—*And I will pray the Father, and he shall give you another Comforter, that he may abide with you for ever;*

John 14:26—*But the Comforter, which is the Holy Ghost, whom the Father will send in my name, he shall teach you all things, and bring all things to your remembrance, whatsoever I have said unto you.*

John 15:26—*But when the Comforter is come, whom I will send unto you from the Father, even the Spirit of truth, which proceedeth from the Father, he shall testify of me:*

John 16:13–14—*Howbeit when he, the Spirit of truth, is come, he will guide you into all truth: for he shall not speak of himself; but whatsoever he shall hear, that shall he speak: and he will shew you things to come. He shall glorify me: for he shall receive of mine, and shall shew it unto you.*

1 Corinthians 3:16—*Know ye not that ye are the temple of God, and that the Spirit of God dwelleth in you?*

Ephesians 4:30—*And grieve not the holy Spirit of God, whereby ye are sealed unto the day of redemption.*

Ephesians 5:18—*And be not drunk with wine, wherein is excess; but be filled with the Spirit;*

Mankind

Genesis 1:26–27—*And God said, Let us make man in our image, after our likeness: and let them have dominion over the fish of the sea, and over the fowl of the air, and over the cattle, and over all the earth, and over every creeping thing that creepeth upon the earth. So God created man in his own image, in the image of God created he him; male and female created he them.*

Job 14:1, 14—*Man that is born of a woman is of few days, and full of trouble. If a man die, shall he live again? all the days of my appointed time will I wait, till my change come.*

Psalm 8:4–5—*What is man, that thou art mindful of him? and the son of man, that thou visitest him? For thou hast made him a little lower than the angels, and hast crowned him with glory and honour.*

Isaiah 64:6—*But we are all as an unclean thing, and all our righteousnesses are as filthy rags; and we all do fade as a leaf; and our iniquities, like the wind, have taken us away.*

Romans 3:10–11—*As it is written, There is none righteous, no, not one: There is none that understandeth, there is none that seeketh after God.*

Romans 3:23—*For all have sinned, and come short of the glory of God.*

Sin

Numbers 32:23—*But if ye will not do so, behold, ye have sinned against the LORD: and be sure your sin will find you out.*

Ezekiel 18:20—*The soul that sinneth, it shall die. The son shall not bear the iniquity of the father, neither shall the father bear the iniquity of the son: the righteousness of the righteous shall be upon him, and the wickedness of the wicked shall be upon him.*

Romans 6:23—*For the wages of sin is death; but the gift of God is eternal life through Jesus Christ our Lord.*

James 1:15—*Then when lust hath conceived, it bringeth forth sin: and sin, when it is finished, bringeth forth death.*

1 John 1:8–10—*If we say that we have no sin, we deceive ourselves, and the truth is not in us. If we confess our sins, he is faithful and just to forgive us our sins, and to cleanse us from all unrighteousness. If we say that we have not sinned, we make him a liar, and his word is not in us.*

1 John 3:4—*Whosoever committeth sin transgresseth also the law: for sin is the transgression of the law.*

Jeremiah 17:9—*The heart is deceitful above all things, and desperately wicked: who can know it?*

Salvation

Isaiah 45:22—*Look unto me, and be ye saved, all the ends of the earth: for I am God, and there is none else.*

Isaiah 43:11–12—*I, even I, am the LORD; and beside me there is no saviour. I have declared, and have saved, and I have shewed, when there was no strange god among you: therefore ye are my witnesses, saith the LORD, that I am God.*

John 14:6—*Jesus saith unto him, I am the way, the truth, and the life: no man cometh unto the Father, but by me.*

Acts 4:12—*Neither is there salvation in any other: for there is none other name under heaven given among men, whereby we must be saved.*

Romans 10:9–10—*That if thou shalt confess with thy mouth the Lord Jesus, and shalt believe in thine heart that God hath raised him from the dead, thou shalt be saved. For with the heart man believeth unto righteousness; and with the mouth confession is made unto salvation.*

Ephesians 2:8–9—*For by grace are ye saved through faith; and that not of yourselves: it is the gift of God: Not of works, lest any man should boast.*

Titus 3:5—*Not by works of righteousness which we have done, but according to his mercy he saved us, by the washing of regeneration, and renewing of the Holy Ghost;*

Church

Matthew 16:18—*And I say also unto thee, That thou art Peter, and upon this rock I will build my church; and the gates of hell shall not prevail against it.*

Colossians 1:18—*And he is the head of the body, the church: who is the beginning, the firstborn from the dead; that in all things he might have the preeminence.*

Ephesians 5:25–27—*Husbands, love your wives, even as Christ also loved the church, and gave himself for it; That he might sanctify and cleanse it with the washing of water by the word, That he might present it to himself a glorious church, not having spot, or wrinkle, or any such thing; but that it should be holy and without blemish.*

Acts 2:46–47—*And they, continuing daily with one accord in the temple, and breaking bread from house to house, did eat their meat with gladness and singleness of heart, Praising God, and having favour with all the people. And the Lord added to the church daily such as should be saved.*

1 Corinthians 12:13—*For by one Spirit are we all baptized into one body, whether we be Jews or Gentiles, whether we be bond or free; and have been all made to drink into one Spirit.*

1 Timothy 3:15—*But if I tarry long, that thou mayest know how thou oughtest to behave thyself in the house of God, which is the church of the living God, the pillar and ground of the truth.*

Angels

Genesis 3:24—*So he drove out the man; and he placed at the east of the garden of Eden Cherubims, and a flaming sword which turned every way, to keep the way of the tree of life.*

Psalm 148:2, 5—*Praise ye him, all his angels: praise ye him, all his hosts. Let them praise the name of the Lord: for he commanded, and they were created.*

Isaiah 6:1–3—*In the year that king Uzziah died I saw also the Lord sitting upon a throne, high and lifted up, and his train filled the temple. Above it stood the seraphims: each one had six wings; with twain he covered his face, and with twain he covered his feet, and with twain he did fly. And one cried unto another, and said, Holy, holy, holy, is the Lord of hosts: the whole earth is full of his glory.*

Mark 13:32—*But of that day and that hour knoweth no man, no, not the angels which are in heaven, neither the Son, but the Father.*

Hebrews 1:5–6—*For unto which of the angels said he at any time, Thou art my Son, this day have I begotten thee? And again, I will be to him a Father, and he shall be to me a Son? And again, when he bringeth in the firstbegotten into the world, he saith, And let all the angels of God worship him.*

1 Thessalonians 4:16—*For the Lord himself shall descend from heaven with a shout, with the voice of the archangel, and with the trump of God: and the dead in Christ shall rise first:*

End Times

1 Thessalonians 4:13–18—*But I would not have you to be ignorant, brethren, concerning them which are asleep, that ye sorrow not, even as others which have no hope. For if we believe that Jesus died and rose again, even so them also which sleep in Jesus will God bring with him. For this we say unto you by the word of the Lord, that we which are alive and remain unto the coming of the Lord shall not prevent them which are asleep. For the Lord himself shall descend from heaven with a shout, with the voice of the archangel, and with the trump of God: and the dead in Christ shall rise first: Then we which are alive and remain shall be caught up together with them in the clouds, to meet the Lord in the air: and so shall we ever be with the Lord. Wherefore comfort one another with these words.*

John 14:1–3—*Let not your heart be troubled: ye believe in God, believe also in me. In my Father's house are many mansions: if it were not so, I would have told you. I go to prepare a place for you. And if I go and prepare a place for you, I will come again, and receive you unto myself; that where I am, there ye may be also.*

Acts 1:10–11—*And while they looked stedfastly toward heaven as he went up, behold, two men stood by them in white apparel; Which also said, Ye men of Galilee, why stand ye gazing up into heaven? this same Jesus, which is taken up from you into heaven, shall so come in like manner as ye have seen him go into heaven.*

Revelation 22:20—*He which testifieth these things saith, Surely I come quickly. Amen. Even so, come, Lord Jesus.*

How to Lead a Person to Christ

Someone once said, "The fruit of a Christian is another Christian." There is a lot of truth in that statement. The Christian leader will influence people to be more soul-conscious. Yet, sometimes a person will be very active in sharing the gospel, but will not see much fruit. It is the responsibility of the Christian leader to train others to not only be available, but effective in their witness. Here are some truths that every soulwinner must remember as he prepares to help another soul spend an eternity with Christ.

1. **A soulwinner should start with the truth of God's love for every individual.**
   John 3:16 is perhaps the most familiar verse in all the New Testament. *"For God so loved the world...."* There are sinners living today who actually believe that God hates them and wants them to go to Hell because of their sin. A sinner will never accept a Saviour who he believes will never love him.

2. **A soulwinner must emphasize the fact that we are all sinners— there are no exceptions.**
   There have been some who understand the "love" of God and feel that He would never send anyone to Hell. These sinners must also understand that the God of "love" is also first, and foremost, holy. All men fall short of the holy standard He has set. As a result of this "falling short," we are condemned to an eternity in Hell. Romans 3:23 includes all men everywhere.

3. **A soulwinner must teach the sinner that his sin carries with it an expensive price tag.**
   According to Romans 6:23, *"the wages of sin is death...."* In Ezekiel 18:20, the Israelites learned that the soul that sinned would die. As a soulwinner, the person you are dealing with has the wrath of God already abiding on him (John 3:36).

4. **A soulwinner should demonstrate the good news that Jesus has already paid this price.**

   Not only does Romans 6:23 deal with the penalty of sin, it also deals with the promise of salvation. Romans 5:8 continues with this theme by showing the sinner that Christ died for us while we were yet sinners.

5. **A soulwinner must remember that a sinner must personally accept Christ as Saviour.**

   This promise is given in Romans 10:13—*"For whosoever shall call upon the name of the Lord shall be saved."* A sinner may believe that God loves him, may understand the fact that he is a sinner, and may further understand that Jesus died to pay his sin debt and still be lost. The soulwinner is not after a simple mental assent to a list of subscribed facts. He is looking for a sinner to repent, to confess, and to know the joy of being a Christian.

6. **Ask the sinner, "Is there anything that would hinder you from trusting Christ right now, today, as your Saviour?"**

   This question will show the soulwinner if there are still any "obstacles" that must be removed before a sinner trusts Christ. It will also serve as a good transition into drawing the gospel net. After a sinner is saved, the Great Commission is still unfulfilled. We are commanded to go, to win, to baptize, and to teach (disciple). An effective soulwinner will determine to see each aspect of the Great Commission come to fruition with those he leads to Christ.

Verses Remembered by Effective Christians

When you lose sight of His greatness:
Jeremiah 32:17; Jeremiah 33:3; Psalm 147:5; Romans 11:33–36; and
1 Chronicles 29:11–14

When you have needs:
Matthew 6:33; Philippians 4:19; Psalm 37:3; Psalm 37:25; and
Deuteronomy 2:7

When you are overwhelmed:
Psalm 55:5; Psalm 55:18; Psalm 107:6–8; and 2 Corinthians 4:16

When problems seem insurmountable:
2 Corinthians 4:15–18; Romans 8:18; Psalm 32:7; Psalm 60:12;
Psalm 61:2; and Psalm 62:6–8

When you need purpose:
1 Corinthians 10:31; Ephesians 3:16–21; John 10:10; and Psalm 139:14

When you have stress:
Philippians 4:4–7; Deuteronomy 20:1–4; and Jeremiah 32:27

When you are under pressure:
Psalm 27:1–2; Psalm 27:13–14; Psalm 46:1–2; and 2 Corinthians 12:9–10

When you worry:
Philippians 4:6–7; 1 Peter 5:7; Psalm 55:22; and Psalm 46:10

When you are afraid:
Psalm 56:3; Genesis 15:1; Psalm 27:1; 2 Timothy 1:7; and John 14:27

When you have a big decision to make:
Psalm 32:8; Psalm 143:10; Psalm 40:8; Proverbs 3:5–6; and
Psalm 37:3–6

When you are discouraged:

1 Samuel 30:6; Joshua 1:9; Isaiah 41:10; Isaiah 40:26–28; and 2 Corinthians 4:15–16

When you are disheartened:

Joshua 1:5–9; Psalm 73:2; Psalm 73:17; and Psalm 73:24–26

When you are facing opposition:

2 Timothy 3:12; 2 Timothy 2:3; 1 Peter 4:12–13; 1 John 4:4; and Romans 8:31–32

When friends seem to let you down:

2 Timothy 4:16–17; Hebrews 12:2–3; Matthew 28:20; and Deuteronomy 32:27

When you are lonely:

Isaiah 41:10; Hebrews 13:5–6; Acts 18:9–10; and Isaiah 43:2

When you ask if it is worth it:

Matthew 25:21; 1 Corinthians 15:58; Galatians 6:9; and 2 Corinthians 4:17.

BIBLE
READING
SCHEDULES

One-Year Bible Reading Schedule

January

- [ ] **1** Gen. 1–3 — Matt. 1
- [ ] **2** Gen. 4–6 — Matt. 2
- [ ] **3** Gen. 7–9 — Matt. 3
- [ ] **4** Gen. 10–12 — Matt. 4
- [ ] **5** Gen. 13–15 — Matt. 5:1–26
- [ ] **6** Gen. 16–17 — Matt. 5:27–48
- [ ] **7** Gen. 18–19 — Matt. 6:1–18
- [ ] **8** Gen. 20–22 — Matt. 6:19–34
- [ ] **9** Gen. 23–24 — Matt. 7
- [ ] **10** Gen. 25–26 — Matt. 8:1–17
- [ ] **11** Gen. 27–28 — Matt. 8:18–34
- [ ] **12** Gen. 29–30 — Matt. 9:1–17
- [ ] **13** Gen. 31–32 — Matt. 9:18–38
- [ ] **14** Gen. 33–35 — Matt. 10:1–20
- [ ] **15** Gen. 36–38 — Matt. 10:21–42
- [ ] **16** Gen. 39–40 — Matt. 11
- [ ] **17** Gen. 41–42 — Matt. 12:1–23
- [ ] **18** Gen. 43–45 — Matt. 12:24–50
- [ ] **19** Gen. 46–48 — Matt. 13:1–30
- [ ] **20** Gen. 49–50 — Matt. 13:31–58
- [ ] **21** Ex. 1–3 — Matt. 14:1–21
- [ ] **22** Ex. 4–6 — Matt. 14:22–36
- [ ] **23** Ex. 7–8 — Matt. 15:1–20
- [ ] **24** Ex. 9–11 — Matt. 15:21–39
- [ ] **25** Ex. 12–13 — Matt. 16
- [ ] **26** Ex. 14–15 — Matt. 17
- [ ] **27** Ex. 16–18 — Matt. 18:1–20
- [ ] **28** Ex. 19–20 — Matt. 18:21–35
- [ ] **29** Ex. 21–22 — Matt. 19
- [ ] **30** Ex. 23–24 — Matt. 20:1–16
- [ ] **31** Ex. 25–26 — Matt. 20:17–34

February

- [ ] **1** Ex. 27–28 — Matt. 21:1–22
- [ ] **2** Ex. 29–30 — Matt. 21:23–46
- [ ] **3** Ex. 31–33 — Matt. 22:1–22
- [ ] **4** Ex. 34–35 — Matt. 22:23–46
- [ ] **5** Ex. 36–38 — Matt. 23:1–22
- [ ] **6** Ex. 39–40 — Matt. 23:23–39
- [ ] **7** Lev. 1–3 — Matt. 24:1–28
- [ ] **8** Lev. 4–5 — Matt. 24:29–51
- [ ] **9** Lev. 6–7 — Matt. 25:1–30
- [ ] **10** Lev. 8–10 — Matt. 25:31–46
- [ ] **11** Lev. 11–12 — Matt. 26:1–25
- [ ] **12** Lev. 13 — Matt. 26:26–50
- [ ] **13** Lev. 14 — Matt. 26:51–75
- [ ] **14** Lev. 15–16 — Matt. 27:1–26
- [ ] **15** Lev. 17–18 — Matt. 27:27–50
- [ ] **16** Lev. 19–20 — Matt. 27:51–66
- [ ] **17** Lev. 21–22 — Matt. 28
- [ ] **18** Lev. 23–24 — Mark 1:1–22
- [ ] **19** Lev. 25 — Mark 1:23–45
- [ ] **20** Lev. 26–27 — Mark 2
- [ ] **21** Num. 1–2 — Mark 3:1–19
- [ ] **22** Num. 3–4 — Mark 3:20–35
- [ ] **23** Num. 5–6 — Mark 4:1–20
- [ ] **24** Num. 7–8 — Mark 4:21–41
- [ ] **25** Num. 9–11 — Mark 5:1–20
- [ ] **26** Num. 12–14 — Mark 5:21–43
- [ ] **27** Num. 15–16 — Mark 6:1–29
- [ ] **28** Num. 17–19 — Mark 6:30–56

March

- [ ] **1** Num. 20–22 — Mark 7:1–13
- [ ] **2** Num. 23–25 — Mark 7:14–37
- [ ] **3** Num. 26–28 — Mark 8
- [ ] **4** Num. 29–31 — Mark 9:1–29
- [ ] **5** Num. 32–34 — Mark 9:30–50
- [ ] **6** Num. 35–36 — Mark 10:1–31
- [ ] **7** Deut. 1–3 — Mark 10:32–52
- [ ] **8** Deut. 4–6 — Mark 11:1–18
- [ ] **9** Deut. 7–9 — Mark 11:19–33
- [ ] **10** Deut. 10–12 — Mark 12:1–27
- [ ] **11** Deut. 13–15 — Mark 12:28–44
- [ ] **12** Deut. 16–18 — Mark 13:1–20
- [ ] **13** Deut. 19–21 — Mark 13:21–37
- [ ] **14** Deut. 22–24 — Mark 14:1–26
- [ ] **15** Deut. 25–27 — Mark 14:27–53
- [ ] **16** Deut. 28–29 — Mark 14:54–72
- [ ] **17** Deut. 30–31 — Mark 15:1–25
- [ ] **18** Deut. 32–34 — Mark 15:26–47
- [ ] **19** Josh. 1–3 — Mark 16
- [ ] **20** Josh. 4–6 — Luke 1:1–20
- [ ] **21** Josh. 7–9 — Luke 1:21–38
- [ ] **22** Josh. 10–12 — Luke 1:39–56
- [ ] **23** Josh. 13–15 — Luke 1:57–80
- [ ] **24** Josh. 16–18 — Luke 2:1–24
- [ ] **25** Josh. 19–21 — Luke 2:25–52
- [ ] **26** Josh. 22–24 — Luke 3
- [ ] **27** Judges 1–3 — Luke 4:1–30
- [ ] **28** Judges 4–6 — Luke 4:31–44
- [ ] **29** Judges 7–8 — Luke 5:1–16
- [ ] **30** Judges 9–10 — Luke 5:17–39
- [ ] **31** Judges 11–12 — Luke 6:1–26

April

- [ ] **1** Judges 13–15 — Luke 6:27–49
- [ ] **2** Judges 16–18 — Luke 7:1–30
- [ ] **3** Judges 19–21 — Luke 7:31–50
- [ ] **4** Ruth 1–4 — Luke 8:1–25
- [ ] **5** 1 Sam. 1–3 — Luke 8:26–56
- [ ] **6** 1 Sam. 4–6 — Luke 9:1–17
- [ ] **7** 1 Sam. 7–9 — Luke 9:18–36
- [ ] **8** 1 Sam. 10–12 — Luke 9:37–62
- [ ] **9** 1 Sam. 13–14 — Luke 10:1–24
- [ ] **10** 1 Sam. 15–16 — Luke 10:25–42
- [ ] **11** 1 Sam. 17–18 — Luke 11:1–28
- [ ] **12** 1 Sam. 19–21 — Luke 11:29–54
- [ ] **13** 1 Sam. 22–24 — Luke 12:1–31
- [ ] **14** 1 Sam. 25–26 — Luke 12:32–59
- [ ] **15** 1 Sam. 27–29 — Luke 13:1–22
- [ ] **16** 1 Sam. 30–31 — Luke 13:23–35
- [ ] **17** 2 Sam. 1–2 — Luke 14:1–24
- [ ] **18** 2 Sam. 3–5 — Luke 14:25–35
- [ ] **19** 2 Sam. 6–8 — Luke 15:1–10
- [ ] **20** 2 Sam. 9–11 — Luke 15:11–32
- [ ] **21** 2 Sam. 12–13 — Luke 16
- [ ] **22** 2 Sam. 14–15 — Luke 17:1–19
- [ ] **23** 2 Sam. 16–18 — Luke 17:20–37
- [ ] **24** 2 Sam. 19–20 — Luke 18:1–23
- [ ] **25** 2 Sam. 21–22 — Luke 18:24–43
- [ ] **26** 2 Sam. 23–24 — Luke 19:1–27
- [ ] **27** 1 Kings 1–2 — Luke 19:28–48
- [ ] **28** 1 Kings 3–5 — Luke 20:1–26
- [ ] **29** 1 Kings 6–7 — Luke 20:27–47
- [ ] **30** 1 Kings 8–9 — Luke 21:1–19

May

- [ ] **1** 1 Kings 10–11 — Luke 21:20–38
- [ ] **2** 1 Kings 12–13 — Luke 22:1–30
- [ ] **3** 1 Kings 14–15 — Luke 22:31–46
- [ ] **4** 1 Kings 16–18 — Luke 22:47–71
- [ ] **5** 1 Kings 19–20 — Luke 23:1–25
- [ ] **6** 1 Kings 21–22 — Luke 23:26–56
- [ ] **7** 2 Kings 1–3 — Luke 24:1–35
- [ ] **8** 2 Kings 4–6 — Luke 24:36–53
- [ ] **9** 2 Kings 7–9 — John 1:1–28
- [ ] **10** 2 Kings 10–12 — John 1:29–51
- [ ] **11** 2 Kings 13–14 — John 2
- [ ] **12** 2 Kings 15–16 — John 3:1–18
- [ ] **13** 2 Kings 17–18 — John 3:19–36
- [ ] **14** 2 Kings 19–21 — John 4:1–30
- [ ] **15** 2 Kings 22–23 — John 4:31–54
- [ ] **16** 2 Kings 24–25 — John 5:1–24
- [ ] **17** 1 Chr. 1–3 — John 5:25–47
- [ ] **18** 1 Chr. 4–6 — John 6:1–21
- [ ] **19** 1 Chr. 7–9 — John 6:22–44
- [ ] **20** 1 Chr. 10–12 — John 6:45–71
- [ ] **21** 1 Chr. 13–15 — John 7:1–27
- [ ] **22** 1 Chr. 16–18 — John 7:28–53
- [ ] **23** 1 Chr. 19–21 — John 8:1–27
- [ ] **24** 1 Chr. 22–24 — John 8:28–59
- [ ] **25** 1 Chr. 25–27 — John 9:1–23
- [ ] **26** 1 Chr. 28–29 — John 9:24–41
- [ ] **27** 2 Chr. 1–3 — John 10:1–23
- [ ] **28** 2 Chr. 4–6 — John 10:24–42
- [ ] **29** 2 Chr. 7–9 — John 11:1–29
- [ ] **30** 2 Chr. 10–12 — John 11:30–57
- [ ] **31** 2 Chr. 13–14 — John 12:1–26

June

- [ ] **1** 2 Chr. 15–16 — John 12:27–50
- [ ] **2** 2 Chr. 17–18 — John 13:1–20
- [ ] **3** 2 Chr. 19–20 — John 13:21–38
- [ ] **4** 2 Chr. 21–22 — John 14
- [ ] **5** 2 Chr. 23–24 — John 15
- [ ] **6** 2 Chr. 25–27 — John 16
- [ ] **7** 2 Chr. 28–29 — John 17
- [ ] **8** 2 Chr. 30–31 — John 18:1–18
- [ ] **9** 2 Chr. 32–33 — John 18:19–40
- [ ] **10** 2 Chr. 34–36 — John 19:1–22
- [ ] **11** Ezra 1–2 — John 19:23–42
- [ ] **12** Ezra 3–5 — John 20
- [ ] **13** Ezra 6–8 — John 21
- [ ] **14** Ezra 9–10 — Acts 1
- [ ] **15** Neh. 1–3 — Acts 2:1–21
- [ ] **16** Neh. 4–6 — Acts 2:22–47
- [ ] **17** Neh. 7–9 — Acts 3
- [ ] **18** Neh. 10–11 — Acts 4:1–22
- [ ] **19** Neh. 12–13 — Acts 4:23–37
- [ ] **20** Esther 1–2 — Acts 5:1–21
- [ ] **21** Esther 3–5 — Acts 5:22–42
- [ ] **22** Esther 6–8 — Acts 6
- [ ] **23** Esther 9–10 — Acts 7:1–21
- [ ] **24** Job 1–2 — Acts 7:22–43
- [ ] **25** Job 3–4 — Acts 7:44–60
- [ ] **26** Job 5–7 — Acts 8:1–25
- [ ] **27** Job 8–10 — Acts 8:26–40
- [ ] **28** Job 11–13 — Acts 9:1–21
- [ ] **29** Job 14–16 — Acts 9:22–43
- [ ] **30** Job 17–19 — Acts 10:1–23

July

❏	1	Job 20–21	Acts 10:24–48
❏	2	Job 22–24	Acts 11
❏	3	Job 25–27	Acts 12
❏	4	Job 28–29	Acts 13:1–25
❏	5	Job 30–31	Acts 13:26–52
❏	6	Job 32–33	Acts 14
❏	7	Job 34–35	Acts 15:1–21
❏	8	Job 36–37	Acts 15:22–41
❏	9	Job 38–40	Acts 16:1–21
❏	10	Job 41–42	Acts 16:22–40
❏	11	Ps. 1–3	Acts 17:1–15
❏	12	Ps. 4–6	Acts 17:16–34
❏	13	Ps. 7–9	Acts 18
❏	14	Ps. 10–12	Acts 19:1–20
❏	15	Ps. 13–15	Acts 19:21–41
❏	16	Ps. 16–17	Acts 20:1–16
❏	17	Ps. 18–19	Acts 20:17–38
❏	18	Ps. 20–22	Acts 21:1–17
❏	19	Ps. 23–25	Acts 21:18–40
❏	20	Ps. 26–28	Acts 22
❏	21	Ps. 29–30	Acts 23:1–15
❏	22	Ps. 31–32	Acts 23:16–35
❏	23	Ps. 33–34	Acts 24
❏	24	Ps. 35–36	Acts 25
❏	25	Ps. 37–39	Acts 26
❏	26	Ps. 40–42	Acts 27:1–26
❏	27	Ps. 43–45	Acts 27:27–44
❏	28	Ps. 46–48	Acts 28
❏	29	Ps. 49–50	Rom. 1
❏	30	Ps. 51–53	Rom. 2
❏	31	Ps. 54–56	Rom. 3

August

❏	1	Ps. 57–59	Rom. 4
❏	2	Ps. 60–62	Rom. 5
❏	3	Ps. 63–65	Rom. 6
❏	4	Ps. 66–67	Rom. 7
❏	5	Ps. 68–69	Rom. 8:1–21
❏	6	Ps. 70–71	Rom. 8:22–39
❏	7	Ps. 72–73	Rom. 9:1–15
❏	8	Ps. 74–76	Rom. 9:16–33
❏	9	Ps. 77–78	Rom. 10
❏	10	Ps. 79–80	Rom. 11:1–18
❏	11	Ps. 81–83	Rom. 11:19–36
❏	12	Ps. 84–86	Rom. 12
❏	13	Ps. 87–88	Rom. 13
❏	14	Ps. 89–90	Rom. 14
❏	15	Ps. 91–93	Rom. 15:1–13
❏	16	Ps. 94–96	Rom. 15:14–33
❏	17	Ps. 97–99	Rom. 16
❏	18	Ps. 100–102	1 Cor. 1
❏	19	Ps. 103–104	1 Cor. 2
❏	20	Ps. 105–106	1 Cor. 3
❏	21	Ps. 107–109	1 Cor. 4
❏	22	Ps. 110–112	1 Cor. 5
❏	23	Ps. 113–115	1 Cor. 6
❏	24	Ps. 116–118	1 Cor. 7:1–19
❏	25	Ps. 119:1–88	1 Cor. 7:20–40
❏	26	Ps. 119:89–176	1 Cor. 8
❏	27	Ps. 120–122	1 Cor. 9
❏	28	Ps.123–125	1 Cor. 10:1–18
❏	29	Ps. 126–128	1 Cor. 10:19–33
❏	30	Ps. 129–131	1 Cor. 11:1–16
❏	31	Ps. 132–134	1 Cor. 11:17–34

September

❏	1	Ps. 135–136	1 Cor. 12
❏	2	Ps. 137–139	1 Cor. 13
❏	3	Ps. 140–142	1 Cor. 14:1–20
❏	4	Ps. 143–145	1 Cor. 14:21–40
❏	5	Ps. 146–147	1 Cor. 15:1–28
❏	6	Ps. 148–150	1 Cor. 15:29–58
❏	7	Prov. 1–2	1 Cor. 16
❏	8	Prov. 3–5	2 Cor. 1
❏	9	Prov. 6–7	2 Cor. 2
❏	10	Prov. 8–9	2 Cor. 3
❏	11	Prov. 10–12	2 Cor. 4
❏	12	Prov. 13–15	2 Cor. 5
❏	13	Prov. 16–18	2 Cor. 6
❏	14	Prov. 19–21	2 Cor. 7
❏	15	Prov. 22–24	2 Cor. 8
❏	16	Prov. 25–26	2 Cor. 9
❏	17	Prov. 27–29	2 Cor. 10
❏	18	Prov. 30–31	2 Cor. 11:1–15
❏	19	Eccl. 1–3	2 Cor. 11:16–33
❏	20	Eccl. 4–6	2 Cor. 12
❏	21	Eccl. 7–9	2 Cor. 13
❏	22	Eccl. 10–12	Gal. 1
❏	23	Song 1–3	Gal. 2
❏	24	Song 4–5	Gal. 3
❏	25	Song 6–8	Gal. 4
❏	26	Isa. 1–2	Gal. 5
❏	27	Isa. 3–4	Gal. 6
❏	28	Isa. 5–6	Eph. 1
❏	29	Isa. 7–8	Eph. 2
❏	30	Isa. 9–10	Eph. 3

October

❏	1	Isa. 11–13	Eph. 4
❏	2	Isa. 14–16	Eph. 5:1–16
❏	3	Isa. 17–19	Eph. 5:17–33
❏	4	Isa. 20–22	Eph. 6
❏	5	Isa. 23–25	Phil. 1
❏	6	Isa. 26–27	Phil. 2
❏	7	Isa. 28–29	Phil. 3
❏	8	Isa. 30–31	Phil. 4
❏	9	Isa. 32–33	Col. 1
❏	10	Isa. 34–36	Col. 2
❏	11	Isa. 37–38	Col. 3
❏	12	Isa. 39–40	Col. 4
❏	13	Isa. 41–42	1 Thess. 1
❏	14	Isa. 43–44	1 Thess. 2
❏	15	Isa. 45–46	1 Thess. 3
❏	16	Isa. 47–49	1 Thess. 4
❏	17	Isa. 50–52	1 Thess. 5
❏	18	Isa. 53–55	2 Thess. 1
❏	19	Isa. 56–58	2 Thess. 2
❏	20	Isa. 59–61	2 Thess. 3
❏	21	Isa. 62–64	1 Tim. 1
❏	22	Isa. 65–66	1 Tim. 2
❏	23	Jer. 1–2	1 Tim. 3
❏	24	Jer. 3–5	1 Tim. 4
❏	25	Jer. 6–8	1 Tim. 5
❏	26	Jer. 9–11	1 Tim. 6
❏	27	Jer. 12–14	2 Tim. 1
❏	28	Jer. 15–17	2 Tim. 2
❏	29	Jer. 18–19	2 Tim. 3
❏	30	Jer. 20–21	2 Tim. 4
❏	31	Jer. 22–23	Titus 1

November

❏	1	Jer. 24–26	Titus 2
❏	2	Jer. 27–29	Titus 3
❏	3	Jer. 30–31	Philemon
❏	4	Jer. 32–33	Heb. 1
❏	5	Jer. 34–36	Heb. 2
❏	6	Jer. 37–39	Heb. 3
❏	7	Jer. 40–42	Heb. 4
❏	8	Jer. 43–45	Heb. 5
❏	9	Jer. 46–47	Heb. 6
❏	10	Jer. 48–49	Heb. 7
❏	11	Jer. 50	Heb. 8
❏	12	Jer. 51–52	Heb. 9
❏	13	Lam. 1–2	Heb. 10:1–18
❏	14	Lam. 3–5	Heb. 10:19–39
❏	15	Ezek. 1–2	Heb. 11:1–19
❏	16	Ezek. 3–4	Heb. 11:20–40
❏	17	Ezek. 5–7	Heb. 12
❏	18	Ezek. 8–10	Heb. 13
❏	19	Ezek. 11–13	James 1
❏	20	Ezek. 14–15	James 2
❏	21	Ezek. 16–17	James 3
❏	22	Ezek. 18–19	James 4
❏	23	Ezek. 20–21	James 5
❏	24	Ezek. 22–23	1 Peter 1
❏	25	Ezek. 24–26	1 Peter 2
❏	26	Ezek. 27–29	1 Peter 3
❏	27	Ezek. 30–32	1 Peter 4
❏	28	Ezek. 33–34	1 Peter 5
❏	29	Ezek. 35–36	2 Peter 1
❏	30	Ezek. 37–39	2 Peter 2

December

❏	1	Ezek. 40–41	2 Peter 3
❏	2	Ezek. 42–44	1 John 1
❏	3	Ezek. 45–46	1 John 2
❏	4	Ezek. 47–48	1 John 3
❏	5	Dan. 1–2	1 John 4
❏	6	Dan. 3–4	1 John 5
❏	7	Dan. 5–7	2 John
❏	8	Dan. 8–10	3 John
❏	9	Dan. 11–12	Jude
❏	10	Hos. 1–4	Rev. 1
❏	11	Hos. 5–8	Rev. 2
❏	12	Hos. 9–11	Rev. 3
❏	13	Hos. 12–14	Rev. 4
❏	14	Joel	Rev. 5
❏	15	Amos 1–3	Rev. 6
❏	16	Amos 4–6	Rev. 7
❏	17	Amos 7–9	Rev. 8
❏	18	Obad.	Rev. 9
❏	19	Jonah	Rev. 10
❏	20	Micah 1–3	Rev. 11
❏	21	Micah 4–5	Rev. 12
❏	22	Micah 6–7	Rev. 13
❏	23	Nahum	Rev. 14
❏	24	Hab.	Rev. 15
❏	25	Zeph.	Rev. 16
❏	26	Hag.	Rev. 17
❏	27	Zech. 1–4	Rev. 18
❏	28	Zech. 5–8	Rev. 19
❏	29	Zech. 9–12	Rev. 20
❏	30	Zech. 13–14	Rev. 21
❏	31	Mal.	Rev. 22

90-Day Bible Reading Schedule

Day	Start	End	✔	Day	Start	End	✔
1	Genesis 1:1	Genesis 16:16	❑	46	Proverbs 7:1	Proverbs 20:21	❑
2	Genesis 17:1	Genesis 28:19	❑	47	Proverbs 20:22	Ecclesiastes 2:26	❑
3	Genesis 28:20	Genesis 40:11	❑	48	Ecclesiastes 3:1	Song 8:14	❑
4	Genesis 40:12	Genesis 50:26	❑	49	Isaiah 1:1	Isaiah 13:22	❑
5	Exodus 1:1	Exodus 15:18	❑	50	Isaiah 14:1	Isaiah 28:29	❑
6	Exodus 15:19	Exodus 28:43	❑	51	Isaiah 29:1	Isaiah 41:18	❑
7	Exodus 29:1	Exodus 40:38	❑	52	Isaiah 41:19	Isaiah 52:12	❑
8	Leviticus 1:1	Leviticus 14:32	❑	53	Isaiah 52:13	Isaiah 66:18	❑
9	Leviticus 14:33	Leviticus 26:26	❑	54	Isaiah 66:19	Jeremiah 10:13	❑
10	Leviticus 26:27	Numbers 8:14	❑	55	Jeremiah 10:14	Jeremiah 23:8	❑
11	Numbers 8:15	Numbers 21:7	❑	56	Jeremiah 23:9	Jeremiah 33:22	❑
12	Numbers 21:8	Numbers 32:19	❑	57	Jeremiah 33:23	Jeremiah 47:7	❑
13	Numbers 32:20	Deuteronomy 7:26	❑	58	Jeremiah 48:1	Lamentations 1:22	❑
14	Deuteronomy 8:1	Deuteronomy 23:11	❑	59	Lamentations 2:1	Ezekiel 12:20	❑
15	Deuteronomy 23:12	Deuteronomy 34:12	❑	60	Ezekiel 12:21	Ezekiel 23:39	❑
16	Joshua 1:1	Joshua 14:15	❑	61	Ezekiel 23:40	Ezekiel 35:15	❑
17	Joshua 15:1	Judges 3:27	❑	62	Ezekiel 36:1	Ezekiel 47:12	❑
18	Judges 3:28	Judges 15:12	❑	63	Ezekiel 47:13	Daniel 8:27	❑
19	Judges 15:13	1 Samuel 2:29	❑	64	Daniel 9:1	Hosea 13:6	❑
20	1 Samuel 2:30	1 Samuel 15:35	❑	65	Hosea 13:7	Amos 9:10	❑
21	1 Samuel 16:1	1 Samuel 28:19	❑	66	Amos 9:11	Nahum 3:19	❑
22	1 Samuel 28:20	2 Samuel 12:10	❑	67	Habakkuk 1:1	Zechariah 10:12	❑
23	2 Samuel 12:11	2 Samuel 22:18	❑	68	Zechariah 11:1	Matthew 4:25	❑
24	2 Samuel 22:19	1 Kings 7:37	❑	69	Matthew 5:1	Matthew 15:39	❑
25	1 Kings 7:38	1 Kings 16:20	❑	70	Matthew 16:1	Matthew 26:56	❑
26	1 Kings 16:21	2 Kings 4:37	❑	71	Matthew 26:57	Mark 9:13	❑
27	2 Kings 4:38	2 Kings 15:26	❑	72	Mark 9:14	Luke 1:80	❑
28	2 Kings 15:27	2 Kings 25:30	❑	73	Luke 2:1	Luke 9:62	❑
29	1 Chronicles 1:1	1 Chronicles 9:44	❑	74	Luke 10:1	Luke 20:19	❑
30	1 Chronicles 10:1	1 Chronicles 23:32	❑	75	Luke 20:20	John 5:47	❑
31	1 Chronicles 24:1	2 Chronicles 7:10	❑	76	John 6:1	John 15:17	❑
32	2 Chronicles 7:11	2 Chronicles 23:15	❑	77	John 15:18	Acts 6:7	❑
33	2 Chronicles 23:16	2 Chronicles 35:15	❑	78	Acts 6:8	Acts 16:37	❑
34	2 Chronicles 35:16	Ezra 10:44	❑	79	Acts 16:38	Acts 28:16	❑
35	Nehemiah 1:1	Nehemiah 13:14	❑	80	Acts 28:17	Romans 14:23	❑
36	Nehemiah 13:15	Job 7:21	❑	81	Romans 15:1	1 Corinthians 14:40	❑
37	Job 8:1	Job 24:25	❑	82	1 Corinthians 15:1	Galatians 3:25	❑
38	Job 25:1	Job 41:34	❑	83	Galatians 3:26	Colossians 4:18	❑
39	Job 42:1	Psalm 24:10	❑	84	1 Thessalonians 1:1	Philemon 25	❑
40	Psalm 25:1	Psalm 45:14	❑	85	Hebrews 1:1	James 3:12	❑
41	Psalm 45:15	Psalm 69:21	❑	86	James 3:13	3 John 14	❑
42	Psalm 69:22	Psalm 89:13	❑	87	Jude 1	Revelation 17:18	❑
43	Psalm 89:14	Psalm 108:13	❑	88	Revelation 18:1	Revelation 22:21	❑
44	Psalm 109:1	Psalm 134:3	❑	89	Grace Day	Grace Day	❑
45	Psalm 135:1	Proverbs 6:35	❑	90	Grace Day	Grace Day	❑

INDEXES

Title Index

Title Index

May

June

September

October

Scripture Index

John

About the Author

Dr. Paul Chappell is the senior pastor of Lancaster Baptist Church and the president of West Coast Baptist College in Lancaster, California. He is a powerful communicator of God's Word and a passionate servant to God's people. He has been married to his wife, Terrie, since 1980, and they have four married children who are all serving in Christian ministry. He enjoys spending time with his family and serving the Lord shoulder to shoulder with a wonderful church family.

Dr. Chappell's preaching is heard on *Daily in the Word*, a radio program that is broadcast across America. You can find a station listing at dailyintheword.org.

You can also connect with Dr. Chappell here:

Blog: paulchappell.com
Twitter: twitter.com/paulchappell
Facebook: facebook.com/pastor.paul.chappell

Other Titles for Your Daily Walk

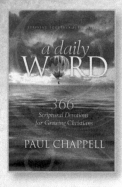

A Daily Word

Designed to complement your daily walk with the Lord, this book from Dr. Paul Chappell features 366 daily devotional thoughts to strengthen and encourage your spiritual life. Each devotion features a one-year Bible reading selection. Also included are helpful reference resources as well as Scripture and title indexes. (424 pages, hardback)

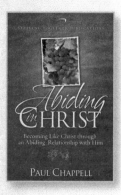

Abiding in Christ

In these pages, Dr. Paul Chappell will lead you on an exciting and encouraging journey to discover the authentic Christian life. You will learn how an intimate relationship with Christ produces a genuine heart and life change. You will find the source of true love, abundant joy, lasting fruit, spiritual maturity, emotional stability, and purpose in life. (168 pages, paperback)

Stewarding Life

God has given you one life and filled it with resources—time, health, finances, relationships, influence, and more. How you steward these resources will determine whether you successfully fulfill God's eternal purpose for your life. This book will challenge and equip you to strategically invest your most valuable resources for God's eternal purposes. (280 pages, hardcover)

strivingtogether.com